Brothers & Sisters

Brothers & Sisters

A Special Part of Exceptional Families

THIRD EDITION

by

Peggy A. Gallagher, Ph.D.
Professor and Chair
Department of Educational Psychology and Special Education
Georgia State University
Atlanta

Thomas H. Powell, Ed.D.
President
Mount St. Mary's University
Emmitsburg, Maryland

and

Cheryl A. Rhodes, M.S., L.M.F.T.
Department of Educational Psychology and Special Education
Georgia State University
Atlanta

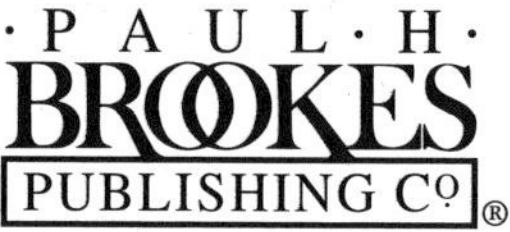

Baltimore • London • Sydney

Paul H. Brookes Publishing Co.
Post Office Box 10624
Baltimore, Maryland 21285-0624

www.brookespublishing.com

Typeset by Integrated Publishing Solutions, Grand Rapids, Michigan.
Manufactured in the United States of America by
Versa Press, Inc., East Peoria, Illinois.

Library of Congress Cataloging-in-Publication Data

Gallagher, Peggy Ahrenhold, 1952-
Brothers & sisters : a special part of exceptional families / by Peggy A. Gallagher, Thomas H. Powell, Cheryl A. Rhodes.—3rd ed.
p. cm.
Rev. ed. of: Brothers & sisters / Thomas H. Powell. 2nd ed. c1993.
Includes bibliographical references.
ISBN-13: 978-1-55766-719-9 (pbk.)
ISBN-10: 1-55766-719-5 (pbk.)
1. Children with disabilities—Family relationships. 2. Brothers and sisters. I. Powell, Thomas H. II. Rhodes, Cheryl A. III. Powell, Thomas H. Brothers & sisters. IV. Title. V. Title: Brothers and sisters.
HV903.G35 2006
362.82—dc22 2006019993

British Library Cataloguing in Publication data are available from the British Library.

Contents

About the Authors

Peggy A. Gallagher, Ph.D., Professor and Chair, Department of Educational Psychology and Special Education, Georgia State University, Post Office Box 3979, Atlanta, Georgia, 30302-3979

In addition to teaching and serving as Chair of the Department of Educational Psychology and Special Education at Georgia State University in Atlanta, Peggy A. Gallagher coordinates the Early Childhood Special Education program and also directs Project SCEIs (Skilled Credentialed Early Interventionists), a collaborative between six universities as part of Georgia's Part C Early Intervention Program, to develop statewide training for parents and professionals. She holds a doctorate in special education from the University of North Carolina at Chapel Hill.

Dr. Gallagher has extensive training and experience in working with families of young children with disabilities and in developing personnel preparation systems. Early in her career, as a teacher of young children with special needs, Dr. Gallagher became interested in sibling relationships as she got to know her students' brothers and sisters. Subsequently, she co-founded the Sibling Information Network in 1981 with one of her co-authors, Dr. Thomas H. Powell. She and her husband Kevin are the parents of two teenagers.

Thomas H. Powell, Ed.D., President, Mount Saint Mary's University, 16300 Old Emmitsburg Road, Emmitsburg, Maryland, 21727-7700

Prior to his appointment as President of Mount Saint Mary's University, Thomas H. Powell was President of Glenville State College in Glenville, West Virginia. Dr. Powell has served as Dean of the College of Education at Winthrop University in Rock Hill, South Carolina, and Dean of the College of Education and Human Services at Montana State University–Billings. He received his doctorate in special education from

Peabody College of Vanderbilt University. Powell founded the Sibling Information Network with Peggy A. Gallagher. He also is the founding director of the University of Connecticut's University Affiliated Program on Disabilities. He and his wife Irene have three children.

Cheryl A. Rhodes, M.S., L.M.F.T., Associate Project Director, Project SCEIs, Department of Educational Psychology and Special Education, Georgia State University, Post Office Box 3979, Atlanta, Georgia, 30302-3979

Cheryl A. Rhodes is a licensed marriage and family therapist and a licensed professional counselor with expertise in working with families of children with disabilities. She holds a master's degree in counseling from City University of New York–Brooklyn College. Ms. Rhodes has been a trainer, project director, consultant, and counselor for more than 25 years. She has designed programs and conducted support groups for siblings of children with disabilities and for grandparents rearing grandchildren with disabilities. She is involved in initiatives for families of children with disabilities at the state and national levels and serves as Chair of the Family Consortium for the Division for Early Childhood of the Council for Exceptional Children. She has worked with Georgia's early intervention program since the mid-1990s. She is the parent of three children, two daughters and a son, ages 22, 20, and 18. Her younger daughter acquired a disability at age 13 months.

Foreword

In my work, I never pass up an opportunity to bend the ears of colleagues and family members about why brothers and sisters are too important to ignore. If nothing else, I try to leave them with the following messages:

- Almost anything that can be said about being the parent of a child with special needs can also be said about being a brother or sister of a child with special needs. Throughout their lives, siblings will have many, if not most, of the same issues that parents will—as well as many that are uniquely theirs.
- These siblings will be in the lives of their brothers and sisters who have disabilities longer than *anyone,* certainly longer than any service provider, but longer even than their parents. In a relationship that may span 60–80 years, siblings will still be around when a favorite teacher is a distant memory and Mom and Dad are no longer available to be primary advocates. As adults, siblings will give new meaning to the phrase "sandwich generation." Most will raise their own children, pursue their careers, look after their aging parents, and do whatever they can to ensure that their siblings with disabilities live and work in their communities with dignity. Call it, as adult siblings often do, life in the "club sandwich" generation.
- With the possible exception of a child's mother, no one spends as much time with a child who has a disability than the child's siblings do. Because of this, siblings will have an enormous influence on their brothers and sisters who have disabilities. As valuable as inclusive classrooms are, no classmate will have a greater impact on the social development of a child with special needs than will the child's siblings.

Despite their concerns and the important roles they play, siblings are often left out of most agencies' and providers' functional definition of "family." They are usually an afterthought at best—even in agencies committed to family-centered services or who write individualized family service plans. Compare the services and considerations given to siblings at most agencies with those routinely offered to parents. In most cases, it is easy to see who is getting the short end of the stick. Siblings—too often left in the literal and figurative waiting rooms of service delivery systems—deserve better.

If we care about families, we have an obligation to learn about siblings and their concerns. And, because sibling issues are life-span issues, there is much to learn. Preschoolers who are siblings will have unique concerns, as will siblings who are senior citizens. Siblings' issues change and evolve throughout their—and their families'—life spans.

Whether you are beginning your education about siblings with brothers and sisters with special needs or furthering it, you have picked up a wonderful resource. When the first edition of *Brothers and Sisters—A Special Part of Exceptional Families* was published in 1993, it was a godsend. There had been few books or resources up until that time that had sought to explain siblings' experiences, and none were as effective in providing readers with both an overview of recent research and helpful, practical information. It was a pleasure to recommend it to colleagues and parents who knew that siblings were too important to ignore and who were seeking to learn about their experiences. I am happy to report that the newest edition makes this same significant contribution. Whether you are a student or a service provider wishing to learn about research on siblings or a parent seeking helpful advice, you will find much of what you are looking for in the pages that follow.

Siblings are an amazingly deserving and a remarkably underserved population. Most have both legitimate concerns and wonderfully generous spirits. As such, they are worthy of everyone's time and attention. But just in case you think their issues aren't sufficiently compelling, think about this: When we attend to siblings' concerns, their brothers and sisters who have disabilities benefit, too—as will parents, agencies, and even taxpayers. Attending to siblings' concerns increases the chances that they will be loving advocates for their brothers and sisters who have disabilities throughout their lives together.

Thank you for your interest in this fascinating community. And thank you, Peggy, Tom, and Cheryl, for your excellent contribution to our understanding of siblings' needs and concerns.

Don Meyer
Director
Sibling Support Project
Seattle

Preface

Siblings play a critical role in our lives. They know us like no one else and have shared our experiences, both good and bad. Siblings constitute our first social network, and their early influence affects us throughout our lives. Our sibling relationships are typically the longest relationships we will have in life. With all of the importance that attends these relationships, however, seldom do we take time to consider them; seldom do we take time to recognize them; seldom do we take time to celebrate them.

This book is devoted to special sibling relationships—that is—relationships between brothers and sisters in which one sibling has a disability. We believe that in such family situations, sibling relationships take on new meaning and significance. Just like parents who have children with disabilities, siblings of these brothers and sisters also are in need of special attention, understanding, and support. Most of all, these siblings need to be recognized for their unique contribution to the family system.

We have spent the last several decades actively engaged in work with brothers and sisters with and without disabilities. Our work has involved both research and the provision of direct services to siblings and their families. During that time, we learned to listen to siblings, to identify some of their needs, and to understand their unique role within exceptional families. Throughout this book, we have included a number of stories that have been shared with us (with identifying details masked to protect confidentiality), as well as a number of our own observations of siblings and their families.

It is important to recognize two fundamental principles that have guided our work with siblings. First, siblings who have brothers or sisters with disabilities—whether they have intellectual disabilities, cerebral palsy, autism spectrum disorders, learning disabilities, hearing/speech/vision loss or disorders, fragile X syndrome, attention-deficit/hyperactivity disorder, or other disabilities—have similar experiences and needs. Siblings typically discuss the same types of feelings and emotions, often sharing their joys, fears, and problems. Many of the special concerns and unique needs of siblings are universal. Second, we have learned to respect that each sibling is unique and has a unique relationship with his or her brother or sister with a disability. At first glance, this may seem to be in conflict with the previous statement; however, although siblings have similar concerns, needs, and experiences, personal aspects may vary from sibling to sibling and may change over time. More important, we are finding that aspects of certain disabilities may have an influence on the sibling relationship. Because each sibling is a member of a unique family system, every sibling experiences life differently and so must be respected as an individual. The immediate and future influence that a sibling with a disability will have on his or her brother or sister will differ depending on a number of the individual characteristics of each family system.

We wrote this book for professionals and parents who wish to learn about special siblings and to help family members. This third edition provides an update of the latest research and service programs that have focused on the needs of brothers and sisters. In addition, we have stressed the need to involve members of the extended family, such as grandparents, and the need to be culturally sensitive in working with families. The model of theory to research to practice, which must guide the development of human services, also provides the format for this revised edition.

Chapters 1–4 present a brief overview of the importance of siblings in the family system and the special aspects of having a brother or sister with a disability. Chapters 5–11 detail a number of strategies to help siblings. Appendices then follow with updated lists of related literature and resources for professionals and parents, which should be helpful in working with siblings.

We hope that this book will provide greater recognition of the needs and experiences of children and adults who have brothers and sisters with disabilities and will continue to stimulate and inspire development of research and services to meet their special needs.

Acknowledgments

Throughout the development and production of the first two editions, and during work on this third edition, we relied on the assistance of many people. We would like to thank staff at the Paul H. Brookes Publishing Co., including Vice President Melissa Behm, who first believed in this project; Acquisitions Editor Rebecca Lazo and Acquisitions Assistant Steve Peterson, for seeing the book through its initial stages; and Senior Book Production Editor Leslie Eckard, for her tireless and compassionate editing.

We would also like to thank Irene Quinn Powell and Kevin Cunningham Gallagher for their advice and guidance, which have improved this edition.

We are grateful to our students, many of whom have brothers and sisters with disabilities and who have chosen careers in teaching because of the desire to help others with similar experiences.

We thank Don Meyer, Director of the Sibling Support Project, for his foreword and for his pioneering work to recognize the importance of brothers and sisters and to serve their unique needs.

We give special thanks to all of the brothers, sisters, and family members who have shared their experiences with us during the past years. The book contains many of your stories. We have changed your names if requested to protect the trust that you placed in us; however, we hope you know how deeply you have influenced us. Thank you for sharing your stories, your wisdom, and your humor. We specifically thank Claire Dees of the SPECTRUM Autism Support Group and the Project SCEIs Part C Early Intervention Parent Educators and Part B Parent Mentors from across Georgia. We also sincerely thank the many families who shared photographs that bring life to the pages that follow.

And finally, we give special thanks to our own children—our greatest teachers—from whom we have learned much about the sibling experience.

To my parents
Henry and Lynn Ahrenhold
—PG

To my children
Stedman, Nick, Tom Henry, and Cate
—TP

To my children
Rachel, Elizabeth, and Douglas Rhodes
—CR

Listening to Siblings

"Although I have emphasized the difficulties of growing up with a sibling with a disability, I don't mean to exclude the love and pride that most of us feel for our brothers and sisters."

—McHugh, 2003, p. 210

Individuals often express that there is something unique, something special, about growing up in a family in which a brother or sister has a disability. Sibling relationships, which play such a critical role in a child's overall development, take on special significance when one of the siblings has a disability. Perhaps this is because the issue is so multifaceted and different for each set of siblings. It may be because of stress experienced by the siblings; perhaps it is because the siblings spend more or less time together; or maybe it is because they rely on each other so much or so little. For many siblings, these factors work in combination with each other to form their own situation that is unlike anyone else's. Considering the multitude of factors involved and the individual nature of each family situation, it may be impossible to clarify the uniqueness of such distinct sibling relationships.

For many years, professionals have maintained a fragmented view of families who have children with disabilities. They have looked mostly at mothers' views while giving scant attention to siblings (Powell & Gallagher, 1993; Powell & Ogle; 1985; Seligman, 1983; Trevino, 1979). More recently, interest has been growing in the experiences of people who have brothers or sisters with disabilities (Burke, 2004; Connors & Stalker, 2003; Glasberg, 2000; Klein & Schleifer, 1993; McHugh, 2003; Meyer & Vadasy, 1996). This interest is clearly evidenced by the increase in research efforts directed toward brothers and sisters, a professional focus on assisting siblings, and programs aimed at providing siblings with information and support services. Most important, parents and professionals are beginning to take the time to listen to siblings. Siblings are being brought together, interviewed, and encouraged to discuss their experiences. Parents and professionals are learning from siblings. In fact, siblings are also learning from each other.

Professionals have begun asking siblings questions in an effort to learn how they can help them to cope effectively with their unique situations. Don Meyer has devoted most of his professional career listening to siblings and developing programs aimed at their special needs. In his book, *The Sibling Slam Book: What It's Really Like to Have a Brother or Sister with Special Needs* (2005), he asked 80 adolescent siblings from five countries to write brief responses to questions he posed to help them consider the fullness of their relationship with their brother or sister. Meyer asked the siblings to react to varied questions such as

- How would you describe your relationship with your sibling?
- How do you like hanging out with your sibling?
- What do you want people to know about your sibling?
- Do you think your sibling knows he or she has a disability?
- Do you think being a sibling has affected your personality? How?
- What makes you proud of your sibling?
- What do you tell your friends about your sibling's disability?
- Has your sibling ever embarrassed you?
- Can you imagine what it would be like if your sibling didn't have a disability?
- What do you see for your sibling's future?
- What life lesson have you learned from being a sibling of a sister or brother with disabilities?
- If you had one wish for your brother or sister, what would it be?

The responses Meyer received from these questions were varied and complex, yet it was evident that living closely and intensely with a sibling who has a disability can be both rewarding and stressful. Reports from many siblings indicate a full range of strong feelings—from joy to sadness, from pride to shame, from understanding to confusion. Despite the variety of feelings, all reports from siblings clearly demonstrate that deep emotions surround the experience of growing up with a brother or sister who has special needs.

The fullness of these responses reminds us that, like all sibling relationships, experiences and reactions are different for each individual.

Rather than assuming that all siblings feel the same way and have the same experiences and reactions, the first strategy for those who wish to help siblings is to listen actively to their stories. Careful listening will provide us with a better understanding of this unique experience.

As we talk with siblings, we must offer them a safe haven to discuss their issues and feelings without reprisal. Such interaction, of course, may be difficult for many parents and professionals because the information shared may cause feelings of pain or guilt. Strohm, whose sister has cerebral palsy, described her feelings when this safe haven was not provided.

> *"As a child I felt much anger: at my sister for being the way she was; at my parents for the special treatment they gave her; at everyone else for staring and not understanding. This anger had to be hidden; there was nowhere to direct it, so it turned in on me. I became self-doubting and frustrated at my perceived inadequacies."*
>
> —Strohm, 2005, p. 47

Siblings have much to share—with parents, professionals, and each other. This sharing provides parents and professionals with opportunities to begin to understand their feelings and needs. Siblings can teach those who are willing to listen to their message, and they can guide the actions of parents and professionals who want to help them. By listening carefully, we can learn how siblings' needs can best be met. By closely listening to their stories and probing their experiences, we can learn to minimize problem situations and maximize opportunities for growth. By learning from siblings' collective experiences, we can begin to help other brothers and sisters turn potentially painful, burdensome experiences into rewarding ones.

In an effort to set the stage for the subsequent chapters of this book, excerpts from several siblings' candid descriptions of their feelings and experiences appear on the following pages. Their insights and comments provide opportunities to learn about the special nature of growing up with a brother or sister who has a disability.

Robert Meyers was one of the first siblings to fully describe his relationship with his brother, Roger, who has intellectual disabilities.

> *"From the time Roger began going to physicians and consultants, it seemed to me that I carried a five-hundred-pound lead weight around in front of my brain. Never out of my mind was the idea that my brother was retarded, needed special attention, needed special care and that I had to provide some of it."*
>
> —1978, p. 36

Conway has a brother with prolonged mental illness. She opened her account of her relationship with a set of mixed feelings that expresses the emotions experienced by many siblings.

> *"Being the sibling of a person with a disability is a paradoxical experience. It can be stressful and difficult, but it can also impart a deep sense of meaning to life. It can provoke concern and compassion, which, these days, seems increasingly rare. It can also elicit feelings which are powerful and contradictory."*
>
> —1986, p. 4

Helsels, although reporting a full range of feelings and emotions, summarized her experience in the most positive way.

> *"All in all . . . I feel that Robin has brought much good into the lives of my family. He has taught us a great deal about acceptance, patience, individual worth, but most of all about love."*
>
> —1985, p. 96

Macfarlane, in writing about her sister Anna, who has autism, may have provided the best statement of the full range of experiences that siblings encounter. Her testimony, while recognizing the challenges, puts these into the type of perspective we want all siblings to experience.

> *"I cannot deny that Anna has been a burden to my family, but the rewards of that burden have been amazing. Anna has taught my family patience, maturity, love and compassion. If it hadn't been for Anna, I don't think that I would have the understanding and love I do for children with special needs and children in general. Anna has touched me in a special way, and I think that I would be a very different person if she weren't in my life."*
>
> —2001, p. 191

Bodenheimer offered a brief description of several of her experiences with her brother, Chris, who also has autism. She tells of her concern over his diagnosis and the etiology of his disability.

> *"I remember the turmoil surrounding the pursuit of his elusive diagnosis. The whole family shared in the knowledge that 'something' was wrong—he doesn't talk, he doesn't seem to hear, yet he loves music and keeps rhythm, he will only eat bananas, he's fascinated with water, never wants to cuddle, won't sleep through the night. . . . Knowing all these things made it even more difficult when those professionals [we] sought out gave confusing and conflicting reports. . . . An especially difficult part of living with an autistic sibling is the ever-present question of etiology. Why??? As a child, it's hard to live with someone who has difficulty learning, gets*

upset, and acts strangely when no one seems to know why. Children expect adults to have the answers, but so often in the case of the autistic child, the siblings are left on their own to grapple with this question."

—1979, pp. 291–292

Hanover, whose brother and child have autism spectrum disorder, offers a poignant description of learning of her son Joshua's disability.

"The day we went to take Joshua to a specialist in New York, he was the worst he could have been. It was heart-wrenching. I will tell you the whole way back I was silent. It was too much for me to absorb, and I started thinking all over, 'Oh no, I'm going to relive the hell I knew as a child.'"

—as quoted in Feiges and Weiss, 2004, pp. 80–81

Consider what Jennifer felt when she learned that her older brother Dick, who had Down syndrome, was diagnosed with cancer.

"Then, one cold, windy day in January, everything crumbled. Dick was diagnosed as having acute lymphoblastic leukemia. Could this be possible? Wasn't Down syndrome enough? . . . Initially Jennifer was angry and greatly saddened. She functioned as if in a trance. She did her assignments, helped her grandmother at home with chores, and watched over her baby brother and sister. All the time, her mind struggled with questions: 'Why?' 'To what purpose?'"

—in Klein and Schleifer, 1993, p. 112

Jennifer's statements, displaying emotions that are not unlike parental feelings, seem typical of those made by other siblings, and provide a clue to the needs that siblings have when children are diagnosed.

All too often it seems that siblings are excluded from information and from the search for answers concerning the disability. Ellifritt, whose sister has Down syndrome, described the situation she faced:

"My parents never sat me down and said, 'This is the problem, this is what's wrong with her. Do you understand? Do you have any questions?' My attempts to communicate were all in vain."

—1984, p. 19

Fortunately, some brothers and sisters have different experiences regarding learning about a sibling's particular disability. Barnett has a brother, Will, who is 11 months younger and has cerebral palsy and severe mental retardation. Barnett recalled,

"I like that my parents were very open and honest with me about what was wrong with my brother and why. I liked that they kept me abreast of his health."

—Personal communication, June 1, 2005

Some siblings tell of the extra responsibilities and burdens they experienced as a result of having a sister or brother with a disability. As one sibling noted,

> *"Having a younger brother with a disability has made me grow up very quickly. I have to do things most kids my age don't have to do. I am expected to practically be an adult toward him. . . . He is sort of training me to be a parent, but I still want to be a kid sometimes."*
>
> —in Adolphson et al., 2003, p. 34

Tara reminds us of the additional responsibility that siblings are often given and of the pressure applied to mature quickly in an interview.

> *"Adults always told me I was so mature for my age, so good to be spending time with my brother and helping my mother. I hated those comments so much; I just wanted to be a child."*
>
> —in Strohm, 2005, p. 82

Klein and Schleifer described interviews with individuals who grew up with siblings with disabilities. Diane, a young college student, recalled her feelings of embarrassment:

> *"I can remember being embarrassed about Cathy because she is really, I guess, quite upsetting to see for the first time. . . . I can remember in a bus terminal we had to spread a blanket on the floor so Cathy could crawl around and get a bit of exercise. A crowd gathered and I hated the people*

so much. I was just terribly embarrassed and I wanted to hide Cathy and I wanted to protect her from these people who were glaring. . . ."

—1993, p. 10

Another sibling, Richard, whose brother had hearing loss and severe physical disabilities, experienced the pain of watching his brother being teased on the playground:

"They made a circle around my brother and started looking at him and I just didn't know what to do. On the one hand I felt like saying, and it upsets me now to think that I would say what I wanted to say, 'Jim, hurry up and get out of here.' Even now that I say it, it is totally disgusting and at the same time I wanted to say to all those little kids, 'If you don't move now, I am going to throw you all over the fence.' Even now I have not resolved it—more than anything else, it shows me that I have not really come to terms with the whole thing. Furthermore, it gives me some appreciation for what my brother has to go through."

—1993, p. 8

McHugh provided a glimpse of some of her feelings about the unequal attention she received.

"Many of us siblings knock ourselves out trying to please our parents, but sometimes it seems the harder you try, the less appreciation you get for your accomplishments. That can make you very angry, but you feel like a spoiled brat if you say, 'Hey, I did something really good here. How about a little appreciation—the kind you give my brother for tying his shoes.'"

—2003, p. 39

Some siblings tell of their initial jealousy and subsequent realization of their brother's or sister's needs. Mark's brother, Chad, had Down syndrome and died at the age of 6 of congestive heart complications. Mark noted,

"One thing I couldn't understand was why Chad got what he wanted more than I did. He got to eat ice cream every morning for breakfast and he got first choice of things that Daddy brought home. When we both wanted the same coloring book, or candy, Chad always got it and it didn't always seem fair back then, but now that I am older I realize why he got them. All this happened years ago and I can remember some things like they were yesterday, while some things I can just barely remember, but now I realize, more than I did years ago, how much Chad meant to me. All of this may have happened long ago but the memories of Chad will always be stored in the very front of my brain and I will never forget him."

—M. Langston, personal communication, April 24, 1984

Bodenheimer shared the important role her parents played in her acceptance of her brother, Chris:

> *"In time I was helped to understand that the best we could do was to meet his needs as we saw them, enjoy his engaging personality, and accept what seemed impossible to change. The model of caring consistently displayed by our parents made it easier for my brother and me to assume this kind of acceptance."*
>
> —1979, p. 292

Over the years, we have found that siblings, like their parents, have hopes and dreams for their brothers and sisters with disabilities. Boisot conducted a structured interview with Michelle, whose brother Ben has a severe disability. Michelle described one hope for her brother:

> *"I want him to communicate. It is really hard for me to think about having all the same worries and concerns, thoughts, dreams and opinions that I have now, but being unable to communicate them to people. So, I know he thinks about the same things I do, and someday he will be able to tell other people what he thinks."*
>
> —2002, p. 31

With regard to the future, siblings definitely have concerns and know that they will be involved in the caregiving of their brother or sister with a disability, even when their eventual role is unclear. Siblings often talk about the future and the chance that they may someday be responsible for their brother or sister. Frank has experienced hopes and expectations regarding his future spouse because of concern for his sister Amy, who has Down syndrome:

> *"I've avoided marriage for a long time—I'm 41—but I considered it briefly just so I could take care of her. My parents decided not to send her to the group home, but when I do get married, I will have to find someone who will be willing to have Amy come and live with us when my parents are no longer here. All my relationships with women, serious or not, include Amy in some way or another."*
>
> —in McHugh, 2003, p. 152

L. Dufford recalled her future husband's feelings on meeting her brother, Eric.

> *"In my junior year of college I met my future husband and was thrilled that he was accepting of Eric and the fact that he would eventually become our responsibility if something ever happens to my mom."*
>
> —Personal communication, May 6, 2005

While many brothers and sisters have shared some of their pain, fears, and frustrations, these stories present only one side of the picture. The sibling experience can also be quite rewarding and have a profound, positive influence on the individual brothers and sisters. Consider these statements from siblings.

> *"There are both positive and negative aspects to having a sister with a disability, but like anything else in life, you have to take the good with the bad. It may take a bit longer for people to think of Corrie as just another little sister, but once they get to know her, they appreciate her for the beautiful, stubborn, funny girl she is."*
>
> —F. Last, personal communication, 2005

> *"Chris has brought us closer in a way you can't describe. He's just brought us closer together. . . . He's the glue, and he's shaped how my sister and I think and act. You can't separate the person I am—or my sister from my brother."*
>
> —in Feiges and Weiss, 2004, p. 104

> *"I always felt there was something very different about our family. Of course, you know, Cathy being that difference. Because of her difference there was a degree of specialness or closeness about us that, I do not know, it was sort of a bond that made us all very, very close."*
>
> —in Klein and Schleifer, 1993, p. 15

In 2004, reporter Jane Gross wrote an article for the *New York Times* describing the many issues surround growing up with a brother or sister with autism. In her article she quoted a teenager named Mark, whose brother Derek has required extraordinary family attention because he has autism. Mark noted that while his brother's disability can be annoying,

> *"He brings us together more, because we are in it as a family."*
>
> —2004

Many siblings tell us about their pride in their parents as a result of parenting a child with a disability. McHugh shared a report from Jayne, the youngest sister of Becky, who has intellectual disabilities:

> *"My father's dedication and the kind of energy he has put into his work at The Arc has affected me and my family. It's inspirational to see him work that hard and have that kind of focus, to get something done. I am really happy that Becky is in our life, and she has made me a better person, able to look at people differently, not just to see them physically, but to see what they can do."*
>
> —1999, p. 43

Many siblings have memories of positive family experiences that will buoy them during the tough times. A work by Adolphson and colleagues surveyed siblings of children with visual impairments about fun and good times. They had a great deal to say, such as the following:

> *"There are so many wonderful times that I have had with my brother that it is hard to pick just one. I love to just play with him. I love to watch him smile. Watching him have a good time is enough to make my day. My family and I try to help him live a happy and normal life. Sometimes I think he does the same for us."*
>
> —in Adolphson et al., 2003, p. 38

And, another very wise sibling advised,

> *"Most people say that love makes the world go round, but I think that fun and good times push it most of the way."*
>
> —in Adolphson et al., 2003, p. 38

Many siblings report learning important lessons from their brother or sister such as humility and compassion, developing a deeper appreciation for family, and knowing the importance of laughter. Indeed, many siblings have a wisdom and humanity way beyond their years. They often describe their brother or sister as their hero. An excerpt from Heroes, a poem by Katie Rousseau, sister of Chris, who died at age 9, reflects this idea of heroism:

> Everyone knows that Superman flies,
> That Batman has his wheels,
> That Cat Woman claws, and Dracula gnaws
> And Ms. Piggy cannot miss her meals.
>
> Spiderman swings all night on his web
> While Wolverine howls to the moon.
> My hero is my brother and yours may be another
> But my hero is not changing soon.
>
> —K. Rousseau, personal communication, June 7, 2005

Although siblings may see their brothers or sisters with disabilities as heroes, in many ways the siblings are the unsung heroes in families of children with disabilities.

SUMMARY

Siblings have much to teach us. We can only learn if we are willing to take the time to listen and to better understand their powerful messages. It seems clear that it is difficult, at best, to make generalizations about the experiences of siblings. Later chapters in this book show that research and clinical practice have proven that although siblings share a number of similar characteristics and feelings, each brother and sister is affected differently by having a sibling with a disability. It is important that neither parents nor professionals make any assumptions without first listening and offering support.

By listening to siblings, we know that the experience of growing up with a brother or sister who has a disability is not easily defined. It is certainly not unidimensional. The experience is complex and changes over time. Like all sisters and brothers, siblings report that they have powerful feelings about their siblings. Whether positive or negative, we have yet to meet a sibling who reported that the experience did not in some way influence his or her life.

By attending to siblings' messages, we can begin learning how to help enhance their experiences so that more will benefit, and so that families will also be strengthened. It all starts by listening.

What We Know About Sibling Relationships

"Still—whether one celebrates or denies the sibling bond—as long as one has a brother or sister alive, there is always another human being who has known one as a child, who has experienced one in a unique and intimate way over which one has had little control, who has been a mirror, however distorted, of one's childhood and youth; someone, in short, who has been a child of, and has shared the same parents."

—Bank and Kahn, 1997, p. 336

• • • Sitting around the kitchen table in Tammy's home seems so comfortable and familiar to her brothers and sisters. Her home is so much like the home they grew up in; in fact, many of their parents' possessions can be found throughout the house. These three siblings have decided to keep their sibling relationship vibrant after their parents died, and keep in touch through phone and e-mail. They also gather together regularly for holidays. At these gatherings, they share news, compare notes, reminisce about the past and, most important, they celebrate their sibling relationship. This time, Erica and Daniel talk about going fishing together with their spouses and children. Tammy and Erica are planning a family vacation together. All three talk openly about their parents, remembering their strong points as well as their weak ones. Each has a slightly novel perspective on their parents, which makes the other siblings think, laugh, and sometimes cry. Each sibling pair had a different relationship. Although the siblings share many experiences as a group, they also share uniquely personal experiences with each other. As adults with growing children of their own, their sibling relationships have taken on a new significance. Each one contributes in different ways to helping the others. Erica helped Tammy and her husband with a down payment on their new house. Daniel helped Erica secure her new job. Tammy always has time to help the others with their computer projects. Their present and past sibling relationships have helped them to find meaning in their current lives. These siblings continue to rely on each other, which emphasizes the value of their unique family relationship. The bond between these siblings ties them together for a lifetime and grows stronger over time. They have shared a special time together—their childhood. They have shared the same parents, and as adults, they continue to share their lives with each other. • • •

Siblings clearly have a powerful influence on the lives of their brothers and sisters. Jiao, Ji, and Jing (1986) found that children with siblings are rated more persistent and cooperative and have greater peer prestige than more "egocentric," only children. What is so critical about siblings? Throughout this chapter, a number of aspects of sibling relationships are reviewed. This chapter focuses on relationships between siblings in general. The special relationship between siblings and their brothers and sisters with disabilities is considered in detail in Chapter 3.

Unlike any other relationship, the sibling relationship provides two or more people with physical and emotional contact at critical life stages. Siblings provide a continuing relationship from which there is no annulment. This permanent relationship allows individuals to exert a considerable influence over each other throughout their lives.

WHAT DO SIBLINGS CONTRIBUTE TO EACH OTHER'S LIVES?

Siblings are socialization agents for each other. They often provide the first and some of the most intense peer relationships for a child. This special relationship provides a context for social development, particularly in early and middle childhood (Deater-Deckard, Dunn, & Lussier, 2002). As Bossard and Boll (1960) noted, the relationship between siblings is one of "mutual interdependency." Downey and Condron (2004) analyzed a sample of kindergarteners to determine if siblings help to promote children's social and interpersonal skills. They found that children negotiate peer relationships more effectively when they grow up with at least one sibling, particularly if the sibling is a full sibling rather than a step or half sibling. Siblings are available as long-term playmates and companions. As such, they help each other and teach each other, either directly or incidentally. The relationship also provides opportunities for sharing and the open and direct expression of their feelings.

Through their social interactions, siblings also learn a "give-and-take" process. Siblings help each other to learn to compromise. They teach each other the benefits of mutual collaboration and learn about resolving differences. This socialization process has a profound influence on the life of the sibling. From these social interactions, the child develops a foundation for later learning and personality development. Siblings also serve as a unique support system for one another. Besides being a playmate, the sibling may be a confidant and a counselor. Siblings typically provide advice to each other and may serve as a source of support in difficult times. This support system, important throughout the sibling relationship, may take on additional significance as the siblings mature and leave home. The sibling support network often continues throughout adulthood.

Siblings are more than just socialization agents for each other, however. Anderson, Hetherington, Reiss, and Howe (1994) found that siblings provide opportunities for the development of sensitivity, social understanding, caregiving, and conflict management in children. Perez-Granados and Callanan (1997a) looked at the role of siblings in young children's semantic language development and found that older siblings (between the ages of 6 and 8 years old) demonstrated early signs of a scaffolding approach to teaching similar to that typically provided by mothers. The siblings could not adjust the approach as well as mothers, of course, and did display a more demonstrative style of teaching versus the more informative style used by mothers. These researchers remind us of the importance of looking at how siblings learn from each other.

An Increasing Significance in Today's Society

Bank and Kahn (1997) discussed the emotional and social landscape of America as being more impersonal, more fragmented, and marked by a sense of alienation that was not noted even back in the 1980s. For siblings, this may mean that their families are more fragmented and they may spend either more or less time together depending on family circumstances. Eggebeen (1992) has reviewed census data to document sibling configurations across five cohorts from the 1940s to the 1980s. He looked at changes across four aspects including number of siblings, birth-order distributions, spacing intervals, and sex composition across groups of African American and Caucasian children. He found sharp declines in the number of siblings through the 1960s and 1970s. This reflected changes in the proportion of each cohort who are firstborn and only children, both of which had increased substantially by the 1980 cohort. There was also a notable decline in the proportion of children who had a sibling of the opposite sex. One racial difference Eggebeen noted is that African American children of preschool age had a higher average number of siblings than did European American children. Changes such as these that indicate a decrease in the number of siblings overall point to the increased importance of the relationship with the sibling or siblings an individual does have.

A Lifelong Relationship

The sibling relationship is perhaps the most long-lasting and influential relationship of a person's life. The sibling relationship begins with the birth of a brother or sister and continues throughout a person's lifetime. The duration of that relationship is certainly substantial. Unlike relationships with parents, which may last 40–60 years, the sibling relationship may last 60–80 years.

The sibling relationship, like any meaningful relationship, changes and develops as do the siblings. As Bank and Kahn (1997) noted, the sibling relationship has periods of intense activity as well as periods of inactivity. Sibling relationships follow a life cycle of their own. In early childhood, siblings provide a constant source of companionship for one another. As young children, they interact with each other frequently and share not only toys, clothes, rooms, parents, and grandparents but also important family experiences. During the school years, siblings begin to reach out to nonfamily members. Siblings use the social skills they have learned from each other to establish relationships with others outside the family constellation. Throughout adolescence, many siblings seem ambivalent about their relationships with brothers and sisters; however, they rely on siblings as confidants and advisors, especially regarding friends, use of drugs, sexuality, and other concerns (Deater-Deckard et al., 2002; Lamb, 1982). These cycles may change if the parents divorce or step siblings are added, of course. For example, teenage siblings who have been raised together from birth may be blended into their mother's new husband's family after a divorce. In an instant, they may now have infant or toddler stepbrothers or stepsisters and experience the early childhood cycles of play and extensive caregiving needs.

In adulthood, the sibling relationship takes on new characteristics as individuals begin to leave home and establish an independent life. Young adult siblings may provide critical support or encouragement. As siblings have their own children, their brothers and sisters, as aunts and uncles, provide unique experiences to each other's children. They provide an additional network of love and support to their siblings' children. In old age, when children move away and spouses die, siblings can provide a support network to each other (Cicirelli, 1982; Seltzer, 1991). They may again re-establish frequent contact and, in some cases, move in together to provide companionship and share the final experiences of life much like they shared the first stages of their lives together.

SIBLINGS WITHIN THE FAMILY SYSTEM

Families have always been a rich and meaningful part of life. From the support of the family, a child develops the strength and spirit to meet the challenges of the future. We first learn of the outside world and ourselves as part of that world from the family. Families provide children with their first opportunities to explore, to communicate, and to interact with other human beings.

Families change as children grow older, as parents change, and as the community changes. Family members' relationships are adjusted and social contacts outside the family expand and mature. In whatever way the family changes, it still remains the social point of departure, however. Children leave the family and go to school, to church, to recreational activities, and on to their adult lives—sometimes marrying and starting their own families. The family is a stepping stone to the future.

Interactional Dynamics

Families can be viewed as an interrelated system that supports the interdependence of the individual family members. Each member of the family is a critical element whose personality and interactions affect those of other family members. As one member of the family changes, so, too, will the other members. As Beckman and Bristol (1991) pointed out, the fundamental concept of a family systems focus is that the family consists of a number of interdependent subsystems. Events or circumstances that affect one part of the system likewise influence the other parts (Fewell, 1986; Minuchin, 1974; Stoneman & Brody, 1984; Turnbull, Turnbull, Erwin, & Soodak, 2006). The extended family, the community, and any policies that regulate resources are all outside influences that affect the nuclear family (Bronfenbrenner, 1977).

Family interactions are never as simple as they may first seem. An interaction between parents often influences future interactions between the parents and children or one parent and child. As a toddler learns to use language, for instance, the child influences the way parents and even siblings relate to him or her. Likewise, the relationship between a father and one of his daughters influences the interaction between his two daughters. Any one family member exerts influence on his or her *individual* relationship with every other family member. This influence, in turn, affects the relationships between other family members.

Schvaneveldt and Ihinger (1979), in their classic analysis of sibling interactions and interdependence, asserted the importance of considering families as systems. They have outlined five basic assumptions in regard to sibling relationships:

1. Within most families, there exist three subsystems of interaction. Each of these subsystems (spouse–spouse, parent–child, and sibling–sibling) operates semi-independently within the family structure.
2. Family members both initiate and receive social interactions. Family interaction is dynamic, with husbands and wives affecting each other, parents and children affecting each other, and siblings affecting each other.
3. Sibling interaction is a continuous process of development that occurs throughout the life span.
4. The personality development and social behaviors of family members are partially determined by family composition and interaction.
5. Sibling groups have properties similar in characteristics to other small groups.

Thus, in conceptualizing sibling relationships, the group or dyad of siblings must be first thought of in the context of the larger family system. These patterns of influence are transactional in nature; that is, one sibling affects the other sibling and vice versa, and this interaction changes across time (Bell, 1968; Sameroff & Chandler, 1975).

Brody, Stoneman, and MacKinnon (1986) looked at studies that have directly focused on the relationship of siblings' interactions to other family subsystems. The findings suggest that such interaction is related to the quality of the sibling relationship. In their 1986 study, Brody and his colleagues observed 24 sibling pairs in their homes. Results revealed several associations between maternal childrearing practices and the behavior of the older sibling toward the younger sibling. Managing and helping behaviors of the older sibling were positively related to maternal child-rearing practices that encouraged curiosity and openness. In contrast, these behaviors were negatively related to maternal inconsistency and anxiety induction. The authors also found that the particular play context influenced the types of behaviors observed and urged other researchers to focus on context as an important variable when looking at sibling interactions.

Family Context

Hetherington, Reiss, and Plomin (1994) reminded us that in order to understand sibling relationships, one must examine them in context of other family relationships such as the parent–child relationship. Other studies (Brody & Stoneman, 1986; Brody, Stoneman, & Burke, 1987a; Bryant & Crockenberg, 1980; Teti & Ablard, 1989) have also suggested that sibling relationships are in large part a function of the parent–child relationship. Wood, Vaughn, and Robb (1988) investigated concordance in the social-emotional and attachment behaviors of firstborn and secondborn siblings in 65 families and found that the quality of infant maternal attachment at 12 months showed significant concordance among siblings and was conditioned by the stability of maternal behavior.

Parental discord may have negative effects on sibling interactions. Brody and colleagues (1987a) found that parental conflict was associated with lower rates of prosocial behavior and greater agonistic behavior among siblings. Brody, Stoneman, McCoy, and Forehand (1992) found that parental perceptions of lack of family cohesiveness, parental inequality of treatment, and family conflict during discussions of sibling problems were linked to higher sibling conflict levels.

Erel, Margolin, and John (1998) examined 73 same-sex sibling pairs ages 3½–8½ during free play to look at whether the link between the marital relationship and sibling interaction is direct or is influenced by the mother–child relationship. They found that older siblings' negative behavior is only linked with negative dimensions of the marital and mother–child relationship, but younger siblings' negative behavior is linked with the mother–child relationship. Older siblings exhibited more negative behavior (e.g., aggression and dominating behaviors) toward their younger siblings than vice-versa. The authors also found an association with age spacing and position in the family such that spacing between siblings was associated with positive sibling behavior, but only that of the younger sibling to the older. The age gap between siblings ranged from 11 months to 4 years with a mean of 2 years and a standard deviation of 9 months. Results indicated that the greater the spacing between siblings, the greater the warmth expressed by the younger toward the older sibling. The authors suggest that this demonstrates an indirect route from marital discord to negative sibling interaction, meaning that the marital relationship affects children because it affects the

parent–child relationship. They suggest that this provides evidence for a model of the family system as a whole that takes into account all three family subsystems including marital, parental, and sibling.

Volling, McElwain, and Miller (2002) examined sibling jealousy and its relations to child and family characteristics in 60 families with a 16-month-old toddler and an older preschool-age sibling. A positive marital relationship quality was a particularly strong predictor of the older siblings' abilities to regulate jealousy. There was also a general pattern of results showing that those children who expressed negative affect were more likely to interfere with the interaction between parent and sibling and were less likely to focus their attention on alternative play activities.

Miller, Volling, and McElwain (2000) found that both older and younger children were more likely to express jealousy during sessions in which a parent's attention was directed toward a child's sibling than when the parent was interacting with the child. Older children were much less likely to show negative affect and were better able to focus attention and to play during the jealousy paradigm than were the younger children. Miller and colleagues pointed to a need for future research on temperament and to social relationships as developmental contexts for young children's emotional regulation.

RESEARCH ON SIBLING RELATIONSHIPS

Exactly what influence do brothers and sisters have on each other? Do birth order and age spacing really affect a child's personality? Research on siblings and their unique relationships with each other is helping to separate the facts from countless myths about siblings.

Levy, in 1934, was one of the first researchers to address the role of family context in shaping sibling relationships, which led to a shift away from the family systems focus. Sibling status (constellation) variables such as age, sex, or birth order became the focal points. This change was likely precipitated by the historical interest in these variables as predictors of intelligence and personality factors (Sutton-Smith & Rosenberg, 1970). The studies on the effects of sibling status variables as predictors of sibling relationships have been inconclusive (Abramovitch, Corter, & Lando, 1979; Dunn & Kendrick, 1982) and, more recently, the trend in studying sibling relationships has again shifted back to a family systems interactional focus, looking at the interactions of sibling and parents in various contexts. These research trends are discussed in this chapter and their impact on families with a child with disabilities is discussed in Chapter 3. Later chapters (5–11) provide descriptions of many strategies useful for children who have a brother or sister with a disability.

Constellation Variables

Much of the earlier research on sibling relationships involving children without disabilities has concentrated on linking certain factors about the individual siblings, such as age spacing, gender, or ordinal position to differences in such variables as achievement, conformity, dependency, intelligence, or personality (Jacobs & Moss, 1976). These variables are known as constellation variables.

Age Spacing Koch (1955) concluded that age spacing was an important consideration in explaining sibling relationships. He found that children closest in age (less than 6 years apart) played both with each other and with each other's friends more, and had more common interests than did children further apart in age.

Gender On the assumption that siblings do, in fact, influence each other's behavior, several authors conducted studies on sibling gender related to learning tasks. Cicirelli (1972) found female siblings more effective than male siblings or female nonsiblings in teaching a simple conceptual task to younger brothers and sisters. In contrast, he also indicated that boys tend to be more effective in teaching younger, unrelated children than in teaching their own brothers and sisters.

Cicirelli (1976) conducted a similar study to determine the differences in mother–child versus sibling–sibling interactions on a problem-solving task. He discovered that the older sibling's behaviors and the younger child's responses depended on the sex of the older sibling. Cicirelli found that mothers tended to help younger children more when the older child in the family was a male, suggesting that when a child

has an older sister, mothers relinquish portions of their helping roles to the older sister.

In this same study, Cicirelli uncovered another pattern revealing that younger children with siblings of the opposite gender were more independent and received more feedback on tasks from the mother or older sibling than did children with the same-sex siblings. A 1980 study of social behaviors of infants by Dunn and Kendrick offered different findings. Namely, these researchers found marked differences between same- and mixed-sex sibling pairs. The authors observed 40 pairs of siblings at various times in their homes. They noted that by the time the younger child was 14 months of age, more frequent positive social behaviors were shown by both siblings in same-sex pairs. In contrast, more negative behaviors were displayed by the first child in different-sex pairs. Two laboratory studies (Lamb, 1978a, 1978b), however, seem to contrast with both the Cicirelli and the Dunn and Kendrick conclusions. Lamb's studies indicated that the gender composition of sibling pairs had no influence on the interactions of the children. Other studies showed that opposite-sex sibling pairs tend to display more negative behaviors than same-sex siblings in early childhood (Dunn & Kendrick, 1982) and middle childhood (Epkins & Dedmon, 1999).

Such diverse findings highlight the difficulties faced by researchers; the issues are complex and hard to distill to single variables. Stoneman, Brody, and MacKinnon (1986) discussed two broad theoretical perspectives of research studies on sibling status in sex-role development. The first (Brim, 1958) focused on sibling modeling of stereotypical sex-role behavior in which researchers predicted that children in same-sex pairs would be the most stereotypically sex typed, whereas children from cross-sex pairs would be more androgynous. Another perspective (Schachter, 1982) proposed a rivalry–defense hypothesis that predicted that individuals in same-sex pairs become more differentitated from each other than do opposite-sex siblings in order to avoid comparison and competition.

Rust, Golombok, Hines, Johnston, and Golding (2000) looked at the role of brothers and sisters in the gender development of preschool children. They found that boys with older brothers and girls with older sisters were more sex-typed than same-sex singletons, who were more sex-typed than children with opposite-sex siblings. The behaviors of children with older brothers were associated with more masculinity and less femininity; whereas boys with older sisters were more feminine but not less masculine. Rust and colleagues noted that, theoretically, both social learning and cognitive developmental perspectives are consistent with the findings that children may be influenced by the presence of same- or other-sex siblings in the family home. Results of this study indicate that gender of older siblings is associated with gender-role behavior of younger siblings and is particularly influenced by the presence of an older brother. It is important to point out that the relationship is reciprocal—younger siblings may influence the gender role behavior of older brothers and sisters, for instance, through encouragement of certain preferred games and toys.

Birth Order Unruh, Grosse, and Zigler, focusing on birth order and number of siblings in a family, compared groups of firstborn, later-born, and only born children on a task used to assess the effectiveness of social reinforcement. Firstborn children played significantly longer without social reinforcement than did later-borns; however, "the number of siblings was not found to be related to playing time" (1971, p. 1154). In their discussion, Unruh and colleagues pointed out that using number of siblings or birth order as a variable has not yielded consistent results, and these researchers suggested that the age gap between siblings might be an important variable for consideration.

Other researchers (Belmont & Marolla, 1973; Bossard & Boll, 1960; Harris, 1964; Weiss, 1970), have tried to establish a pattern of personality characteristics for individuals falling in a certain birth order, such as the "first child" or the "baby" of the family. Some children seem to fit easily into these typical stereotypes. Studies (Belmont, Stein, & Zybert, 1978; Davis, Cahan & Bashi, 1977; Sutton-Smith & Rosenberg, 1970; Zajonc & Bargh, 1980) suggested that sibling birth order variables do influence individual styles, preferences, and adult self-esteem, but the importance of such patterns may have been overestimated. The constructs are inadequate in explaining the complexity of sibling relationships.

Number of Children Downey (1995) reviewed the literature on typical sibling relationships and found that in almost every case, children do better in school and on cognitive tests when they have fewer versus many siblings and that siblings provide opportunities for play (Brody, 1998). Downey and Condron (2004) described two theories regarding siblings. One, the resource dilution theory, suggests that siblings dilute resources from rather than provide resources for each other, and are therefore not advantageous to each other. Another theory is that siblings provide resources to each other; that is, with everything else being equal, the more siblings a child has, the better he or she is able to develop play skills. Downey and Condron suggested that although siblings may provide opportunities for each other, there may be a threshold, and even one sibling may be enough to reach the advantages.

Beyond the Constellation Variables Researchers of varying backgrounds, from sociology to medicine, have stressed the importance of the sibling relationship. The key word here may be *relationship.* Factors beyond sibling age spacing or ordinal position are now believed to be important in describing and explaining the nature of sibling relationships. The literature has shifted from the study of sibling-status constellation variables (e.g., birth order, age spacing) to a study of the formative process of developing sibling relationships and the complexity of those relationships within a systems framework. Researchers have also looked at the developmental nature of those relationships across time to study sibling relationships in focused time periods, such as in the preschool years, the elementary years, middle childhood and adolescence, and adulthood. A particularly large increase has occurred in the number of studies looking at sibling relationships in the middle childhood and adolescent years over the past decade.

Another trend in the sibling literature is the study of parental differential treatment (PDT) as a component of the nonshared environment (Daniels & Plomin, 1985; Dunn & Plomin, 1990, 1991; Plomin & Daniels, 1987), which is described in more detail later in this chapter. In other words, what makes siblings who come from the same parents and who are raised in the same home environment so different from each other? Research is now also trying to take into account the various family configurations, such as step- or blended families, which may affect sibling outcomes. Although most of the earlier sibling studies were of families of European-American descent, more recent studies have looked at sibling relationships in the African American community. Two other major new areas of interest in sibling research are that of temperament and conflict. All of these areas of research are outlined next.

Developmental/Age Patterns Vandell and Wilson (1987) noted that studies on early relationships involving siblings have focused on the content and affective quality of sibling interactions. Young siblings are naturally influenced by the presence of a brother or sister, and the actions of one child influence the actions and reactions of others. Some of the effects of these sibling–sibling interactions have been described in this chapter already. Researchers are also documenting the patterns of sibling relationships at various stages throughout the life cycle—from children in the elementary years through adulthood—a departure from early studies that looked at sibling relationships only during the infancy and preschool years.

Studies of Infant and Preschool-Age Siblings

Studies in the early years of children's lives have looked specifically at language development and reciprocal and complimentary interactions, as well as the content and affective quality of the sibling interactions from a longitudinal perspective.

Language Several studies (Barton & Tomasello, 1991; Mannle & Tomasello, 1987; Tomasello & Mannle, 1985) have investigated the effects of brothers and sisters on their younger siblings' (24 months and younger) language development. In looking at triads with a parent and two siblings present, it seems that—compared with the mother–infant dyad—siblings are highly directive in their linguistic interactions with younger siblings and show little skill (or inclination) to provide nonverbal information to the infant. They neither adjust their sentence length and complexity nor add conversation-maintaining devices.

Jones and Adamson (1987) also investigated language use in mother–child–sibling interactions. They found that, in their mother's presence, later-borns made significantly fewer utterances when siblings were present than when they played alone. Although there were no qualitative differences in maternal speech during dyadic as compared with triadic situations, a striking quantitative difference was found. Mothers spoke much less to the younger sibling when the older sibling was present, and the older sibling's language did not seem to compensate for the decrease. Woolett (1986) maintained that—although there may be a decrease in adult sensitivity to individual children and their needs when an older sibling is present—a more stimulating linguistic environment also is often found, perhaps because mothers are speaking to their children as a group and perhaps talking about more mature themes or holding more vocabulary-rich conversations to incorporate the various age groups.

In a study of siblings who were preschool age (at the study's inception), Brown and Dunn (1992) looked at developmental changes in the patterns of family conversations and children's talk about feelings over a 14-month period. They found significant increases in total amount of talk and frequency of talk about feelings between sibling pairs. Siblings gained prominence as conversational partners and sibling pairs directed significantly more conversation to each other when the younger siblings had reached 47 months of age than when the study started. Brown and Dunn cautioned that the siblings were all from middle-class families, who tend to reflect the value of viewing older siblings as playmates rather than caretakers.

Howe (1991) looked at the relationship between internal state, perspective taking, and affective behavior in siblings ages 36–58 months (oldest child) and 14 months (younger child). She found that a large portion of preschoolers' conversations directed to younger siblings contains references to internal states such as feelings, wants, and abilities. Preschoolers who directed more positive affective behavior and more total affective behavior to their younger siblings also engaged in more frequent sibling-directed internal state language. Howe suggested that this internal state language may be a way of regulating sibling interaction and also a potential means for siblings to construct shared meaning in their worlds.

Interactions Young siblings interact in interesting ways. For instance, Samuels (1980) assessed the effect of an older sibling's presence on numerous 23-month-old infants while they were exploring a new environment. Samuels found that, when older siblings were present, the infants tended to leave their mothers more quickly, stay away longer, and move farther away from their mothers than they did when no older siblings were present. Infants also inspected and manipulated objects more in the presence of their older siblings. Dunn (1983) concluded that sibling relationships provide a context for social learning and understanding. Sibling influence can be seen in the imitative behaviors of younger siblings as well as in the development of social and intellectual skills. Dunn suggested that the complementary features of sibling interactions are areas of importance in the developmental patterns of sibling relationships.

Newman (1994) presented an overview of the literature on sibling caregiving interactions, which shows that older siblings can impart skills and care that can be helpful to a younger sibling. Garner, Jones, and Palmer (1994) looked specifically at the social cognitive correlates of preschool children's sibling caregiving behavior using 55 sibling dyads. They recorded the frequency of preschooler's caregiving acts and the number of seconds the younger sibling was distressed. The researchers found that emotional role taking, knowledge of caregiving scripts, and toddler distress were positively related to sibling caregiving behavior. This level of affective knowledge and skills was more clearly related to sibling caregiving than was cognitive perspective taking.

Garner, Jones, and Miner (1994) described a study that looked at the role of caregiving by preschool-age siblings from families with low incomes in order to better understand the development of social competence within the family. The mothers' positive expressions of emotion within the family were related to higher levels of caregiving by the sibling, whereas more negative emotional expressions led to less caregiving behaviors by the sibling. Garner and colleagues found that redirecting was the most frequent type of caregiving behavior followed by verbal comforting and physical comforting, a pattern similar to patterns reported for middle-income children (Garner, 1993). This study again highlights the importance of the parent role in influencing the tone of sibling relationships.

Howe, Petrakos, and Rinaldi (1998) looked at how sibling relationship quality was associated with children's play patterns. The target siblings (who were the older siblings) were kindergarten age. They concluded that the sibling relationship is a rich context for pretend play and negotiation, with some sibling partners engaged in frequent, extended, elaborate play sequences.

Cummings and Smith (1993) studied the impact of anger between adults (mother and a male adult) on siblings' and peers' emotions and social behavior. The older siblings studied ranged from 5 to 7 years old, whereas the younger siblings in the dyads ranged from 2 to 5 years old. They found that expressions of positive affect increased among female siblings during an anger period between adults and continued in the resolution period, and that prosocial behaviors among male siblings greatly increased in resolution periods. Cummings and Smith suggested that siblings may attempt to buffer each other from the stress of adult discord and may thus play an important role in families regarding coping with stress. Siblings' primary means of buffering the other sibling from stress was an increase in helping, sharing, and cooperating.

Longitudinal Studies Abramovitch and her colleagues (Abramovitch et al., 1979; Abramovitch, Corter, & Pepler, 1980; Abramovitch, Corter, Pepler, & Stanhope, 1986; Corter, Abramovitch, & Pepler, 1983; Pepler, Abramovitch, & Corter, 1981) conducted a notable series of research projects documenting the relationships of young siblings over time. Their basic goal has been to provide information on the content and affective quality of sibling interactions in the preschool years. They have looked at how variables such as gender or age affected these patterns.

In the first study of this series (Abramovitch et al., 1979), the younger siblings averaged 20 months of age, and age intervals between the siblings were either extensive (2½–4 years) or minimal (1–2 years). Using observational ratings, the authors found that the oldest children in the sibling dyad initiated prosocial acts more often than did the younger siblings, whereas younger siblings imitated more often. These effects were found regardless of age-spacing between siblings.

These researchers also looked at interactional patterns in both same-sex and mixed-sex sibling pairs and found girls to be more prosocial than boys in both the 1979 and 1980 studies. In the same-sex (Abramovitch et al., 1979) study, pairs of sisters responded more positively overall in terms of prosocial behavior than did brothers. In the mixed-sex (Abramovitch et al., 1980) study, younger siblings responded more positively to social initiations than did their older siblings. Also, in the same-sex pairs, older boys were more physically aggressive than were older girls, whereas no differences emerged on any measures of aggression in mixed-sex pairs.

Corter, Abramovitch, and colleagues (1983) found that mothers are less consistent in their treatment of children in mixed-sex sibling dyads, and the researchers proposed increasingly sex-typed interests and activities as factors in less-positive interactions between mixed-sex dyads. Overall, though, they documented reciprocity in the sibling relationship from an early age, with prosocial and play-oriented behaviors constituting a majority of sibling interactions in the preschool years.

In a first longitudinal follow-up study by Pepler and colleagues (1981) of 28 pairs of mixed-sex and 28 pairs of same-sex siblings, it was found that the pattern of interaction just described remained quite stable during the 18 months following the initial observations. Older children still initiated more prosocial behaviors, whereas younger siblings imitated more often. However, a marked increase in prosocial behavior by both the older and younger siblings was noted over the 18-month time period. Of note, gender differences found in the earlier study, in which girls initiated more prosocial behaviors, were not found in the follow-up observations.

Abramovitch and colleagues (1986), in a second follow-up study of sibling interaction, observed 24 pairs of same-sex and 24 pairs of mixed-sex sibling dyads in their homes. This study, conducted 18 months after a first follow-up study and 3 years after their initial observations, found patterns of interaction similar to those observed earlier. In their ongoing longitudinal observations in naturalistic and laboratory settings, Abramovitch and colleagues have observed that older siblings consistently initiate more aggressive and prosocial behaviors, whereas the younger siblings display more imitative behaviors. The older sibling thus dominate the relationship even as both siblings grow older. They suggest that birth order is a critical component of sibling interaction. Neither age spacing nor gender composition showed consistent effects.

Dunn and Kendrick (1979), Lamb (1978a), Samuels (1980), and Wishart (1986) also found that older children served as models for initiating actions, whereas younger siblings pay attention to and tend to imitate their older brothers and sisters. Wishart found that sibling modeling was an effective method of facilitating cognitive development in infants.

Another longitudinal study (Dunn, Slomkowski, & Beardsall, 1994) extended from preschool to middle childhood. Dunn and colleagues studied the sibling relationship using home observations and maternal and child interviews. They found that scores on preschool measures of sibling interaction contributed to individual differences in positive aspects of the relationship in early adolescence, independent of gender and socioeconomic status (SES). The differences in warmth and intimacy of siblings at preschool age showed significant links with sibling interaction 7 years later. The results showed substantial continuity in the siblings' positive and negative behaviors toward one another over the time period. The authors remind us of the significance of the sibling relationship in the younger years, particularly in terms of shaping aggression or conflict (which will be discussed in more detail in this chapter).

Studies on Elementary School-Age Siblings

Many studies of sibling interactions have looked at preschool-age children and their younger infant or toddler siblings. Older siblings tend to offer toys to their siblings and attempt to engage in verbal exchanges (Abramovitch et al., 1979; Abramovitch et al., 1980; Lamb, 1978a, 1978b; Samuels, 1980), whereas the younger siblings tend to model and monitor the behavior of their older brother or sister. Studies have also investigated the interactions of school-age siblings. Sutton-Smith and Rosenberg (1968), for instance, found that on the one hand, older preadolescent-age siblings (fifth and sixth graders) were perceived by themselves and their younger siblings as being more "powerful" in social-structural terms. On the other hand, the younger siblings were perceived as showing more resentment and as having a tendency to turn more often to their parents for help.

Brody and Stoneman (1986) and Stoneman and colleagues (1986) noted the importance of context in studying role relationships and gender differences in sibling interactions for school-age children.

Role Relationships A *role* is a patterned sequence of actions performed in an interactive or social context (Stoneman & Brody, 1982), which appears to have important developmental outcomes. The role relationships that occur during sibling interactions are important to explore. Studies of school-age siblings by Brody, Stoneman, and MacKinnon (1982); Brody, Stoneman, MacKinnon, and MacKinnon (1985); and Stoneman and colleagues (1984, 1986), looked at the roles of teacher, learner (or observer), manager, and managee in semistructured and naturalistic contexts. Consistent with earlier reported studies of preschool-age sibling dyads, older school-age siblings assumed teacher and manager roles more often, whereas the younger siblings were in the reciprocal roles of managee and learner. They also found greater role asymmetries in sibling interactions as contrasted with peer interactions, and in dyads having an older sister as contrasted with those containing an older brother.

Minnett, Vandell, and Santrock (1983) observed 73 pairs of siblings in the school setting, focusing on the 7- to 8-year-old firstborn siblings. The sibling pairs participated in unstructured, cooperative, and competitive contests. The authors found that firstborn siblings were significantly more likely than their younger siblings to praise, teach, and display dominant behaviors. The authors also noted that more positive behaviors were associated with siblings in pairs more widely spaced in age (3–4 years), whereas aggression was more common in pairs more closely spaced in age (1–2 years). This contrasts with a finding of Abramovitch, Pepler, and Corter (1982), who found that in preschool-age siblings, the age differences in dyads made little or no difference in their social interactions.

Kosonen (1996) reported a study on 69 Scottish primary school children. The siblings of these children were perceived to be a significant source of support and help and were regarded proportionally as of almost equal importance to the children as were their parents. Children were most likely to turn to their older siblings for support and help; younger siblings were rarely sought out in this regard.

Gender Differences Stoneman and colleagues (1986) discussed gender differences in the role relationships of school-age children. Generally, female sibling pairs play together more than do males (Brody et al., 1985; Stoneman et al., 1984), and among same-sex sibling pairs, older girls assume more of a teacher role than do boys. In Stoneman and colleagues' (1986) descriptive study of same-sex and cross-sex school-age sibling pairs, activities selected in the home by same-sex pairs were the most stereotypically sex-typed. Types of activities in cross-sex pairs tended to be influenced mostly by the gender of the older child. Arliss (1997) looked at sibling communication for early elementary age children outside the home and found that siblings frequently chose to sit near one another during lunch and provide emotional support. She found that sibling interaction outside the home was more likely to occur when siblings were of the same gender and were close in age. Interaction was also more likely to occur when the siblings were engaged in activities associated with rituals of the home, such as eating.

Studies of Siblings in Middle Childhood and Adolescence

The number of research studies conducted with siblings during the middle childhood and adolescent years has increased substantially. Dunn, Slomkowski, and Beardsall (1994) noted that most of the sibling studies focusing on middle childhood and adolescence have been cross-sectional in design rather than longitudinal.

Bryant's (1982) early work on sibling relationships in middle childhood suggested that ambivalence, as well as rivalry and conflict, characterize the relationship of siblings during these years. Dunn (1983) reviewed several important longitudinal studies and concluded that even if a sibling relationship is close, harmonious, and conflict-free in the early years, it may not continue to be so in middle childhood and adolescence. Changes in sibling relationships highlight the importance of the wider social context in which children are growing up, and normative life events such as transition to high school for one may affect the relationship between siblings.

In an attempt to clarify developmental trends, Buhrmester and Furman administered the Sibling Relationship Questionnaire (Buhrmester & Furman, 1990; Furman & Buhrmester, 1985) to children in grades 3, 6, 9, and 12. They found that relationships were rated as progressively more egalitarian across the age groups. Adolescents reported reduced levels of dominance, nurturance, companionship, intimacy, and affection from their older siblings when compared with younger participants. Whereas levels of perceived conflict with younger siblings were moderately high across all four grades, ratings of conflict with older siblings were progressively lower. Buhrmester and Furman suggested that as siblings become more competent and their developmental

status becomes more similar, their relationship becomes more symmetrical and egalitarian. The relationship may become less intense because brothers and sisters spend decreasing amounts of time together. Generally, same-sex sibling pairs report feeling closer than do opposite-sex dyads.

Dunn (1996) reported that individual differences in positivity and negativity toward siblings are moderately to highly stable over the course of middle childhood. McHale, Updegraff, Helms-Erikson, and Crouter (2001) looked at sibling influences on gender development in middle childhood and early adolescent years. This study looked at qualites of gender roles (i.e., attitudes, personality and leisure activities) to determine if one sibling's qualities could predict those of his or her brothers or sisters. Families were interviewed over 3 years. The qualities of the firstborn siblings in year 1 did predict the qualities of second-born siblings in the third year. Thus, the older sibling may be a relevant role model for the younger sibling, but the reverse was not found. It seems that the socialization process may work differently for two siblings within the same familiy. There appeared to be more evidence of sibling influence than parental influence during the middle childhood developmental period.

Whereas past literature has found that parenting appears to be a critical factor in understanding negative child outcomes, it seems that sibling relationships may be another important influence. Slomkowski, Rende, Conger, Simons, and Conger (2001) looked at delinquency and sibling relationships. They reviewed the literature that shows that sibling effects on delinquency are independent of the impact of other salient factors such as parental and peer influences (Farrington & West, 1993; Lauritsen, 1993; Rowe & Gulley, 1992). Most of these studies have focused on brothers and suggest a social influence process that occurs from oldest to youngest. It seems that an older sibling's delinquency at one point in time may influence the later expression of delinquency by the younger sibling (Farrington, 1995; Farrington & West, 1993), regardless of gender. For sister–sister relationships, it seems that low levels of warmth/support led to older–younger sister delinquency, whereas for brothers it was high levels of warmth/support. The authors caution that sibling effects may change across adolescence and that they can be independent of parental influence (Farrington & West, 1993).

Moser and Jacob (2002) also examined the differential effects of parenting and sibling influences in predicting adolescents' problem behaviors and found that sibling behavior was a significant predictor of deviant behavior, even when parenting effects were statistically controlled. Specifically, sibling conflict appears to be important in understanding internalizing behaviors such as depression or anxiety. Ardelt and Day (2002) also studied the importance of older siblings as role models in adolescence, in terms of both positive and deviant behaviors. They found that younger siblings whose older siblings were reported and perceived to be deviant were more likely to have lower feelings of competence than were peers with an older sibling reported to be within normative bounds of behavior. The older siblings' influence appears to be a pervasive influence for younger siblings. Widmer and Weiss (2000) investigated the association between older siblings' support, older siblings' adjustment, and younger siblings' adjustment in areas of delinquency, academic success, and mental health for adolescents considered to be at risk. They found that sibling support was not correlated to any of the areas of development for younger siblings but that older sibling support influenced the outcomes of the younger only when accompanied by a positive image of the older sibling—that is—the younger sibling's perception of the older sibling's adjustment.

Evidence also indicates that older siblings can be positive role models. Kowal and Blinn-Pike (2004) looked at sibling influences on adolescents' attitudes toward safe sex practices and found that perceptions of the quality of the sibling relationship (as more positive) were more closely associated with sibling discussions about safer sex than were older siblings' general attitudes toward safer sex. The closer that siblings report they are to each other, the more likely they are to be self-disclosive and provide support (Tucker, McHale, & Crouter, 2001). Updegraff, McHale, and Crouter (2002) looked at developmental patterns and relationship linkages in adolescents' sibling relationships. Adolescents reported more intimacy with friends than with siblings and more control with siblings than with friends. Their research indicated that, over time, sibling intimacy increased for the siblings studied, however.

McCoy, Brody, and Stoneman (2002) looked at how sibling relationships provide an environment for exploring important social skills, such as caregiving, compromise, and negotiation while at the same time providing a context in which to learn about competition, dominance, and aggression. Tucker, McHale, and Crouter (2001) looked at the nature of and the extent of adolescent siblings' supportive roles and under which conditions siblings provide support to one another regarding familial and nonfamilial issues. They used data from 185 firstborn adolescents (with a mean of 16 years) and secondborn (with a mean of 13 years) sibling pairs. The results showed that both older and younger siblings reported the older sibling as a source of support about nonfamilial issues (e.g., social, scholastic), whereas siblings assume equally supportive roles in familial issues. Previous research had shown that older sisters are frequent confidants, particularly for younger sisters (Buhrmester, 1992; Tucker et al., 1997) and that same-sex siblings receive support from each other more often than opposite sex siblings do (Buhrmester, 1992; Tucker, Barber, & Eccles, 1997). Howe, Aquan-Assee, Bukowski, Lehoux, and Rinaldi (2001) looked at early adolescent-aged (fifth and sixth grade) siblings as confidants. They found that siblings who tended to engage in self-disclosure were more likely to feel good about sharing with each other, but that those pairs who did not self-disclose reported not trusting or not receiving emotional support from each other. In concordance with Buhrmester and Prager (1995), warmth in the sibling relationship was the key association for both emotional understanding and self-disclosure. The authors conclude that the sibling relationship provides an important context for the development of self-disclosure skills and socioemotional understanding.

Dunn, Slomkowski, Beardsall, and Rende (1994) looked at links between earlier sibling relationships and adjustment in middle childhood and early adolescence. They conducted a longitudinal study of siblings spanning 7–8 years to examine the issues of whether sibling relationship differences are stable over time between toddlerhood and middle childhood, and whether the quality of the relationship over time relates to children's self-esteem in adolescence. For both older and younger siblings, the quality of their sister or brother's behavior toward them is related to a later sense of their own competence and attractiveness (Dunn et al., 1994). Over time, the authors found clear patterns of association between the quality of sibling relationships in preschool years and adjustment 7 years later. They found older siblings' internalizing behavior in early adolescence was associated with lack of friendly behavior shown to siblings at earlier times; thus, differences in the affection and support shown by 5-year-olds to their younger siblings provide quite a sensitive predictor for their later internalizing behavior. Associations over time were clearer for the older siblings than for the younger siblings. The hypothesis that younger siblings may be more vulnerable to a lack of affection from older siblings than vice versa was supported. Lack of friendly behavior (rather than high levels of conflict) between siblings in middle childhood was associated with later adjustment difficulties.

Studies of Siblings in Adulthood

Researchers have also focused on the important stage of siblings in adulthood. A classic study by Aldous, Klaus, and Klein (1985) looked at aging parents and their relationships with adult children. They found that although social prescriptions regulate a norm of equal attachment to each child in order to encourage family harmony and eliminate sibling rivalry, parents do, in fact, differentiate between children. In addition, the factors of proximity and gender were found to consistently promote close kinship ties.

Bank and Kahn (1982) and Cicirelli (1982) also have documented sibling relationships throughout the life span. Cicirelli described the process of development for these ongoing relationships, suggesting that by the middle childhood years, sibling roles determined by the position in the family and various personality characteristics have been clearly established. He suggested that although siblings may be close throughout their adolescent years, supporting each other in new steps such as dating, they often experience a period of separation in early adulthood, when contact is more dependent on external circumstances such as holidays. Later in their lives, siblings may share in the care for their older parents and the dismantling of the parents' home and possessions when they relocate into senior housing or after their deaths (Cicirelli, 1982).

Pulakos (1989) found that women perceived their sibling relationships to be closer and more important than did men, but it was unclear if the important factor was same-sex or cross-sex relationships. Using gender as a variable, Floyd (1995) studied closeness in adult sibling relationships. Floyd used questionnaires with college students who reported closeness with siblings through activities such as doing favors for each other or providing help in an emergency, but also through personal accounts such as "We just know we are close." Thus, siblings reported closeness in purely instrumental ways such as helping each other and doing favors for each other as opposed to reports of peer/friend closeness that seem to revolve around like interests and activities.

Martin, Anderson, Burant, and Weber (1997) looked at verbal aggression in adult sibling relationships and found that when verbal aggressiveness is present in a relationship, the parties involved experienced less satisfaction and trust. White (2001) used pooled time series analysis on 9,000 individuals from the National Survey of Families and Households study to look at four measures of sibling relationships over the course of the lifetime. These measures—proximity, contact, and the likelihood of giving and receiving help—decline significantly during early adulthood, but proximity and contact then stabilize in middle age with no further declines. Sibling exchanges increase slightly after age 70. White concludes that the dominant pattern of sibling relationships over the adult life span is reduced contact and exchange, coupled with strong staying power. Siblings who have children of their own tend to be energized in sharing their sibling relationships. They may, for instance, be more inclined to get families together over holidays if there are children involved. Connidis (1994) and Rossi and Rossi (1990) found that most adults perceive significant reciprocal obligations between siblings.

THE NONSHARED ENVIRONMENT AND PARENTAL DIFFERENTIAL TREATMENT

Research has shown that although most siblings grow up in the same family, this does not mean that they are having the same experiences. In fact, much research points to the existence of what is termed the *nonshared environment* and that siblings often experience what researchers term *parental differential treatment* (PDT). Turkheimer and Waldron (2000) discussed what many define as the most influential article ever written in the field of developmental behavior genetics, that of Plomin and Daniels (1987), which showed that a substantial portion of the variability in behavioral outcomes of siblings could not be explained by the additive effects of genetics or the environmental influences of families. Indeed, Daniels and Plomin (1985), Plomin and Daniels (1987), and Rowe and Plomin (1981) all argued that events within a family are often experienced in very different ways by individual children, creating what they call *nonshared environmental influences.* Similarly, Schachter and Stone (1985) defined the *nonshared, within-family environment* as the environment that children in the same family do *not* share in common. Prior to these studies, researchers had neglected this nonshared influence. Instead, they had focused on socioeconomic status, parenting styles, and other such factors that were shared by siblings and could account for similarities but not differences. Since the classic Plomin and Daniels article, however, an entire field of research has been generated in an attempt to answer why children in the same family are so different.

Dunn and Plomin (1990, 1991), for example, completed a series of research studies and concluded that siblings, even though they may grow up in the same family with the same parents, experience their environments quite differently. These researchers believed that any similarity among siblings is due to heredity and not to the experience of growing up in the same family. Their premise is that siblings are remarkably different from each other, that they are treated differently by parents and siblings, and that they experience this treatment differently. Whether siblings actually are treated differently by parents or that they only perceive that they are being treated differently is unclear. For instance, children as young as 14 months of age appear to be vigilant monitors of their mothers' interactions with older siblings. Even though a mother may treat her children similarly at a particular age or stage (Dunn, Plomin, & Daniels, 1986), the siblings (unless they are twins) are not at the same age or stage at the same time, and thus, focus on the differential parental behavior (Dunn & Plomin, 1990). Dunn and colleagues (1986) found little stability in maternal behavior toward the same child during the course of a year. Although consistent in their responses to developmental advances in their children at the same age, mothers differed in their responses to the same child over time as the child aged.

Indeed, this parental differential treatment is viewed as a major component of the nonshared environment (Daniels & Plomin, 1985; Plomin & Daniels, 1987). Researchers have begun establishing links between such differential treatment and differences in siblings' adjustment (Dunn & Plomin, 1990; McHale & Pawletko, 1992). As Kowal and Kramer (1997) noted, a host of studies using differing methods have shown links between parental differential treatment and the quality of sibling relationships in the family (Brody, Stoneman, & Burke, 1987b; Brody, Stoneman, & McCoy, 1992 a, b; Brody et al., 1992; Conger & Conger, 1994; McHale, Crouter, McGuire, & Updegraff, 1995; McHale & Pawletko, 1992; Stocker, Dunn, & Plomin, 1989). Stewart, Mobley, VanTuyl, and Salvador (1987) conducted a longitudinal assessment of firstborn children's adjustment to the birth of a sibling. At the time of the birth, the older children ranged from 2 to 4 years of age. Observations conducted at intervals of 1, 4, 8, and 12 months after the birth showed the older sibling responding by imitating the infant or by confronting the mother or infant. Over time, interactions were primarily confrontations with the increasingly "intrusive" infant. Observational data supported earlier results found by Dunn and Kendrick (1982). The data indicated that mothers had dramatically decreased their interactions with the firstborn over time, whereas fathers' relative frequency of interaction with the older child had remained stable (Stewart et al., 1987).

These results confirm those of previous studies showing connections between differential parental behavior and conflictual sibling relationships. They found that, as in the previous studies by Bryant and Crockenberg (1980) and Brody, Stoneman, and Burke (1987b), most mothers directed more affection, attention, control, and responsiveness to the younger sibling. This powerful predictor, maternal differential behavior, provides support for the significance of nonshared environmental factors. The causal direction, of course, is still unclear because maternal behavior may be a consequence of the negative relationship between siblings rather than its cause.

Graham-Bermann (1991) chose to look at differential treatment from the child's point of view; namely, the link between children's perceptions of the sibling relationship to their actual behavior within a specific sibling relationship. In this way, she could assess whether and in what ways the siblings' perceptions of being similar to or different from one another are reflected in the way they behave together or in individual self-perceptions. Siblings rated themselves as similar to or very much like their sibling 26% of the time; they rated themselves in the middle range between similar and different 31% of the time; and they rated themselves as dissimilar 43% of the time. Mothers rated siblings as more unlike than the siblings themselves did.

Pike, Manke, Reiss, and Plomin (2000) conducted research with adolescent siblings to see how siblings perceived differential experiences in terms of parental treatment, sibling treatment, and peer characteristics (i.e., to see if siblings shared a perception that they were treated differently). Siblings in the study appeared to share some common understanding, but their perceptions did differ and siblings perceived lasting differences between their environmental contexts. Pike and colleagues (2000) suggested that genetic propensities cause siblings to actively construct different experiences for themselves, and in turn, parents and siblings react differently to each other.

McHale, Updegraff, Tucker, and Crouter (2000) compared the extent of PDT and girls' and boys' perceptions of parents' fairness in middle childhood and adolescence as a function of gender constellation of the sibling dyad (e.g., boy–boy, boy–girl, girl–girl). The researchers hypothesized that equal treatment was best, but concluded that it is actually not the norm and may not result in the most positive outcomes. Evidently, the meanings that children give to PDT matter. Kowal and Kramer (1997) confirmed that siblings who rated PDT as fair, though not necessarily equal, also reported more positive sibling relationships.

Most of the research on parental differential treatment has concentrated how mothers treat children differently. Very little research looks specifically at paternal differential treatment or at the comparison of maternal versus paternal differential treatment. Researchers have found that fathers are more apt to treat boys and girls differently than are mothers, particularly in the areas of discipline, activity involvement, and affection (Lytton & Romney, 1991; Siegal, 1987). A study by Tucker, McHale, and Crouter (2003) found differences in mothers' versus fathers' reported patterns of differential treatment, particularly in the areas of affection and amount of time spent with the children. Their research also showed that mothers and fathers often treat adolescent offspring differently and that these patterns are related to personal qualities of children, including gender differences.

Brody, Stoneman, and McCoy (1992a) reported that the rates of direct positive paternal behaviors in a game-playing situation were associated with positive sibling behaviors, whereas rates of direct negative paternal behavior were associated with negative sibling behavior. They found only one difference in the rates of maternal and paternal behavior toward the children, yet that one paternal behavior accounted for the unique variance in the sibling relationship quality. Brody and colleagues (1992a) speculated that the difference may be tied to the relative scarcity of paternal behavior.

Brody, Stoneman, and McCoy (1992b) looked at maternal and paternal differential treatment of siblings and sibling differences in negative emotionality. They found that adolescent and young adult siblings believed that they experienced different family environments than their siblings and that parents perceived differences in their own treatment of children. Also, young children perceived differences in parent behavior toward them and their siblings. Indeed, these researchers found that when parents are together with both children, they direct higher rates of affectionate, controlling, and responsive behavior to the youngest child. It also seems that mothers and fathers direct different rates of behavior toward siblings during parent–sibling interactions and that high levels of differential treatment are linked with variations in child adjustment and sibling relationships. They thought temperament might be associated with maternal and paternal PDT. In this study, they looked specifically at children rated by parents as expressing vigorous and high levels of negative emotions such as frustration or anger. They found that both mothers and fathers showed the highest rates of PDT when the younger sibling was rated as higher on negative emotionality than the older child. Parent time and resources appeared to be more equally distributed when the older child was rated as more negative. The researchers suggested that the important factor might be the differences in levels of emotionality between siblings rather than the exact level, and that a cyclical process might be occurring in which sibling differences in negative emotionality elicit higher levels of PDT and, in turn, foster larger differences in negative emotions.

Mekos, Hetherington, and Reiss (1996) took an ecological approach to looking at PDT in two different family contexts, families in which divorce had not taken place and families in which the parents had remarried. They found that parents in remarried families with a biological child and a stepchild showed greater differential warmth (i.e., tended to show more warmth to one child over another) and monitoring and mothers showed more differential negativity than in nondivorced families. PDT did not differ, though, if both children in the remarried families were the mother's biological and the father's stepchildren. This research suggests that links between differential treatment and consequent differences in sibling adjustment are more apparent in families that are remarried. This situation might magnify differences in treatment and adjustment.

In summary, consensus exists between Plomin and his colleagues (Plomin, Asbury, & Dunn, 1991) and other researchers that children growing up in the same family experience different environments. One aspect of this difference appears to be PDT, which, in turn, appears to interact with the quality of the sibling relationships. Future research in the area of PDT must look at the effects of maternal versus paternal differential treatment and at the effects of age because it is likely that nonshared environmental influences at one age are largely different from nonshared environmental influences at another age (Plomin, Asbury, & Dunn, 2001). Future studies must also look at the gender of the siblings because most of the research thus far has looked at same-sex rather than opposite-sex pairs.

Future research will no doubt turn to other factors as well. Turkheimer and Waldron (2000) conducted a meta-analysis on nonshared environments and concluded that measured nonshared environmental variables do not account for a substantial portion of the nonshared variability. They suggest that genetics contribute substantially to experience, and that the way parents treat children may be more a result of genetically influenced differences between the siblings. They agree that siblings experience very different family environments and that these differential experiences are strongly associated with differential outcomes for siblings. They argue that genetic mediation largely accounts for these associations.

From another perspective, Feinberg and Hetherington (2001) stressed that it is important to look at shared environments because although there may be dissimilar environments that lead to dissimilar outcomes (nonshared environment), similar environments may also lead to dissimilar outcomes. They argue that the second possibility has been relatively neglected.

Bussell and colleagues (1999) noted that research has consistently demonstrated that children's behavior toward their siblings tends to resemble the interactions that occur in the parent–child relationship (Stocker & McHale, 1992; Brody & Stoneman, 1994; Brody, Stoneman, & MacKinnon, 1986; Brody, Stoneman, & McCoy, 1992a). They suggested that this could occur because siblings model parent behavior or because parent–child interactions become internalized and are used as a working model for the siblings. The research by Bussell and colleagues looked at positivity and negativity in mother–adolescent, and sibling dyads. The adolescents tended to have consistent experiences in their relationships with mothers and siblings, in part, the authors argue, because of some common environmental influence, the general family climate. They argue that their findings do not indicate that nonshared environment significantly contributes to observed resemblances between mother–adolescent and sibling relationships, except when adolescent reports are used. Instead, they say that the results argue for the importance of shared environmental influences on similarity between maternal–adolescent and sibling relationships. Neale (1999) responded to Bussell and colleagues (1999), noting that their results showed a substantial effect of the shared family environment on measures of social interaction are unusual, especially since the common finding has been the absence of large effects of the family environment on individual differences in behavioral traits (Rowe, 1994). Neiderhiser and colleagues (1999) replied back to Neale and said they were most intrigued by findings that the correlation between mother–child and sibling relationships could largely be explained by shared environmental influences, because that is what their previous study had argued for.

Obviously, the issue of the importance of the shared and nonshared environment within a family is an important one for those looking at sibling relationships. Plomin, Asbury, and Dunn (2001) suggested that some degree of nonshared environment may be due to the fact that siblings react differently to ostensiblingly shared environmental influences. Goldsmith (1993) suggested that researchers in this area must distinguish between objective and effective environments. The objective environments are events that might be observed by a researcher, whereas effective environments are defined by the outcomes they produce. A mother's depression might be an example. The fact of the diagnosis of depression is objective to a degree, but different siblings may feel the effects of this depression differently. Goldsmith suggested that if the effect is different, then the effect is nonshared. Feinberg and

Hetherington (2000), in their review of the literature on sibling "differentiating processes," also suggest that the same event can affect siblings in different ways. For instance, one sibling may become very proactive in dealing with his mother's depression and in ensuring that he does not become depressed himself, whereas another sibling may become depressed himself.

RESEARCH ON SIBLINGS IN DIFFERENT TYPES OF FAMILIES

Many researchers have looked at families from different circumstances, races, and cultures to determine sibling experiences and factors related to relationships.

Siblings in Step Families

An aspect of the current sibling literature that is being investigated is that of sibling relationships in blended or step families. Sturgess, Dunn, and Davies (2001) discussed studies by Deater-Deckard & Dunn (1999) that showed that although many full siblings express considerable hostility and dislike for each other, many half and step siblings are less intensely involved, either negatively or positively. Deater-Deckard and Dunn in 2002 also found that more conflict and aggression occurred between full siblings than with half or step siblings. Deater-Deckard, Dunn, and Lussier (2002) studied sibling relationships in different family contexts such as households with a stepparent and single-mother households with half-sibling relationships. They found there were no significant differences in sibling negativity or positivity. Siblings raised in single mother families were the most negative compared to children in other types of families, but there were no differences found in terms of positivity. The authors suggest that positivity and negativity may be two separate dimensions rather than a continuum.

As Kier and Lewis (1998) noted, some researchers have looked at the importance of major life stresses on children such as parental conflict and separation. They noted that opinion is divided; some say that separation from parents may draw siblings closer together in order to cope with stress, whereas others suggest that turmoil in the parents' relationship can spill over and negatively affect the siblings' relationship. Their research looked at preschool sibling interactions in separated and married families and found that for both groups, the gender configuration of the sibling pairs was important. Same-sex pairs seemed to show closer patterns of interaction, and sister–sister dyads were particularly prosocial. Also, preschool sibling dyads from separated families interacted more, suggesting that negative life experiences might promote greater sibling closeness.

Dunn, Deater-Deckard, Pickering, Golding, and the ALSPAC Study Team (1999) looked at family relationships longitudinally, including sibling relationships. They found that individual differences in sibling relationship quality were related to mother–partner affection, and that hostility (e.g., parents toward children, children toward each other, children toward parents) assessed 4 years earlier was related to current parent–child negativity. They found evidence for both direct and indirect pathways (via parent–child relationships) linking mother–partner and sibling relations. In families in which a stepfather was present, according to this study, mother–partner hostility was unrelated to parent–child negativity and sibling relationship quality, whereas it was believed to be related when the natural parents were involved. Positivity and negativity toward younger siblings decreased with the age of the older siblings; in other words, emotions were not as intense as the siblings got older. Also, older sisters were more positive to their younger siblings than were older brothers.

Siblings in African American Families

Studies have increasingly been looking at sibling issues in families beyond those of European American descent. Brody and Murry (2001) looked at older siblings' contributions to younger siblings' competence in single-parent African American (AA) families. The authors noted that AA families have a long tradition of assigning child care and socialization roles to older siblings, whereas past research with European American children has shown older siblings acting as teachers, managers, and helpers. The Brody and Murry study found that older sibling competence significantly predicted younger sibling competence, and that younger sibling competence was higher when the older sibling was more competent. An association was found with conflict in that in AA families, conflict moderates the association between older and younger sibling competence. They also found that just as in European American families, older sisters and younger sisters are more likely than siblings in other combinations to engage in play matched at the developmental level of the younger sibling, and that the younger siblings were more self-regulated than siblings in other combinations.

Brody, Kim, Murry, and Brown (2004) studied protective paths linking competence to behavioral problems among rural AA siblings. The firstborn siblings were approaching early adolescence and the secondborn siblings were in middle childhood. They predicted that child competence would indirectly contribute to the parenting received by the child by influencing positive effects on the mothers' psychological functioning. The researchers did find that the competence of the older sibling was positively associated with maternal psychological functioning, but that the competence of the younger sibling was not found to be significantly associated to the competence of the older sibling. Obviously, much research still needs to be done in this complex area.

Siblings in Latino and Mexican American Families

Perez-Granados & Callanan (1997b) looked at parents and siblings as resources for learning in young children of Mexican descent. According to parent reports conducted for this study, younger siblings in these Mexican American families learn mostly academic skills from older (4- to 6-year-old) siblings, but also some social and self-care skills, whereas older siblings learn mostly social skills such as sharing and communicating from their younger (2- to 3-year-old) siblings. This echoes previous research with European American siblings that showed that siblings serve as social agents for one another and that older siblings frequently play the role of teacher.

Parents reported that siblings in Mexican families learn through indirect methods such as observing and imitating rather than direct methods such as teaching each other. The authors found that siblings in these families are rich learning resources for one another. This was consistent with another study (Perez-Granados & Callanan, 1997a), which found that when asked to help the younger sibling play a game, the older siblings in Mexican American families focused on making the correct choices, whereas mothers tried to give the younger siblings helpful information or hints so they could make the correct choice themselves.

Ortiz, Innocenti, and Roggman (2005) studied early language development of young children from low-income Spanish-speaking families and found that the amount of child–sibling interaction in English and the mother's report of the siblings' English knowledge was positively correlated with both receptive and expressive vocabulary scores for the younger children in English. However, the children's English interaction was negatively correlated with the younger siblings' expressive (but not receptive) vocabulary scores in Spanish, and the sibling's English knowledge (as reported by the mother) was negatively correlated with the younger children's receptive (but not expressive) vocabulary scores in Spanish.

RESEARCH ON THE INFLUENCE OF TEMPERAMENT

Beyond mother–child interactions, it seems that temperament of individual siblings also plays an important role in sibling relationships. Stocker and colleagues (1989) stressed the importance of looking at temperamental and personality characteristics of each sibling as likely factors in the relationship that develops between them. These authors examined the links with child temperament, maternal behavior, and family structure in sibling relationships. Home visits included interviews and observations of 96 families with siblings grouped by ages 3–6 and 5–10 years. They found that differences in sibling relationships are, to a significant extent, related to maternal behavior, temperamental characteristics of the children, their age, and family structure variables. The child's temperamental characteristics accounted for a significant amount of the unique variance in sibling relationships. Groups in which the second-born siblings were older had more cooperative and less conflictual relationships than those groups in which siblings were younger.

Brody, Stoneman, and Burke (1988) conducted a study of child temperament and parents' perceptions of children's adjustment. Seventy married couples with two children of the same gender were studied. They found that the perception of a child's adjustment was associated with the temperament of both siblings. Thus, for example, a child's absolute level of persistence or emotional intensity may be less important to parental perceptions than are the *differences* in absolute levels of temperament compared with the sibling. The authors urge researchers to continue focusing on the intrafamilial perspective and the family processes that create similar or dissimilar environments for children in the same family.

Volling, Herrera, and Poris (2004) looked at the issue of temperament as it relates to sibling caregiving. They looked at preschool-age children's caregiving behavior toward their younger siblings during a brief separation from the parents. They found that the temperament of the older sibling and younger toddler did account for variance in prediction of the older sibling's caregiving behaviors. In fact, sibling caregiving behavior was more strongly associated with parent ratings of sibling and toddler temperament than to distress in the younger sibling. The older sibling's social fear was positively related to providing care. Thus, if the older sibling had a temperament that showed social fear, the sibling tried more strategies to ease the younger sibling's distress perhaps because he or she was more likely to experience anxiety and guilt. The younger siblings' temperamental anger and soothability were positively associated with receiving care from older siblings. On the one hand, the older sibling's activity level was also a significant predictor of older sibling's comforting behaviors in that the more the older sibling's activity level increased, the less chance he or she would provide comfort to a younger sibling. On the other hand, an older sibling's positive, happy disposition did not seem to affect caregiving one way or other.

McCoy, Brody, and Stoneman (2002) looked at the effect of same-sex sibling relationships on temperament and the quality of best friendships. They wanted to see if early adolescents' sibling relationships moderated the link between their temperamental styles and the quality of their relationships with best friends. They proposed that siblings may serve as a useful buffer against negative consequences of a difficult temperament in areas such as friendships.

RESEARCH ON SIBLINGS AND PEER RELATIONSHIPS

Several researchers have looked at direct links between children's sibling and peer relationships. McCoy and colleagues (2002) discussed the congruence and the compensatory models of relationship similarity. A congruence model is based on the work of Bandura's social learning theory (1977) and Patterson's social interaction model (1982), and postulated that relationships in one context should reflect the quality of relationships in other contexts. Research supporting a congruence model include the Kramer and Gottman (1992) and McCoy, Brody, and Stoneman (1994) articles that found that more positive sibling relationships were associated with more postitive friendships and general peer relations. A compensatory model, however, suggests that individuals who have poor relationships in one context may compensate for them by establishing stronger relationships in other contexts (Hertz-Lazarowitz, Rosenberg, & Guttman, 1989). Several studies have demonstrated support for this model as well. McCoy and colleagues (2002) suggested that age or gender links may play mediating roles in these relationships, and purported that at least for early adolescent girls, siblings may do more than fill the void created by poor peer relationships. They also may provide a context in which the negative effects of a difficult temperament may be diminished. It seems that for girls, if they experience a warm sibling relationship with little conflict with their sister, that can generalize to their nonfamilial relationships even if their own temperaments make social relations difficult.

McCoy, Brody, and Stoneman (2002) also looked at whether early adolescents' sibling relationships ameliorate the effects of a difficult temperament on best friendships. Data was collected from parents on temperament ratings for 73 later born siblings whose mean age was 7 years. Five years later, these siblings, who were now adolescents, provided information about support and discord in their best friendships. Older siblings also provided information about the warmth and/or conflict in same-sex sibling dyads. They found that support and discord in girls' best friendships were negatively and positively predicted by the level of temperamental difficulty only when relationships with older sisters were respectively lower in warmth or higher in conflict. Thus, early adolescents with more difficult temperaments experience less positive relationships with both their siblings and their best friends when their relationships were conflictual. The authors purport that siblings may serve as a buffer against negative consequences that a difficult temperament can have for early adolescent-aged friendships.

Other studies have looked at issues of temperament as it related to sibling conflict. Generally, children who are active, intense, or unadaptable in temperament have more conflicted relationships with siblings (Boer, 1990; Brody & Stoneman, 1987). Brody, Stoneman, and Gauger (1996) looked at the moderating role of sibling temperament for parent–child and sibling relationships. Sibling ages were 10 years and 7½ years. The links among mother–older child relationship quality, father–older child relationship quality, and sibling relationship quality were moderated by the older sibling's temperament. They report that children with difficult temperaments have consistently been shown to be at risk for experiencing high levels of conflict and negative activity in their sibling relationships. They also found that an association between father–younger child and sibling relationship quality occurred primarily for dyads in which the older sibling had a difficult temperament and the younger one had an easy temperament.

Stoneman and Brody (1993) found greater conflict and rivalry between siblings high on negative emotionality. They found that preschoolers with higher activity levels exhibited more agonistic behaviors toward siblings and were more involved in sibling conflict than if they had lower activity levels. They noted that the highest levels of conflict-negativity occurred when both siblings were high in activity (temperament trait) and when the oldest sibling was rated as more active than the younger sibling, whereas conflict was lowest when both were rated low in activity. Some gender effects do appear to have occurred in that male sibling pairs were less interactive and engaged in more negative interactions than did female siblings.

RESEARCH ON SIBLING CONFLICT

A plethora of research has been conducted regarding sibling conflict since the mid-1990s. Newman (1994) has reviewed research on conflict and friendships in sibling relationships and noted that although conflict is common, the more predominant patterns are more positive socialization experiences in which siblings practice social cognition skills. These skills include insight into another's motives and feelings, tolerance, self-control, and understanding reasons for others' behaviors. Although studies have shown many positive aspects of sibling relationships, considerable amounts of negativity and conflict have been found as well (DeHart, 1999). As Brody (1998) noted in his excellent review, sibling conflict and aggression are linked to child maladjustment. For instance, children in sibling relationships that are hostile and lack warmth tend to show higher levels of adjustment problems. Other data indicates that chronically conflicted sibling relationships may serve as a training ground for the development and maintenance of aggressive behavior and conduct problems in younger siblings (Bank, Patterson, & Reid, 1996; Garcia, Shaw, Winslow, & Yaggi, 2000). Garcia and colleagues (2000) used a longitudinal design and looked at parenting and sibling effects on aggressive and delinquent behaviors in 5-year-old children in a target group. The siblings' conflict explained a significant and unique amount of variance in outcome measures even when controlling parent effects, socioeconomic status, and previous problem behaviors of the target child. Indeed, siblings' warmth and conflict appear to be significant predictors of child outcomes, though researchers caution that the studies have been mostly correlational so far and that cause and effect remain unclear.

Vespo, Pedersen, and Hay (1995) outlined the literature relative to young children's conflicts with siblings, and stressed that conflict is not necessarily destructive and can have constructive aspects. Their study found an interaction between gender of older and younger siblings revealing that boys had twice as many conflicts with younger brothers as they did with younger sisters. Older girls had slightly more conflicts with younger sisters than they did with younger brothers. Again, it seems that conflict occurs more often in same gender versus mixed gender dyads of siblings, at least at preschool age. They also noted that conflict occurs routinely during ongoing harmonious social interactions, and is generally brief and easily resolved.

McGuire, Manke, Eftekhari, and Dunn (2000) focused on the context rather than frequency of sibling conflict, conflict initiation, and conflict resolution in middle childhood years. They found that disagreements in these years revolved around issues between siblings (such as possessions or physical aggression) rather than issues of favoritism by the parents.

Other studies indicate that the rate of sibling conflict decreases from preschool to school-age years (Brody, Stoneman, MacKinnon, & MacKinnon, 1985; Vandell & Bailey, 1992), and that the relationships tend to become more egalitarian. Perhaps school-age siblings tend to solve their arguments more constructively as their social–cognitive skills increase (Dunn & Slomkowski, 1992). Ram and Ross (2001) also outline literature on conflict that shows that both older children and older sibling pairs use more sophisticated and constructive negotiation strategies such as cooperation or questioning and fewer destructive tactics such as crying or aggression. At the same time, the more sophisticated strategies help older siblings achieve self-serving goals rather than win-win outcomes for both. The literature also showed that positive conflict management strategies and resolution were used far less frequently than were self-centered ones. The Ram and Ross overview indicates that siblings can negotiate conflicts of interest skillfully and with little hostility. The degree of conflict of interest, the existing sibling relationship, and the types of strategies used are all important factors in studying conflict in sibling relationships.

Ram and Ross (2001) looked at sibling dyads (of children 4–6 years and 6–8 years) in a laboratory setting regarding negotiation of division of toys. They found that generally, children use a variety of constructive problem-solving strategies rather than contentious tactics. Rinaldi and Howe (1998) found that constructive tactics are associated with sibling interactions that were less conflictual and relationships that are rated as more positive, whereas destructive and prolonged conflicts are associated with negative sibling relationships.

Rinaldi and Howe (2003) also explored family members' (e.g., mothers, fathers, siblings) perceptions of the frequency and types of constructive and destructive conflict strategies used within family subsystems; parents and children disagreed about the relative level of sibling conflict. Constructive conflict involves the process of negotation and collaboration, whereas destructive conflict occurs when partners are not satisfied with the outcome, or use physical or verbal threats or actions. Siblings' reports of conflict were negatively correlated with parental assessment of warmth of sibling relationships. Siblings' reports of warmth were positively corrrelated with parental assessment of warmth of sibling relationship. They did find that negative parent–child relationships were associated with negative sibling relations. It is important to emphasize that this type of research is still in its beginning stages and no conclusions can yet be drawn.

Howe, Rinaldi, Jennings, and Petrakos (2002) looked at conflict resolution in sibling pretend play conflicts and found that conflict issues and aggression were associated with specific resolution strategies. They discussed the sibling conflict literature that shows that conflict can be associated with coping and management, but if it is destructive to either party, it may be detrimental to children's relationships (Vandell & Bailey, 1992). In a previous study, Rinaldi and Howe (1998) found that siblings who reported using more frequent constructive strategies or who managed conflict more positively reported warmer sibling relationships. Firstborn siblings appeared to take a more dominant role by initiating procedural types of conflicts and passive resolutions, whereas with younger siblings, conflict was significantly more strongly associated with third-party resolutions. The issue of whether particular kinds of conflict issues are resolved by siblings in differential ways remains largely unstudied, although DeHart and colleagues (2001) found developmental shifts from early childhood to adolescence in strategies used such that distraction and surrender strategies increased over time.

Brody, Stoneman, McCoy, and Forehand (1992) looked at sibling conflict and found that paternal equality of treatment and family harmony during family discussions about sibling problems as well as parents' perceptions of family cohesiveness are associated with lower sibling conflict levels. These researchers believed that sibling conflict is multiply determined. School-age siblings, for instance, whose fathers treat them impartially during problem-solving discussions, whose families are generally harmonious, and whose parents are generally close, are more likely than siblings in less positively functioning families to develop relationships with few conflicts.

Siddiqui and Ross (1999) looked specifically at how the endings of sibling conflicts occur and found four major types: 1) compromise, 2) reconciliation, 3) submission, and 4) no resolution. They found that conflicts typically ended with no resolution for preschoolers and again when siblings were between the ages of 4½ and 6½. They also stressed that although conflict may often be seen as negative, it is important to the development of social and interpersonal skills. A study conducted by Raffaelli (1992) with siblings in early adolescence found the same general results—that most sibling conflicts ended with no overt resolution. Unlike with peers, there seems to be little compromise or reconciliation between siblings, possibly owing to a power difference between them (Siddiqui & Ross, 1999).

Ross, Siddiqui, Ram, and Ward (2004) interviewed 3- to 9-year-old siblings regarding their recent conflicts and found that children were adept at describing their own and their sibling's behaviors, goals, and actions. These reports showed that the perspectives of siblings were that the conflicts were not one-sided; it seems they did understand others and their needs and wants.

McHale, Updegraff, Tucker, and Crouter (2000) examined parents' roles in adolescent siblings' relationships and found three general reactions to sibling conflict, including noninvolvement, intervening, or coaching. They noted mother–father differences in conflict reactions and time spent with siblings, and found that the time spent by parents in the company of both siblings is associated with positive sibling relationship qualities. They also found that parental involvement in conflict did not promote positive sibling relationship qualities but instead, the parents' efforts to resolve conflicts may give rise to more negativity in the relationship. The gender of both the parent and the child seemed to affect a parent's likelihood of getting involved in siblings conflicts, too. Mothers were more likely than fathers to stay out of sibling conflicts, especially when the dyad was an older brother and a younger sister (McHale et al., 2000).

Conflict is obviously an important feature of the sibling relationship. It is important to remember, however, that in a review of sibling studies by Newman (1994), children reported that positive qualities were at least as likely or even more likely to be present in their relationships with their siblings. Newman reminds us of the earlier observational studies of siblings (Abramovitch, Corter, & Lando, 1979; Abramovitch, Corter, & Pepler, 1980; Corter, Pepler, & Abramovitch, 1983) in which, despite considerable evidence of conflict, conflict was not seen as the predominant sibling interaction pattern. The issue of conflict is a complex one that needs much further investigation.

SUMMARY

Siblings play an important role in each other's development during their lifetimes. Social interactions with siblings provide a context and foundation for the development of social and related skills such as language or motor skills. The sibling relationship is a foundation from which brothers and sisters are prepared for experiences with others outside the family constellation.

Early research efforts focusing on the relationship between and among siblings were concerned primarily with the structure of the sibling relationship. Variables such as birth order and age spacing were considered important in defining sibling relationships. More recent research has focused on the patterns of interaction within sibling and family relationships. Research in developmental patterns for preschool and school-age children shows a role pattern of initiation on the part of the firstborn child and one of imitation for the secondborn sibling, a pattern that becomes more egalitarian over time. Recent research on typical siblings has also looked specifically at sibling relationships in middle childhood and adolescence and found continuing powerful interactions. The adult sibling relationship shows separation and then a rich and close relationship again for many siblings toward the end of life.

Perceived or actual differential treatment of siblings by parents affects the quality of the sibling relationship as well as the quality of parent–child interactions. The influence of divorce, separation, and remarriage on sibling relationships is beginning to be addressed and should continue because of the large percentage of families affected by these circumstances. Cultural heritage may contribute to this context, and much research in this area is needed. Future research must contend with myriad issues. Research must focus on the importance of the sibling relationship within the family context, and should take into consideration that there is often more than one sibling dyad in a family. In reality, of course, many families have more than two children and patterns of interaction between all siblings should be documented. Additional research must also continue to examine nonshared environmental factors and the influence of the father or male caregiver in sibling and mother–child relationships. Brody and Stoneman (1986) and Stoneman and colleagues (1986) argued for the importance of context in describing sibling interactions. It has become clear that the temperament of the siblings is part of this context as well as conflict within the interactions.

3

What We Know About Special Brothers and Sisters in the Family System

"Eric has really affected my life from my childhood throughout adulthood. Before my husband, I was closer to Eric than anyone else in the world . . . Eric and I used to have our own language to communicate . . . I can remember playing for hours with him, just like other children do with their siblings. I remember 'sticking up' for Eric when other children would tease him. I think I always put myself in the protector mode with respect to him. I think the responsibility of caring for Eric helped me mature faster and I was always viewed as responsible and dependable."

—L. Dufford, personal communication, May 6, 2005

Grace and Ian wanted a large family. Judi, their third child, was born with Down syndrome. The doctors diagnosed Judi's condition at birth and were encouraging about her chances of attending school and of being accepted as part of their small, rural community. The doctors had no idea of the effects, if any, Judi would have on the rest of the family, particularly Alicia and Marissa, the oldest daughters, and any other children to come. A year after her birth, Judi was also diagnosed with vision impairment, but despite this setback, the family had a relatively easy adjustment. Then Grace became pregnant again. Grace and Ian decided it was time to find out what influence a child with a disability might have on brothers and sisters and vice versa.

The next few weeks were devoted to earnest research concerning what effects children with disabilities have on their siblings. Grace and Ian read quite a few research reports. Some of the reports noted negative effects, others noted no significant effects, and still others claimed that the effects were positive. Grace and Ian began to wonder about the value of such research if definitive answers were not to be found, so Grace decided to visit with other parents and inquire about sibling problems and the outcomes that other families had experienced. They heard some heartwarming stories and some sad ones, too. Finally, Grace and Ian realized that they had to rely on their own feelings and judgment. They wanted a large family, and Judi was an integral part of that family already. Her older sisters sometimes got frustrated when they couldn't understand Judi, but they also seemed to take great pride in her accomplishments. The couple resolved to try their best to create a loving family environment that fostered acceptance.

Like other parents in similar situations, Grace and Ian came to realize that the time they spent reviewing some of the literature was worthwhile. They were convinced that if siblings' experiences could be both positive and negative, then they, as parents, could make a difference. Their readings and interviews gave them a new understanding of problems experienced by siblings and what parents could do to limit and/or minimize those problems.

Now, many years later, Judi attends the local public high school with support from special education programs—the same high school attended by her two younger brothers. Her two older sisters are working. Grace and Ian look back and know that they, indeed, made a difference. Judi is a very special part of their family.

THE FAMILY: A SOCIAL SYSTEM

When discussing a subset of families such as siblings, it is helpful to start with a broad perspective. Several authors have reviewed the general literature on families and have adapted it to develop a framework that includes individuals with disabilities (Beckman & Bristol, 1991; Fewell, 1986; Mackeith, 1973; Minuchin, 1974; Stoneman & Brody, 1984; Turnbull & Turnbull, 2001; Turnbull, Turnbull, Erwin, & Soodak, 2006). The fundamental concept of such a theory is that the family consists of a variety of subsystems, each of which is interrelated. Of course, such a framework takes on an added dimension when one of the members in the system has a disability. For many families, the realization that a child has a disability is unexpected. For example, no one imagined that Jon would be born with multiple disabilities; it was a surprise when Bethany was diagnosed as having a learning disability; Andre's parents cried when they learned that he had developmental delays. However difficult, most families find ways to cope with new situations and new problems. The news of a disability forces families, particularly parents and siblings, to confront their dreams and expectations for the child. Those dreams may be altered by the reality of the disability. Learning about such a disability permanently changes the life of each family member. The adjustment period in which family members learn to revise their dreams and accept the child with a disability into their framework differs from family to family. In some families, the process is long and difficult; for others, it seems to occur easily; in most families, it is a recurring process (Gallagher, Fialka, Rhodes, & Arceneaux, 2002).

Turnbull and Turnbull (1990, 2001) and Turnbull and colleagues (2006) have outlined a systems framework for the family of a person with a disability. This model includes four components as seen in Figure 3.1: 1) family characteristics, 2) family interaction, 3) family function, and 4) family life cycle. Each of these components is described briefly below.

Family characteristics are the descriptive factors such as size and makeup, cultural background, or socioeconomic status that describe a family and give input on family interaction. *Family interaction* is the ongoing process of family relationships that is responsive to individual and family needs; *family function* refers to the varying taks that a family performs to meet the individual and collective needs of its members. Finally, the *family life cycle* component represents the sequence of changes that affects families during the children's early childhood and school-age years as well as during adolescence and adulthood. Each of these components is important in considering the nature of sibling relationships. Elements of the family life cycle are addressed in more detail next.

All families face a number of critical transitional periods in their lives that may create stress. The birth of a new child, school entrance, or a change in those living in the household are all transition stages in a family life cycle. For the family with a child who has a disability, the stress of these transitional times may be particularly acute. Turnbull and Turnbull (2001) have described four such periods:

1. *Birth and early childhood,* when parents initially find out that the child has a disability and begin participation in services
2. *Childhood,* when the child with a disability becomes eligible for school-age services and, thus, faces academic expectations
3. *Adolescence and young adulthood,* when the family member with a disability and his or her family confronts choices of career options in high school, develops self-determination skills, and confronts dating and sexualtiy issues
4. *Adulthood,* when the family member with a disability and his or her parents are involved in making decisions on postsecondary educa-

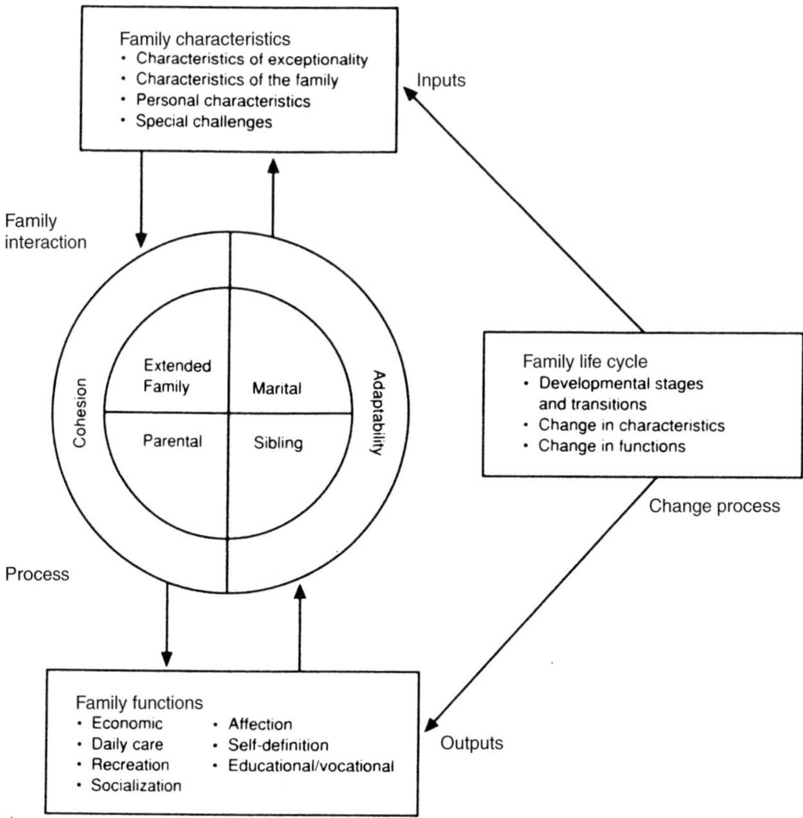

Figure 3.1. Family systems conceptual framework. (From TURNBULL, ANN; TURNBULL, RUD; ERWIN, ELIZABETH J.; SOODAK, LESLIE C., FAMILIES, PROFESSIONALS AND EXCEPTIONALITY: POSITIVE OUTCOMES THROUGH PARTNERSHIP AND TRUST, 5th Edition, © 2006, p. 6. Reprinted by permission of Pearson Education, Inc., Upper Saddle River, NJ.

tional programs and supports and employment and living options as well as in thinking about what happens when the parents age and can no longer assume the responsibility and/or care for the person with a disability.

These points in family life serve as a framework to help service providers to identify potential periods in which family members, particularly parents and siblings, experience intense stress (Simeonsson & Simeonsson, 1981). All families must face times of decision, but transitions at these points may be more difficult for families with a member who has a disability. Changes in the family characteristics may occur such as in the child's self-care abilities; or changes in family interactions may occur, such as an increase in interactions between siblings when the child with

disabilities is able to communicate more. And, intensifying matters, critical periods for siblings without disabilities may occur simultaneously, forcing the family to deal with the differing needs of individual family members at the same time (Turnbull & Turnbull, 1990, 2001).

Knowing when stress is likely to occur enables professionals to direct their services to alleviate or minimize the problems for family members during these critical times. Stress need not have completely negative effects, but can be turned into a positive force.The resiliency model of family stress, adjustment, and adaptation by McCubbin and McCubbin (1993) helps to explain why some families adapt and become stronger in the face of stressful circumstances, whereas others remain vulnerable and some even deteriorate. Family adaptation is defined as the outcome of family efforts to bring a new level of balance, harmony, coherence, and functioning to a stressful or crisis family situation. Families with more resources have a better chance of managing stress and restoring balance to their lives.

Like all other families, families that have a member with a disability are facing the societal pressures and demands of today (Simeonsson & Simeonsson, 1981). Each family is unique and has varying needs. Families display both vulnerability and extreme strength, and when that family includes a child with a disability, the family may be both stressed and strengthened by the experience. Featherstone (1980) speaks of the solitude, loneliness, and fear of being the parent of a child with a disability. She reminds us, however, that parents and families do endure and learn to live with difficult circumstances and, as Perske (1981) suggested, they often turn a tough situation into a rich and rewarding experience.

A SPECIAL RELATIONSHIP

A special part of the family is, of course, siblings. The brothers and sisters of people with disabilities are vital components in the family system. They influence the individual through their interactions and are, likewise, influenced by their brother or sister. This influence has preoccupied researchers, who have sought to describe the effects that individuals with disabilities have on their siblings. The following pages review some of that research. Much of the early research efforts concentrated on the varying effects that the child with a disability would have on brothers and sisters if the child lived at home or was institutionalized. Later research has been devoted to the process of the sibling relationship because most siblings now live together at home, at least in the early years of their lives.

This chapter reviews research that shows negative, mixed, and positive results regarding the effects a child with a disability has on his or her siblings, as well as factors that contribute to the varied outcomes. Then, more recent literature on actual interactional processes is discussed, and the research in context/role considerations, differential treatment, and stress/coping styles is reviewed.

Past research (Cerreto & Miller, 1981; Hannah & Midlarsky, 1999; Kaminsky & Dewey, 2002; Lobato, 1990; Mandelco, Olsen, Dyches, & Marshall, 2003; McHale, Simeonsson, & Sloan, 1984; Seligman, 1983; Senapti & Hayes, 1988; Simeonsson & McHale, 1981; Taunt & Hastings, 2002) on the relationships between children with disabilities and their siblings shows that there can be both positive and negative effects for the child without a disability. On the positive side, some siblings report satisfaction in learning to live and cope with the demands of a child with a disability. They experience genuine joy and pleasure at the smallest accomplishments of the child, and they feel a warmth and compassion for all people as individuals with unique needs and abilities.

Negative Effects

Having a sibling with a disability is a situation ripe for mixed emotions, however, and siblings also report negative effects such as feelings of bitterness and resentment because of the extra attention given to the child with the disability. Some siblings explain that they feel fearful and anxious about how to interact with the child, or even feel guilty because of their own good health.

Farber (1959, 1960, 1968), one of the pioneers in exploring the psychosocial adjustment of siblings of a child with a disability, suggested that the more independent and higher functioning the child with the disability, the better adjusted the siblings tend to be. He also found that older sisters, who often had greater caregiving responsibilities for the child, scored higher in "role tension" when the child with a disability lived at home rather than in an institution; Fowle (1968) concurred. It is important to note that Farber's data came from parental assessments of their children, not from the siblings themselves. As Cerreto and Miller (1981) have pointed out, subsequent research has produced a set of complex observations that partly support and partly refute Farber's original contentions.

Some corroboration of potential deleterious effects comes from an extensive study conducted by Grossman (1972). In her exploratory study, she interviewed college students whose siblings had varying degrees of mental retardation. Her data revealed that about one-half of the group she interviewed had difficulties associated with having a sibling with a disability. These included ignorance concerning the feelings of the child with mental retardation and uneasiness about their own future children. Grossman also found that some siblings felt guilty for being in good health while, at the same time, they felt neglected because of their parents' preoccupation with the child who had a disability.

McHale and Gamble (1987) found that older sisters of children with mental retardation showed somewhat poorer adjustment in four measured areas than did siblings of children without disabilities. Older brothers were also more anxious and had lower levels of perceived competence in the areas of social acceptance and conduct when they had a sibling with a disability.

Lobato, Barbour, Hall, and Miller (1987) found no differences in self-competence and acceptance, understanding of developmental disability, or childcare responsibility in 46 preschool-age children, 24 of whom had a sibling with a disability and 22 of whom had a sibling without a disability. Interestingly enough, significant group differences were found in behavior ratings by mothers. Mothers rated their children, whether they were boys or girls, as more aggressive when they had a sibling with a disability.

More recently, Fisman, Wolf, Ellison, and Freeman (2000) compared adjustment in Canadian children categorized into three groups: siblings of children with pervasive developmental disorder (PDD), siblings of children with Down syndrome, and siblings of a control group of children who were typically developing. The siblings, who were ages 8–16 years at onset of the research, were studied twice with a span of 3 years in between. The researchers found significantly more adjustment problems in siblings of children with PDD at time 1 and again 3 years later compared with siblings of those with Down syndrome and the control siblings.

Mixed Outcomes

Cleveland and Miller (1977) conducted a mail survey to obtain information on the long-range influences that a child with a disability would have on family members. The authors analyzed 90 surveys of adult siblings and focused particularly on their life commitments and career choices. Female siblings who were the oldest in the family reported having significantly more responsibility for the child with a disability. The older siblings also tended to enter the helping professions more often and sought professional counseling for personal problems. The authors found, too, that the adult siblings perceived the presence of the individual with a disability as affecting their social relationships because, in the course of almost daily contact with the individual with a disability, they placed less emphasis on close friendships, marriage and family, and community membership. Female siblings reported having closer relationships with the individual with a disability than did their brothers. They also reported being more knowledgeable about the disability—in this study it focused on mental retardation—than were their brothers. Self-reports from siblings in this study also suggested that siblings assumed responsibilities for inferred parental psychological needs, for example, and tended to overachieve. Thus, the siblings tended to try to compensate for the limitations of the child with the disability.

As Cerreto and Miller (1981) emphasized, a major finding of the Cleveland and Miller study is that there may, in fact, be a positive outcome for the sibling without a disability who has a brother or sister with a disability. In general, adult siblings agreed that their families coped successfully, that they were adequately informed, and that both they and their parents had adapted successfully to the presence of the child with mental retardation. Other, more recent studies have also found mixed outcomes in sibling relationships.

McHale and Gamble (1987) have supplemented behavior ratings with self-reports of sibling interactions and activities. Telephone interviews, conducted on a daily basis, found no differences between children who had a younger sibling with a disability and those without in terms of number of negative or positive behaviors directed at the siblings. Siblings having a brother or sister with a disability did report greater intensity of any problems; that is, the events were seen as more troublesome. McHale and Gamble also pointed out that such intensity often leads to "'internalized problems" involving worries and anxieties about the child's welfare. These researchers have found that such adjustment problems often become more negative with age.

Wilson, Blacher, and Baker (1989) found that, although siblings expressed a high degree of perceived responsibility for the child's welfare and a high proportion of siblings viewed their interactions as successful, the reports were not entirely positive. Most siblings did acknowledge some degree of sadness, anxiety, and anger, and for a small number of siblings, such negative feelings were predominant.

Kirkman (1986), an Australian researcher, conducted a survey of adults who had a brother or sister with a disability and organized their responses around the following themes: family relationships, schooling, friendships and social life, difficult and easy times, self-concept, and sibling relationships. She stressed that all siblings cause problems for their other siblings whether or not a child with a disability exists in the pair. She also found that although the problems or concerns may be more pronounced when a child in the family has a disability, these problems are not necessarily of a different nature than those in other sibling relationships.

Lobato (1990) also found that, in general, siblings of children with disabilities do not appear to have a higher incidence of major personality or behavior disorders than their sibling peers. Granted, they are affected by the experience of living with a child who has a disability and may have special concerns and feelings; however, these do not often translate into measurable psychological adjustment problems.

More recently, Rodrigue, Geffken, and Morgan (1993) compared 19 siblings of children with severe autism with siblings of children with Down syndrome and siblings who were typically developing. The siblings studied were 10 years old, on average. The siblings of children with autism displayed more internalizing and externalizing behavior problems than did siblings in the other two groups, but all mean scores still fell within the normative range. Older siblings had higher rates of both internalizing (i.e., inhibited, very shy, or anxious behaviors) and externalizing (i.e., aggression or other acting-out behaviors) when their sibling had autism. The three groups did not differ significantly on measures of self-competence or parent reports of social competence. Rodrigue and colleagues concluded that siblings of children with autism are not especially vulnerable to adjustment problems, although they did find that sibling age is a variable. Likewise, higher levels of marital satisfaction between parents were also associated with higher levels of self-esteem in siblings of children with autism.

Hannah and Midlarsky (1999) looked at the competence and adjustment of siblings of children with mental retardation. Compared with siblings in a control group, the authors found no overall differences for internalizing disorders, externalizing disorders, or self-esteem and competence based on group membership, gender, or gender match. They suggest that being in a family that has a child with mental retardation does not lead to a greater degree of mental distress or pathology than may be found in families with children who are typically developing. They did pinpoint that boys with a brother or sister with mental retardation had more difficulty in school functioning, and that a greater number of girls with siblings with mental retardation expressed distress through internalizing behaviors.

Bagenholm and Gillberg (1991) found that Swedish siblings of children with autism have high levels of loneliness and problems with peers. They also found that overall, siblings of children with autism as well as siblings who were typically developing reported quite good relationships with their siblings, and that siblings of children with autism reported significantly less positive attitudes toward their siblings and significantly fewer descriptions of the sibling's role in the family relative to other siblings. Mates (1990), however, included only the oldest siblings of children with autism and found no differences between brothers and sisters on measures of self-concept, academic achievement, or school or home adjustment.

Guite, Lobato, Kao, and Plante (2004) looked at the relationship between sibling and parent reports of sibling adjustment to children with developmental disabilities and/or ongoing medical conditions. They found that differences between parent and sibling reports were common, and parents were more likely to report more sibling adjustment problems than were siblings. When parents and siblings differ in their opinions of sibling relationship or adjustment, it is more likely that parents report more negative adjustment issues for siblings than do the siblings, and that parents report the situation as being more burdensome in general on the sibling and family than do the siblings.

Dyson and her colleagues have conducted a series of sibling studies in Canada. Dyson, Edgar, and Crnic (1989) sent a questionnaire to 110 families, one-half of whom had a child with a disability and the other half of whom made up a control group of families with children having no disabilities. In the families having a child with a disability, they found that a combination of factors such as parental attitude, social support, and family psychological environment predicted the self-concept, presence or absence of behavior problems, and social competence of the older siblings. The same combination of factors was predictive only of social competence in the families in which there were no children with disabilities. These siblings were also negatively affected (e.g., had lower self-concepts) by parental stress related to the condition or challenges related to the sibling with the disability.

Dyson and Fewell (1989) compared the self-concept of 37 siblings who had brothers or sisters with disabilities to a control group who had siblings without disabilities. These groups were matched by gender, geographical region, socioeconomic status (SES), and age. They found no differences in the levels of self-concept between the two groups and no significant effects for gender, birth order, SES, or type of disability. Dyson (1989) and Ferrari (1984) also found that siblings of children with a disability were comparable with children who had siblings with no disabilities in measures of self-concept, behavior problems, and social competencies. Dyson did find differences along psychological dimensions such as aggression and hyperactivity, and great variations within each group of siblings. Dyson and Fewell hypothesized that the actual effect of a sibling with a disability is slight because either the nature of self-concept is permanent or because siblings have developed positive concepts through certain transactional processes. These processes include adaptive coping and additional responsibilities leading to increased competence. Dyson and Fewell concluded that the effect of a sibling with a disability on a person's self-worth is individualized and that further studies should investigate the importance of the type of disability as well as expand on the instrumentation used. Ten years later, in 1999, Dyson again found no differences in level of self-concept, social competence, or behavior adjustment between siblings of children with disabilities and siblings of children without disabilities.

Grissom and Borkowski (2002) looked at self-efficacy in adolescents who have siblings with or without disabilities. Self-efficacy is defined as the belief that one is capable of organizing and executing the actions necessary to attain certain goals. None of the adolescent measures comparing self-efficacy or peer competence differed significantly between those who had a sibling with a disability and those who did not. For those with siblings with disabilities, interpersonal competence and maternal attitudes and modeling were significantly related to self-efficacy; that is, those with mothers who put a greater emphasis on and modeling of prosocial and empathic behaviors had siblings with higher scores on self-efficacy. These results point to the need to increase mothers' awareness of the importance of their attitude and actions. When sibling research started, the model was that the sibling would be expected to experience adjustment problems. The focus has changed to looking at possible beneficial effects as well. Self-efficacy may be a way to identify these positive outcomes because it is a process-oriented variable rather than a static one such as gender or age.

Positive Effects

Although Grossman (1972) found some negative effects on siblings, she also found a number of positive outcomes. She reported that about one-half of college students interviewed described the presence of a child with a disability as a positive, integrative experience in their family. These siblings showed increased tolerance for differences as well as higher levels of empathy and altruism. Grossman proposed that the manner in which a disability was interpreted and accepted delineated its impact on the siblings involved. Taylor (1974) suggested that a positive communication pattern between siblings without disabilities and mothers of children with mental retardation is instrumental in achieving optimal sibling adjustment. Grossman pointed out that the "humanness" of people with mental retardation, as viewed by siblings, was influenced by the severity of the retardation, the extent to which the mother seemed to accept the child, and the amount of time the sibling played with the brother or sister with a disability.

Other authors have also concluded that there are positive aspects associated with the presence of a child with a disability in the family (Graliker, Fishler, & Koch, 1962; Schipper, 1959). Lobato (1983, 1990), for instance, maintains that extra caregiving responsibilities do not necessarily lead to negative adjustment. Such responsibilities may be balanced by an increase in the quantity or quality of attention given to the siblings by parents. Schreiber and Feeley (1965) concluded that, for some siblings of children with disabilities, there is an increased sense of maturity and responsibility resulting from growing up with the child. Mates's (1982) study of 32 children with autism found that, as a group, their siblings displayed higher than average levels of self-concept. In addition, Lloyd-Bostock (1976) found that parents reported that their child with a disability was generally loved and accepted by the other siblings in the family.

McHale, Sloan, and Simeonsson (1986) compared the sibling relationships of three groups of 6- to 15-year-olds: those with siblings who had autism, mental retardation, or no known disabilities. All sibling relationships were rated by the siblings as generally positive, with no significant differences found among groups. Mothers of children with a disability rated the sibling relationship more positively than did mothers of the comparison group. It is important to note that the data indicated that the experience of having a child with a disability in the family is highly variable, with a range of responses displayed. Children who have siblings without disabilities, however, tended to have responses that clustered around the mean.

More recently, Van Riper (2000) reported on the well-being of siblings of children with Down syndrome through mailed questionnaires completed by mothers and siblings. Results showed that the siblings had favorable self-concepts, and mothers reported that the siblings were socially competent, with a low incidence of behavior problems. As a group, sibling well-being was higher in these families, as indicated by lower levels of demands, greater resources, and higher levels of family coping.

Taunt and Hastings (2002) asked parents about the positive impacts their child with disabilities had on themselves, siblings, and the extended family. Parents mentioned an increased sensitivity and caring on the part of siblings and other relatives, especially grandparents. They also reported increased closeness and support in the extended family. The parents reported that siblings developed greater maturity and a greater sense of responsibility. A caution of this study is that the results were based on parent report, which may influence how the siblings interact or at least the perception of these interactions.

Kaminsky and Dewey (2002) looked at the psychosocial adjustment of siblings of children with autism compared with siblings of children with Down syndrome and others who were typically developing. Results indicated that siblings of children with autism, as well as the other groups, were well adjusted and reported low levels of loneliness. The siblings of children with autism reported that they received high levels of social support, but these reports did not differ from those given by other siblings. Pilowsky, Yirmiya, Doppelt, Gross-Tsur, and Shalev (2004) also conducted research on the social and emotional adjustment of siblings of children with autism. Their study was conducted in Israel. They found that the adjustment of the siblings was positive, "noteworthy even," and did not differ from siblings of children with mental retardation or those with language delay.

Gath and Gumley (1987) compared three groups of sibling pairs: The first included a child with Down syndrome; the second included a child with mild, nonspecific mental retardation; and the third consisted of siblings with no known disabilities. Children with a sibling with Down syndrome had fewer behavior problems and did better in school than those with siblings with nonspecific mental retardation. Furthermore, the pairs with nonspecific mental retardation were also more likely to be associated with lower socioeconomic status (SES) groups. Gender did not appear to have an impact. Sisters did not exhibit any more adjustment problems than brothers in this study.

Mandleco, Olsen, Dyches, and Marshall (2003) looked at the relationship between family and sibling functioning in families of a child with a disability. They investigated the relationship between parental perceptions of family functioning and the social skills of school-age siblings and found that control siblings and those with disabilities demonstrated more social skills than problem behaviors, and that siblings of children with disabilities scored higher in cooperation and self-control than did control siblings, demonstrating positive adaptations for siblings of children with disabilities. Father and mother perceptions affected sisters of children with disability ratings on externalizing behaviors, suggesting that sisters are more at risk for adjustment problems than are brothers.

Cox, Marshall, Mandleco, and Olsen (2003) looked at the coping responses to daily life stressors of siblings, ages 6–18 years, who have a sibling with a disability. Siblings responded verbally to a sentence-completion activity regarding coping responses to stressful situations. A content analysis found four overall categories of responses including proactive (i.e., used problem solving and reasoning), interactive (i.e., sought out social support to manage the problem), internally reactive (i.e., expressed feelings of emotion), and nonactive (i.e., no response; reported by only a small number of siblings). The most popular reactions reported were proactive and interactive for both boys and girls, reminding us that increased sibling responsibility may have positive outcomes and lead the siblings to be more proactive.

FACTORS CONTRIBUTING TO SIBLINGS' ADJUSTMENT PATTERNS

The impact that a child with a disability has on siblings may vary a great deal. The relevance of research conducted during the 1960s and 1970s is subject to question, especially given the increase in family support services (e.g., respite care and public school programs). Negative effects on siblings may be ameliorated by increased openness about, acceptance of, and services for those with disabilities. However, it is generally agreed that, even today, it can be stressful to have a brother or sister with a disability.

Cerreto and Miller (1981) and Trevino (1979) have noted that siblings of children with disabilities are potentially at risk for a wide variety of behavior or emotional problems, which may be long-lasting and may influence career choices and future family patterns. Past research has shown that myriad factors may contribute to the adjustment patterns of the child without a disability. As Cate and Loots noted,

> The impact of a child's impairment on siblings may be best conceptualized as a risk factor, the significance of which is mediated by sociodemographic features, individual and family adaptive and functional

> patterns, sibling constellation variables, and impairment characteristics. (2000, p. 399)

Many people find it helpful to envision the effects a child with a disability has on the sibling in terms of a continuum, with very positive outcomes at one end and very negative outcomes (e.g., psychological disturbance) at the other. Many different factors seem to contribute to where the sibling without a disability functions on this continuum. Family characteristics, including size, SES, and religion, appear to be factors contributing to sibling adjustment. In addition, parental attitudes and expectations as well as characteristics of both of the siblings, such as age, gender, temperament, and the severity of the child's disability, also significantly influence the sibling relationship and affect sibling adjustment. A discussion of these four major contributing factors follows. Although all of these variables have not been studied extensively, it is thought that they often interact with each other to influence different feelings and relationships. It is important to remember that this continuum of outcomes for siblings is not static. Simply because a sibling seems to have a very healthy, positive relationship at one time does not mean that, at another time, the same sibling may not express some very negative behaviors and feelings.

Family Characteristics

Characteristics of the nuclear family appear to be important factors contributing to sibling adjustment. Family size, the socioeconomic status of the family, and religious involvement must also be considered as unique variables that influence the sibling relationship.

Family Size Taylor (1974) has suggested that siblings from larger families are generally better adjusted than those from smaller families. It seems natural that in two-child families in which one child has a disability, parents are more likely to rest all of their hopes and expectations on the other sibling. In larger families, however, these hopes and desires can be distributed to several children and, thus, prevent the pressure from resting on the one child. McHale and colleagues (1984) found that children from larger families are better adjusted, provided that the families have adequate financial resources. Dyson (1989) also found that the greater the number of children in the family, the better the psychological adjustment of the siblings. More recently, Kaminsky and Dewey (2002) found that better psychosocial adjustment in siblings of children with autism was associated with a greater number of siblings in the family and suggested that more siblings may help individual siblings feel less pressure in terms of responsibilities. Pilowsky and colleagues (2004), however, found that the greater the family size, the greater the delay in siblings' socialization skills for siblings of children with autism. The researchers speculate that perhaps family dynamics are different depending on the number of children. More children may lead to decreased availability of the parents to individual children.

Socioeconomic Status Family SES also can affect sibling responses toward a child with a disability. Grossman (1972) found that siblings from middle-income families generally had a range of positive and negative feelings that were predictable based on their parents' attitudes. Middle-income families often have problems lowering their high expectations for their child with a disability (McHale et al., 1984). At the same time, middle-income families tend to be more financially secure and better prepared to utilize outside resources such as camps, respite care services, and a wide range of professionals in securing help for any family needs. Conversely, families of lower SES typically have limited financial resources. Thus, siblings, especially females, who are from poorer families may be overwhelmed with extra caregiving responsibilities that cannot be provided for through other channels.

Stoneman, Brody, Davis, and Crapps (1988) found that in families with greater income, siblings participated more in out-of-home activities and spent more time with friends. They also found that more educated parents placed fewer caregiving responsibilities on older siblings and facilitated more out-of-home activities.

Religion No recent or current research was available at the time this book was published on the variable of religion and its effects on siblings with disabilities; nevertheless the construct showed up as important in past research. In a review of the literature regarding the role of religion in parental acceptance of a child with a disability conducted in the mid-1960s, Stubblefield (1965) noted that the birth of such a child often precipitated a theological crisis for many parents at that time. Religious faith affects parents' responses to the birth of a child with disabilities. Zuk, Miller, Bartram, and Kling (1961) established moderate but positive correlations between measures of religious background and maternal acceptance of a child with a disability. They found that at that time, Roman Catholic families tended to be more accepting of a child with mental retardation than were Jewish or Protestant families, and they explained such acceptance as deriving from the explicit definitions supporting the home and family life decreed by the Roman Catholic Church. McHale and Gamble (1987) found that mothers who were more involved in religious activities used more coping strategies for dealing with the stress of having a child with a disability. The religious involvement of the mother was also related to higher self-esteem and fewer depression and anxiety symptoms in the siblings.

Parental Attitudes and Expectations Siblings' perceptions of their parents' attitudes regarding the child with a disability can indeed be a powerful influence on their adjustment. In a study conducted in 1960 on the adjustment of parents and siblings of a family member with a disability, Caldwell and Guze (1960) looked at 32 families, one-half of which had a child with a disability living in the home and one-half of which had a child with a disability living in an institution. They found that, generally, the two groups were similar in terms of adjustment. One area in which the two groups were clearly different was in the sibling's perception of the ideal living arrangement for the child with mental retardation. Both groups felt that the environment in which their sibling was living was the best living situation for that sibling. Holt (1958) also conducted personal interviews with parents in the homes of 201 families that included a child with mental retardation. Holt noted that 5% of the parents reported feelings of embarrassment and shame on the part of the children without a disability toward their sibling with mental retardation, and that such feelings were, to some extent, related to the parents' own adjustment.

Other researchers have stressed the importance of parental attitudes in sibling adjustment. Graliker and colleagues (1962) found that siblings without disabilities had fewer behavior challenges in home, school, and social activities when both parents had the same positive attitude toward their child with mental retardation than did children of parents who did not share such a positive attitude. In her study a decade later, Grossman (1972) suggested that one of the strongest factors affecting the sibling's acceptance of the child with a disability is the feelings of the parents, particularly the mother. She proposed that the manner in which parents interpret and respond to a disability determines the impact on the siblings involved. Clearly, parental attitudes exert a significant influence on a sibling's acceptance of a child with a disability. Siblings are better adjusted when their parents are more accepting of the condition of the child (McHale et al., 1984). As Lobato (1990) noted, a positive marriage with good communication predicts good psychological adjustment for the children. Rodrigue, Geffken, and Morgan (1993) also found that higher levels of marital satisfaction were associated with higher levels of self-esteem in siblings of children with autism. Lobato saw both good communication and closeness acting as critical buffers between the siblings and the stresses of having a brother or sister with a disability. Grissom and Borkowski (2002) recently confirmed that maternal attitudes and modeling were significantly related to self-efficacy for adolescents with siblings with disabilities. They found that siblings with mothers who put a greater emphasis on the modeling of prosocial and empathic behaviors toward the child with disabilities had higher scores on self-efficacy.

Characteristics of the Sibling without a Disability

Demographic characteristics in families who have a child with a disability are difficult to separate from those birth order characteristics found in all other families (Lobato, 1983). However, the gender and age of the sibling without a disability in relation to the child with a disability seem to be factors that contribute to the sibling's adjustment.

Gender and Caregiving As mentioned previously, several authors found that female siblings who are the oldest in the family rather than male siblings in this birth order are most adversely affected by the presence of a child with a disability (Cleveland & Miller, 1977; Gath, 1974; Graliker et al., 1962; Grossman, 1972; McHale et al., 1984). Older siblings, particularly females, may experience adverse reactions because they usually assume child care responsibilities, and these responsibilities are often compounded when one of the children has a disability. Stoneman and colleagues (1988) found that the changes in the role of women in our society appear to have had minimal impact on the disproportionate role that older sisters of children with mental retardation still bear in child care responsibilities. Their study found that the older sisters' responsibilities were associated with an increase in observed sibling conflict and a decrease in positive sibling interactions, as well as decreased opportunities for peer contacts and activities outside the home. As a group, though, the siblings of brothers and sisters with disabilities did not differ significantly from comparison peers in the frequency of contact with friends or participation in activities outside the home.

In semi-structured home interviews with 24 siblings (ages 9–13), all of whom had a younger sibling with severe disabilities, Wilson and colleagues (1989) found that caregiving (e.g., teaching, dressing, feeding, babysitting, disciplining) appears to be a regular and significant feature of the siblings' relationship. In this qualitative and descriptive study, siblings reported that they interacted with the child with disabilities on a daily basis and were conversant regarding the school activities of the child. McHale and Gamble (1987) also found that children who had brothers or sisters with disabilities spent significantly more time taking care of their siblings, whereas those who had siblings without disabilities spent more time doing chores together. Thus, while the amount of time spent together was relatively the same, the tasks and activities were different.

In a more recent study, Cuskelly and Gunn (1993) found that there was no difference in the amount of household responsibilitiy between brothers and sisters of those with Down syndrome and those with siblings who were typically developing; however, sisters of children with Down syndrome who provided more assistance around the home were reported to have fewer adjustment problems than those who did fewer household chores.

McHale and Harris (1992), in an effort to look at the extent and nature of sibling interactions, found that children (ages 8–14) with younger siblings, particularly girls, spent more time in caregiving activities with their siblings who had a disability. In contrast, children who have siblings without disabilities spent more time performing chores together. They did not find any differences among families in the total time spent with a brother or sister who had a disability versus a brother or sister who did not have a disability, but did find that girls perform more caregiving activities and boys, more play activities. The researchers also found that more time spent in caregiving was significantly correlated to reports of anxiety symptoms; however, no other significant correlations between activities and the quality of the relationship were found. These researchers speculated that perhaps the slightly higher ratings of anxiety and lower self-esteem may be offset by a more mature self and broader outlook (McHale & Gamble, 1989; McHale & Harris, 1992).

Gender and Age Some research shows that the psychological adjustment of siblings is more positive when the child with a disability is of the opposite gender from the sibling. Grossman (1972) found that siblings reported more embarrassment when the sibling with a disability was of the same gender and of close age to the child. Likewise, Schreiber and Feeley (1965) and Simeonsson and Bailey (1983) found that the greater the age difference between the child with a disability and the sibling, the more likely it was that the sibling was well adjusted. This may be because wider age-spacing of children is associated with less parental stress and reports of better marital relationships (Wagner, Schubert, & Schubert, 1985), which can lead to smoother sibling relationships.

Wilson and colleagues (1989), however, found that children who were of the same gender and relatively closer in age to the child with the disability described a more positive impact of having a sibling with a disability—a sense of connectedness. Wilson and colleagues viewed this connectedness as being a salient finding. Although children of the same age and gender may enjoy the benefit of close companionship, such "togetherness" is also fertile ground for conflict (Lobato, 1990).

It also appears that when the sibling without a disability is much older than the sibling with a disability, particularly more than 10 years older, he or she will be better adjusted (McHale et al., 1984; Simeonsson & Bailey, 1983). As Lobato noted, both Breslau (1982) and Dyson (1989) also found fewer indications of adjustment problems as differences in siblings' ages increased. Simeonsson and Bailey (1983) believed that the poorer adjustment found in siblings who are younger or closer in age may be attributable to identity problems. These siblings may have difficulty, for instance, adjusting expectations of what an older brother should be able to do when the brother has a disability and may not even be able to feed himself. The sibling must learn to adjust his or her own identity in relation to a sibling who has a disability and, therefore, does not perform as a person that same age would typically perform. Simeonsson and Bailey (1983) have also proposed that the extent to which siblings perceive themselves as competent in relation to the sibling with disabilities will help determine their adjustment. In effect, then, they suggest that older siblings, being innately more competent, or siblings who have been given information and training related to the sibling's disabilities and thus, who feel competent with the child with a disability may be better adjusted than those who do not feel such confidence. These researchers also believed that characteristics such as temperament may be of major importance when looking at the relationship between two siblings.

Characteristics of the Child with a Disability

The child with the disability, of course, also brings a unique personality and set of characteristics to the sibling relationship. Previously, it was thought that the specific type of disability was not a major factor in sibling adjustment, but rather that the important factor was the severity of the disability and associated caregiving requirements. However, more recent research has focused on differences among siblings of children with specific disabilities, and it does appear that diagnosis (or the characteristics of persons with a particular disabilitiy) may be a factor. Another factor is the ever-increasing age of the person with the disability.

Type of Disability Lobato (1983) outlined a series of studies on siblings of children with Down syndrome, cystic fibrosis, hearing impairments, autism, cerebral palsy, and childhood cancers, noting that all of the researchers described similar results regarding the psychosocial adjustment of the siblings and hypothesizing that there must be factors other than the type of disability that determine adjustment for the siblings without disabilities. Although it is true that other factors such as sex or age relative to the child with disabilities or even individual traits such as temperament (Simeonsson & Bailey, 1983) are indeed important variables affecting the outcome of the sibling relationship, it does appear that the specific disability of the child may play a factor in that relationship as well, according to other studies. The following text looks at several studies of siblings of children with several different types of disabilities and how these disabilities may relate to siblings' adjustment and challenges.

Siblings of Children with Mental Retardation Cuskelly and her colleagues have conducted a series of articles regarding siblings of children with Down syndrome in Australia. Cuskelly and Dadds (1992) and Cuskelly and Gunn (1993) reported that the sisters of children with Down syndrome had significantly more conduct problems than did brothers of children with Down syndrome or a comparison group with no disabilities. No differences were found in the amount of household responsibility between brothers and sisters of those with Down syndrome or with a comparison group with no disabilities (Cuskelly & Gunn, 1993). Cuskelly and Gunn also found that sisters of a child with Down syndrome who provided more assistance around the home were reported to have fewer problems than those who did less. The authors speculated that perhaps mothers of girls who had siblings with Down syndrome expect their daughters without disabilities to take more responsibility and when they do not, mothers may perceive them as more of a behavior problem. In contrast, Cuskelly, Chant, and Hayes (1998) looked at behavior problems of 4- to 18-year-old siblings of children with Down syndrome compared with a control group of siblings of children who were typically developing. They found that mothers and fathers from both groups reported no differences with the siblings in terms of behavior problems. Likewise, the siblings of children with Down syndrome did not differ in their contribution to family tasks from the siblings of children who were typically developing.

Others have also studied children with Down syndrome and their siblings. Van Riper (2000), as mentioned previously, used mailed questionnaires completed by mothers and siblings and reported that siblings had favorable self-concepts and were reported by their mothers to have a low incidence of behavior problems. Kaminsky and Dewey (2001) found that siblings of children with Down syndrome (their study included siblings of children with autism as well) reported greater admiration for their sibling and less quarreling and competition in their relationships than in sibling dyads of typically developing children, whereas Kaminsky and Dewey (2002) reported that siblings of children with Down syndrome were well adjusted and reported low levels of loneliness.

Eisenberg, Baker, and Blacher (1998) compared adolescent siblings of children with mental retardation living at home or in residential placements with siblings of children who were typically developing. Siblings in the study had a mean age of 13 years. Despite different situations, siblings were remarkably similar on measures of psychological adjustment, self-esteem, and family environment. When the child with mental retardation lived out of the home, sibling relationships were found to be less intense and less warm, but also not as conflictual. Siblings of children with mental retardation had beliefs and attitudes about placement that were highly consistent with the child's current living situation (and likely with parental attitudes). Siblings of children with mental retardation indicated that they would like to be more involved in conversations about the child, and that it would be helpful to have family conversations about future plans. These children felt that such conversations would reduce—not increase, their anxiety about their siblings. The siblings of children with mental retardation differed from control group siblings in that they perceived themselves as having more power in the relationship. This is consistent with other findings that show more hierarchical and less egalitarian relationships when there is a sibling with a disability in the dyad.

Brody, Stoneman, Davis, and Crapps (1991) observed older children with mental retardation and their younger siblings in home settings during toy play, television viewing, and snacks. They also observed comparison groups of siblings without mental retardation. Interactions between children with mental retardation and their siblings were characterized by accentuated role asymmetries that favored the younger sibling, whereas in the comparison group, the older sibling was the dominant one. When the older child had mental retardation, the younger brother or sister played more manager, teacher, and helper roles than did other younger siblings. An interesting twist, though, is that older children with mental retardation assumed teacher and helper roles for their younger siblings more often than did older siblings in a control group. This was especially true in the snack context. It also seems that the competence of the child with mental retardation predicted the sibling role asymmetries. The study also showed that context is an important variable; dyads all engaged in similar amounts of interaction during television and snack, whereas the dyads with the older child with mental retardation interacted less during toy play than did the other dyads.

Stoneman, Brody, Davis, Crapps, and Malone (1991) looked at roles of younger children (ages 4–10 years) with siblings with mental retardation compared with a control group of typically developing sibling dyads. The older siblings ranged from 7 to 12 years. Role reversals were evident in the younger children who had siblings with mental retardation because they assumed ascribed roles such as babysitting normally given to the older child. The researchers did not find that this affected the quality of the sibling relationship however; in fact, they found less role conflict in the dyads in which the older sibling had mental retardation. Younger siblings of children with mental retardation assumed more responsibilities for child care than did comparison younger siblings, particularly if they were sisters. Interestingly, younger siblings of children with mental retardation had fewer household chores than did comparison siblings, perhaps because they were already adding on caregiving roles. The severity of mental retardation did matter as the younger siblings of less adaptively competent children with mental retardation were called on to take greater responsibility for their own personal care and for assisting with meal preparation.

Hannah and Midlarsky (1999) found that being a sibling in a family with a child with mental retardation does not lead to more mental distress or pathology than does being in a family with typically developing children, although a greater number of girls with siblings with mental retardation did express distress through internalizing behaviors.

Siblings of Children with Emotional Disturbance and/or Behavior Disorders Litzelfelner (1995) looked at the perceptions of siblings of children with emotional disabilities, a group about which there is little research. This study was exploratory and used a focus group method. The following themes emerged from the siblings' descriptions of their behaviors:

- Most said that having a sibling with emotional disabilities did not affect them, although they did point out the aggressive behaviors of their siblings.
- They said that their family was like other families and that they did not know anything different.
- They did not have much information or understanding about emotional disabilities and wanted that information.
- They were mostly optimistic about the future for their sibling and family.

Stormshak, Bellanti, and Bierman (1996) looked at the quality of the sibling relationship and the development of social competence and behavioral control in children labeled aggressive. The children with aggression were in first and second grade. Three types of sibling interactions emerged: 1) conflictual (high conflict/low warmth), 2) involved (moderate levels of conflict and warmth) and 3) supportive (low conflict, high warmth). Approximately half had conflictual interactions, but the other half had involved or supportive interactions, suggesting that the sibling relationship may be an important context for social learning. Not surprisingly, children in involved relationships showed better adjustment than did those in conflictual ones.

East and Rook (1992) assessed the sibling relationships of children who were isolated in school and found that if they had a supportive sibling relationship, they were more likely to have higher levels of maturity at home, again suggesting that positive sibling relationships can be a support for children with behavior disorders.

Epkins and Dedmon (1999) looked at siblings as observers of their siblings with depression, anxiety, and aggression. They found no significant differences in siblings' reports and self-reports of the children with these disorders regarding their behaviors. The siblings, though, did report significantly higher levels of aggression in the target children than did the self-reports by the target children, leading the researchers to conclude that siblings may be especially good informants.

Siblings of Children with Autism Kaminsky and Dewey (2001) reported on the sibling relationships of children with autism compared with those with Down syndrome and those who were typically developing. They found that sibling relationships of children with autism were characterized by less intimacy, prosocial behavior, and nurturance than were sibling dyads in the other two groups. The authors speculated that the lack of intimacy in sibling relationships with a child with autism could be related to the social and communication deficits of those with autism. They also found that siblings of children with autism or Down syndrome reported greater admiration for their sibling and less quarreling and competition in their relationships than in typical sibling dyads. Knott, Lewis, and Williams (1995) found that children with autism spent less time with their sibling, used a smaller number and less variety of both prosocial and antagonistic initiations toward their sibling, and imitated their sibling less than did children with Down syndrome. The interaction patterns of siblings with a brother or sister who had autism, though, were at similar levels of initation and responding to those of siblings with a brother or sister with Down syndrome; the interactions of the siblings with a brother or sister with disabilities were more similar to each other than those of a comparative group of siblings with a brother or sister who was typically developing.

Little (2002) looked at mothers' perceptions of victimization among children with Asperger syndrome and nonverbal learning disorders.

The findings showed that of the mothers of a child with Asperger syndrome and/or nonverbal learning disorder, 75% reported that their child had been hit by peers or siblings in the past year and had been emotionally bullied.

Gold (1993) looked at depression and social adjustment in siblings (mean age of 13 years) of boys with autism. Siblings of boys with autism scored significantly higher on depression than a comparison group, but not on problems of social adjustment. As noted earlier, Rodrigue, Geffken, and Morgan (1993) found that siblings of children with autism displayed more internalizing and externalizing behaviors than did siblings of children with Down syndrome or a control group of siblings of children who were typically developing, although all scores fell within the normative range. Fisman and colleages (2000) found that the siblings of children with pervasive developmental disorder (of which autism is on the spectrum) had significantly more adjustment problems than did those with siblings with Down syndrome or a control group with typically developing siblings.

As previously noted, a study in Sweden (Bagenholm & Gillberg, 1991) found that siblings of children with autism have high levels of loneliness and problems with peers and that they reported less positive attitudes toward their siblings than did those with siblings who were typically developing or those with mental retardation. An earlier study by Mates (1990), however, had found no differences on measures of self-concept, academic achievement, or school or home adjustment for older siblings of a child with autism. In their 2002 study, Kaminsky and Dewey looked at the psychosocial adjustment of siblings of children with autism compared with those with siblings with Down syndrome or a typical control group. The siblings of children with autism were reported to be well-adjusted, as was found in another study in Israel (Pilowsky et al., 2004). These mixed results found in studies of siblings of children with autism indicate varying and sometimes conflicting levels of adjustment.

Siblings of Children with Physical Disabilities Cate and Loots (2000) looked at siblings of children with certain physical disabilities (spina bifida or cerebral palsy) in Holland. Siblings reported difficulties in undertaking mutual activities and in communicating with siblings with a physical disability, although overall they reported few significant problems. Most siblings in the study also expressed concern for the future and for the health of the sibling with the disability. The siblings did not report that having a sibling with a disability caused problems in their relationships with friends, although the siblings did report annoyance and distress at the awkward reactions of strangers. Siblings also noted that they enjoyed doing things together such as building blocks, and described certain "perks" of having a sibling with a disability, such as being allowed to go to the front of amusement park lines. The siblings in this study reported that they accept that the sibling with the disability gets more attention from parents, although they do not always like it. Sixty-five percent of the siblings spontaneously indicated that they appreciate their parents' attempts to be equitable.

Dallas, Stevenson, and McGurk (1993) compared Greek children with cerebral palsy with a control group of children without a disability in terms of these children's interactions with siblings. The children with cerebral palsy were more passive and lacking in assertiveness than were childen in the control group, and their siblings were correspondingly more directive. As expected, the interactions in the pairs with a child with a disability were predominantly hierarchical in nature, with the child with the disability assuming the role of the younger child regardless of his or her chronological age. The researchers also found more maternal intervention in sibling pairs with a child with a disability, particularly when the child with a disability was younger.

Siblings of Children who are Deaf or Hard of Hearing Little is known about siblings of children who are deaf or hard of hearing. Raghuraman (2002) did a literature review and found reports that many hearing siblings enjoy being interpreters, role models, and caregivers for their brother or sister who is deaf or hard of hearing. Meyer and Vadasy (1996) reported that hearing siblings can experience sadness, anger, or guilt, and some may worry about "catching" the deafness of their brother or sister.

Siblings of Children with Traumatic Brain Injury McMabon, Noll, Michaud, and Johnson (2001) looked at how siblings adjust when a sibling experienced pediatric traumatic brain injury (TBI). These researchers found no statistical differences in depressive symptoms, self-concept, or behavior between siblings and their peers in a control group 3–18 months after the injury. As a group, the siblings of children with TBI did not have many parent-reported behavior problems. If the child with TBI had poorer functional outcomes, however, it correlated significantly with lower self-concept and more symptoms of depression in the siblings. Rivara (1994) suggested that siblings commonly feel neglected by their parents because of the overwhelming needs and care for the child with TBI.

Siblings of Children with Learning Disabilities Research in the area of siblings of students with learning disabilities is scarce. Dyson (1996) researched the sibling self-concept of children with siblings with learning disabilities. She found that the self-concept of the siblings was comparable with that of siblings of children with no disabilities. However, while the relationships between siblings with and without learning disabilities were generally positive, 19% of the siblings reported various negative experiences. These experiences included being teased by, being fearful of, and imitating inappropriate behaviors of the child with learning disabilities. Several of the parents in the study expressed a need for a group support activity for the siblings.

Dyson (2003) also compared children with learning disabilities to their siblings. According to parents surveyed, their children did not differ in global self-concept and academic self-perceptions, but parents rated the children with learning disabilities as having less social competence and more behavior problems than their siblings with no disabilities.

Siblings of Children Who Are Deafblind or Visually Impaired Again, little research exists in the area of siblings of those who are deafblind. Heller, Gallagher, and Fredrick (1999) reported on the perceptions of parents from 36 families who had a child with deafblindness. The parents reported that the siblings' roles were unequal, with siblings who were typically developing primarily taking on a helping role. Of note was the fact that 25% of the participants reported that the sibling without a disability interacted very little or even avoided the child with deafblindness. Parents also reported that siblings did not typically use unique modifications needed to effectively interact with individuals who are deafblind, such as communication systems.

Harland and Cuskelly (2000) explored the responsibilities and concerns of young adults in Australia who had siblings with vision and/or hearing difficulties. They found that although mothers tended to be the primary caregivers, siblings played an important secondary role in supporting the sibling with hearing and/or vision difficulties. Some siblings expressed guilt about not being able to do more with their brother or sister with disabilities. All of the siblings expressed anxiety about their role in caregiving in the future when their parents would not be able to do so. Siblings also tended to be concerned about how their interactions with the siblings with vision and/or hearing impairments might affect their other roles in professional jobs or in marriage. Siblings also expressed concern about the possibility of having a child with a disability and wanted more information about programs for their siblings.

Laman and Davidson (personal communication, June 14, 2005) discussed a study in which they compared the siblings of children with visual impairments or blindness with 10 control group families, all of whom lived in rural areas. These researchers compared three areas of responsibility for the child who was typically developing including involvement in home tasks, degree of independence, and extent of social activities. On the one hand, children with siblings without visual impairments described having more responsibilities in the home, except for getting the sibling ready for the day. It seems that siblings with brothers and sisters who were blind or had vision impairments spent more time helping their sibling get ready or dressing him or her. The siblings of children who were blind or had vision impairments also reported that they visited friends' homes less and were less involved in extracurricular activities than did children in the control group. On the other hand, siblings of children who were blind or had visual impairments reported that they had more freedom and attended more social events than did the control group siblings.

Severity of Disability Researchers have found that the variable of the severity of a child's disability interacts with the child's age and type of disability. Farber (1959), Grossman (1972), and Kirk and Bateman (1964) found that siblings were more adversely affected when the child's disability was more severe and, thus, required more care. Again, the state of a family's financial resources interacts with the severity of the disability. In families of lower socioeconomic status (SES), in which the financial resources for support such as babysitters or tutors are limited or unavailable, siblings typically have more caregiving responsibilities. Caregiving responsibilities, which include such tasks as feeding and bathing, have been discussed by several authors (Battle, 1974; Fotheringham & Creal, 1974; Korner, 1971; Robson & Moss, 1970; Schaffer & Emerson, 1964) as having an effect on mother–child interaction, on the mother's self-concept, and on parental stress (Beckman, 1983; Beckman-Bell, 1980; Harris & McHale, 1989). Parents of children with disabilities must cope with the aspects of child care often in unusual circumstances and for an extended period of time (Battle, 1974; Beckman-Bell, 1980; Fotheringham & Creal, 1974; Harris & McHale, 1989). Indeed, Beckman-Bell (1980), in a study examining the relationship between characteristics of infants with developmental disabilities and maternal stress, found that caregiving demands alone accounted for 66% of the variance in perceived parent and family problems.

In Harris and McHale's (1989) study, mothers who participated the most in activities, whether leisure or caregiving, with their child with a severe disability, rated their family problems as more intense. They were concerned with the present and future well-being of their child, as well as with the excessive time demands associated with caregiving.

It follows that such caregiving demands might also influence sibling relationships.

Several researchers found no differences in sibling and parental adjustment related to the severity of the disability (Breslau, 1982; Kolin, Scherzer, New, & Garfield, 1971). Tew and Laurence (1973) found that siblings often react more poorly toward siblings with mild disabilities than toward those with more severe disabilities, perhaps because the child with a mild disability does not act like he or she "looks" like he or she should act. In other words, with hidden disabilities such as Asperger syndrome, a sibling looks typical but may act in a way that is annoying or unexplainable to others, including siblings. The siblings may also feel that the child with a disability is receiving more parental time and attention for no justifiable reason (see differential treatment sections).

Children with certain disabilities tend to have behavior problems, and these issues might also contribute to the perceived severity of the disability. Fisman and colleagues (2000), for instance, noted that caregivers of children with pervasive developmental disorders reported the highest levels of distress and depression (compared with caregivers of children with Down syndrome or a typical control group) and that these reports persisted over time. Although a parent may not, in this situation, be overinvolved in specific caregiving responsibilities, he or she may have to be more vigilant in overseeing interactions and behaviors, thus taking time away from the sibling.

Age of Child with the Disability The age of the child with a disability also seems to influence the adjustment of the siblings. Researchers (Farber, 1964; McHale & Gamble, 1987; Miller, 1969) have found that as individuals with disabilities grow older, their siblings experience more difficulties. This may be due to the fact that the child becomes increasingly difficult to care for and his or her behavior becomes increasingly difficult to manage, while the differences between the siblings become more noticeable (Bristol, 1979; Wikler, 1983). Parents report that the family's isolation grows as the child matures physically but not mentally or socially (Lobato, 1990).

In a study of individuals with mental retardation living outside the home in family care homes, Stoneman and Crapps (1990) assessed the relationship of parents and siblings with their relative who lived in the family care home. Although only about one half of the individuals with mental retardation had any contact with their families, the providers noted that parent and sibling relationships were closer when the individuals with disabilities were older and more able. Siblings visited from increasingly greater distances as their siblings with disabilities aged. Home care providers also reported a significantly lower amount of stress for the resident when siblings visited more frequently.

Zeitlin (1986), in a study of 35 adults with mental retardation, found that the vast majority of their siblings remained in contact when the sibling with mental retardation moved into community-based living. Most of the contact was provided by sisters, through hierarchical, helping behaviors with their brother or sister with mental retardation. An interesting finding was that younger siblings were more likely than older siblings to act as caretakers for the sibling with mental retardation. Zetlin found that the adult siblings' concern for their brothers or sisters mimicked the expressed wishes of the parents. Many studies have occurred since the mid 1990s that look at the factor of age and siblings with disabilities. These will be discussed in detail at the end of this chapter under adult interactions.

SIBLING INTERACTIONS

Although much research on siblings of children with disabilities has focused on the adjustment of the child without a disability and on interventions to facilitate that adjustment, researchers also are beginning to explore another aspect of the process of sibling relationships: *interactions.* As Senapti and Hayes (1988) pointed out, although the focus had been on the products of the relationships rather than on the interaction process, it makes sense that the focus should turn to the actual interactions, especially since many of the factors described earlier (e.g., age-spacing, gender, severity of disability) are not factors a parent or service provider may have any particular control over.

Researchers are studying these interactions in the same way that they are examining sibling dyads when no child with a disability is present. The following are four broad areas of research in interactions with sibling dyads that include a child with a disability:

1. The extent and quality of sibling interaction
2. Differential treatment by parents
3. Stress/coping styles
4. Adult interactions

Each of these areas are outlined next.

Extent and Quality of Interactions

Stoneman, Brody, Davis, and Crapps (1987, 1989) have argued for the importance of contextual considerations in the study of sibling interactions. They have looked specifically at the roles siblings take and activities in which siblings are engaged, as described in their research studies that follow.

Stoneman and colleagues (1987, 1989) collected observational data on sibling interactions. The 1987 study looked at same-sex sibling interactions in natural in-home contexts. Whether there was a sibling with mental retardation in the pair, they found that there was a high level of interaction. The types of activities siblings engaged in were related to the gender of the siblings and to whether the younger sibling had mental retardation. In sibling pairs in which there was a younger child who had mental retardation, the pairs of boys were likely to be playing with toys, whereas the female pairs engaged in noncompetitive physical activities such as swinging or tumble play. Comparison pairs were more likely to be playing games or watching television. Older brothers and sisters with a younger sibling who had mental retardation were more likely than comparison siblings to be engaged in asymmetrical roles, such as managing, teaching, and helping.

Stoneman and colleagues' 1989 study looked at sibling interactions in standardized observational contexts (e.g., snacking, playing with toys, watching television) in an effort to further determine role asymmetry, egalitarianism, and the affective quality of sibling relationships. This study also found heightened role asymmetries between older siblings when their younger brothers or sisters had mental retardation. Older siblings took greater responsibility for teaching, helping, and directing than did a comparison group. Differing amounts of interaction and various patterns of relationships were noted, depending on the activity contexts.

Abramovitch, Stanhope, Pepler, and Corter (1987) compared sibling pairs including a child with Down syndrome to pairs including a child with no known disability and found results similar to those of Stoneman, Brody, and colleagues. In the groups with a sibling with a disability, the children without disabilities assumed the dominant leadership roles even when they were the younger siblings. These siblings also displayed significantly more nurturing and affectionate behaviors toward their siblings than did the children whose siblings did not have a disability.

Stoneman and colleagues (1987) also found a link between competency and role asymmetry in sibling pairs. It seemed that the less competent in language and adaptive skills the siblings with disabilities were, the greater was the role asymmetry in the pair. Stoneman and colleagues' study found that language and adaptive skills of the children with mental retardation positively predicted the amount of time spent playing with older siblings as well as the possibility of less role asymmetry. In the 1989 study, the level of role asymmetry increased with the age of the child with mental retardation. These findings support Farber's (1960) contention that when siblings are younger, sibling interactions tend to be more egalitarian. As they grow older, however, children without disabilities assume increasingly dominant positions when their sibling has a disability, whereas in families with two children without disabilities, sibling relationships become more egalitarian with age (Cicirelli, 1982). As Dunn (1983) noted, there is less reciprocity in the relationship when a sibling with a disability is present. Stoneman and her colleagues suggested that the greater role asymmetry with age eventually paves the way for the advocacy role that many siblings of people with disabilities assume as adults.

Lobato, Miller, Barbour, Hall, and Pezzullo (1991) looked at preschool siblings of children with disabilities and their interactions with mothers and brothers and sisters to look at similarities and differences in their behaviors and interactions as compared with a control group. They found few differences in sibling groups in quantity or quality of interactions with family members. They did find that siblings with a brother or sister with a disability engaged in more parallel play and social play and were more nurturing than were children in sibling dyads who were typically developing. Sisters of children with disabilities engaged in the most social play. Interestingly, the interactions between mothers and their children differed in that regardless of gender, siblings of children with disabilities received twice as many directives, scolds, and reprimands from mothers as did children in the control group even though few differences in rates of problematic behavior such as aggression were noted in the siblings.

Caro and Derevensky (1997) conducted an exploratory study between siblings with and without disabilities to look at sibling interactions using the Sibling Interaction Scale. They did not find any differences in behaviors of preschool and school-age siblings (i.e., the intensity of their involvement, their choice of activities, or their amount of pleasure during interactions) regardless of whether the child had a sibling with a disability. They did find significant differences between the dyads in the complexity of sentences and roles engaged in, with sibling interactions mostly found to be positive. The behaviors of siblings with disabilities were found to influence the responses of siblings without disabilities. Of note, when siblings with disabilities chose to act, they assumed equal roles almost as often as did their siblings without disabilities. Overall, siblings who were typically developing were more likely to engage in directive roles in which they managed, taught, or helped, whereas the siblings with disabilities were more likely to engage in no role or a passive role.

Caro and Derevensky (1997) suggested the importance of fostering more equal roles between siblings in order to facilitate increased assertiveness on the part of the child with disabilities. Perhaps the more directive roles displayed by siblings who are typically developing reflect compliance with parental expectations, and yet the quality of the sibling interaction may be negatively affected.

McHale and Harris (1992) looked at the affective tone of sibling interactions and reported differences in what siblings perceive as contributing to the relationship. These findings were similar to Begun's (1989) study, which compared females' evaluations of their relationship with a sibling who had a disability with a sibling who did not. The experiences with siblings who had a disability were characterized as involving less intimacy, similarity, admiration, and competition, as well as more dominance by the sister without the disability. The sisters also reported less reciprocity from the brother or sister with a disability than from the siblings with no disability, while at the same time they reported engaging in more nurturance with those with disabilities.

It is important to view interactions in the context of several other studies that have noted more nurturing behaviors and less reciprocity in sibling relationships that involve a child with a disability. Several authors (McHale et al., 1986; Ogle, 1982; Schaefer & Edgerton, 1981) found that parents rated sibling dyads higher (i.e., more positively and kindly) on the Sibling Inventory of Behavior (Schaefer & Edgerton, 1979) when the dyad contained a child with a disability than when both children in a dyad did not have disabilities. Miller (1974), likewise, found that children tended to engage in activities of a more instrumental nature (e.g., helping, teaching) when their siblings had disabilities, and in activities of a more expressive nature (e.g., self-fulfillment, mutual satisfaction) with their siblings who did not have disabilities.

Thus, it seems that children who may feel stress or have problems with a sibling who has a disability will not "take out" such feelings on that sibling. If anything, the research shows that children are kinder and more positive toward their siblings with disabilities. This is in concordance with the teaching/helping roles observed by Stoneman and her colleagues discussed in this chapter. Although this is a positive finding, the reader is cautioned that it may be important for the sibling relationship to evolve into more of an equal one so that the child with disabilities is not always in a subordinate role.

Differential Treatment

A common concern for children and adults is the way in which they are treated by their parents in comparison with the way their siblings are treated (see Chapter 2 on parental differential treatment). Children begin at an early age to monitor their parents' behavior toward themselves and their siblings and to detect differences in the ways they are treated (Dunn & Stocker, 1989). As noted by Dunn, Stocker, and Plomin (1990) and McHale and Pawletko (1992), in addition to the actual differences in the ways parents treat their children, the *realization* by the sibling that he or she is being treated differently may also have effects on their well-being and development. Parents should be keenly aware of children's perceptions of parental fairness and its effects on sibling adjustment.

As discussed by McHale and Pawletko (1992), a related set of studies by Brody and colleagues (1987b), Bryant and Crockenberg (1980), and Stocker and colleagues (1989) have focused on differential treatment and its effect on the sibling relationship. Bryant and Crockenberg (1980) concluded that siblings do compare parental interest and attention, and that evidence of preferential treatment toward one child can result in ill will and emotional conflict in the sibling relationship. Brody and colleagues (1987b) and Stocker and colleagues (1989) found similar results implying that preferential treatment may have negative implications in a child's relationships with his or her sibling while simultaneously having positive consequences for the child's own adjustment.

McHale and Harris (1992) and McHale and Pawletko (1992) reported on the differential treatment of siblings in four dimensions. These four dimensions are maternal involvement in activities with the older versus the younger child, household responsibilities assigned to the older versus the younger child, disciplinary responses employed by the mother in response to conflict, and the older child's satisfaction with parental differential treatment. They found greater levels of differential treatment in families with a child who has a disability. Mothers spent more time with younger siblings overall, but the differences were greater when the younger sibling had a disability. In terms of disciplinary strategies, mothers used more positive strategies such as reasoning or compromise with older siblings, and more power (assertive) strategies with younger siblings when the siblings had a disability. The 1992 McHale and Pawletko study found that children who had a sibling with a disability and who were relatively more involved in younger sibling activities (e.g., help, play, outings), or who performed relatively more chores, experienced the highest levels of depression and anxiety. Children whose siblings did not have disabilities and who were the least involved in their activities reported the fewest symptoms of anxiety and depression.

Although McHale and her colleagues did find greater levels of differential treatment in families having a child with a disability, they found no group differences in children's satisfaction with the differential treatment (McHale & Gamble, 1989). Satisfaction with differential treatment correlated only with differential maternal involvement; that is, the more satisfied children were, the less time they spent (relative to younger siblings) with their mothers. In addition, children's satisfaction with differential treatment was systematically related to their well-being and their evaluations of the sibling relationship. McHale and her colleagues urge more research in the area of differential treatment. They suggest that a child might have mixed feelings: pleasure about better treatment and yet also guilt or even negativity because the sibling is receiving the poorer treatment. McHale and Pawletko (1992) concluded that differential treatment of siblings is a complicated phenomenon that depends on 1) the domain of differential treatment being considered (e.g., mother–child activities versus disciplinary activities), 2) the potential consequences of differential treatment under consideration (well-being versus relationship measures), and 3) the family context.

McHale and Pawletko (1992) suggested that although some forms of differential treatment may imply clear favoritism on a parent's part (in this study it was primarily the mother's part), other forms—such as higher involvement in care or play—may be viewed as an imposition by older children. Thus, children may evaluate different forms of treatment in various ways. In children who receive more positive attention (reasoning, compromise) and have siblings who have a disability, a higher level of anxiety coincides with the guilt these children have expressed at receiving more favorable treatment. Such feelings can also motivate the child toward more kindness and concern in the sibling relationship.

Although McHale and Pawletko's (1992) study provides evidence that siblings of children who have disabilities do experience greater differential treatment than do other siblings, the authors caution that such discrepancies arise not because the children are neglected but rather, because their younger siblings with disabilities are treated so differently from other children their same age. It is important to be aware that mixed emotional reactions can arise. Although a child may be able to understand and justify the differential treatment, he may still harbor feelings of neglect or isolation.

Stress/Coping Styles

Some researchers are beginning to look at stress factors and siblings' coping styles in an effort to understand adjustment in children who have a sibling with a disability. Gamble and McHale (1989) gathered ratings of the nature of stress and coping styles in 62 children ages 7–14 years, divided equally between those with a sister or brother who had a mental disability and those with a sibling without a disability. They found no significant group or gender differences for the overall frequency of stressful events or for the amount of anger felt between the two groups. However, the comparison group did report that their siblings "teased or bugged" them more often, and children who had siblings with a disability showed significantly higher affect ratings in response to their sibling getting hurt or sick.

Children, in general, reported responding to stressful events in different ways, and these various reactions and coping strategies were important in determining self-ratings of well-being (Gamble & McHale, 1989; McHale & Harris, 1992). Children who had a sibling with a disability and girls who had a sibling without a disability used coping responses characterized as "other-directed cognitions" (e.g., my brother is a creep) more frequently. Boys who had siblings without disabilities tended to use "self-directed" strategies more often (e.g., trying to calm down or think about ways to solve the problem). These strategies were positively related to adjustment and relationship reports. Perhaps, as Gamble and McHale noted, the siblings of children with disabilities react less directly because their siblings may not understand and/or their parents are less tolerant of such behavior. Girls, of course, may have similar sanctions placed on their behaviors.

Both stressor frequency and the use of cognitive coping strategies accounted for significant portions of the variance in sibling relationship measures. Self-directed strategies (e.g., doing something fun to forget about it) were positively associated with relationship measures whereas other-directed cognitions were negatively related.

Interactions as Siblings Become Adults

The coexisting facts of the aging of the world's population and the increase in the life expectancies of people with disabilities are driving interest in siblings of adults with disabilities, as is evidenced by the wealth of studies that have occurred since the mid 1990s. Cuskelly and Gunn (1993), in an overview of research on adult responsibilities toward brothers or sisters with special needs, highlighted common themes as follows:

- Most adult siblings do maintain regular contact with brother/sister with a disability and provide him or her with affective support (Krauss, Seltzer, Gordon, & Friedman, 1996; Seltzer, Begun, Seltzer, & Krauss, 1991)
- Adult siblings tend to provide much less instrumental assistance than emotional support for their brother or sister with a disability (Pruchno, Patrick, & Burant, 1996)
- Female siblings as opposed to males are often more involved with the sibling with disabilities and take greater care with associated responsibilities (Pruchno, Patrick, & Burant, 1996).

In an early study, Seltzer, Begun, Seltzer, and Krauss (1991) provided information about the nature of sibling and intergenerational relationships for adults with mental retardation. The most involved sibling was typically older than and of the same gender as the adult with mental retardation, lived near the family home, and had at least weekly contact in person or by phone. The adults with disabilities in this study lived at home and, it is interesting to note, maternal well-being was associated with the siblings' active involvement in the life of the adult with mental retardation. Families with high levels of sibling involvement tended to be more expressive and cohesive, more oriented toward achievement and independence, and more likely to participate in active recreational activities than did families with lower levels of sibling involvement. However, they did find an imbalance in the exchange of affect between the sibling and the adult with mental retardation. The siblings were giving more than twice the support they received in return from their brother or sister. The authors also noted that at this stage, siblings tended to give more affective support (showing concern for welfare) than instrumental support (helping with daily tasks or self-care activities).

Similarly, Begun (1989), in a study of adult and adolescent females and their siblings with mental retardation, found a lack of balanced reciprocity in the relationship, with sisters without mental retardation giving more instrumentally and affectively than their siblings with mental retardation. She also found that siblings who did not live together had less conflictual relationships.

Postschool Transition and Sibling Relationships Siblings have been referred to as the "next generation of family caregivers" (Krauss, Seltzer, Gordon, & Friedman, 1996), but they may not be prepared or willing to assume such roles. Griffiths and Unger (1994) surveyed parents and siblings of adults with mental retardation to better understand family perceptions regarding future caregiving.

Chambers, Hughes, and Carter (2004) gathered parent and sibling perspectives on the transition to adulthood for family members with significant cognitive disabilities. Parents and siblings perceived that they lacked knowledge about postschool options. Not surprisingly, parents assumed a more active role in learning about postschool options than did siblings. Parents and siblings both felt that the family member with disabilities would continue to live in the parents' home. Both groups indicated that they rarely discussed postschool options with each other or with their family members with cognitive disabilities. Chambers and colleagues urged professionals to be sure to involve the sibling in the transition process.

Ramifications for the Future Krauss, Seltzer, Gordon, and Friedman (1996) pointed out the importance of understanding the sibling perspective because the siblings without disabilites are the potential future caregivers of the siblings with disabilities. These researchers looked at the roles of adult siblings of individuals with mental retardation. In this study, the people with mental retardation were still living in their parents' homes, and the parents were aging. Results indicated that the siblings without mental retardation maintained regular and personal contact with, provided emotional support to, and felt knowledgeable about the needs of their brother or sister with mental retardation. Of the siblings without disabilities studied, 64% intended to live apart, whereas 36% thought they would co-reside with the brother or sister with mental retardation. Sisters without mental retardation were most inclined to co-reside with their sisters with mental retardation. The severity of mental retardation appeared to affect the nature of future living arrangements, because those with less severe mental retardation had siblings who predicted a greater chance of co-residence. According to this study, too, the greater the current number of shared activities, the more likely the sibling was to say he or she would co-reside with the adult with disabilities. It is important to point out that even those who said they planned to live apart maintained an impressive amount of contact with their brother or sister with mental retardation; at least half saw each other on a weekly basis.

Many adults with disabilities continue to live in their parents' home, and there is not much research about what happens when adults move away from home. Seltzer, Krauss, Hong, and Orsmond (2001) looked at family involvement of adults with mental retardation following a transition in residence to a living situation without parents. They also wanted to look at patterns of sibling involvement after the adult with mental retardation moved from the family home. A control group of siblings had a brother or sister with disabilities who remained in the parental home. The siblings in the control group reported greater levels of emotional involvement than those whose siblings moved from the family home. For both groups, adult siblings reported improved sibling relationships over time. Those whose brothers or sisters moved out of the parental home increased their shared activities over time and felt less pessimistic about the future care of siblings over time. Seltzer and colleagues stressed that these confirm the importance of siblings to the quality of life of adults with mental retardation and urge service providers to include siblings in plans for moves.

Rimmerman and Raif (2001) looked at the involvement with and role perception toward adult siblings with mental retardation in Israel. They compared siblings of those with mental retardation with those without mental retardation on frequency of contact, role perception, and engagement activities. Generally, siblings of people with mental retardation had more frequent contact with their siblings, especially when their parents were no longer living. However, siblings of people who were typically developing reported that they received more instrumental and affective assistance and affective giving from their siblings.

Seltzer, Greenberg, Krauss, Gordon, and Judge (1997) focused on the effects of lifestyle and psychological well-being of siblings of adults with mental retardation or mental illness. They contrasted siblings of adults with mental retardation to siblings of adults with serious mental illness with respect to pervasiveness of the impact the brother or sister had on a sibling's life; the closeness of their current relationship and the frequency of contact; and the factors related to sibling's level of psychological well-being. The siblings of adults with mental retardation were significantly more likely than siblings of those with mental illness to perceive that their brother or sister had had a pervasive influence on their life decisions and to evaluate their sibling experience as mostly positive. These siblings of adults with mental retardation also reported a closer relationship with their brother or sister with a disability than did siblings of those with serious mental illness. The siblings of adults with mental retardation had better psychological well-being when they had a closer relationship with their brother or sister, whereas the siblings of adults with a serious mental illness reported more favorable psychological well-being when they perceived that their brother or sister had a less pervasive impact on their lives. These siblings reported the experience of having a sibling with mental illness as mostly negative. The authors speculate that because mental retardation is usually diagnosed much earlier in life, has a more stable course than does mental illness, and may be viewed by some as more socially acceptable, perhaps it is easier for siblings of individuals with mental retardation than it is for siblings of individuals with mental illness to cope with the myriad issues that occur in adulthood.

Although this section of this chapter has centered on research on adult interactions of siblings with and without disabilities since the mid 1990s, many other issues related to disabilitiess in adulthood concern families. These topics are discussed further in Chapter 10 on adults.

SUPPORT FOR FAMILIES

Undoubtedly, recent efforts to provide community support to families who have a member with a disability will have a substantial impact on lessening the stress faced by parents and siblings. Community services may help to minimize and, in some cases, alleviate problems experienced by siblings, but only when they are comprehensive in nature and flexible enough to meet the varying and ever-changing needs of families and their individual members.

The development and implementation of a full continuum of community-based services has been the goal of many parents, siblings, and professionals working together to improve the quality of life for people with disabilities and their families. This full continuum may include the following family-oriented services:

- Respite care
- Home health service
- Transportation programs
- Sibling counseling and training
- Parent counseling and training
- Recreational programs
- Community living programs (e.g., supported living)
- Financial assistance

- Social work
- Advocacy services

Later chapters in this book more closely examine the issue of support services for families.

SUMMARY AND FUTURE DIRECTIONS

The review of the literature in this chapter should clarify the complexity and importance of families and the significance of sibling relationships to the family system and to individual family members. Early studies of siblings without disabilities focused on demographic characteristics, such as birth order, in relation to personality characteristics. The focus of recent investigations has shifted, however, to observational studies of the interactions between siblings. A similar trend in the literature involving siblings of children with disabilities has evolved.

The literature involving siblings of children with disabilities looked first at sibling-status variables that contribute to the psychosocial adjustment of siblings without a disability. Siblings without disabilities were affected by the presence of a child with a disability in both positive and negative ways. It seems that there is a continuum of positive and negative outcomes for siblings, and that their position on this continuum is related to a number of variables that have been discussed in detail. A sibling's status on such a continuum can change over time. Such research does, of course, have its limitations. Hannah and Midlarsky (1985) noted that many of the early studies reporting negative effects not only failed to use comparison groups but also used various methods of observation from sources other than the siblings themselves. As mentioned earlier, these variables are often hard to control or change.

It seems that variables such as context, roles, and parental differential treatment are important considerations in looking at the interactional processes of siblings. As they grow older, siblings assume increasingly dominant positions when their sibling has a disability, whereas in families with two children without disabilities, sibling relationships become more egalitarian with age (Cicirelli, 1982). As Dunn (1983) noted, relationships are characterized by less reciprocity when a sibling with a disability is present.

Children know by an early age that their parents treat them differently from their brothers and sisters. In families having a child with a disability, differential treatment is sometimes exaggerated. Whatever their feelings as a result of being treated differently, it seems that for the most part, siblings do not vent their frustrations on their brothers or sisters with disabilities. If anything, siblings are kinder to their brothers and sisters than they are to other siblings, often taking a teacher or helper role. Their relationship seems to become even less "equal" as the children grow older. What this relationship means for the child with a disability remains to be seen. Would it be more helpful for that child to learn the "give-and-take" of the real world from their siblings? And what does it eventually mean for the sibling without a disability? As Bell (1968) reminds us, interaction is a two-way process.

Future research must continue to explore the domain of differential treatment. We need to assess children's perceptions of differential treatment and how this perception varies with certain children (McHale & Harris, 1992). We need to know at what ages children understand why they are treated differently, and how having a disability mitigates the perception of differential treatment (McHale & Pawletko, 1992).

Future research must also consider the development of sibling relationships and interactions throughout their lifetimes and in natural environments. Many studies of adults with brothers or sisters with disabilities have been conducted since the 1990s, and it is hoped that this trend will continue as more siblings age and researchers are able to measure the effects of sibling relationships in the older years. We also need to know more about the role of the father and extended family members because most of the research in sibling relationships that has used parent ratings or looked at parent qualities has involved only the mother's perspective. Research also is needed that includes the perspectives of people with disabilities regarding sibling relationships and interactions.

Research has shown that specific disabilities (or at least the concomitant behaviors and skills found within a certain disability) may lead to different reactions among siblings. It is encumbent upon the field to continue to conduct disability-specific research with siblings to find the common issues as well as any disability-specific ones.

McHale and Harris (1992) also suggest longitudinal designs to measure the potential positive benefits of growing up with a child who has a disability because these positive aspects might not be exhibited until adolescence or even adulthood. New measurement instruments would also be helpful in furthering sibling research, as would different designs and methodologies, including ethnographic, case study, and qualitative perspectives. Cuskelly (1999) discussed methodological issues in researching the adjustment of siblings of children with a disability because the literature on the psychological adjustment of siblings leads to contradiction and confusion. Methodological differences such as the ages of children being studied as well as differences in the sensitivity of measurement instruments leads to varying results, for example.

In addition, an important variable may be the issue of the amount of time that has transpired since a child's diagnosis as well as the fact that siblings may have very different experiences from each other, even in the same family. It is important to remember, too, that dynamic variables exist such as parental response, temperament, parental relationship, services provided, or differential treatment that are probably more relevant mediators and moderators of sibling adjustment than are static factors such as gender or age.

Certain broader family issues should also be examined. Stoneman and colleagues (1988) suggested that research needs to be conducted on the special demands placed on the sibling without a disability when two or more children in the same family have a disability. Likewise, single mothers of children with disabilities experience more general stress and financial difficulties than do married mothers (Bristol, Reichle, & Thomas, 1987). Siblings in these families should be observed and finding on them reported. It is also important that researchers look at the relationships and interactions of all of the siblings within a family and not just the dynamics with one child. Critical, too, is the need to explore sibling issues in families beyond those of European-American descent.

When a brother or sister has a disability, will the effects on siblings be negative or positive? The complexity of this question prohibits answering quickly or easily. Research that draws a single conclusion presents too simplistic a solution for the resolution of such a compound issue. On the basis of what we now know, perhaps the best answer is still, "It depends." A number of contributing factors enter into the equation, including parental attitudes and expectations, parental differential treatment, family size, family resources, religion, severity of the child's disability, and the pattern of interactions between the siblings. With new family-oriented services, professionals' understanding of the unique need of families, especially of siblings, is increasing. It is hoped that programs will help to ensure that the experience of having a brother or sister with a disability will be positive for all family members.

Concerns and Needs of Siblings Living with Brothers and Sisters with Disabilities

"I was a very sensitive child, and I felt a great deal of responsibility. . . . I definitely felt like a caretaker for my brother and responsibility for him in ways that are difficult to explain. Looking back, I think I tried to be the perfect child in many ways to make up for what my brother could not do. My parents and I are very close, and I was also very mature for my age. I was very involved and 'in the know' about my brother. . . . My parents were very active in my upbringing and aware of everything going on in my life, but at different points of my childhood I can remember emotions regarding my brother ranging from embarrassment, sadness, anger, and rage that it has happened to him. I didn't want to make my parents upset so I didn't talk about it much."

—A. Barnett, personal communication, June 1, 2005

Many siblings find it difficult to talk about a brother or sister with a disability. They keep their concerns to themselves, never daring to share an integral part of their lives with others. McHugh explained,

> *"The reluctance to talk about negative feelings is only natural, as most of us are taught as children that we must love and help those less fortunate than ourselves. When siblings in typical families get mad at each other, they say, 'I hate you,' 'I wish you'd go away and never come back,' or 'Mom and Dad aren't your real parents—you're adopted.' But you can't say things like that to someone who may die by the age of 20 or whose disability is not her fault."*
>
> —2003, p. 130

When siblings are able to find a "kindred spirit" in friends or colleagues with whom they have shared interests and experiences on many levels, however, their friendship and mutual experiences provide a source of support for the special joys and challenges common to siblings of individuals with disabilities.

All siblings who have sisters and brothers with disabilities express a number of special concerns they have about themselves, their families, their communities, and the future. Their emotions are mixed (some positive, some negative), and their questions, although sometimes unvoiced, are many. They often have problems talking with their parents, grandparents or other relatives, and/or friends about their brothers or sisters. Some siblings have extraordinary responsibilities for the child with a disability. These responsibilities produce a number of specific worries and needs. Like Anna, some siblings do not know how or with whom to share their feelings, problems, and needs. Other siblings need basic information about their brothers or sisters, or training to learn how to better communicate or interact with their brothers or sisters or even to work on how to be a good advocate for their adult brother or sister with special needs.

This chapter focuses on the special concerns and unique needs of siblings. It provides a foundation for succeeding chapters, which will detail methods to meet the special needs of siblings who have brothers and sisters with disabilities.

SIBLINGS' SPECIAL CONCERNS

Siblings who have brothers and sisters with disabilities are, first and foremost, people. They share the same concerns and problems most other siblings experience as children and adults; however, it is important for professionals to recognize siblings' special concerns and needs and to acknowledge that such needs will vary according to certain factors such as the age of the sibling. Kutner (n.d.) agreed that as siblings age, their need for information about their siblings continues to increase. Younger siblings need support primarily from the family unit. As siblings grow older, their need for respite services, counseling, and school services becomes more important, and as siblings grow into adulthood, different needs emerge.

The studies reviewed in Chapter 3 and our own extensive interviews with siblings demonstrate that siblings tend to share a number of special concerns. These concerns are independent of family size, the sex of the sibling, or the birth order of the sibling. Siblings typically discuss concerns about:

1. The child with a disability
2. Their parents
3. Themselves
4. Their friends
5. The community (the school in particular)
6. Adulthood

The Child with a Disability

Naturally, siblings have a number of special concerns about their brother or sister with a disability and his or her particular condition. Their concerns focus on the cause of the disability, the child's feelings and thoughts, prognosis for a cure or improvement, the services the child with a disability needs, how they can help their brother or sister, where the person with disabilities resides or will reside, and what the future holds. These major areas of concern give rise to questions like those in the following list, which siblings may ask openly or sometimes hesitate to ask. It is important to help siblings address these concerns.

Concern	Question
Cause of the disability	Why does my sister have a disability?
	Did I cause the disability?
	What caused the disability?
	Will future brothers and sisters also have disabilities?
	Whose fault is it?
The child's feelings	Is my brother in pain?
	Does he have the same feelings I do?
	What does he think about?
	Does he know me?
	Does he love me and my parents?
	Why does he behave so strangely?
Prognosis	Can my sister be cured?
	Will she improve?
	Can she grow out of this?
	Can treatment really help?
Needed services	What special help will he need?
	Who are these professionals who work with him?
	What do they do with him?
How to help	What am I supposed to do with my sister?
	What can I expect from her?
	Can I help teach her?
	How can I interact with her?
	Should I protect her?
Where the child lives	Why does my brother still live at home?

	Wouldn't a group home be better for him?
	Why do people come to our house to work with my sister?
The future	What will happen to my sister in the future?
	Will she always be with us?
	Will she go to school?
	Will she have a job?
	Will she get married and have a family?
	Will she ever live on her own?

Their Parents and Other Relatives

When siblings talk about their family, whether informally, formally, privately, or in groups, much of the discussion centers on their parents. Siblings tend to have concerns about parental expectations, communicating with parents, their parents' feelings, their parents' time, helping their parents, and their participation in child-rearing. They also have questions about talking with other relatives such as grandparents, aunts and uncles, or cousins.

Concern	**Question**
Parental expectations	What do my parents expect of me?
	Why are my parents so hard on me?
	Why do they expect so much of me?
	Why do they overprotect me?
	Are my parents using me to compensate for my sibling's shortcomings?
	Why do they let my brother "get away"' with so much?
	Will they treat me normally?

Communicating with parents and relatives	How can I discuss my feelings about my sister with my parents?
	How should I handle disagreements with my cousins and my sister?
	How can we openly talk about my sister, her problems, and what we are going to do about them?
Their parents' and other relatives' feelings	How do my parents or grandparents feel about my brother?
	Are they afraid, sad, happy, lonely, confused or excited like I am?
	Do they love me as much as my brother?
	Why do they fight so much about my brother?
	Do my parents know why this has happened to our family?
	Why doesn't my aunt bring her baby to our house?
Their parents' time	Why must all of their time be given to my sister?
	Why won't they spend more time with me?
	Why must we always do something that involves my sister?
	Why can't I have some private time with them?
Helping their parents	What can I do to help Mom and Dad?
Participation in child-rearing	Should I express my views on raising my brother?

	Why do they always ask me to babysit?
	Why am I always responsible?
	Do they want me to control his behavior?

Themselves

Privately (usually when discussing a related topic), some siblings begin to share special concerns they have about themselves. They are concerned with their feelings, their health, and their relationship to the sibling.

Concern	**Question**
Their feelings	Why do I have such mixed feelings about my sister?
	Why doesn't anyone else I know have to deal with this in their family?
	Do I really love her or really hate her?
	Why does she make me so happy and also so angry?
	Am I jealous of the attention she receives?
	Why do I feel guilty because reading is so easy for me and so hard for him?
	How can I deal with my mixed feelings?
Their health	Will I "catch" the disability?
	Is there something wrong with me?
Their relationship to the sibling	How can I get along better with my brother?
	Will we have a normal brother–sister relationship?

	Why am I smarter and stronger than my older brother?
	How can I be a better, more loving sister?

Their Friends

Almost all siblings discuss their relationships with their friends and the special problems encountered as a result of the disability. Siblings are concerned with informing their friends about the child with a disability, whether their friends will tease and/or accept the child, and how dating will be affected.

Concern	Question
Informing their friends	How can I tell my best friend about my brother?
	Should I invite the friend over to meet my brother?
	Will my friends understand?
	Will they think I have a disability too?
	Will they tell everyone at school?
Teasing	What should I do when my friends tease my sister?
	Why are they so mean to her?
	Why do they tease me about my sister?
	What should I say to them?
	What should I do when other kids are making fun of people with disabilities?
Their friends' acceptance	Should I invite my brother to play with us?
	Can my friends accept my brother?

Concern	Question
	Will they like him?
	Will they be afraid of him?
Dating	What will my boyfriend think of my sister?
	Will my sister frighten my girlfriend away?
	Will my boyfriend think there is something wrong with me?
	What if my sister makes a scene when my girlfriend comes over?
	How much should I tell my boyfriend about my sister?

The Community

Naturally, siblings are preoccupied about concerns involving the child and the community. In particular, siblings have special concerns regarding school, community acceptance, and community living.

Concern	**Question**
School	Will my brother be able to keep up with "regular" classes and assignments?
	What happens in special education classes?
	What does my sister learn?
	Do my teachers treat me differently in school?
	Will kids at school treat my sister okay?
	What should I do when kids say "retard"?
	Will I be compared with my sister?

	Will I be responsible for my sister's problems and her behavior?
	Why do teachers always call me when there is a problem?
	Do I have to associate with my brother at the after-school program?
Community acceptance	Will my brother be accepted in public?
	Why do people stare at us?
	What should I tell strangers?
	What should I do when I feel embarrassed by how my sister talks?
	What if my brother has a seizure on the playground or in the store?
	Will people take advantage of him?
	Will he be exploited or cheated by others?
	Will anyone outside of the family be my brother's friend?
Community living	What is a group home?
	Will my brother have a girlfriend there?
	Will my sister ever have sex?
	Will the neighbors accept my sister?
	Will my brother get and hold a job?

Adulthood

As siblings get older, their special concerns focus on the unique problems associated with adulthood. These concerns typically involve guardianship, their own family, and the nature of their continuing involvement.

Concern	Question
Guardianship	Will I be responsible for my brother when my parents die?
	What will be expected of me?
	Will I be financially responsible for my brother?
	Will my brother have to live with me?
	Who will be my sister's guardian if I am unable or unwilling?
Their own family	Will my spouse accept my sister?
	Does the presence of a disability affect my chances for having healthy children?
	Do I need genetic counseling?
	How do I provide a proper balance in my responsibilities to my sibling and to my spouse and children?
	How will my children be affected by their aunt who has a disability?
	Can I be fair to both my family and my sibling?
	What will happen if my sister comes to live with us?
Continuing involvement	How should I continue to be involved with my brother?

Should I visit his group home?

Should I advocate on his behalf?

Should I join a parents' and/or siblings' group?

Am I selfish if I don't want to see my brother every weekend and holiday?

SIBLINGS' UNIQUE NEEDS

The special concerns expressed by most siblings provide a way of gauging the nature and intensity of a sibling's individual needs, special problems, and worries. Of course, each sibling's needs vary; not every sibling encounters the same challenges and joys or to the same degree, and family responses (as discussed in Chapter 3) will differ. Some siblings have few, if any, special needs; others have many needs that will change over time. These needs demand respect and understanding. Information, counseling, and training must be available for siblings as well as their parents.

Respect

Like all people, siblings who have brothers and sisters with disabilities have a need to be recognized and respected as individuals. They should be recognized for their own accomplishments, characteristics, feelings, and joys. Siblings have a need to not be compared with the other child. They need to stand on their own and to develop an identity outside of their family and especially outside of their brothers and sisters. Siblings have a major need to be respected as individuals by their parents. They need to neither be pushed too hard in an attempt to overcompensate for lost parental hopes nor overprotected because the parent applies blanket restrictions to all of the children. These needs are not unlike the needs experienced by all siblings; however, they may be intensified by the presence of a child with a disability and the family structure that has developed to accommodate that child.

Understanding

Siblings who have sisters and brothers with disabilities need understanding. Unlike other siblings, their lives may be altered by the added pressures and problems associated with living with a child with a dis-

ability. They need to know that their special concerns are recognized and respected as legitimate. They need affirmation that others (especially adults) understand their problems and are willing to help.

Information

Siblings have a unique need for honest, direct, and comprehensible information in order to answer questions about their brothers or sisters, their entire family, themselves, school, special services, guardianship, treatment, and so forth. Siblings need different information at various stages of their lives. They need a system to gather such information in an easy-to-access manner; a system that is responsive to their personal questions rather than to predetermined, generic questions. Siblings need an information system that is longitudinal rather than episodic in nature, one that adapts to their changing needs and is readily available throughout their lives. Chapter 5 explores this more in-depth.

Support and Counseling

Some siblings need to share their feelings with trained counselors to enable them to understand and accept their feelings. Others need a mechanism to help them deal effectively with their behavior and to change their behavior. Some siblings need formal and individualized counseling, whereas others require a more informal approach with a social service professional. Some siblings need to be involved with other siblings so that they can share their feelings and learn from one another.

Training

Training represents yet another broad category of needs. Many siblings have a strong desire to help their parents with the child who has a disability. In order to serve as an effective helper, the sibling often needs special training. Some siblings seek education to learn how to teach specific skills to their sister or brother; others want to learn how to manage the child's behavior; still others want to learn how to plan and interact with the child. As siblings age, their need for information and training changes as they gather information on housing, guardianship, self-determination, and so forth.

An analysis of these special needs implies the development and implementation of a diversified service system that offers training, guidance, and support to siblings with brothers and sisters who have disabilities. Siblings may need different services at various stages in their lives. Not all siblings will require outside services, but those who do should have access to services that will meet their varying needs across their life spans.

SUMMARY

As this chapter has illustrated briefly, siblings who have brothers and sisters with disabilities experience a number of special concerns and, consequently, have special needs. Although it is impossible to generalize one set of concerns to all siblings, many siblings worry about the child with a disability, their parents, themselves, their friends, the community, and adulthood. These concerns lead to a set of specific needs in regard to respect, understanding, information, counseling, and training. Although the concerns and needs presented in this chapter are not an exhaustive list of all possible worries and requirements, they reflect the scope and range of the concerns and needs experienced by most siblings who have brothers and sisters with disabilities.

The following chapters specifically address ways in which the needs of siblings can be met. These chapters suggest ways to provide information to siblings, counsel and support siblings, facilitate social interaction between the child with a disability and the sibling, train the sibling to teach the child, develop positive community programs, and help adult siblings deal with their concerns.

Providing Information to Children with Siblings with Disabilities

"We siblings have a hunger for information about our brother or sister's disability. . . . When parents don't give a child a chance to ask questions, don't set the tone that no subject is taboo, it affects the way he reacts to his brother or sister with a disability for the rest of his life . . . Open, frank communication gives the sibling the feeling of participation in addressing the disability, a healthy interest in ways in which the family can work together to lighten the load of everyday household chores and medical treatments."

—McHugh, 2003, pp. 15, 18.

When Jim Angelo's brother Johnny was born 30 years ago with Down syndrome, his parents were clear about how the rest of their children would adjust to his special needs. Jim, 39, recalls,

> *"They sat all six of us down and said, 'God gave us Johnny, and we're going to pitch in.' Johnny was included in everything we did. Johnny helped make me who I am today. He's touched the lives of my brothers and sisters and made us better people."*
>
> —Calabro, 2003

Although Jim's acceptance of his brother's disability is a result of many factors and may not be universal, his account illustrates how parents set the tone early on by including siblings and giving them information about their sibling's disability. Compare this story to Kathy's relationship with her brother.

• • • Kathy was in her senior year of college when she met Chad. She hadn't dated much over the past 4 years; it took most of her time and energy to maintain an A average while working part time. Now she felt like she had finally met someone special and soon she and Chad were spending lots of time together. Everything was going so well that over the next few months Kathy and Chad started talking about marriage. Chad brought Kathy to meet his parents twice before she agreed to bring him to meet hers. She kept putting off the inevitable. As much as she thought she was over the past, she found herself worrying about what Chad would think about her brother Buddy. Buddy was 4 years younger than Kathy and attended special education classes in high school. Buddy had very serious seizures that required careful monitoring, medications, close supervision, and almost all of her mother's attention. Kathy couldn't remember a time when she spent more than a few stolen minutes alone with her mom. Kathy really didn't have much to do with Buddy's care as she was growing up. When she was younger and she'd offer to help, her mom usually said, "Don't worry about it. You go play with your friends."

She hadn't told Chad much about Buddy. On the drive to her house, she decided to tell Chad a little more to prepare him. As she spoke, she couldn't help smiling as she heard herself say exactly the same story her mother helped her craft years ago when she had trouble explaining Buddy to friends who came over for play dates.

"Buddy had seizures that damaged his brain. He understands things, but he understands them *his* way. He loves music, basketball, and is awesome at puzzles. When he meets people, Buddy is very friendly but he doesn't always act the way you or I would."

Chad didn't say much, but Kathy could tell he was listening carefully. He nodded his head as she talked about Buddy's likes and asked her to explain how Buddy might act.

Kathy explained, "He gets very excited and sometimes comes on too strong. He might get too close or try to hug and kiss you, especially if he's happy to see you. If you feel uncomfortable, Chad, tell him. Say something like, 'Hey, Buddy. I'm glad to see you, too; can you give me a high five?'"

"Like this?" Chad said, grinning and raising his hand high in the air. "Sounds good to me," he added. Chad's good humor and acceptance made Kathy feel closer to him.

The visit went better than expected. Buddy didn't overwhelm Chad and Chad didn't freak out about a 17-year-old boy wearing a helmet and mismatched shirt and pants who was unable to say more than a few words at a time. On the ride home, Chad asked a lot of questions about Buddy. He was especially interested in exactly what "was wrong" with Buddy. Chad asked how it happened and if it was something that "ran in the family." As they talked, Kathy realized that she really didn't have all of the answers. Of course she knew her brother had seizures, but somehow his programs, therapists, medications—even his disability—had little to do with her as she was growing up and she just didn't know how to respond to Chad.

Now that she was thinking about her future, including getting married and having children, Kathy needed more information about Buddy's disability. She called her mother the next day. They talked about other things until Kathy finally worked up the courage to ask, "How come we never really talked about Buddy's condition?" Her mother's answer surprised her. "I didn't want to burden you. I wanted you to have a normal childhood. Besides, you never asked any questions, so I thought you weren't interested." "Well, I am now!" Kathy declared. With that opening, Kathy began what she jokingly referred to as Buddy 101, her personal disabilities awareness course. She spent time with Buddy, talked openly with her mother and father, searched the Internet, and even invited Chad to accompany her to a meeting for adult siblings. In the process she learned a lot about herself and her family. She gained a greater appreciation for her parents' dedication, their hopes and dreams for her and her brother, and a deeper understanding of how having a sibling with a disability had influenced who she was today. • • •

Kathy's story illustrates the need for information commonly experienced by siblings who have brothers and sisters with disabilities. As noted in Chapter 4, siblings are anxious about the cause of and prognosis for their brother or sister's disability, their sibling's feelings, what services will be needed, and how their relationship with this brother or sister will be affected. Unlike the straightforward approach Kathy was able to take as an adult, most requests for information from children are less direct and are woven into the daily fabric of family life. Parents may get questions such as "Mom, why can't Kenyon talk yet?" "What does cerebral palsy mean?" "Does it hurt to be blind?" "Why won't he play with me?" "Will I get sick, too?" Some children, however, have trouble even asking these questions or may not get the answers they need if they do ask.

THE NEED FOR INFORMATION

"Should I ask my father?" "What will he say?" "Will he be hurt if I talk about Don's disability?" "Does Mom know what Heather's problem is?" "Should I ask?" All siblings ask questions such as these in their

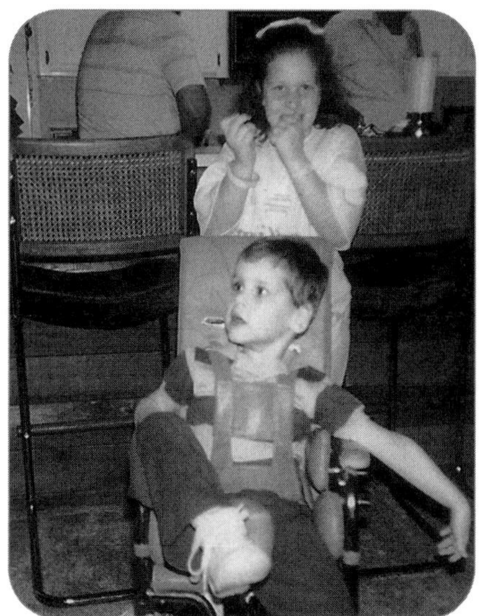

minds, and some ask them out loud. Some families live in silence. Silent questions seldom get answers. Without answers, many children fabricate their own stories and explanations for various disabilities. Often, their explanations and interpretations are far from the truth. Some families prefer silence to the possible risks of communication. Such families may never have experienced the value of candid discussion or felt the benefits of searching together for answers to shared questions.

Why do some siblings fail to ask questions about their siblings with disabilities? Burton (1975), in reviewing the lack of questioning on the part of children who have siblings with cystic fibrosis, postulated that children's silence might reflect their desire to protect their parents from the pain of the disability. He suggested that some children do not question because of fears that the parents may break down or may reject the questioning child.

Sometimes parents unintentionally set up barriers to communication because they may be at a loss as how to answer siblings' questions.

> *"Finding out such an important detail of my life when I was only four years old was hard. I was confused, surprised, and didn't know what to do. What made it even harder was seeing my parents not knowing what to do."*
>
> —Adolphson et al., 2003

One child, Tim stated at a sibling group,

> *"I asked my parents, 'Why is my brother acting weird?' but they wouldn't tell me. They said 'wait 'til you're older.'"*
>
> —Personal communication, January 6, 2005

In a preliminary survey on siblings of children in early intervention, when asked what they needed to ensure a healthy sibling relationship, parents expressed a desire to know how to explain the disability in understandable terms that would not frighten or cause siblings to think differently about their brother or sister (Gallagher & Rhodes, 2005).

In their research of siblings of children with autism, Harris and Glasberg (2003) reported that parents might be reluctant to talk with siblings because they want to protect them and keep them from confronting the reality of the sibling's disability. Many families with a chronically ill child do not communicate well about the disease (Fanos, 1996).

Others have also found that siblings are poorly informed about a brother or sister's disability (Chintz, 1981; Crnic & Leconte, 1986; McKeever, 1983). This lack of information is often the result of parents who either do not recognize the child's condition or who simply do not actively provide information to siblings, perhaps because they may not have been fully informed. Parental silence typically blocks the flow of information and leaves siblings' questions unvoiced and unanswered once again.

Lobato (1990) noted that for some siblings, especially very young siblings, their understanding of the disability represents a unique combination of what they have been told, what they have overheard and observed, and what they have conjured up on their own. In an older study of families with children who have cystic fibrosis, Burton (1975) found that 53% of parents did not discuss the disability with the siblings. Of the 47% who did, information that was shared was simplistic and, thus, the explanations were minimal. Several researchers suggested that information needs to be repeated frequently because some children do not retain much information about the specifics of disabilities (Burbach & Peterson, 1986; Potter & Roberts, 1984).

For most parents who have a child with a disability, in general, sharing information about the disability can be problematic (Seligman, 1983). Parents experience a range of mixed feelings about their children with disabilities (Featherstone, 1980). The topic of disability may be confusing and is usually painful. Sharing information with their other children can be a source of stress for parents. It is important to help parents to move beyond their personal feelings of confusion and sorrow and on to a more realistic understanding of the disability and a readiness to begin working as a family to adjust to their special circumstances.

Siblings' needs for information are much like those of their parents. Just as parents feel a need to gather a variety of information to help them adjust, so, too, will their children. Wilson and colleagues (1989) found that of siblings they surveyed, 87% expressed interest in participating in a sibling group to learn more information and coping strategies. Itzkowitz (1989) also found that a significant majority of siblings expressed a desire to receive information in a structured format. A lack of information or misinformation about a disability can lead to unwarranted worries or fears. For both parents and siblings, the need for information changes as the child with a disability grows older. Confronting the different periods of transition in a child's life, as discussed in Chapter 2, will call for new kinds of information.

Featherstone (1980) noted, however, that although siblings have needs that parallel those of their parents, these needs are not exactly the same because, obviously, siblings are not parents. Siblings interact with and react to their brothers and sisters in ways different from those of their parents. Their sense of identity is usually more closely tied to siblings. Siblings, unlike parents, have limited life experiences to help put a disability into perspective and may never know life without the brother or sister who has a disability. The sibling relationship, unlike the parental relationship, is usually lifelong.

As discussed in Chapter 4, siblings typically need and want specific information about the following:

- The child with a disability (in particular, aspects of the disability, prognosis, and implications)
- Their parents
- The services the sibling will require
- The future

In addition, siblings need information about themselves. They need to know about their role, their responsibilities, their feelings, and how relationships with their friends may be affected. Like their parents, siblings' information needs change over time. As a result, instead of episodic information, they need to receive information throughout their lives. They need information that changes as they change. Young children have informational needs that are vastly different from those of adolescents. Recognizing their changing needs will help parents and professionals provide varying and more sophisticated information resources as the siblings grow up. As they mature, their ongoing need for more information on different topics and for more detail underscores the fact that the delivery of answers to questions must be viewed as a longitudinal, or lifelong, need.

Parents and professionals need to anticipate hearing sibling questions and concerns expressed in different ways over time and should be prepared to give answers that are developmentally appropriate. Kutner (2005) advised that children need increasing amounts of information about their siblings with disabilities as well as other family issues. This information has to be presented in ways that match children's developmental needs and abilities.

TALKING WITH SIBLINGS—THE KEYS TO EFFECTIVE COMMUNICATION

Providing clear, concise information to siblings is the key to effective communication between the sibling and parent or sibling and professional. Effective communication can be enhanced by attending to the following 12 points.

1. *Actively listen to siblings.* The first step in providing information is to listen actively to the sibling. The importance of active listening cannot be overstated. Siblings often report unequal balance in parental attention. When parents make time in a demanding schedule to listen, they communicate care, concern, and respect for the needs of their typical child. Active listening implies that the listener put other projects and tasks aside while the sibling talks. An active listener questions the sibling to make sure he or she understands the message. An active listener also repeats or paraphrases the communication to let the sibling know he or she has correctly heard what was said or asked.

2. *Take your time.* Siblings find it difficult to learn everything in one sitting or with one explanation. Parents and professionals should be patient with questions as well as answers. It may be difficult for siblings to ask questions, especially those they view as embarrassing or painful. A sibling should have plenty of time to talk, ask questions, and interpret information. Likewise, parents and professionals should not feel that they need to share all of their information at one time. Gradual assimilation will most likely help to ensure that the sibling retains the information.

3. *Serve as a model.* Parents and professionals should act as models by openly asking questions and seeking information themselves. Parents and professionals should demonstrate that asking questions and seeking information is a healthy and a valued behavior. In addition, parents and professionals can model effective communication by honestly expressing their feelings and thoughts. Parents and professionals can also serve as models in terms of their acceptance of and interactions with the child who has a disability. Models continually communicate information more strongly through their actions than they do their words. Encourage and respond to children's questions in an honest, open manner.

4. *Be knowledgeable.* Parents should become informed about the disability themselves and seek information from those who have a substantial knowledge base. Parents and professionals should always strive to increase what they know about specific disabilities, not only for their own benefit but also so that they can serve as a source of information for siblings and for the child with a disability. As parents increase their knowledge about a specific disability, they soon acquire a new vocabulary of terms, descriptions, programs, and interventions. When talking with siblings, use correct terminology to describe conditions but do not overwhelm siblings with overly technical explanations.

5. *Be sincere and honest.* Even when parents have developed a thorough knowledge base, it is likely that siblings will pose questions that cannot be easily answered. Answers should always be accurate. Simplistic answers to complex questions or untruthful responses will only hamper future communication. If the answer to a particular question is unknown or complex, the parent or professional should say so. "I don't know" is an acceptable answer and far better than incomplete, vague, or inaccurate information. If an answer is not known, it may be beneficial for both the sibling and parent or professional to undertake some joint research to seek the answer. A trip together to the library or a dual Internet search will clearly communicate an interest in the siblings' questioning. If appropriate, invite the sibling to attend his or her sibling's IEP meeting, medical appointments, or offer to ask the sibling's questions for him or her.

6. *Provide understandable answers.* Providing too much information to a youngster or inadequate or overly simplistic information to adolescents or adults will hinder effective communication. Consideration must be given to the age of the sibling and the specific question being asked. (Does the sibling want a quick yes or no, or does he or she want detail?) A wise approach may be to provide some information and then to ask, "Do you understand? Can I tell you more?" Remember, too, to use age-appropriate language and examples when answering questions. When a 4-year-old asks, "What does mental retardation mean?" a simple response might provide the needed information and set the stage for additional understanding. "'It means Jarred learns more slowly. Like learning to count to 10; it took him longer to learn than it did for you, but he can do it now." When a 10-year-old asks the same question, a more detailed response is usually needed. "When someone says a person has mental retardation, it means he has a disability that affects his

brain. Your brother Jarred has mental retardation because part of his brain works differently. People who have mental retardation take a longer time to learn things. Remember how quickly you learned all of the names of the birds for your science project? It's going to take Jarred much longer to learn all of those names. He still likes birds the way you do; he just will have trouble remembering their names. Does that make sense?"

7. *Have an open attitude.* Parents and professionals should expect questions of all sorts from siblings. They should have an open attitude in terms of accepting questions on all topics related to the disability. No question should be treated as insignificant or "dumb." Each question should be answered with care and understanding. Listen carefully for the "question behind the question." Ask, "Is there anything else you want to know?" or "Does that make sense?" If siblings trust that their questions will be accepted, they are more likely to express concerns, especially when these questions reflect intense feelings such as "Why does he have different rules?" or "When will he get better?"

8. *Provide balanced information.* Information can be presented in many ways. Concentration on the negative aspects will present a skewed picture of a disability and its related implications. A balanced approach, in which both the positive and negative aspects of a disability are openly discussed, is always preferred. Siblings need to have both sides, not information that is overly biased in one direction. This is especially important given research data that reveals how children with disabilities are responsible for many positive contributions to the family constellation (Summers, Behr, & Turnbull, 1989). Although it may be natural for a brother or sister to stress the negative aspects of having a sibling with a disability, parents and other adults have a responsibility to stress the positive contributions of the child with the disability. Such information will help siblings develop a balanced and, it is hoped, positive outlook regarding their relationship with their brother or sister.

9. *Capitalize on nonverbal communication.* Body language including facial expressions, body movements, sitting position, and standing location all communicate interest and respect to siblings. Parents and professionals should be aware of their nonverbal communication when talking with siblings. Siblings, like all other people, recognize those who respect their concerns and inquiries via the nonverbal communication expressed.

10. *Facilitate questions.* Some siblings will not ask questions aloud. Parents and professionals can facilitate questions by:

    a. Posing questions themselves ("I wonder what will happen when Alex leaves school?")

    b. Directing questions to siblings ("Have you ever thought about what it would be like to be blind?" or "Do you ever wonder why your brother goes to a different school than you do?")

    c. Initiating a discussion about specific sibling issues using natural events, television shows, videos and movies, and books and magazine articles that depict disabilities or family problems ("The girl in this book has a hearing aid like Manuel" or "Do you think we could try this with Shamika?")

    d. Introducing kids to Internet sites and listservs especially for (or by) siblings of children with disabilities. To start, parents may want to visit the sites with their child. Younger siblings may need help setting passwords, logging on, or learning the art of "conversation" on discussion boards where one person posts a question and others read and reply. Reading other siblings' questions can stimulate new thinking as well as give permission to ask tough questions. See Appendix B, Sibling Listservs and websites for more information.

    All of these situations can help facilitate discussions in which information may be shared. These opportunities help to provide a context for the information and may also motivate both parents and siblings to share information with each other.

11. *Anticipate questions.* At certain times in the life of a person with a disability, family members may have more need for information than at other times. For example, when a child with a disability first attends school, approaches puberty, or leaves home, family members' questions may be more intense or urgent. It is important to anticipate these times of uncertainty and provide special information (e.g., "John is going to work at the grocery store. Have you ever thought about John going to work when he gets older?" Or, "John has to start now to learn good work skills if he is going to be successfully employed later on. Do you want to talk about what John will do at his job?").

    In addition to major transitions, certain day-to-day situations may call for more information or discussion than usual. For example, when a child wants to bring friends home, this may raise concerns about what others will think of the sibling with a disability (e.g., "Your Brownie troop is meeting at our house next week. Are you comfortable introducing Elizabeth to the girls? Do you want to talk about what to say?").

12. *Follow up on earlier communication.* Parents and professionals should not expect that a sibling will understand the answers to complex questions after one explanation. To ensure that the sibling understands and to deal with related questions, it is wise to follow up on conversations (e.g., "Andre, I told you about the new way we're going to work with Tommy when he screams. Did you think of any other questions about how to ignore him or what will happen when he screams at school?") Follow-up provides an opportunity to clarify information and leads naturally to additional questions.

Talking to Siblings: Getting Started

All parents wonder how they will respond when they are asked for the first time, "Why can't my brother talk?" or "What's wrong with Katie?" Experienced parents advise parents to prepare for questions from siblings because such questions do typically get asked. Frequently, parents find the anticipation leading up to these questions to be the hardest part of starting what will become a lifelong conversation. Janice Fialka, clinical social worker and mother of a child with disabilities, described her thoughts the day her daughter asked "the tough question":

> *"At the age of 7 my daughter Emma asked me about her eleven year old brother's differences. As parents we had always focused on our son Micah's strengths and abilities which were similar in many ways to his peers. As both Micah and Emma grew, his differences and her ability to see the differences increased. 'Mom, Micah doesn't read. I read. It seems like I should be older than him.' I remember to breathe slowly—to take in the air and let it out lightly as if my lungs are tip-toeing to a lullaby. 'You're right. Micah can only read a few words. You are reading many words.' And then I take the plunge. I know I must begin but part of me wants to stay in the old way of pretending that maybe you don't have to know. 'Micah is in special education.' I feel dizzy. Can I really be saying this now? Wait, I'm not ready. I haven't practiced exactly what I will say. And yet words are coming out of my mouth . . . and they even sound coherent."*
>
> —Fialka, 1997, p. 23

Glasberg (2000) interviewed siblings of children with autism to learn how children think about autism at different ages. Results of the study indicated a lack of information or even misinformation about autism,

even when parents reported that they had shared information with siblings. Siblings reported that it was helpful to them when they had a clearer understanding of their sibling's challenging behavior. Results of this study further suggested that accurate information can increase the time siblings spend with their brother or sister with autism.

> *"One time my brother asked for help by sign language. I didn't know what it meant so I was confused, but then my mom showed me some signs and now I understand him."*
>
> —J. Graves, personal communication, January 6, 2006

Based on their research designed to assess how children think about autism at different ages, Harris and Glasberg (2003) offered some suggestions for initiating conversations with siblings that should be helpful to parents and professionals regardless of the specific disability:

- Hear the child out before making corrections.
- Stay neutral regardless of what the child says. Try not to judge what the child tells you.
- Praise the child for sharing feelings with you.
- Prepare for the child to share intense emotions, which may vary from sympathy to guilt to anger. Respect whatever feelings are there.

INNOVATIVE APPROACHES TO INFORMATION SHARING

In response to the increasing awareness of the needs of siblings for clear, concise information and to moderate some of the problems related to siblings' lack of information or misinformation, a number of professionals have initiated informational programs for siblings. As a result of these collective efforts, a number of aspects critical to the successful establishment of informational programs have come to light.

Programs and Workshops

In the mid 1960s, Kaplan and Colombatto (1966) conducted a study to provide information and activities to siblings who have brothers and sisters with mental retardation. In a pilot project during the summer, young siblings (ages 2½–5 years) participated in a series of enrichment activities and field trips. Because the siblings were too young to participate in discussion groups, the activities provided an informal context for the siblings to bring up problems and to share their thoughts and misconceptions. Teachers in this project were trained to listen for such statements and to provide understandable, age-appropriate information to the siblings. Discussing mental retardation with siblings and providing them with ample opportunity to ask questions about the disability in a comfortable atmosphere benefited the young siblings participating in the program.

Murphy, Pueschel, Duffy, and Brady (1976) pioneered informational workshops for siblings of children with Down syndrome who were being seen at the Developmental Evaluation Clinic of Children's Hospital Boston. During parental interviews, staff inquired about sibling relationships and encouraged parents to bring siblings to the clinic. When the siblings arrived, they observed clinic activities and met with professional staff members who answered their questions. To more fully meet the needs of siblings, a series of Saturday workshops was designed to provide more comprehensive information to siblings. In these Saturday workshops, siblings were divided into age groups and participated in a number of discussions, presentations, and demonstrations. These included meetings with a physician to discuss chromosomes and characteristics of Down syndrome, a physical therapist to discuss muscle tone and activities to help children with Down syndrome develop their motor skills, and a psychologist to discuss learning characteristics of children with Down syndrome. In addition, siblings observed teaching demonstrations and had the opportunity to look at chromosomes through a microscope. Within the context of these workshops, siblings met other siblings, saw other children with Down syndrome, and shared their feelings and problems with professionals. Murphy and her colleagues (1976) reported that siblings often discussed telling their friends about Down syndrome and problems related to the future. Within the context of the informational workshop, siblings had the opportunity to learn from one another as well as from professionals.

Feigon (1981) developed sibling information-sharing groups in a hospital in Chicago. These groups of siblings (ages 10–18) met for 12 weekly sessions. The groups were structured to provide both information and a support system to the siblings. Each group received information about the disability and discussed their family, their feelings, and their social needs and responsibilities. Specific information on working with the child was provided as requested by group members. Feigon suggested that programs of this type be voluntary and heterogeneous (not limited to a specific disability). Given the nature of the group, it is necessary to provide flexibility in terms of length of meetings, structure, and content.

Lobato (1981) conducted a systematic training program for young siblings (ages 4–7) of children with a wide range of disabilities (e.g., Down syndrome, cerebral palsy, epilepsy, heart defects). This program was designed to 1) teach the siblings factual information about developmental disabilities, 2) increase the siblings' recognition of the personal strengths and positive characteristics of their sibling with a disability and other family members, and 3) teach the siblings to constructively express their reactions to stressful family situations.

The training consisted of having the siblings attend small-group training sessions for 1½ hours for 6 weeks. During the training sessions, the leader presented information about developmental disabilities to the siblings, role-played, and discussed feelings and problems related to their family situations. Evaluation of these informational training sessions revealed that the siblings were able to accurately define developmental disabilities. Most of the siblings increased their positive self-reference statements and made positive verbalizations regarding their brother or sister with a disability and other family members. In addition, Lobato found that for some participants, social interactions at home were positively influenced.

Benson (1982) described a series of workshops for siblings (ages 8–15) of children with developmental disabilities. The workshops were developed to help siblings learn about disabilities and to facilitate sharing of experiences among siblings. Each workshop was implemented over a weekend. During the first day, siblings were engaged in sessions in which the basic nature and causes of developmental disabilities were explained. In addition, siblings took part in structured discussions that focused on the experiences of their families. During the second day of the workshop, the siblings were provided an opportunity to participate in recreational activities with each other, their parents, and their siblings with disabilities. Overall, this workshop structure had a positive effect on the siblings. They increased their knowledge about disabilities and developed more positive attitudes toward people with disabilities.

Byrnes and Love (1983) directed a series of workshops for siblings of children who are deafblind. These workshops focused on information sharing via age-appropriate recreational activities. The authors provided a detailed activity analysis for each of the workshop's four objectives. Strategies used to meet each objective are outlined here.

1. *Explain the educational program.* To address the first objective, the siblings toured the school, met with professionals to learn about special services, observed their brother or sister in the classroom, discussed specific educational programs, experimented with special equipment, and observed other children with different disabilities.

2. *Provide specific factual information.* To meet this objective, siblings participated in group discussions on the cause of the disability, discussed genetic aspects of specific disabilities, learned the meaning of unfamiliar technical terms, and discussed the roles of professionals.

3. *Provide an understanding of the problems associated with a condition underlying a disability.* The siblings met and talked with people with various disabilities, did activities that simulated the experience of having disabilities, used a variety of adaptive and prosthetic equipment, and role-played situational barriers to mobility.

4. *Provide information about community resources.* To accomplish this fourth objective, siblings discussed community-based support groups, toured community-based programs for adults with disabilities, and discussed community placements for their brothers and sisters.

Based on their work, Byrnes and Love (1983) believed that no *direct* counseling or therapeutic activities should be introduced in the workshop agenda. Through the planned activities, they found that siblings often spontaneously share their feelings and problems. Group leaders should respond to these natural expressions with the help of the other siblings who may have the same feelings or experience similar problems.

Willenz-Issacs (1983) designed an information project for siblings of children who are deaf and hard of hearing who were attending the Kendall Demonstration School at Gallaudet College in Washington, D.C. Because deafness impairs communication between family members, the workshop focused on communication. After an introductory activity, the siblings received a detailed tour of the school, listened to an auditory simulation of what a person who is hard of hearing might experience, and experimented with an audiology booth. During the workshop, the adult leaders presented a skit depicting play between children who were deaf and their siblings. The skit focused on problems related to play and asked the siblings to suggest various resolutions that were then acted out. Finally, the older siblings attended a discussion group while younger siblings participated in art activities.

An innovative program initiated at the University of Washington has provided a number of resources to assist siblings who have brothers and sisters with disabilities. This program, originally called Supporting Extended Family Members (SEFAM), was designed to provide ecological support to families with children and adults with disabilities. This information workshop consisted of two simultaneous sessions—one for siblings and one for parents (Meyer, Vadasy, & Fewell, 1985). The program later developed into Sibshops (Meyer & Vadasy, 1994).

Meyer and Vadasy have detailed the components of a Sibshop in their 1994 book, *Sibshops: Workshops for Siblings of Children with Special Needs* (Paul H. Brookes Publishing Co.) Their book provides comprehensive information on how to organize and run Sibshops, suggestions for introductions; discussions; recreational and food activities; sibling concerns and opportunities; the information needs of siblings, parents, and providers; and ideas for programs for adult siblings. The model originally designed for school-age children has been adapted for older and younger children and for brothers and sisters of children with other special needs, including special health concerns, deafness, emotional disturbance, and so forth. Sibshops sponsors include schools, hospitals, specific disability groups, and community mental health agencies. See Appendix B for information on the Sibling Support Project (Sibshops, listservs, publications, resources for professionals, and locations of Sibshop programs).

The goals of a Sibshop are to provide siblings with an opportunity to

- Meet other siblings in a relaxed, recreational setting
- Discuss common joys and concerns with other siblings of children with special needs
- Learn how other people handle situations commonly experienced by siblings of children with special needs
- Learn more about the implications of the sibling's special needs

- Provide parents and other professionals with opportunities to learn more about the concerns and opportunities frequently experienced by brothers and sisters of people with special needs

The session for siblings consists of small-group discussions run by professionals who encourage questions about and provide information on disabilities. Within the group, siblings are encouraged to talk about themselves, to share their interests, and to discuss aspects of living with a brother or sister who has a disability. In addition, group leaders model ways to play with siblings and discuss problems related to interacting with brothers and sisters.

While the siblings are engaged in the Sibshop program, parents have an opportunity to increase their understanding of the unique needs of siblings by interacting with a panel of older siblings (ages 15–32). Panel members talk about themselves, their parents, and their brother or sister with a disability. They discuss aspects of being a sibling that they found both rewarding and distressing. The parents have an opportunity to ask the panelists questions and to seek advice.

> *"The panel was great. They provide so much insight. We are the parents and we will never truly know what it is like to have a sibling with special needs. It is hard enough being an adult with a child with special needs, let alone going through it as a child with a sibling."*
>
> —T. McCarthy, personal communication, May 18, 2005

Sibshops can be offered in a variety of formats for siblings including periodic single events, multisession groups, and special recreational activities such as camp-outs. The workshops give siblings an opportunity to come together, share information, relax, laugh, and develop interpersonal relationships.

Darcy and colleagues (2005) evaluated the effectiveness of an interagency sponsored Sibshop program in Cork, Ireland. Qualitative and quantitative data were obtained using semi-structured interviews of siblings and parents and the Piers-Harris Children's Self-Concept Scale (Piers, 1986). A majority of the siblings interviewed reported that they enjoyed and benefited from the Sibshops. Parents reported benefits to their children as well. However, the data as measured by the Piers-Harris showed no significant increase in self-esteem.

Lobato (1985) reported on the development and evaluation of a training program to address the information and support needs of preschool-age siblings. A 6-week workshop was designed to help preschoolers to increase their understanding of developmental disabilities, recognize their strengths and those of other family members, and learn ways to express their feelings. The strategies of modeling, coaching, role-playing with puppets, and reading children's literature were used. Preschoolers became more accurate in their definitions of various disabilities, and most of the children increased their positive statements about themselves and their families including their brother or sister with special needs. In 1990, Lobato developed workshops designed to address the developmental characteristics of young children, including the young child's limited ability to generalize information and new skills, and to apply these skills in everyday situations. This attention to generalization should be an ingredient in any workshop for siblings.

Burton (1991) developed a unique workshop for siblings called KIDPOWER. It is designed for children between the ages of 8 and 12. The workshop focuses on the strengths that siblings possess and the positive impact that they can have on their friends and the general community. KIDPOWER was developed at the University of Idaho to focus on

- Creating a social support network
- Sharing experiences
- Developing behavior management skills
- Learning about disabilities
- Integrating children with disabilities into community programs

In the workshops, children are encouraged to draw pictures and write about their needs while learning about people with disabilities. KIDPOWER focuses on the positive contributions of brothers and sisters with disabilities and tries to instill a sense of optimism toward the experience of being part of a special family.

Phillips (1999) evaluated a community-based intervention with siblings of children with developmental disabilities who were from economically disadvantaged families. The intervention was for African American children who had siblings with a developmental disability. A control group received no intervention. The 15-week after-school program included group discussions about developmental disabilities, recreational activities, and homework assistance. The goal was to alleviate the siblings' stress by providing information about disabilities and by creating a context of social support. The group who participated in the afternoon intervention program showed significantly improved socioemotional adjustment compared with the other group. Specifically, the intervention group showed decreased ratings of depression and anxiety, improved self-esteem ratings, and significantly less sibling-related stress. It is important to note that the intervention alone showed substantial benefits to children even though no direct intervention with parents or family was provided.

Munch and Levick (2001) described an innovative Sibling Night program developed to address the psychosocial needs of siblings of newborns hospitalized in neonatal intensive care units (NICU). As parents and professionals understandably focus their attention and care on the infant in the NICU, the daily lives of siblings may be unintentionally overlooked. The NICU "Sibling Night" takes place every 6 to 8 weeks. Social workers serve as group facilitators and co-facilitators with nurses, social work interns, and trained volunteers. Parents, other caregivers, and children ages 3 to 16 are invited to attend. After an introductory session for parents and siblings together, parents and siblings meet separately for the remainder of the meeting. Suggestions for supporting siblings of hospitalized newborns are shared with parents during the parent group. The sibling group uses art—drawing and coloring—in a specially developed coloring book to facilitate the primary goal of providing an atmosphere of importance to siblings. The other goals are to encourage siblings and parents to laugh and have fun, express their feelings, enhance self-esteem, and identify individual needs that parents can follow-up on at a later time.

Special Groups

In addition to workshops, special groups that address the needs of siblings who have brothers or sisters with disabilities can be found through specific disability groups (e.g., local chapters of the Down Syndrome Association, Autism Society of America, United Cerebral Palsy), community service agencies, and medical or hospital-based programs for children with chronic or life-threatening illness. State Parent-to-Parent organizations can also be an excellent source of information, resources, and support programs for parents and siblings of children with disabilities. They maintain an extensive database that parents can access for disability, program, and parent matching information.

Adult Siblings

"As wonderful as my husband is, there's nobody who really knows how I feel or cares about my concerns the way other siblings do. They've been there."

—Janet in McHugh, 2003, p.133

Programs for adult siblings also deserve special consideration (Meyer & Vadasy, 1994). One way to acknowledge the important role adult siblings play in the family is to create programs that reflect their interests. These usually include a need for information, peer support, and advocacy skills. The National Association of Sibling Programs (NASP) (n.d.) includes a variety of community programs for adult siblings in many states. Formats range from annual conferences, informal meetings, and periodic formal meetings with a specific topic to structured, multisession programs.

To meet the three main needs above, the NASP has developed the following goals:

1. *Information*

   Make programs and services available for brothers and sisters of individuals with disabilities

   Provide information on how other adult siblings have resolved issues commonly faced by brothers and sisters

2. *Peer support*

   Meet other adult siblings

   Share common joys and concerns with other adult brothers and sisters

   Examine the impact of the sibling's disability on the entire family

   Discuss relationships with other brothers and sisters with a sibling with a disability

   Offer understanding to participants who are experiencing a crisis with their siblings

3. *Advocacy*

   Acquire necessary skills to become effective advocates for their brothers and sisters

   Advocate for services for their brothers and sisters

   Consider creation of services to assure that siblings' needs are met (e.g., housing, training, or respite).

For more information about Adult Siblings, see Chapter 10.

ESTABLISHING PROGRAMS TO PROVIDE INFORMATION

From the innovative efforts described in the previous section, a number of components of information-sharing programs for siblings can be identified. The guidelines that follow are specifically intended for professionals developing information workshops for siblings.

Workshop Goals

Naturally, the goals and objectives of individual workshops vary according to the needs of the siblings. Generally, however, workshops should focus on the following nine goals:

1. To teach specific information about the nature and cause of the disability
2. To teach siblings current philosophy directing services for persons with disabilities
3. To share information about services and materials needed by people with disabilities
4. To provide information on the roles of professionals who work with people with disabilities
5. To demonstrate teaching or other intervention techniques used with people with disabilities
6. To identify community resources that provide services to people with disabilities and their families
7. To facilitate the sharing of ideas, problems, solutions, and information among siblings
8. To help siblings develop a positive self-image by recognizing their unique contribution to the lives of their brothers and sisters with disabilities
9. To facilitate positive interactions among family members

Program Content

The content of such workshops should focus on providing information rather than on providing counseling or therapy (discussed further in Chapter 6). As a natural outcome of information sharing, siblings typically discuss their feelings, problems, and attitudes toward their brother or sister. Within the context of information sharing, these feelings and problems can be addressed in a positive way. Several program models and general information about program content and design are offered next. Opportunities should also be supplied for socializing and group leisure activities, particularly for weekend workshops. The entire program should not be too intense or too rigidly structured, leaving siblings ample time to talk to other siblings.

Table 5.1. Suggested workshop topics on disability-related issues

Topic	Information covered
Developmental disabilities	Characteristics of the specific disability including physical, medical, learning, and social aspects
	Causes of the disability
	General prognosis for the disability
	Prevalence of the disorder
	Definitions of medical and technical terms
Program philosophies	Natural environments
	Least restrictive environment (LRE)
	Inclusion
	Community-based services
	Legal and human rights of people with disabilities
Services	Educational services
	Medical services
	Social services
	Financial services
	Adaptive equipment needs and use
	Legal services
Professionals	The role of and services provided by educators, physicians, physical therapists, social workers, nurses, mobility specialists, occupational therapists, psychologists, audiologists, speech pathologists, and so forth
	Special equipment used by professionals
Intervention techniques	Special instructional strategies
	Special communication strategies
	Mobility procedures
	Behavioral intervention strategies
	Physical and occupational therapy
	Techniques to assist with adaptive skills (e.g., dressing, eating)
	Aspects of special therapies (e.g., music, play therapy)
Community resources	Group homes and supported living
	Vocational programs, especially supported employment
	Social Security
	Family support programs
	Respite care services
	Advocacy services
	Community recreational programs
Interpersonal sharing	Problems and feelings encountered by siblings
	Advantages of being a sibling
	Challenges of being a sibling
	Interacting with siblings
Contributions	Ways to help siblings at home
	Helping siblings in the community

Family communication	Needs of parents Asking parents questions Discussing ideas with parents
Friends	Telling friends about siblings Coping with teasing Teaching friends about disabilities Playing with friends and siblings
The future	Guardianship Financial planning Estate planning Advocacy Self determination Living arrangements

The specific content of workshops will vary according to the goals adopted, the disability addressed, the age of the siblings, and the time allocated. It is, therefore, impossible to provide a comprehensive list of all of the topics that can be addressed in informational workshops. Table 5.1 provides a list of generic topics that could be included in a series of sessions for siblings. Because the material is generic, it can be adapted for specific disabilities and different age groups. Above all, be sure that a workshop's content is based on the most up-to-date information. Providing information that is out of date will only serve to hamper siblings in their understanding of the disability and their adjustment to having a member in the family who has a disability.

Activities The best information workshops provide a number of varied activities for siblings, including socializing, games, and structured activities. Lecture-only formats will not hold the attention of most children or teenagers and will limit the important discussions that can occur. Table 5.2 lists a number of activities for siblings. Some of the activities are especially suited for young children (e.g., puppet shows and skits), whereas others are particularly appropriate for older children (e.g., discussion groups).

Recreation A number of successful information workshops have provided structured opportunities for siblings to interact with each other by engaging in recreational activities. Table 5.3 presents a number of recreational activities that can be used within the context of a workshop. Again, some of the activities are better suited for young children, whereas others are more appropriate for adolescents or young adults.

Table 5.2. Suggested activities for information workshops for siblings

Tours of school programs
Observations of the sibling at school
Observations of therapy sessions
Interviews with professionals
Using special equipment and materials
Simulating various disabling conditions
Discussion groups
Panels to address specific topics
Role-playing
Films, computer simulations, and other media
Stories
Puppet shows and skits
Presentations by professionals

Parental Involvement

Some parents will be apprehensive about their child's participation in a workshop. Most parents will want to be assured that the information presented is in agreement with their own information, understanding, and values related to the child with the disability. To help parents reach a decision and become involved, details regarding the goals, content, and structure of the workshop should be sent to parents well in advance of the scheduled sessions. Opportunities for parents to talk with workshop leaders should be provided.

Table 5.3. Suggested recreational activities for information workshops for siblings

Barbecues
Arts and crafts activities
Team sports (e.g., basketball, bowling, soccer, volleyball, softball)
Relay races
Field trips
Overnight camp-outs
Pizza or other food-themed parties
Parties
Swimming
Group games
Dances
Read-a-thons
Theme days (e.g., water day, Cinco de Mayo day)

Siblings need time by themselves to discuss problems and seek information without parental influence. Many workshops include a special component for parents. These sessions can provide helpful information to parents about siblings and to foster discussion on issues related to siblings. Panels of adult siblings who talk with parents powerfully convey the unique needs of siblings. At the conclusion of the major portion of the workshop, parent and sibling groups should come together for a mutual sharing of information gained or for more informal recreational activities.

Age Grouping

Workshops should be organized to meet the varying needs of the different age levels of siblings. Arranging groups of similar age siblings will facilitate discussion and help the participants focus on common needs and concerns. Six basic age groups are recommended:

1. Preschool: 3–5 years
2. School-age: 6–9 years
3. Preadolescent: 10–13 years
4. Adolescent: 14–18 years
5. Young Adult: 18–22 years
6. Adult:
    a. Adult Siblings
    b. Sibling Caregivers and/or Guardians

Group Leaders

Group leaders can be professionals, older siblings, parents, or interested adults. Leaders should be knowledgeable about the topic to be addressed, able to facilitate discussion, and able to present information in an enjoyable manner. Two leaders per group are highly recommended.

Group Size

Depending on the goals of the information workshop, size is a critical variable. Typically, the most productive groups include five or more siblings and do not exceed twenty. Ideal groups have between 10 and 12 members.

Gender Configuration of Group

Most sibling groups are open to both boys and girls, although we recommend that consideration be given to limiting attendance to same-sex groups when planning sibling groups for certain ages, specifically preteens and adolescents. Younger teens' interest and activity preferences vary by gender. For example, a sibling group held at an Autism Parent Support program was, by chance and not design, most often attended by female siblings ages 8–13. They loved craft activities, art projects, and music. A favorite game was called American Idol. The girls reported playing this with friends. Three members were the judges (they did a great job of imitating the stars!); those who wanted to compete were the contestants, and the rest became the audience. In addition to being fun, the activity provided opportunities to build self-confidence and practice risk-taking behavior. One time, when a brother came to the group, the girls refused to play American Idol when it was suggested. At adolescence, the influence of attraction, competition, and approval may make it more difficult for females and males to stay on task or feel comfortable sharing feelings. Conversely, mixed-sex groups are more like family groupings, giving teens a better opportunity to model and practice conflict resolution, communication skills, and problem-solving strategies. Also, there may be logistical difficulties in planning same sex groups due to limited space, staff, and numbers of siblings attending programs.

Workshop Location

Sometimes it is helpful to provide workshops in locations where the siblings with disabilities receive services. In this way, the participating siblings can observe the surroundings and equipment firsthand. By conducting the workshop in the school or clinic, the program will have more significance to the children because they will come in direct contact with the environment experienced daily by their brother or sister who has a disability. A social worker in a school for children with disabilities saw benefits to holding programs for siblings at the school. Siblings preferred an annual program over ongoing workshops. Siblings were able to visit classes, try out equipment, and talk with therapists. The highlight of the program for most was the show put on by students who attend the school for their siblings and families. The show was an opportunity for siblings to see their brothers' and sisters' talents and strengths (J. Galail, personal communication, May 19, 2005). However, sometimes being in a more neutral or informal environment can facilitate better discussion and learning.

Longitudinal Programs

Successful programs provide opportunities for siblings to gather information over time. As their needs change and siblings mature and assimilate new knowledge, new and more sophisticated questions arise. Comprehensive information programs will be able to meet these varying needs. One-time, episodic information sharing, although a vast improvement over no service provision, will not satisfy the siblings' ongoing needs for information.

Follow-Up

An essential component of information workshops is follow-up. Program leaders should actively contact participants (perhaps through telephone, e-mail, or chat rooms) to assess the degree to which siblings understood the information presented and can use the information. These follow-up contacts also provide opportunities to clarify misconceptions and to provide additional information and resources as needed.

Evaluation

Siblings and parents should evaluate information workshops. The evaluation might include

- Content-related questions to assess comprehension
- Analysis of the strengths and weaknesses of the program
- Additional information needs
- Suggestions for future workshops

A sample evaluation form is reproduced in Figure 5.1.

Role of Grandparents and Extended Family Members

The special role of grandparents of children with disabilities is beginning to be addressed in articles (e.g., Sandler, 1998), books (e.g., Jones, 2001), and programs such as Grandparent-to-Grandparent (PACER CENTER

The Sibling Information Workshop for Adolescents

Post-Evaluation

Session # ___ Date: _______

1. Age: ___
2. Why did you come to the workshop? ______________________
3. The best part of today's meeting was: ______________________
4. The worst part of today's meeting was: ______________________
5. Name one thing you learned today: ______________________
6. How will this help you and/or your sibling? ______________________
7. Is there something you want to know that we did not address? _______
8. Was the workshop leader: a) helpful? ___ b) interesting? ___ c) boring? ___
9. Do you plan to come back again? ______________________
10. How can we make these workshops better? ______________________

Figure 5.1. Sample evaluation form for sibling workshops.

http://www.pacer.org/parent/grand.htm). Information on grandparents and their grandchildren with special needs may also be found in specific disability organizations, the American Association of Retired Persons' (AARP) Grandparent Information Center, and the Georgia State University National Center on Grandparents Raising Grandchildren (http://chhs.gsu.edu/nationalcenter/).

Grandparents and extended family members play an important role in supporting siblings. Grandparents can give special time, bring siblings to activities they might otherwise miss, or provide respite for their grandchild with special needs so that parents can have special time with the other sibling or siblings. Grandparents provide a great deal of practical and emotional support to parents of children with disabilities. In many families, grandparents and other extended family members are the main source of support available to families. More research is needed to explore how grandparents might support families of children with special needs, especially siblings.

Angela is mother to 8-year-old twins, Shelby (who has cerebral palsy) and Sydney. Her story may be unusual because both her parents and in-laws are very involved in her children's lives, but it illustrates the many ways grandparents can contribute to families of children with special needs.

> *"Grandparents level the playing field. I can't spend as much time as I would like with Sydney. Shelby's care is really involved and it pulls me away from doing things with Sydney. Her grandparents are able to give Sydney more attention and support to make her feel equally special. My mother and father are like an extra set of hands. They're there to back me, to help me out. They're able to help me purchase therapy equipment that Shelby would not be able to have otherwise. My mother-in-law found a different way to be supportive. She's older, not in good health, and doesn't have the financial resources of my parents, but she collected money in her town to help fund special therapy for Shelby. She went around town telling people about her granddaughter and through word of mouth, raised a lot of money that would have come out of my pocket. I have to make sure to make my children realize that both sets of grandparents are equally important. Since my mother-in-law can't take my kids alone, I bring the girls to her house for sleepovers so they can say, 'I stayed the night at my Nanny's.'"*
>
> —A. Sanders, personal communication, May 19, 2005

Another mother said,

> *"The grandparent role is a great one. I know that often grandparents feel inadequate to help with the disabled sibling, not knowing what to do, how to do it, but they are more equipped to help with the others. My mom has my typical son and daughter come spend a few days each summer, each by themselves with her, and they get lots of individual time with her. Another friend sends her typical daughter to spend several weeks each summer with her grandparents and relatives. The nice thing is they can be the center of attention and also get a break from the sibling who might cause a lot of disruption in the home. I know my son has kept my kids up*

at night due to his sleep issues; they have had to ride around with us to therapies or be our main sitters. This is a great way for grandparents to help the entire family in a way they are able and comfortable doing. My mom also takes me on a weekend trip each year to give me a nice break and getaway! Grandparents have been great to attend events like plays, basketball games, or track meets for my kids, too, when often I cannot attend with Blake. They get family support in those activities, making them not feel neglected in their areas of interest or talent."

—C. Dees, personal communication, May 17, 2005

PROVIDING INFORMATION THROUGH BOOKS, INTERNET, AND OTHER SOURCES

A rather informal, although powerful, way to provide important information to siblings is through reading material. Numerous books have been written to help explain disabilities to children and adolescents. In particular, a number of books are devoted to the special needs of siblings. A good resource that provides information on disabilities in a straightforward, easy-to-understand manner is *Living with a Brother or Sister with Special Needs: A Book for Sibs* (1996) by Donald Meyer and Patricia Vadasy. This book is written for younger children and explains many different disabilities and the full range of common feelings experienced by siblings. Services and therapies typically provided to children with disabilities are also described to help siblings understand and appreciate the need for these services. *The Sibling Slam Book: What It's Really Like to Have a Brother or Sister with Special Needs* (Meyer, 2004), is noted in Appendix A.

Appendix A lists and reviews available literature that siblings may find helpful. These include books that explain specific disabilities, books about the sibling experience, general children's literature that contains disability themes, and books written by siblings. Most of these titles are available in local libraries. Schools and clinics that have special education and/or sibling programs should maintain a collection of these books to lend to families. This is an inexpensive, yet effective, way to provide information to siblings. The value of the Internet as a resource for siblings is significant in terms of access to information and support. Appendix B lists web sites of disability organizations that offer specific information and programs for siblings as well as Internet discussion groups for younger, teen, and adult siblings.

Other information sources may include television programs and films, videotapes or movies, and even commercials and printed advertisements. Television shows have featured children, adolescents, and adults with varying disabilities. For the most part, these presentations have addressed some of the problems and needs of people with disabilities in a sensitive manner. These story lines may help to stimulate discussion about similar situations in the sibling's family as well as offer factual information. Other audiovisual materials and documentaries specifically based on various disabilities may be available through school libraries or some social service agencies. A list of films, television movies, and documentaries with disability and sibling themes is included in Appendix A.

SUMMARY

Individuals, young or old, who have a sibling with a disability have unanimously expressed a need for information. This need is for information that is factual, objective, and up to date, and that touches on more subjective and emotional issues. Some siblings never voice their questions; therefore, they never become informed. Misconceptions that begin in childhood can last into adulthood.

It is essential that questions and honest communication be encouraged in order to eliminate fears and misconceptions. Parents and professionals should be aware of effective communication skills, such as listening actively, being accepting and respectful of all questions, knowing how to facilitate questions and discussion, and answering questions honestly and in a manner that is both age appropriate and developmentally appropriate.

Many innovative approaches to disseminate information to groups of siblings have been designed. Several models for a variety of ages, preschool through adolescence and adulthood, have been developed across the United States. Some programs offer similar opportunities for parents to become more aware of the special needs of siblings. Numerous organizational aspects must be considered when planning information workshops or sessions. Workshop and program content, including varied activities and socializing opportunities, should be carefully outlined. Other factors to consider in developing a program include parental involvement, age grouping, group size, gender configuration, leadership, location, follow-up, and evaluation.

Grandparents and extended family have an important and often overlooked role in supporting siblings. Like siblings, they have unique information needs that can be addressed through strategies and programs described in this chapter.

Another efficient and effective means for sharing information with siblings is through books and other media. Books, both nonfiction and fiction, are available for all ages to describe specific disabilities and/or offer insight into the lives of individuals with disabilities, their families, and their siblings. Television programs, web sites, videotapes and DVDs, films, and other audiovisual materials may also be accessible and provide another avenue to information sharing.

The need expressed by siblings for information is universal, compelling, and lifelong. The information provided in this chapter describes an array of books, programs, media, and other innovative approaches that are available. Parents and siblings are encouraged to look through Appendix A and Appendix B for helpful resources.

6

Providing Support to Siblings with Brothers and Sisters with Disabilities

"In high school I was popular and able to carry out many normal activities but inside I was full of self-doubt. I became an expert at hiding the panic that was eating away at me. My parents took me at different times to a psychologist, a hypnotherapist, and psychiatrist. They all said there was nothing wrong with me. . . . No one thought to explore my family situation."

—Strohm, 2005, p. 9

Two overarching areas of need have been identified for children with siblings with disabilities: information and support (Powell-Smith & Stollar, 1997). These areas of need are so connected that it is often difficult to distinguish where one ends and the other begins. Chapter 5 examines the need for information; Chapter 6 considers types of support available to siblings.

For the purposes of this discussion, the term *counselor* will be used to describe a variety of mental health practitioners including counselors, social workers, marriage and family therapists, psychotherapists, psychologists, and psychiatrists working in a variety of community and clinical settings. It is assumed that counselors possess knowledge and skills in the counseling process, familiarity with various counseling modalities, interviewing techniques, and diagnosis of psychological disorders.

Professionals from all programs and agencies that serve families of children with special needs, from health, mental health, and educational perspectives, play an important role in supporting siblings. Professionals can help siblings to learn new problem-solving skills and to be resilient. Siblings can learn about their own strengths and limitations—lessons they will use throughout their lives. Increased appreciation of the special needs of siblings helps siblings to feel included and valued. Professionals can provide information, listen to siblings' points of view (because siblings' ideas may be different from those of their parents!), and try to understand how their daily lives are affected. These professionals can be very helpful in giving siblings accurate information and in helping them to talk about their emotions and experience of guilt, embarrassment, isolation, resentment, jealousy, anger, fairness, attention seeking, and perfectionism. Traditionally, medical and educational services have focused on the person with the illness or disability. However, research makes it clear that the other family members are most likely feeling even greater anxiety and stress than the person with the identified needs (May, 2001) and may benefit from special attention. That special attention may include counseling. Consider the following examples:

Lisa's brother, Bill, has a learning disability. He had great trouble reading and comprehending written symbols. Lisa's parents, in their efforts to assist Bill, helped to form a parents' group for others who have children with learning disabilities. Lisa's mother had been busy with the organization at least 3 nights per week and spent considerable time providing Bill with enrichment activities to help compensate for his learning disability. In 1981, Lisa wrote to the Sibling Information Network for some help and to share her turmoil. She wrote her letter from a psychiatric hospital in New England. At the young age of 16, Lisa decided to commit suicide by ingesting a bottle of aspirin. After swallowing the pills, she called her mother for help. Recovered physically, she is now attempting to recover emotionally. Her letter states her case plainly:

> *"No one ever has time for me. My Mom and Dad are so concerned about Bill and his problems, I am ignored. Don't they know that I hurt inside? Don't they know that I need help? I don't like my brother. I wish he were dead. At times I want to kill myself. I really need help. Can you help me? Will you talk to me?"*

Lisa's parents are distraught over her attempted suicide. As Lisa describes her reasons for this drastic call for help, her parents feel the pain she was experiencing acutely. They feel guilty and confused. Lisa and her parents know the stress that can occur when a family member has a disability.

Lisa's story is certainly not characteristic of all siblings with brothers and sisters who have disabilities. It is, however, a powerful reminder that siblings often experience intense feelings that they may feel unable to express when they have a brother or sister with special needs. Because such intense emotion is not usually expected in a family having a member with a learning disability, Lisa reminds us that no matter how mild the disability, family dynamics may produce intense emotions.

Unfortunately, Lisa had nowhere to turn for help. In desperation, she resorted to a guaranteed method of drawing her parents' attention to her feelings and needs, although it almost proved fatal. It can only be speculated that a more positive scenario might have ensued if Lisa had access to someone who could help her before she reached this critical point.

Kevin wrote a letter to the Sibling Information Network requesting similar assistance:

> *"I'm 14 and my brother, Gary, is 12. Gary is my only brother. He has autism and most days, he drives me crazy. We sleep in the same room. If I ever forget to put my homework away the minute I finish, he goes after it. Remember the story, 'the dog ate my homework'? At my house, it's my brother who ate my homework! I really want to talk or write to other kids who have a brother like mine. There's no one here I can talk to about my brother. Sometimes I just need to tell someone who can understand how I feel. Another kid who has a brother with autism will know what I am talking about. Can you help me?"*

Kevin's concerns, like those of so many others, clearly indicate that siblings need an open channel of communication to express their feelings, particularly to people who will take the time to listen and understand.

In a moving essay, Zatlow described her feelings toward her brother, Douglas, a young adult with autism:

> *"We [siblings] all adapt as best we can but sometimes the penalty for our constant accommodation is considerable."*
>
> —1982, p. 2

For Zatlow, the responsibility of helping to raise her brother was an arduous struggle at great emotional expense. Zatlow mentioned specific concerns she had about her brother's future and her possible role as his guardian if she were to inherit the responsibility of caring for him. She urged the development of alternatives for families so that siblings will not be denied their own lives and will be given an opportunity to develop their own separate identities.

Kelly, writing about his experiences as a brother of a child with Down syndrome, has also provided some insight into a sibling's feelings:

> *"Terry was always one of us, and Mom and Dad never understated the fact, even though his other brothers knew he was different. Little did I suspect that I would grow to hate the difference before I learned to respect it. 'Maybe we're lucky in a way to have been blessed with a special needs child,' I'd hear my parents say to themselves. Often, we would be forced to contain our personal problems and focus attention on a truly needy kid. . . . Terry and I were in it together. We'd play together. Sometimes I'd*

> *fantasize rather than analyze what it was like to be him. In fact, I'd wonder and fantasize so hard that I'd wish I were him and he me. It hurt. 'Why can't he be like me?' and 'I'd do anything so he could know what it was like to be normal.' What I believe I was doing then was assuming a sympathetic nature that was blind to love."*
>
> —Kelly, 1982

Kelly's experience of not revealing his personal problems and his fantasies is certainly not unusual to siblings with brothers and sisters who have disabilities. Indeed, these are feelings commonly experienced by siblings.

SIBLINGS AND THEIR FEELINGS

As discussed in Chapter 4, siblings who have brothers and sisters with disabilities experience a full range of feelings related to the sibling, the parents, the entire family, themselves, other people, and the world in general. They feel excitement, anger, joy, frustration, sadness, guilt, loneliness, fear, and jealousy. These feelings vary in intensity and meaning and may occur in response to isolated events or to the overall family situation.

Of course, such feelings are not unique to siblings who have brothers or sisters with disabilities. Many siblings experience similar emotions toward brothers and sisters without disabilities (Dyson, 1999; Hannah & Midlarsky, 1999; Rodrigue, Geffken, & Morgan, 1993). Most siblings experience jealousy and rivalry, in particular (Kirkman, 1986; McDermott, 1980). However common these feelings may be, when left unresolved or suppressed, they may cause substantial life problems and most certainly will interfere with the development of positive sibling relationships.

When trying to understand the feelings of siblings, it is important to acknowledge that different perspectives influence what is reported. Burke (2004) interviewed families of children with disabilities. In his study, siblings and parents reported different areas of concern. Siblings shared concerns about the future whereas parents were most concerned about everyday events. Guite, Lobato, Kao, and Plante (2004) looked at the relationship between sibling and parent reports of sibling adjustment. They found that parents were more likely than siblings to report sibling adjustment problems. The siblings who report more negative adjustment than their parents do tend to be younger and male. Guite and colleagues stressed that it is important to gain information on sibling relationships from multiple sources such as mothers, fathers, siblings, and the sibling with a disability.

Some of the intense feelings that may be experienced by siblings of children with disabilities include the following:

Fear

Siblings may be afraid of "catching" the disability (Binger, 1973; Burbach & Peterson, 1986; Meyer & Vadasy, 1996; Trevino, 1979).

Siblings may be overly concerned and frightened about possible futures for their brother or sister, their parents, and themselves (Harland & Cuskelly, 2000; McHale & Gamble, 1987; Seligman, 1983).

Many siblings fear the reaction of their friends, especially future or present spouses, when they learn about their brother or sister.

Siblings may be afraid to have their own children for fear that they, too, will be born with disabilities (Klein & Schleifer, 1993).

Loneliness

Siblings may feel isolated from peers and, in some cases, may be rejected by their friends (Meyer, Vadasy, & Fewell, 1985).

Siblings may feel isolated from other family members.

Siblings may feel different from other children and may believe that their family experiences are not shared by other families (Bagenholm & Gillberg, 1991).

Anger

Siblings of children with disabilities experience greater degrees of anger than do other siblings (Seligman, 1983).

Typically, siblings feel anger toward the child with the disability, their parents, society, and God (Featherstone, 1980).

Anger may be the result of feeling ignored and unappreciated.

Anger may be directed toward peers who treat the child cruelly.

Resentment

Siblings may feel resentment as parents spend excessive amounts of time and resources with the child who has the disability (McHugh, 2003; Rivara, 1994).

Siblings may resent curtailment of social activities as a result of the presence of the brother or sister.

Siblings may feel resentment at the unfairness of the family situation and the different expectations parents hold for their children (Walker, Garber, & Van Slyke, 1995).

Siblings may feel resentment at constantly having to assume the teacher or helper role (McHale & Harris, 1992).

Embarrassment

Most siblings, at some time, feel embarrassed about their brothers and sisters with disabilities.

Siblings may feel embarrassed when the child with the disability behaves inappropriately in public, causing attention to be directed toward the family (Cate & Loots, 2000).

Siblings often express embarrassment when introducing the child to peers, boyfriends or girlfriends, and so forth.

Extensive adaptive equipment used by a sibling with a disability may cause embarrassment.

Confusion

Siblings may feel confused about their role as sibling and "surrogate parent."

Siblings experience confusion over intervention priorities for the child with a disability and lack of concern for their own needs.

Confusion may be heightened when parents disagree about rearing the child, treat the child differently, or are not at the same stage of acceptance of the disability.

Jealousy

Siblings may be jealous of the attention the child with the disability receives (McHale & Pawletko, 1992). Jealousy is commonly focused on the unfairness or unevenness of parental attention.

> *"Having twins (age 8) makes for even greater jealousy. Sydney is jealous that she doesn't have a wheel chair or a walker because she sees the attention her sister Shelby gets by having them. There is no way of making it fair. You have to compromise. When Shelby gets a wheel chair if I can do it, I'll get Sydney a new bike or something special. They're in that 'me' stage. She sees what she has to do without and not what she is blessed with. Over time, I think the tables will turn and Shelby will be jealous of her sister because she won't be able to do the things physically that her sister can do."*
>
> —A. Sanders, personal communication, May 19, 2005

Pressure

Some parents apply excessive amounts of pressure to achieve on the siblings in order to help them to compensate for the parents' own disappointments (Schild, 1976).

Siblings may be pressured to care for the child with the disability, which results in the taking on of responsibilities that are beyond what is normally expected in sibling relationships (Farber, 1959; Grossman, 1972; Krauss, Seltzer, Gordon, & Friedman, 1996).

Older female siblings typically experience greater demands to help care for the child with the disability (Breslau, Weitzman, & Messenger, 1981; Cleveland & Miller, 1977; Farber, 1959; Pruchno, Patrick, & Burant, 1996).

Siblings in large families experience less pressure than do siblings in small families (Grossman, 1972).

Siblings from less financially stable families may experience more pressure due to their inability to afford outside assistance to aid in the child's care.

Siblings of chronically ill children are often given the responsibility of extensive physical care activities (Travis, 1976).

Guilt

Siblings may feel guilty about their emotions of anger, jealousy, and hostility (San Martino & Newman, 1974).

Guilt feelings may be repressed when negative thoughts and feelings have been punished.

Excessive guilt may be manifested in overly helpful acts directed toward the child with the disability (Seligman, 1983).

Frustration

Attempting to establish what is perceived to be a normal sibling relationship with a brother or sister who has a disability may lead to great levels of frustration (Featherstone, 1980).

Not all siblings experience such intense negative feelings. Many siblings have predominantly positive feelings toward their experiences with their brothers and sisters who have disabilities. Some of these positive attitudes are reflected in several of the excerpts in Chapters 1 and 3. Families are so complex that it is difficult to identify feelings common to all

siblings who have brothers and sisters with disabilities, and it is perhaps impossible to pinpoint why positive or negative feelings take hold. Burke found that it is likely that siblings "will be affected in some way and, as a consequence, they will have to learn to live with their disabled brother or sister and experience some association with the disability itself" (2004, p. 43).

The degree to which and how siblings are affected by their experience of living with a brother or sister with disabilities may be influenced by many factors, including:

1. Severity of the disability
2. Age of the child who has the disability
3. Age-spacing between the child with the disability and the other siblings
4. Birth order
5. Size of the family
6. Pressures exerted by the parents and professionals who are working with the child with the disability
7. Financial status of the family and amount of financial resources needed to help the child with the disability
8. Residence of the sibling who has the disability
9. Sex of the child who has the disability
10. External services needed by the child who has the disability

11. Physical and social adjustments the family has made to accommodate the child with the disability
12. External resources available to help family members
13. Amount and type of responsibility placed on the siblings for the care and treatment of the child with the disability
14. Extent to which the child with the disability manipulates or mistreats the other siblings
15. Extent to which the parents have adjusted to the disability
16. Parental feelings toward the child with the disability
17. Temperament of both or all of the children in the family
18. The perception and experience of being treated differently from the other siblings by one's parents
19. The actual interactions among siblings

When negative feelings develop, they need to be addressed in an open and honest fashion. Suppressed or repressed negative feelings can result in significant adjustment problems and may impede the establishment and maintenance of other social relationships. Murphy and Corte (1989) noted that siblings who harbor unexpressed emotions may be at risk for developing problems. They described several ways siblings may respond to this lack of expression. Some siblings may regress and act like young children, often mimicking the child with the disability. Siblings may become more vulnerable to illness and cling to their symptoms for extended periods of time. Other siblings may act out with fighting, tantrums, lying, cheating, stealing, or other acts of defiance. Still other siblings may adopt the "model child syndrome" as a way of compensating for the brother or sister. When siblings have such negative feelings or act out those feelings, they are in need of support to help them understand, accept, and handle their thoughts and emotions in proactive ways. One source of support is counseling.

WHAT IS COUNSELING?

The term *counseling* is used freely in everyday language. Counseling services are available on a range of diverse topics such as marriage reconciliation, taxes and mortgages, weight loss, or the purchase of an automobile. Counseling means giving advice, encouragement, information, or some sort of general assistance to an individual or group. Counseling also denotes a particular helping relationship between a person and a skilled professional aimed at remedying specific problems. Through this helping relationship, individuals have an opportunity to examine their values, feelings, attitudes, and beliefs, as well as the way in which these are reflected in their behavior (Munson, 1971). Counseling implies a learning process in which people develop an understanding of themselves and learn specific skills to deal effectively with their problems and concerns. Counseling siblings of people with special needs, as in all counseling, implies the establishment of a helping relationship between the sibling and a competent counselor. This relationship is founded on respect for the sibling and his or her problems and needs. An honest, caring relationship between the counselor and the sibling is basic to the counseling process. Counseling can take place in individual, family, and group settings. The choice will be determined by personal preference and the nature of the problem.

Goals for Siblings

When siblings have adjustment problems related to their brother or sister, counseling services should be provided (Post-Kramer & Nickolai, 1985; Slade, 1988). This counseling must be focused on the attainment of specific goals. First, the sibling should come to a deeper and broader understanding of personal feelings and problems. As siblings participate in the counseling process, they should realize the cause of their feelings and problems. Second, siblings should develop skills and attitudes that enable them to cope with their problems and feelings in a constructive manner. They should exit the counseling relationship with a specific course of action that will help to prevent potential problems from escalating to troublesome levels in the future. Third, counseling should enable siblings to pursue their life goals as fully functioning members of society. Counseling should lead to personal growth and fulfillment that will enhance both individual and overall family functioning. Fourth, counseling should allow the sibling to strengthen the relationship with the brother or sister who has the disability. As the sibling experiences personal growth and develops new skills, he or she should learn to relate in more positive ways to the brother or sister with the disability as well as to other family members.

Psychotherapy and Counseling

At this point, it may be helpful to distinguish between psychotherapy and counseling. Both psychotherapy and counseling are essentially concerned with the same intervention goals (e.g., self-exploration, self-understanding, behavior change), and both hinge on the relationship between the professional and the person seeking help. However, there are important differences between the two interventions.

Psychotherapy Brammer and Shostrom (1982) explained that psychotherapy is more concerned with severe life problems than counseling and involves a greater level of intensity and time involvement than counseling. According to George and Christiani (1981), the goals of psychotherapy are more likely to involve a quite complete change of basic character structure, whereas the goals of counseling are apt to be more limited and more directed toward growth and change for an immediate situation.

Bank and Kahn (1982) have described the use of psychotherapy with siblings, primarily siblings of brothers and sisters without disabilities. The goal of their therapy was to uncover the nature of the bond between the siblings—whether it was close or distant—and how it developed. These therapists established a psychotherapy process to handle *severe* life problems experienced by adult siblings. Their approach is clearly beyond the scope and purpose of this book. The majority of siblings will not need psychotherapy to handle their feelings and concerns or to learn new ways to solve their problems. Less intense, more informal counseling is recommended for most siblings who have brothers and sisters with disabilities.

Counseling Counseling is the establishment of a helping relationship between two people. A successful counselor must possess skills to develop and maintain that relationship. Typically, counselors receive professional training to develop specific skills that fulfill the goals of counseling. Although counselors are usually thought of as psychiatrists and psychologists who are highly skilled in behavioral and medical sciences, acceptance of counselors from a broader population who may have only minimal training in counseling techniques is growing (Brammer, 1977; Stewart, 1986). These more informal counselors may include peer counselors at the high school and college-age level, crisis-line telephone counselors, ministers or other religious personnel, teachers, and family members. In any case, it is important for counselors to be fully aware of their skills and the limits of their competence so that they will not attempt to overstep their boundaries. Occasionally, counselors may be asked to help with serious emotional problems, such as severe depression, which require treatment from highly skilled professionals. Competent counselors must quickly make referrals to other professionals as appropriate.

Professionally trained counselors of siblings may be social workers, psychologists (clinical, counseling, and school), psychiatrists, nurses, and educators, as long as they have attained specific competencies and skills.

Professional counselors of siblings must be knowledgeable of the full array of social services and community resources available to families of children with disabilities as well as cognizant of state-of-the-art philosophies concerning human development, behavioral principles, and grief reactions in children (loss and death). They must also be fully informed regarding disability-related conditions of children, including developmental disabilities, chronic and life-threatening illness, and genetic and emotional disorders. Successful counselors are fully aware of current research related to siblings and families, as well as innovative service programs aimed at meeting siblings' needs. Many disability organizations offer educational material and training for professionals.

Counselors also need to be sensitive to and knowledgeable about cultural and language differences because cultural attitudes might be relevant for the counseling process. These might include attitudes about disability, attitudes about caring roles within the family, or attitudes regarding the use of support services (Strohm, 2005).

The Counseling Process

Effective counseling is a purposeful activity involving several steps or stages through which siblings are able to develop new perspectives and skills in a systematic and secure manner. Whether counseling occurs individually or in small groups, the counseling process is generally the same. Seven steps are typically used in counseling siblings who have brothers and sisters with disabilities.

Step 1: Establish a Relationship This step begins as soon as the sibling and the counselor first meet and will continue until the relationship is terminated. The counselor should communicate a sincere respect for the sibling and an attitude of acceptance toward him or her. The relationship will be enhanced as the counselor demonstrates skills in relating to the sibling and an understanding of the sibling's experience. It may be helpful to ask the sibling to complete an introductory card and a sentence completion form like those shown in Figures 6.1 and 6.2. These forms were prepared for adolescents and help to focus the discussion on the sibling's concerns, feelings, problems, and needs, which will be addressed throughout the counseling process. Of course, if this activity will in any way interfere with establishing a friendly, open relationship it should not be considered. The counselor should offer to complete the forms for younger siblings or siblings who have difficulty with reading or writing, as the added pressure might impede the establishment of rapport.

My name is: ______________________________
Address: ______________________________
____
Telephone: ______________________________
School: ______________________________ Grade: ____
Favorite subject: ______________________________
Least favorite subject: ______________________________

My brother/sister's name is: ______________________________
What type of disability does he/she have? ______________________________
____

What do you hope to accomplish here? ______________________________
____
____

Figure 6.1. Introductory card for sibling groups.

Step 2: Understand the Sibling's Feelings and Needs The sibling is encouraged to identify and express feelings about him- or herself and toward his or her siblings, friends, and parents; and to describe any unmet needs. At this stage, the counselor is concerned with the sibling's perception of his or her difficulties and the child's feelings about them (Stewart, 1986). Together, the counselor and sibling examine the problems and feelings from many different vantage points so that the best course of action can be planned.

Step 3: Explore Options The sibling is supported to make progress toward the counseling goal through exploring alternatives. The counselor must not make the decision as to which alternative is best but rather, should suggest many viable options. The parameters of each option in terms of time, effort, cost, risk, sacrifice, and so forth should be discussed during this step. The sibling's analysis of the implications of each option must be carefully reviewed.

Step 4: Plan a Strategy As the sibling analyzes the various options presented earlier, he or she will gradually begin to adopt a suitable strategy. The sibling should be encouraged to *choose* a strategy, rather than just accept the advice of the counselor. Implementation and eventual success of the strategy will require personal commitment. At this time,

Name: ______________________________ Date: ________

1. I am most happy when ______________________________
____
2. Life is easiest when ______________________________
____
3. The most important thing in my life right now is ______________
____
4. If only ______________________________
____
5. On Saturdays I usually ______________________________
____
6. Life is hardest when ______________________________
____
7. It's not easy to ______________________________
____
8. Sometimes I really need ______________________________
____
9. When I get older ______________________________
____
10. It makes me angry ______________________________
____
11. Sometimes I feel sad when ______________________________
____
12. The best thing about my family is ______________________
____

Figure 6.2. Sentence completion form.

the resources needed to carry out the strategy should be identified and located. A written plan of action, generated by the sibling and reviewed by the counselor, may help to structure and determine what will be done to meet the goals of the counseling sessions.

Step 5: Practice New Skills Throughout the counseling process, the sibling has been developing new insights about his or her behavior, feelings, and concerns, and reaching a new level of understanding and acceptance. The counselor must help the sibling to practice the strategy and the new skills before they are actually implemented outside of the counseling environment. Role-playing is useful to help siblings practice newly learned skills. The counselor and sibling establish a realistic situation and practice various roles and behaviors to deal with the problem presented. To ensure that the new skills are generalized to many situations, several role-play sessions are recommended.

Step 6: Terminate the Sessions Typically, the counseling relationship is short term. As a result, termination should be discussed early as the sibling and counselor prepare to conclude the counseling relationship. The decision to terminate must be mutual, although the sibling should assume the major responsibility (Stewart, 1986). It is important that the sibling leave the relationship feeling that the counseling has been constructive. A review of the sessions, initial problems, chosen strategies, and new skills is highly recommended. If the counseling has been successful, the sibling will leave with a positive attitude and with specific skills that can be used to help him or her to cope effectively with problems in the future. The counselor should make sure that the sibling feels valuable by recognizing the achievements and skills mastered through the sessions.

Step 7: Follow-Up Follow-up should not be neglected in the counseling process; in fact, it is an important part of all sibling counseling and should be planned for accordingly. It is unrealistic to expect siblings to maintain changes in their feelings, attitudes, and behavior unless they receive periodic support. Follow-up should be viewed as a "booster shot" to help the sibling carry through with what was accomplished in the counseling sessions. Telephone calls, brief visits, written notes, or e-mails from the counselor help to remind the sibling of the accomplishments achieved earlier, and will communicate an honest concern for the sibling. Suggesting that the sibling send a note or e-mail or call periodically to keep in touch so as to let the counselor know how he or she is feeling may be helpful.

Structured Group Counseling for Siblings

The most predominant counseling approach for siblings of children with disabilities documented in the literature entails structured group discussions. These groups operate on the premise that siblings need an opportunity to express their feelings and thoughts with other siblings who have similar experiences.

Schreiber and Feeley (1965) have reported on the successful implementation of a structured (or guided) group experience for siblings (ages 13–17) of children with mental retardation who were living at home. This sibling group was formed as one part of a broader effort to strengthen overall family life. It focused on the following goals:

1. To assist siblings in identifying their reactions to their brothers or sisters who have disabilities
2. To help individual siblings examine and determine strategies for understanding and dealing with their siblings, parents, and peers, as well as problems related to living with a brother or sister who has a disability
3. To discover siblings' strengths and weaknesses

This group met every 2 weeks over an 8-month period and was led by a social worker. At the conclusion of this group experience, Schreiber and Feeley (1965) noted that it was not the severity of the disability that seemed to affect the adolescents' lives or happiness as much as it was the way the adolescents felt about themselves and their sibling. The participants in this group requested specific information on what they could do to help their families and the sibling with a disability. These researchers concluded that when parents have dealt constructively with problems regarding the child with a disability, the sibling tends to develop greater maturity, tolerance, patience, and responsibility than is typical for children of a similar age. They assert that the sibling of a child with a disability needs reassurance, support, and specific information regarding the disabling condition.

Feigon (1981) described the formation of sibling groups for adolescents who had brothers and sisters with varying disabilities. The groups met weekly for 12 sessions and were set up in discussion-group style. Feigon analyzed the content of these group sessions and identified four common themes. The first theme centered on the family and the sibling's responsibility to the child with a disability. Within this topic, siblings discussed issues such as embarrassment, anger, resentment, loyalty, and commitment. The second theme, intrapsychic feelings, attempted to help the adolescents to focus on their own feelings. Many siblings expressed concerns about their own health and achievements. The third theme, interpersonal information, focused on sharing information regarding disabling conditions, genetic concerns, and behavior management and on introducing the child to friends. The fourth theme revolved around the social needs of the adolescents. In this context, the siblings discussed general topics such as high school, friends, and special events.

Feigon (1981) has noted that such groups have two major functions. One function is purely informational. The siblings want specific information and the group sessions provide a forum for its receipt. Second, the group provides a therapeutic and supportive experience in which the siblings can address their individual needs. By focusing on their needs, group members "seemed to promote a greater understanding of themselves in relation to their sibling" (1981, p. 2).

Borders, Borders, Borders, Watts, and Watts (1982) founded a sibling group at United Cerebral Palsy of Greater Louisville, Kentucky, with the aim of meeting other siblings who have brothers and sisters with disabilities. This group met every other week for 1½ hours over a several-month period. The group used role-playing to learn how to react to stressful situations. These siblings noted, "Through acting out, we are able to discuss everyone's viewpoint and begin to understand why people act or think the way they do" (Borders et al., 1982, p. 2). During their guided group experience, these siblings were able to share and discuss a number of feelings, including anger, happiness, jealousy, worry, and excitement. These siblings encouraged other siblings to join similar groups noting, "You will like your sibling more, and you will like yourself more" (p. 2).

> *"The reality is while we try to give our other children as typical an upbringing as possible, they will be different from their sib experience. I took my daughter to a sib project event when she was 12 and it ended her sense of isolation, and feeling as if she was the only one who has had her life changed."*
>
> —Personal communication, June 19, 2003

Summers, Bridge, and Summers (1991) reported their work with siblings in structured support group sessions. The focus of their groups is to have siblings shift from "other-directed cognitions" (e.g., thinking one's sister is a burden to the family) to "self-directed cognitions" (e.g., developing proactive strategies to address challenges related to the sibling). They detail the goals of a six-session approach to sibling support groups:

Session 1: Allow children to become acquainted and feel comfortable with each other.

Session 2: Discuss what it is like to live with a disability.

Session 3: Learn specifics about disabilities.

Session 4: Explore feelings that individuals have regarding their brother or sister with a disability.

Session 5: Observe the child who has the disability in an intervention setting.

Session 6: Remind children of what they have learned and help them to feel comfortable.

The Sibling Center at California Pacific Medical Center supports siblings of children with chronic or life-threatening medical conditions including cystic fibrosis (CF) and familial amyotrophic lateral sclerosis (ALS). The program was developed by Dr. Joanna Fanos (n.d.), a research psychologist who has extensively studied the impact of growing up with and possibly surviving a sibling who has chronic illness. The five-session program combines joint parent and child meetings as well as a time for siblings to meet alone with a counselor. Parents and their children without disabilities meet with a counselor for evaluation and the development of an intervention plan in the first session. In Sessions 2–3, the sibling(s) meet with the counselor to identify communication difficulties in the family, to minimize emotional distress, and to strengthen coping skills. During Session 4, the first half of the session is conducted with the sibling(s) who are typically developing and the second half is held with the parents to review and develop future plans. Families then attend follow-up sessions for 3 to 6 months to review the emotional needs of the sibling(s) who are typically developing. If a sibling is identified as likely to benefit from additional assistance, referral is made to a child/adolescent therapist.

Research indicates that support groups benefit siblings of children with disabilities and chronic illness. Siblings can benefit from support and information about the disability (Seltzer, et. al. 1997). Phillips (1999) reported decreases in stress, increases in perceived social support, and reduced depression and anxiety and higher self-esteem. In a study of social support intervention for siblings of chronically ill children, Dauz-Williams and colleagues (1997) reported that support group intervention helped siblings to cope better with their own emotions and to better understand their sibling's illness. In their pilot study of the needs of siblings with disabilities, Burke and Montgomery (2000) noted the popularity and need for a sibling support group. Stewart (1986) noted that group counseling typically renders its greatest outcome by demonstrating that others have similar difficulties and problems.

Sibling support groups, such as those described in Sibshops (see Chapter 5) are designed to provide information, problem-solving and communication skills, stress management, and relationship support. The group situation provides an opportunity for a sibling to interact with other siblings who face similar problems and experience similar feelings, and to give and receive help from them as well as from the counselor. These programs do not typically provide counseling support on a formal level, but can make referrals as necessary.

An excerpt of a conversation by members of a support group for siblings of children with autism illustrates how children learn from each other through the group process. In this instance, Sarita was attending the group for the first time. When she dropped off her daughter, Sarita's mother remarked that this was the first time she had come to a sibling program and worried that she might be shy. The group leader wanted to make sure that Sarita felt included, so she encouraged the other girls to talk about their experience.

Sheila (age 10): It's fun.

Ashanti: (age 9): We make things and play games.

Jennifer (age 12): You can say whatever you want.

Judith (age 8): We're autism.

Jennifer: You mean your *brother* has autism, don't you?

Ashanti: I have a brother with autism.

Judith: No, *we're* autism too.

Sheila: Like, we're part of it? Is that what you mean?

Jennifer: You mean we're all autism because we have a brother with autism?

Judith: (nods vigorously): Yes, we're *all* autism.

Group leader: Having a brother or sister with autism does affect everyone in the family.

(There are other nods as everyone agrees and the conversation shifts again.)

Sheila: And we make friends.

Ashanti: Do you want to play?

Sarita (age 9): I think I will like this group.

Advantages and Limitations of Group Counseling Group counseling, like any tactic to help people systematically solve their problems, has both advantages and limitations. Group counseling cannot be considered a cure-all treatment (Schneider-Corey & Corey, 1987). Careful consideration of the advantages and limitations of this type of treatment will help set initial parameters for what can be expected through group counseling, help anticipate what might be potential problems for a particular group, and provide a stronger base for choosing a counseling approach.

Advantages

Group counseling is efficient. Counselors can provide service to more siblings (George & Christiani, 1981).

Siblings provide a support system for each other.

Use of a group allows siblings to use a real-life setting to experiment with and to practice new behavioral strategies during the counseling sessions.

Siblings receive acceptance and validation of their feelings from others, not just the counselor.

Siblings learn interpersonal communication skills beyond those that can be developed in one-to-one relationships.

Groups allow siblings to put their own problems into perspective and to understand how similar and unique they are compared with others.

Siblings may be more receptive to suggestions made by other siblings than by a professional. According to Pietrofesa and colleagues (1984), learning about the commonality of problems, life events, and situations often allows the development of solutions to have more credence.

In groups, siblings can both receive and provide help.

Limitations

Some siblings' personalities do not lend themselves to the demands of the group setting. A quiet and shy sibling may simply get "lost in the crowd"; a domineering sibling may manipulate the group and impede the group process.

Some siblings may have problems and needs that require in-depth attention. Group counseling implies a diluted relationship between the client and a professional (Shertzer & Stone, 1980).

Sibling groups may concentrate on the mechanics of the group process, which detracts from individual concerns.

In groups, cliques can develop. This excludes some members and, thus, divides the group (Pietrofesa et al., 1984).

Some siblings may find it difficult to trust other members and, thus, not fully express feelings, thoughts, and concerns.

Group counseling requires advanced professional skill; sometimes, leadership may be weak and ineffective due to poor counselor training in group techniques (Schneider-Corey & Corey, 1987).

Sometimes parents will respond more to programs with an educational focus than a support group. This needs to be kept in mind when planning programs. Not all siblings will want to join a group or have the chance to do so. Sometimes supporting the sibling individually instead of or in addition to group work may be indicated.

Family Counseling

Family counseling includes a variety of assessment and intervention approaches and may be helpful in supporting siblings of children with disabilities. The family is viewed as a system, with each part of the system related to all of the other parts. A change in one part of the system will result in changes throughout the system. The goals of family counseling are to promote and strengthen the well-being of the family system of relationships and can include an emphasis on sibling relationships.

WHEN TO SEEK PROFESSIONAL SUPPORT

When siblings have adjustment problems related to their brother or sister, counseling services should be provided (Post-Kramer & Nickolai, 1985; Slade, 1988). In her research on the siblings of children with autism, Sandra Harris (n.d.) found that while most siblings are much like other children their age, a small subgroup of siblings are more vulnerable to worry and anxiety or to acting out types of behavior. The child who is often worried, moody, sad, or angry for extended periods of time might benefit from the services of a mental health professional.

Opperman and Alant (2003) looked at coping strategies of 19 adolescent siblings of children with severe disabilities. The findings indicated that siblings were struggling with their situation. They reported limited family interaction, difficulty expressing their feelings about the sibling with a disability, guilt, and limited information about their sibling's disability. Professional support to facilitate adolescents' coping and facilitate establishing strong support networks was recommended.

The following example by a clinical social worker who specializes in working with families of children with disabilities underscores the importance of obtaining a complete family history as part of the counseling interview. It will give a more complete picture of the family and may identify sibling needs.

• • • Mrs. Black sought help with her son Andrew, 5, who has autism. One major struggle occurred over the hand-held electronic game belonging to Andrew's older brother John, 14. Andrew would tantrum uncontrollably whenever he saw the game. No longer able to control her son's aggressive behavior, Mrs. Black was resigned to take away John's game, although she felt she was punishing John for Andrew's disability. Taking away the game caused John a great deal of distress and his intense reaction surprised his mother. While the initial focus of the discussion was on how to modify Andrew's behavior, further interviewing revealed that both boys were inappropriately attached to the game for different reasons. John would go up to his room to play for hours at a time, using the game to escape and control a generally out of control situation. John's behavior was a reaction to what is going on at home, whether or not he was able to talk about it with his parents. The counselor helped Mrs. Black recognize and address John's needs at home and John was referred to meet with a counselor who could help him to express and deal with his mixed strong feelings. • • •

Special Considerations for Groups

Implementing successful therapeutic groups for siblings who have brothers and sisters with disabilities requires attention to a number of considerations. These include manner of participation, group size, age, gender, disability of the sibling, educational and socioeconomic level, meeting location, duration of the group and length of time for individual gatherings, and group leadership.

Participation Siblings must volunteer to come to group sessions. Some children are more comfortable than others in expressing their thoughts and feelings. Those who are coerced or required to attend will most likely not benefit from the experience and may disrupt or hamper the group process.

Group Size It is generally recommended that groups range from six to eight members (George & Christiani, 1981). Of course, size depends on the goals that the group hopes to realize. Some goals require more members than others.

Age Homogeneity in terms of age is more critical for children and adolescents than for adults. The age of the participants should be kept relatively similar for children and within a 2- or 3-year age range for adolescents. Siblings of different ages have different problems and concerns that are best shared by those of a similar age.

Gender Single-sex groups may be preferred over mixed-sex groups in some instances; however, our experience with mixed sexes has been quite positive. Gazda (1978) suggested homogeneous groups, particularly preadolescents who may be reluctant to talk in mixed groups.

Disability of the Sibling Siblings who have brothers or sisters with disabilities share many of the same concerns. It may be helpful, though, to organize sibling groups around the severity and/or nature of the disability experienced by the child. Groups could be organized around a particular disability (e.g., blindness, cerebral palsy, deafness, mental retardation, emotional disturbance, autism) or could be more generic in nature (e.g., severity of the disability). In addition, group composition could focus on where the person with the disability resides (e.g., natural homes, group homes, residential schools).

Location It is essential that the location selected for group meetings provides a comfortable, calm atmosphere. The area should be free from disruptions (e.g., telephone calls, messages, visitors) and should offer privacy. If group members know that the people in the next room can hear what is being said, it is doubtful that they will be open and express their true feelings. A useful arrangement for adolescents or adults is composed of comfortable chairs around a table. Children often seem to prefer to meet in a small circle on chairs or on the floor.

Group Duration and Meeting Time Groups can meet over a relatively brief period of time or for longer terms. We have found that our most successful groups tend to meet weekly for 5–7 weeks for preadolescents, weekly for 8- to 10-week sessions for adolescents, and bi-weekly for 8–10 sessions for adults. Naturally, the length of each session will vary according to the group's needs. It is recommended that groups for adolescents and adults meet for 1½ hours and groups for children meet for 40–50 minutes at a time. A time frame should be established at the onset of the meeting, with the provision that the session may be ended early but should not be lengthened.

Leadership The counselor leading the group needs advanced helping skills if the group is to successfully meet its goals. Most important, the leader needs to model effective communication skills and be able to demonstrate respect and empathy for each group member. The group leader must be able to encourage participation, clarify communication, and provide a source of information for the group members. Group leaders must be skilled in group dynamics and must be able to participate in communication while also observing what is happening. George and Christiani (1981) noted that effective group leaders are skilled in listening, feedback, clarifying statements, linking the commonalities of the group, questioning to generate discussion, and summarizing group communications.

ADDITIONAL CONSIDERATIONS

Throughout this chapter, we have discussed the important role that counseling can play in helping siblings to recognize, understand, and deal with their feelings and problems. Final considerations to be reviewed concern counseling younger children, discussions with parents, stepfamilies, loss and grief, referral, and innovative methods of support including Internet resources, art, books, and journaling.

Counseling Young Children

The counseling process described in this chapter seems best suited to adolescents and adults who strive to find and develop their own identities and solve critical life problems. Adolescents and adults typically have the verbal and cognitive skills to benefit from the counseling process. However, younger children may also experience a number of emotions and have problems that are similar to their older counterparts. Children who have brothers and sisters with disabilities may benefit from counseling, provided that the counselor uses the special skills and understanding necessary for this age group.

Basically, the counseling process with young children is similar to the generic counseling skills outlined previously, except that these special clients have limited verbal and cognitive skills. Young children are limited in their behavioral repertoires and often have limited vocabulary to express feelings. Patterson and Eisenberg (1983) provided the following recommendations for counseling young children:

Help young children label their feelings; children benefit from hearing their feelings restated by the counselor.

Take the young child seriously and give him or her your undivided attention during counseling.

Do not necessarily expect a lot of conversation from young children.

Use graphic materials and play with children to foster communication during the counseling session.

Unstructured play materials, such as puppets and dolls, are recommended; structured games are not necessarily very helpful to foster communication.

During play, observe and reflect on the emotions that are revealed; encourage the child to add verbal expression as appropriate.

Engage the young child in conversation about daily life events as a way of building trust and rapport.

Discussions with Parents

Counselors working with children or adolescents face a dilemma regarding their parents. How much should the counselor share with parents without violating the siblings' trust and confidence? The counselor may recognize that the parents also approach the counseling process with some apprehension. Feigon (1981), in describing a sibling group, noted that many of the families were suspicious of what their child would be told by the counselor, and many parents wanted to control the information that would be shared about the sibling. Most parents want to provide the best environment for all of their children and may be looking toward the counselor as a source of information and support to help them cope effectively with their child.

Sensitive counselors approach this dilemma in a straightforward, honest manner. They should

Meet with parents prior to the counseling session and explain in detail the counseling process and its limits, as well as describe a typical counseling scenario

Involve parents of young children in helping to establish the counseling goal (such involvement may not be appropriate for most adolescents who need to identify their own needs)

Ensure the family that strict confidentiality will be maintained regarding all communications

Provide follow-up reports to the parents. These reports should focus on the general outcome of the counseling without violating the child's trust

Provide parents with written guidelines and suggestions for developing positive family communication and for strengthening the sibling bond

Wasserman (1983) noted that when siblings are unwilling to participate in counseling, parents may serve as a go-between to reach the sibling. For example, the counselor, through parent education programs, can teach parents techniques to facilitate communication between the parent and child. Counselors can focus their attention on helping parents to learn strategies to deal with siblings' concerns, feelings, and actions.

Networking

As noted in Chapter 5, one of the important goals of information sharing is the opportunity for siblings to network with others. Siblings need to know that they are part of larger systems (immediate and extended family, friends, community) that can serve as a source of support. The counselor plays a critical role in helping the sibling to establish networks of support by linking the individual with others and with services that can provide longitudinal support. Often, extended family members (e.g., grandparents, aunts, uncles) can be utilized in a network to support the sibling. Establishing the link among siblings and other resources may not only provide support to the sibling but also to the other willing helpers in the community. Counselors should not overlook the powerful influence of these networks.

Referrals

Some siblings have problems that go beyond the counseling approach; they may be in need of psychotherapy or other more intense treatment. The counselor should refer those siblings to competent colleagues as appropriate. In the case of children and adolescents, prior to referral, the counselor must discuss the reason for referral with the parents and provide them with resources to meet their child's needs.

Stepfamilies

A stepfamily is a family in which one or both of the adult partners have children from a previous relationship. Citing U.S. Census Bureau data, the Stepfamily Foundation (n.d.) reported that more than 50% of U.S. families are remarried or re-coupled and an estimated 1,300 new stepfamilies form each day. Another study posited that one out of every three people in the United States is a stepparent, a stepchild, a stepsibling, or some other member of a stepfamily (Larson, 1992).

A stepfamily household can take many forms and represent many different sibling relationships, including siblings (biologically related), stepsiblings (not biologically related), or half-siblings (share one biological parent). Children who live in the household with the remarried couple most of the time are called *residential stepchildren,* whereas those living in the household less than half time are called *nonresidential* (or visiting) stepchildren. Stepfamilies follow an adjustment process that goes through stages of development. The time it takes for people to get to know each other, to create positive relationships, and to develop some family history is significant, usually at least 4 years, according to the Stepfamily Association of America (n.d.).

Children living with stepparents often live in two households that have different rules, routines, and expectations. Stepfamilies in which children only visit occasionally are hampered by the lack of time to work on relationships. There is less time for one-to-one time between the stepchild and stepparent and less time for family activities. "Where do I belong?" and "Where do I fit in?" are questions asked by many stepchildren. Block and Bartell acknowledged early in their book, *Stepliving for Teens: Getting Along with Stepparents, Parents, and Siblings,* the mixed feelings teens have: "My mom is getting remarried and I'm scared and angry and I don't know why" (2001, p. 5). The book serves to help adolescents regain control through advice they and other teens offer.

When a stepfamily has a child with special needs, an already complicated situation becomes even more challenging. The predictable adjustment issues of stepsiblings can take on greater importance when there is a sibling with a disability. These issues might include discipline, rules, privacy, time spent with stepparent/biological parent, finances, housing/sharing rooms, or jealousy. The impact on siblings may be different depending on the living arrangements of the sibling with disabilities—such as when the child lives with the family, visits occasionally, or has a regular visitation schedule—or when the child with disabilities is a half-sibling who is the biological child of both adult partners. Furthermore, a sibling may find himself suddenly living with a difficult situation without adequate preparation or understanding. Sibling adjustment to a stepsibling with special needs will vary as discussed here under siblings and their feelings. Consider these examples:

Doug, a sibling of a residential stepbrother	"My stepbrother won't stay out of my stuff and it's driving me crazy!"
Beth, a nonresidential sibling	"Now that my dad has remarried, it seems like I have no time with him. When I go to visit at his house, he's so busy helping Marie with Joey we don't get to do things like we used to. Dad says it's hard for them to go out with all that equipment. Besides, it's embarrassing going places with a kid in a wheel chair. It's not fair!"

Carol and Don's story illustrates how parents can help a sibling adjust to a stepsibling with special needs.

• • • Carol and Don knew it would take time for their children to get used to the idea of their marriage, but they were optimistic. Carol's son Sam, age 10, would be the only child living with them full time because Carol's daughter

Abby was away at college in another state. Don's three children, who were all teenagers, lived with their mother in the same town. Because Don was very close to his children, it was especially important to him that Steven, 16, who has Down syndrome, be included in their family even though he would not be living with them full time. Initially, Carol wasn't sure what that would be like for her and Sam. She did a lot of reading, attended programs for parents of children with Down syndrome, and spent time getting to know Steven. She even checked out For Step Kids Only and Bonus Kids, Listservs for children living in stepfamilies (see Appendix A for some examples of web sites).

The first year was a time of adjustment for everyone. Don helped a lot by making sure he maintained primary caregiving responsibility for Steven. When a decision was made about rules, it was Carol who explained it to Sam. They made sure Sam had his own room and they didn't pressure him to share his things with Steven. Now, 2 years after the marriage, Carol can honestly say they are one happy family. Sam really enjoys the times Steven comes over. Steven has a great sense of humor and makes Sam laugh with his jokes. He also likes to cook and is teaching Sam how to make his famous three-alarm chili. Although they see each other less frequently, Carol's older daughter is getting to know each of her stepbrothers and slowly becoming part of the family as well. • • •

Sibling Grief

Just as a parent of a child with special needs grieves the loss of a dream, so do the siblings. The child's sense of loss is real and deserves to be recognized. From their extensive work with families of children with disabilities, Bruce and Schultz concluded, "The traditional view of grieving as involving a series of clearly identifiable stages leading to 'acceptance' is of limited value" (2001, p. 41). Instead, the authors settled on the term, *nonfinite loss* to describe the life-span grief of these families. The cyclical nature of nonfinite loss is key to understanding how people experiencing this type of loss are feeling. The cycles are not linear; they do not have an ending point, and they are prone to recycling over and over. This model should be useful to counselors in working with siblings of children with disabilities.

Finite loss refers to grief as the result of the death of a loved one. While difficult to consider, the possibility is very real that some siblings of children with special needs will experience the death of that brother or sister at some point in their lives. We may not know completely how sibling loss affects an individual over time; however, the loss of a sibling is a profound experience with lifelong effects (White, n.d.).

In a very moving account, Katie, a young teen, describes losing her brother Chris, her initial grief over his death, and its eventual resolution:

"My heart stopped beating and I could taste sand in my mouth. Father Cliff kept talking, but I couldn't hear him. I could only hear the sound of my broken heart beating slower, and slower, and slower. I grabbed a tissue and joined my mom for the chorus of tears. I loved Chris very much and nothing would keep me from not having him as a brother. Even though I have lost Chris and there will be a hole in my heart where he should be, he is never really gone. Then, I realize that he will always watch over me, which means that I will never be alone."

—K. Rousseau, personal communication, June 7, 2005

Although children may experience many of the same feelings as adults—sadness, anxiety, anger, guilt, disbelief, confusion, and helplessness—they are more likely to express their feelings through behavior. Some behavioral signs of children's grief include

- Restlessness
- Changes in sleep patterns—sleeping more or trouble sleeping
- Difficulty concentrating at school
- Crying
- Loss of appetite
- Withdrawal from friends and previously enjoyable activities
- Increased fearfulness or sense of dread

Many excellent resources such as books and web sites are available for adults and children who are grieving the death of a child or a sibling. See the appendices for resources on grief.

Impact on Friendships

Friendships are one of the most significant relationships one has in life. Sometimes, friends can be more helpful than relatives to siblings. Parents can help in several ways. One parent found that the older sibling of a child with autism who she initially hired as a caregiver for her daughter with disabilities became a friend and mentor for her typically developing sibling. Then 8 years old, her daughter was just starting to deal with questions from peers, and was very receptive to learning from an older teen. Another parent wanted her son to feel comfortable attending individualized education program (IEP) meetings and found that her typical child benefited from inviting a friend to come with him to the meetings. Parents can also foster friendships by making sure siblings have alone time when their friends visit and giving siblings permission to spend time away from home attending activities with friends.

Listservs

"I don't know why, but outside of support groups, many siblings rarely talk about their brothers or sisters with special needs. It's not so much that we hide the fact that we have a sibling with a disability. We just don't discuss it with most people, and psychologists tell us that's not healthy. We need to talk to someone—a therapist,a best friend, other siblings in a support group, or siblings on the Internet."

—McHugh, 2003, p. 130

The internet can be a very useful source of support. Individuals who don't want to talk about their sibling in a support group can make use of Sibling Listservs available on the Internet. They give younger siblings and adults a safe place to talk, listen, ask questions, or vent. Several web sites offer Listserv discussion sites for children, teens, and adult siblings including SibKid and Sibnet, sponsored by the Sibling Support Project and SuperSib!, for siblings of children with cancer. Other Listservs may be available through specific disability organizations. A relatively new source of support, Internet Listservs are gaining acceptance and popularity. Parents of younger children will probably want to visit the sites along with their children until they feel comfortable with the process and content. The sites mentioned here are monitored and divided by age. Listservs provide a sense of community and an instant group of understanding peers that can be especially helpful to siblings who may not have support groups available in their community or siblings of children with rare conditions or other unusual situations.

"When I first found (SibNET), I thought, 'Wow! Here's a forum that's never existed before for siblings to talk to other siblings who understand completely what they've been going through. You don't have to explain yourself because they know.'"

—Lucy in McHugh, 2003, p. 138

Sibling Listserv addresses and Internet resources can be found in Appendix B.

Art

Drawing is a powerful medium of expression for many children. Art therapy has been used successfully with many populations. Raghuraman (2002) offered art therapy during a summer camp program for siblings of children with hearing impairments to recognize and talk about feelings. Through a variety of art activities, siblings learned alternate ways of communicating feelings, expressed their individuality, and made new friends. Successful art therapy topics included family pictures, things you like or dislike most about your sibling with a hearing loss, a life-sized self-portrait, and a feeling chart. Baumann, Dyches, and Braddick (2005) used art along with interviews to gain information about the sibling experience.

Touretta (2003) developed a Family Memory Book to facilitate healthy communication among family members. Designed for use in a family-strengthening program, the memory book can assist families in understanding abstract concepts such as acceptance, family values, and trust. It helps to acknowledge the importance of each family member. Art activities from The Family Memory Book can be adapted for siblings.

Books

Books can be used effectively at home, at school, and by counselors to teach about a specific disability, promote social awareness and acceptance of differences, or for bibliotherapy. *Bibliotherapy* means using books to help people solve their problems. By reading literature on a specific topic or theme, identifying with the characters and events in a story, youngsters become aware that others have the same feelings and problems that they do (Internet School Library Media Center [ISLMC], n.d.). Parents and professionals can use bibliotherapy techniques to help siblings of children with special needs to gain knowledge about specific disabilities, identify feelings, express concerns, and resolve personal problems. The child's needs must be identified and then matched to appropriate reading material. The book must be at the child's reading and interest level and the theme should match the needs of the youngster (ISLMC, n.d.).

The ISLMC Bibliotherapy and Children's Books page (http:www://falcon.jmu.edu/~ramseyil/bibliotherapy.htm) is an excellent resource for information on the history and use of literature to help children cope with a variety of problems. A wide range of children's books, disability-specific and general, with characters with disabilities is available through bookstores, libraries, and on the web. Appendix A offers an extensive bibliography of books for young children through young adult. Particularly helpful is a book by Dyches and Prater (2000) titled *Developmental Disability in Children's Literature.*

Specific uses of books vary by desired outcome. A teacher could assign a disability-themed story for a book report or read to the class when a sibling or individual has been teased. A counselor who works with children with autism may suggest books to families to help a sibling understand his or her brother's challenging behaviors. Community agen-

cies and schools can have relevant children's books available as part of a resource library. It is important that libraries, especially at schools, avoid having a separate section labeled "special needs." Organize books about disabilities in a family section or with other books sorted by type (fiction/non-fiction, biography) or reading level rather than disability.

Journaling

Older siblings may find keeping a diary, or practice "journaling," a good way to express and organize thoughts and feelings and to release tension. A good way to get started is to let siblings respond to a question or complete a sentence stem. Counselors and parents can suggest questions or sentence stems that encourage the child to think about his or her experience of having a brother or sister with a disability. For example: What do you think the future will be like for (your brother)? or My family had a great time together when we ________ (Naseef, n.d.)

SUMMARY

This chapter focuses on providing support to siblings who have brothers and sisters with disabilities to assist them in dealing with their feelings and problems more effectively. Siblings typically experience a full range of feelings, including anger, joy, sadness, excitement, frustration, jealousy, and fear. Siblings also have a number of unique problems related to their experiences with their brothers and sisters who have disabilities. Counseling is a common and direct way to help many siblings with their feelings and problems. Effective counseling enables the sibling to develop a number of skills to recognize and understand problems and to solve them in a constructive manner. The goal of counseling is to help siblings deal with their feelings and problems independently. Whether siblings are counseled individually or in groups, it is important that the counselor be someone who has the needed professional competencies to ensure an effective counseling process so that siblings reach their individual goals as quickly as possible.

Providing support to siblings is an essential and lifelong process that should begin as early as possible. Support is critical to ensure that siblings become "enabled" and not "disabled" by the circumstances of their lives. Professionals who work with children with special needs will do much to support siblings by asking one simple question: "Does he have any brothers or sisters?" and consider sibling support an important part of the services they provide.

Social Interaction Between Brothers, Sisters, and Others

How Relationships are Formed and Maintained

"I always love it when I play with my brother and he begins to grin. It is so funny when he grins, and when he laughs he makes me laugh with him. When he starts to smile and laugh, I forget all the times I was mad at him. I think to myself, 'How could I ever be irritated with this face.'"
—Adolphson et al., 2003, p.3

• • • Octavia's older brother, Monroe, has Fragile X syndrome, a genetic disability that results in mental retardation and impulsive behaviors. Monroe is 7 years old and attends first grade in a general education classroom co-taught by two educators. Octavia has just entered kindergarten at the same school.

When Octavia and Monroe are together at home, either in the playroom or in the backyard, they often quarrel. Monroe typically goes after whatever Octavia is playing with, usually resulting in screams or a tugging match. When Octavia wants Monroe to play a game, Octavia's initiations and instructions are not very effective, and she usually gives up trying to play with Monroe after a few attempts. Watching these attempts, their parents are saddened by what might have been and feel the frustration of not knowing how to reverse the situation. Monroe plays by himself; Octavia wants a playmate. • • •

• • • Ellen, age 7, is deafblind. She and her 10-year-old sister, Liz, seldom seem to interact. They don't communicate or play together. Ellen uses a computer screen to communicate and Liz has never understood how it works or how to respond back. Ellen goes away almost every summer to a camp with other children with hearing or visual impairments. • • •

• • • Morgan's younger brother, Qiom, has Down syndrome. Both boys are teenagers (ages 17 and 15, respectively) at the same high school. Qiom likes to follow Morgan around, even running out on the basketball court with him when the team comes out of the locker room. Qiom always asks to do everything Morgan does, and if he doesn't get to go with Morgan, he pouts and occasionally cries. Morgan responds with mixed emotions. On the one hand, he wants to include his brother in some of his activities; on the other hand, he wants some relief from Qiom's constant demands and hanging on. Morgan wants Qiom to know that he loves him, yet, he does not know how to reasonably share his time and activities with his brother. • • •

All three sets of siblings described above share common problems relating to brothers and sisters with disabilities. These problems focus on social interactions related to play and leisure time. Although such problems are universal in sibling relationships, siblings who have brothers and sisters with disabilities may experience unique problems related to social interaction. Some siblings with disabilities may be nonresponsive to a sibling's initiations. Other siblings may be aggressive, whereas others may be withdrawn. Some may not comprehend play instructions. Others cannot manipulate toys and games. Some siblings may never be physically able to run, jump, or wrestle; others may need to be taught play skills. This chapter focuses on social interactions between siblings, with the primary emphasis on ways in which positive social interactions between siblings can be enhanced.

THE IMPORTANCE OF SOCIAL INTERACTION

Almost all children enjoy having friends and social acquaintances. Social interactions contribute more than just opportunities to hang out and play or share confidences, however; they spur a child's development. The importance of social interaction in a child's overall development has been well documented (Dunn, 1983; Guralnick, 1976, 1978; Hartup, 1978, 1979; Kohl & Beckman, 1990; Shores, 1987; Strain & Fox, 1981). Social interactions among children provide a context in which other critical learning experiences take place. Several authors (Strain, Cooke, & Apolloni, 1976; Van Hasselt, Hersen, Whitehill, & Bellack, 1979) have discussed the demonstrated relationship between a child's level of so-

cial interaction and successful learning experiences, which leads to long-term social adjustment. Through social interaction with peers, the child has a basis for learning in the areas of sex-role development (Mischel, 1970), moral development (Hoffman, 1970), and motor and language development (Apolloni & Cooke, 1975), as well as the opportunity to develop self-esteem (Frank, 1988).

Benefits from social interaction are reciprocal in nature. That is, both children engaged in a social relationship benefit from the interaction. Children without disabilities also receive a number of benefits from their interaction with children who have disabilities (Peck, Donaldson, & Pezzoli, 1990). They develop a sense of self and learn to appreciate human differences as well as their own individuality.

Through social interaction, siblings are provided the foundation for a strong, long-lasting relationship. It is hoped that through social interactions, siblings will go beyond their family bonds and become lifelong friends. What parent does not want their children to grow in friendship with each other? Perske (1990) noted that many positive and powerful outcomes have been founded on friendships. Strully and Bartholomew-Lorimer (1988) detailed the many reasons why people with disabilities need friends. Many individuals with disabilities will have a greater likelihood of community acceptance and participation when they are engaged in friendships that extend and enhance the human services system.

Stainback and Stainback (1987) detailed strategies that have helped children with disabilities to develop and sustain friendships. These strategies have tremendous implications for brothers and sisters. Even though one often thinks about friendships as being outside of family relationships, when brothers and sisters become real friends, something special happens within the relationship. Siblings who have become friends share a unique intimacy; they enjoy each other's company and move beyond biological and legal bonds. Friendship between a sibling and a brother or sister with a disability also serves as an example to other children and the community. This example helps set the occasion for others to develop friendships with the person with the disability, thus building important social relationships outside the family. The person with disabilities who has many friends will be less dependent on the human services system (Perske, 1990). Friendships between and among siblings is the real focus of this chapter's attention to social interaction.

Turnbull, Turnbull, Erwin, and Soodak (2006) described the Circle of Friends approach to building friendships for children with disabilities. This approach includes peers (and could include siblings) who come together to form a support network to give advice, insight, and opportunities for the child with special needs in order to build friendships.

Unfortunately, some children do not socially interact with their peers. These children are often referred to as being socially withdrawn or socially isolated. In Strain and colleagues' (1976) view of childhood social adjustment, preschool children are developmentally "at risk" if they do not experience positive, reciprocal social encounters with their peers. They are at risk due to exclusion from an informal, albeit important, source of instruction and learning. Strain and his associates (1976) maintained that children who are socially withdrawn experience difficulties in acquiring appropriate language skills, moral values, motor skills, and socially acceptable methods for expressing anger and sexual feelings. Strain and Fox concurred in assessing the importance of social interaction and pointed out that children identified as socially withdrawn during their early school years are "represented disproportionally in groups of juvenile delinquents, school dropouts during adolescence, and adults who experience adjustment problems" (1981, p. 168). It has also been reported that children who interact very little with peers exhibit greater problems in school achievement (Kohn & Rosman, 1972), in interpersonal social skills during adolescence and adulthood (Ausubel, 1958), and with delinquency (Roff, Sells, & Golden, 1972), and may have greater mental health problems as adults (Cowan, Pederson, Babigan, Izzo, & Trost, 1973).

Peer social interaction seems to be a necessary ingredient for learning various social skills. If children do not interact socially, it is unlikely that they will simply "outgrow" this predisposition. Strain and Fox (1981) and McGee, Feldman, and Morrier (1997) asserted that the vast majority of evidence suggests that social withdrawal in young children can become a persistent and serious problem, and that an absence of peer interaction can contribute to behavioral maladjustment in adulthood.

SOCIAL INTERACTION BETWEEN BROTHERS AND SISTERS

When considering social withdrawal in young children, much of the professional literature deals with social interaction between a child and nonfamily members in environments outside of the home. As Hartup (1979) has pointed out, however, it is family social interaction that provides the foundation for a child's exploration of the social world so necessary for the child's social development. Siblings, in particular, provide the child with the major source of social interaction in his or her first few years of life (Kaplan & McHale, 1980). Similar to interaction with peers, social interaction between siblings can provide a basis for later achievement and development (Sutton-Smith & Rosenberg, 1970). Geisthardt, Brotherson, and Cook (2002), in their study of the friendships of children with disabilities in the home environment, noted the importance of siblings' friends in the peers/play pals of those with disabilities.

In an effort to investigate the extent of social interaction between siblings, Abramovitch and colleagues (1979) conducted a naturalistic study of sibling interaction in the home environment. Abramovitch and her colleagues observed 34 pairs of same-sex siblings in their homes and looked at social interaction along the dimensions of age, sex, and age interval between the siblings. Due to the nature of this pilot study, the researchers only looked at first- and secondborn children who were of preschool age or younger. The age intervals between the children were different for the two groups: in one group, the age interval was considered long (2.5–4 years), and in the other group, it was considered short (1–2 years). Abramovitch and colleagues (1979) observed and categorized the social interactions or lack of them by observing each pair of siblings for two 1-hour sessions. They concluded that children interact with their siblings in the home and, by so doing, acquire their first extensive social experience with other children. The male sibling pairs exhibited more aggressive play behaviors than did the female pairs. Younger siblings tended to observe and imitate their older brothers and sisters more, independent of the age interval between them. Abramovitch and colleagues (1986), in their ongoing longitudinal observations of siblings, found that the older sibling consistently initiated more aggressive and prosocial behaviors, whereas the younger sibling displayed more imitative behaviors. Thus, the older sibling dominated the relationship even as both grew older.

Lamb (1978a), in another study, observed and categorized the social interactions of 24 dyads of siblings in a laboratory setting. These dyads were composed of an 18-month-old child and his or her preschool-age sibling. Lamb found that the older siblings were more likely to vocalize and offer toys to the other child, whereas the younger siblings were more likely to watch, approach, and imitate the older siblings. Lamb concluded that older siblings serve as a model for younger siblings and that their social interaction is critical in the socialization process.

Some studies have looked specifically at the social interactions of siblings and their brothers or sisters with a disability. For example, Brody, Stoneman, Davis, and Crapps (1991) observed older children with mental retardation and their younger siblings in home settings during toy play, television viewing, and snack time. They also observed comparison groups of siblings without mental retardation. Interactions between children with mental retardation and their siblings were characterized by accentuated role differences that favored the younger sibling, whereas in the comparison group, the older sibling was the dominant one. When the older sibling had mental retardation, the younger brother or sister played more manager, teacher, and helper roles than did younger siblings in the comparison group. An interesting twist, though, is that older children with mental retardation assumed teacher and helper roles for their younger siblings more often than did older siblings in the control group. This was especially true during snack time. It also seems that the competence of the child with mental retardation predicted whether the siblings saw themselves as more equal in roles. The study also showed that context is an important variable. Dyads all engaged in similar amounts of interaction during television and snack, whereas the dyads with the older child with mental retardation interacted less during toy play than did other dyads.

Stoneman, Brody, Davis, Crapps, and Malone (1991) looked at roles of younger children (ages 4–10 years) with siblings with mental retardation compared with a control group composed of sibling dyads with children who were typically developing. The older siblings were ages 7–12 years. Role reversals were evident in the younger children who had siblings with mental retardation, most likely because these younger children assumed ascribed roles such as babysitting normally given to the older child. The researchers did not find that this affected the quality of the sibling relationship however; in fact, they found less role conflict in the dyads in which the older sibling had mental retardation. Younger siblings of children with mental retardation assumed more responsibilities for child care than did comparison younger siblings, particularly if they were sisters. Interestingly, younger siblings of children with mental retardation had fewer household chores than did comparison siblings, perhaps because they were already adding on caregiving roles. The greater the competence of the sibling with mental reatardation in adaptive and language skills, the less difference was seen in roles. The severity of mental retardation did matter because the younger siblings of less adaptively competent children with mental retardation were called on to take greater responsibility for their own personal care and for assisting with meal preparation.

Harry, Day, and Quist (1998) conducted an ethnographic study (i.e., case study) of a 12 year-old boy with Down syndrome and his three brothers in a Hispanic family. They discovered that within the family context, the siblings took on a range of sibling roles and activities to compensate for the limited participation of the child with Down syndrome. The three brothers played distinctly different roles in relation to the child with Down syndrome. These roles included "big brothering," with activities such as protecting, helping, reprimanding, keeping an eye out for the sibling, facilitating the child's inclusion (although this role was rare), parallel play, and reciprocal play. The researchers also observed the child with Down syndrome (i.e., the "target" child, which was a rare occurrence in sibling research), and found that his behaviors featured acquiescence and reliance, participation, and withdrawal. The older siblings played predominantly supervisory and facilitating types of roles and the sibling who was closer to the age of the child with Down syndrome played more parallel play with him, suggesting that neither the target child nor his siblings had much expectation of extended reciprocal play. The child with Down syndrome willingly participated when reciprocal play was initiated by brothers. Harry and colleagues noted that this study highlighted a model of the traditional Hispanic family showing hierarchical sibling authority and an emphasis on group versus individual responsibilities. They believe that because the sibling relationships were premised on hierarchy rather than equity, they automatically provided the structure and supports for the target child to participate at his level, with unconditional acceptance.

Knott, Lewis, and Williams (1995) found that children with autism spent less time with their siblings, used a smaller number and less variety of both prosocial and antagonistic initiations toward their sibling, and imitated their sibling less than did children with siblings with Down syndrome. The sibling interaction patterns of children with autism, though, were at similar levels of initiation and responding to those of siblings with a brother or sister with Down syndrome. The interactions of the siblings with a child with disabilities were more similar to each other than a comparative group of typical siblings.

Lobato, Miller, Barbour, Hall, and Pezzullo (1991) looked at preschool siblings of children with disabilities and their interactions with mothers and brothers and sisters to look at similarities and differences in behaviors and interactions. The ages of the children were 3 years to 6 years, 9 months. Disabilities represented included Down syndrome, hearing loss, and spina bifida, among others. The authors found few differences in sibling groups in either the quantity or quality of interactions with family members. They did find that siblings with a brother or sister with a disability engaged in more parallel play and social play and were more nurturing, but were not more likely to interact aggressively or be commanding or directive than in sibling dyads with two siblings who were typically developing. Sisters of children with disabilities engaged in the most social play. Interestingly, the interactions of the mothers differed: Regardless of sex, siblings of children with disabilities received twice as many directives, scolds, and reprimands from mothers as did children in the control group, even though few differences in rates of behavior (e.g., aggression) were found. At the same time, the mothers of children with special needs also displayed more nurturing behaviors, too.

Caro and Derevensky (1997) conducted an exploratory study to observe interactions between siblings with and without disabilities using the Sibling Interaction Scale. They did not find any differences in behaviors of preschool and school-age siblings that were based on having a sibling with a disability. They did find, however, that the behaviors of siblings with disabilities were found to influence the responses of siblings without disabilities. When siblings with disabilities chose to act, they assumed equal roles almost as often as siblings without disabilities. The siblings without disabilities were more likely to engage in directive roles, whereas a sibling with a disability was more likely to display no role or a passive role. Caro and Derevensky suggested that if the more directive roles displayed by siblings without disabilities reflect compliance with parental expectations, then the quality of the sibling interaction may be negatively affected. Perhaps, in order to facilitate more equal roles, parents should not give siblings so many caregiving responsibilities.

Another perspective is that, for whatever reason, the sibling with a disability plays more of a passive role, perhaps due to capability, temperament, skills, or learned helplessness, when the child has been taught over time not to be aggressive and assertive. Age did make a difference; older children were more capable of skills and were more effective at eye contact, physical proximity, and involvement.

Summers, Hahs, and Summers (1997) looked at the conversational patterns of siblings of children with disabilities and those without disabilities. The siblings of children with disabilities appeared to be less sensitive to conversations with brothers or sisters than were siblings in the control group who did not have siblings with disabilities. These researchers found significant differences between types of disabilities, too. For instance, siblings of children with Down syndrome had the highest number of total utterances and their brothers and sisters with Down syndrome had the lowest number of total utterances, indicating that the siblings were talking *at* rather than *with* the child with special needs. Siblings of children with hearing impairment showed much more typical language patterns; these brothers and sisters had learned and used sign language effectively. Interestingly, social scores were an important predictor as well. Children with better social abilities are more likely to have siblings who are more sensitive in their conversations with them. The authors suggest that perhaps siblings work harder at the relationship if the quality of the interactions is higher (or perhaps the siblings work harder because the quality is high).

Soutter and colleagues (2004) looked at information technology as a social intervention for boys with Duchenne muscular dystrophy and their families in the United Kingdom. They provided computers with e-mail capability and Internet connectivity to 74 families in an attempt to reduce social isolation. Indeed, social isolation was reduced for the children with muscular dystrophy. The greatest reported computer use was for schoolwork with siblings, and the technology fostered sibling engagement and interaction. It was noted that family life plays a huge part in the lives of children with physical disabilities, and the technology provided an outlet for the children with muscular dystrophy to be proficient and to be able to teach their siblings.

In 1996, Stormshak, Bellanti, and Bierman looked at the quality of the sibling relationship as it related to social competence and behavior control in children labeled as aggressive in first and second grade. Children who were in involved relationships with their siblings (moderate levels of conflict and warmth) showed better adjustment than did those in conflictual relationships.

Positive social interaction among children with disabilities and their siblings, however, seems to be a problem in some families. Many siblings have requested specific help in this area (Graliker et al., 1962; Schreiber & Feeley, 1965; Sullivan, 1979). Parents of children with disabilities also recognize the value of social interaction and often wish to optimize social interaction between their children. If the sibling and the child with a disability do not socialize well with each other, the loss of the benefits of such a relationship will be more detrimental for the child with the disability than for the other child. Because the child with a disability may have limited opportunities to interact with other children, social interaction with siblings often takes on increased importance. Efforts to facilitate this interaction will be important to the child's development.

A REVIEW OF METHODS TO FACILITATE SOCIAL INTERACTION

Recognizing that a problem with social interaction exists for siblings is the first step toward remediation. Questions can then be posed and intervention begun. What are the causal factors behind sibling relationships? How can interaction be enhanced? An examination of studies of peer relationships can be helpful. Although few studies have dealt directly with siblings, some researchers have been vigorously pursuing methods to help facilitate social interaction among children with disabilities and their peers. Many of their tested techniques have met with success and appear applicable to family situations. The suggestions that follow are derived directly from this literature.

Work on the facilitation of interaction between children with and without disabilities provides a foundation for parents who wish to increase interactions between siblings. Allen, Hart, Buell, Harris, and Wolf (1964) worked with a 4-year-old "socially isolate" [sic] girl who demonstrated poor articulation and frequent imaginary health-related complaints. When the child's teacher was taught to ignore socially isolate behavior and attend to positive peer contacts, the child's social interaction increased rapidly. In a related study, Buell, Stoddard, Harris, and Baer (1968) observed a 3-year-old child who rarely interacted appropriately with peers. Because this child did not play appropriately with outdoor play equipment either, the researchers began to prompt and reinforce the child's use of these materials. As the child's play on the outdoor equipment increased, she began to touch, talk to, and associate with her peers. In this study, the child maintained these social interaction behaviors, even when the teacher's prompting and reinforcement were discontinued.

In a study conducted by Strain and Timm (1974), a withdrawn 4-year-old girl with language and behavior problems was taught to play with peers. Her peers seldom engaged in positive social interaction with each other. To increase positive social interaction, the experimenters used an intensive schedule of praise for all of the children when they interacted. As a result, the child and her peers exhibited accelerated levels of social play.

Strain, Shores, and Timm conducted a study in which they trained children to increase their social initiations with withdrawn preschool children. The training of these peers primarily consisted of several sessions in which the experimenter told the peers "to try their best to get the older children to play with them" (1977, p. 291). Role-playing, in which an adult assumed the role of the withdrawn child, was also incorporated into the training program. The results of this study indicated that the peers were able to increase their social behaviors directed toward the withdrawn children, and as a result, the positive social behaviors of the withdrawn children were increased. Also, the increase in peer initiations resulted in an increase in the social initiations made by the withdrawn children. These researchers concluded that peers can be taught to increase positive social behaviors of withdrawn children.

Work conducted by several researchers (e.g., Day, Powell, & Stowitscheck, 1981; Shores, 1981; Tremblay, Strain, Hendrickson, & Shores, 1981) has led to the development of specific techniques that may enhance social interactions between children with and without disabilities. In an initial study (Tremblay et al., 1981), a group of preschoolers was observed during free-play sessions to determine which behaviors exhibited by children would facilitate social interaction. The results indicated that five specific social behaviors had a good chance of setting the occasion for positive social interaction: sharing, physical assistance, affection, rough-and-tumble play, and verbal invitations to play (e.g., "Let's have a tea party"). In other related studies, these researchers experimentally investigated the effectiveness of these behaviors with children having disabilities who did not interact with other children. In these studies, age peers were trained to initiate the identified social behaviors to the withdrawn children. When the age peers used the identified behaviors, marked increases in positive social behaviors in the withdrawn children were noted. All of the withdrawn children in these studies responded positively and consistently to verbal invitations to play, to share, and to receive physical assistance. The researchers concluded that such behavior can be used to set the standard for future, positive social behavior by children.

Similar studies were conducted to investigate specific methods that adults could employ to directly teach social behaviors to withdrawn children. Imitation-based procedures, in which adults employed modeling, prompting, and praising to encourage social interaction, were found to be effective with children who had varying levels of disability (Shores, 1981). To help teachers utilize the results of this research, a curriculum called Social Competence Intervention Package for Preschool Youngsters, or SCIPPY (Day et al., 1981), was developed and tested. Curriculum components of SCIPPY include specific instructional targets, teaching procedures, and specific activities designed to set the occasion for social interaction. Results of field tests have indicated that teachers could successfully increase positive social interaction between children with and without disabilities (Day et al., 1984).

Knapczyk (1989) conducted a study in which cooperative play among school-age children was increased. Knapczyk instructed peer mentors to participate in play activities and to adapt them to the needs of the children with moderate mental retardation. After the instructional period, the peers assisted the children with their participation in school play activities. As a result, the social interactions between the child with the disability and other children increased and were maintained over several months.

In another demonstration of how reciprocal social interactions can also be taught to children who have disabilities, Kohl and Beckman (1990) demonstrated how social interactions among preschool children with moderate disabilities could be increased using direct instructional tactics. In this investigation, six preschool children with mental retardation were instructed in reciprocal play via modeling, verbal prompting, social praise, and corrective feedback. The children were taught in dyads for 5-minute instructional periods. The prompting and social praise were gradually reduced until they were eliminated altogether.

These same training components were applied in a home setting, in which parents successfully taught their children with and without disabilities to play together (Powell, Salzberg, Rule, Levy, & Itzkowitz, 1983). In this study, a social-training package (Powell, 1982) was developed and tested with several families who had young children (ages 3–9). This training package required parents to systematically train their children to interact using specific materials and teaching methods (e.g., prompting and praising). After they learned how to teach social interactions, all of the parents were able to increase the positive interactions between the siblings during both structured and informal play sessions.

In order to increase social interactions between preschool-age children with and without autism in naturally occurring free-play activities, McGee, Almeida, Sulzer-Azaroff, and Feldman (1992) taught three children who were typically developing to use a modified version of incidental teaching. Results indicated that reciprocal peer interactions continued between dyads even when teachers' verbal praise to the peer teachers was faded across the classroom to occur only occasionally. Similar results were found with siblings in the home context (Harris, Sulzer-Azaroff, & McGee, 1992), increasing sibling–child interactions even when parents were busy in another part of the house.

James and Egle (1986) conducted a study to investigate a direct teaching approach to facilitate social interaction between children with disabilities and their brothers and sisters. In their study, they increased social interactions by teaching the sibling without a disability to initiate and maintain play. These experimenters taught the siblings during 12- to 15-minute sessions using modeling, practice, and feedback. The direct instruction included the use of prompts to the sibling, role playing, and positive social reinforcement. After the siblings were taught, the experimenters instructed the child with the disability in how to initiate play with the brother or sister. James and Egle noted that the direct prompting strategy was effective in increasing reciprocal interactions and that these interactions generalized to other settings and times. It is interesting to note that these siblings were able to maintain their interaction at a 6-month review. The remainder of this chapter highlights many of the aspects of this work as well as other specific suggestions for other age groups of siblings.

Kramer and Radey (1997) tried to directly improve sibling relationships by formal social skills training to coach siblings in prosocial sibling behaviors. The group that got the formal training was reported by mothers and fathers to show increased warmth, decreased rivalry, stable levels of agonism and competition, fewer problematic sibling behaviors, and a reduced status/power differential between siblings. The coached children were 4 to 6 years old and their siblings were younger.

A great deal of evidence indicates that parents play a major role in shaping the quality of the sibling relationship (Brody, Stoneman, McCoy, & Forehand, 1992), particularly as they respond to conflicts. Tiedemann and Johnston (1992) found improved sibling behaviors when mothers were taught strategies for promoting sharing among children. The study previoiusly mentioned by Kramer and Radey tried to directly teach these behaviors.

Hancock and Kaiser (1996) taught three older siblings to use two milieu teaching (i.e., a teaching procedure that is based on conversation and the child's interests) procedures: modeling and mand modeling (i.e., the teacher or parent models or requests a response from the child, such as "Tell me what you want") for teaching language. Single-subject multiple baselines across subjects showed that siblings were able to apply milieu teaching techniques while playing with younger siblings with language delays. Overall interactions between siblings became more positive and balanced during the intervention. Siblings in the study were at least 8 years of age because previous studies suggested that training children younger than age 8 to carry out instructional techniques can be difficult. In addition, two of the three sibling dyads generalized from the play setting to a snack setting for most of the newly acquired behaviors.

A few studies have looked at whether sibling or child behaviors generalized to a setting outside the training setting (James & Egel, 1986;

McGee et al., 1992; Powell et al., 1983). All three studies reported some generalization effects. Powell reported a generalized effect of sustained play between siblings even when parents were not present, and James and Egel reported that two of three sibling pairs generalized positive reciprocal interactions to a larger play group. No previous studies focused on siblings as communication interventionists, and only a few studied siblings in any type of role in family-based intervention.

Koegel, Stiebel, and Koegel (1998) looked at teaching preschool-age children with autism to reduce their aggression toward their infant or toddler sibling. They examined the use of functional assessment and individualized, parent-implemented intervention plans in the home setting. After the intervention, children's aggressive behaviors toward their infant or toddler sibling were largely reduced. Similarly, Belchic and Harris (1994) trained three children with autism to initiate social interactions with their peers who were typically developing and then to generalize the skills to their brother or sister at home.

These studies support the theory that children with disabilities can be taught appropriate behavior with younger siblings. Most intervention work with siblings is designed for children who are typically developing, but children with disabilities can and should be taught appropriate behaviors, interactions, and initiations, as well.

ENCOURAGING SIBLING SOCIAL INTERACTION

Most parents expect their children to play together naturally and to enjoy each other's company. Experienced parents know that this is often unrealistic. Some siblings have trouble playing with one another. When one sibling has a disability, special efforts may be needed to teach the siblings to play together. Through some simple teaching techniques and a basic understanding of how children differ in their interactions at various ages, parents can effectively facilitate social interaction (Powell, et al., 1983).

Developmental Considerations

Lefrancois (1973) has noted that children engage in three general types of play behavior: sensorimotor, imaginative, and social. Sensorimotor play involves the manipulation of toys or engaging in physical activity (running, jumping, crawling) simply for the sensations experienced. Infants typically engage only in sensorimotor play because they are un-

able to perform more sophisticated activities. Imaginative play includes a wide variety of fantasy games. Preschoolers and children in elementary school often engage in imaginative play. Social play involves interaction between two or more children. Typically, social play is governed by explicit or implicit rules that direct the children's activities.

Children do not naturally play together. They learn to interact cooperatively as they mature. The type of play interaction between siblings varies according to their age and ability. To provide a context for facilitating social interaction, it is important to consider some basic differences among four age groups of children.

Birth–3 Years Infants and very young children (birth to age 3) seldom interact socially with their siblings. Most of their play is sensorimotor and their interactions are usually directed toward parents and other adults. Occasionally, they will play with siblings, but most of their play at this stage is parallel (Parten, 1932) in that they play side by side with no real interaction. In parallel play, the children do not share nor do they employ mutually accepted rules to govern their play. This stage of parallel play is a transitional time for children, who are going from isolated play to cooperative interactions. Simple structured games and activities (finger plays, dancing, hide and seek) help the transition from parallel play to more advanced play in the next stage.

3–6 Years As children reach preschool age (3–6 years old), cooperative interactions increase. A child learns to be less selfish and begins to realize that mutual collaboration with other children can increase the enjoyment of play. During the preschool years, children learn to share, to organize fantasy games, to engage in rough-and-tumble activities, and to help one another. Also during this time, children first develop the language and communication skills needed to facilitate and maintain social interaction. Play at this stage is still simple, yet some rules and protocol are required to maintain interactions. Cooperative play at this stage typically occurs in a series of short episodes as opposed to extended durations of play.

6–12 Years When a child reaches school age (6–12), cooperative interactions with siblings and other children become more sophisticated. During this time, children engage in many forms of social play that include cooperative and imaginative activities. Rule-governed play, in which the children agree on rules and protocol, is more frequent. Sports, commercial board games, video games, and rough-and-tumble activities as well as fantasy games provide a context for social interactions. One mother described how her 9-year-old twins play together.

> *"Sydney is just wonderful at adapting games so that she and Shelby, who has cerebral palsy, can play together. That is one of the best things about them being the same age and same sex and being twins—they get along and they learn to adapt to the way each other is. In the beginning, I created games or activities for them to do together but as they've grown, I've only had to show them small ways to adapt regular toys so they can both play. On the trampoline where Shelby is stationary in a bungee jump, Sydney creates games like 'Ring around Shelby,' or they do gymnastics with Shelby in her harness on the trampoline."*
>
> —A. Sanders, personal communication, May 12, 2005

13–18 Years Cooperative interactions for adolescents (ages 13–18) involve a wide variety of activities. During this period, team sports and other sporting activities (e.g., Frisbee) comprise a large portion of social interactions. Adolescents also interact in more subtle ways. They listen to music, watch television shows, and "hang out" together. At first glance, these activities seem to be simply parallel acts; however, they usually involve more sophisticated behaviors, including sharing and verbal interactions. More overt social interactions, like going out for ice cream, participating in sports, going to dances, or developing a hobby, are just some ways in which adolescents interact with their peers.

What Parents Can Do

Within the home, parents can influence the rate and nature of social interaction between siblings. By systematically "setting the stage," parents can encourage social interaction. Through social praise and attention, parents can teach their children to increase their cooperative play behaviors. Although it is not always easy, parents can effectively teach social interaction skills to their children. Prizant, Wetherby, and Rydell (2000) suggested using developmental and ecological features of the environment to design sibling play interventions with children with autism. They suggested that naturally occurring play routines should be consistent and predictable, should foster shared control and reciprocity among the partners, and should create multiple opportunities for expressing communicative intent.

Siblings can be encouraged to interact socially with each other by focusing on the following five techniques: 1) establish reasonable expectations, 2) set *realistic* play time limits, 3) select activities and toys that lead to interactions, 4) arrange the appropriate play environment, and 5) praise the siblings for interaction. Each will be described next.

Establish Reasonable Expectations Parents should not expect siblings to interact all of the time. As mentioned earlier, social interaction between siblings seldom occurs before age 3, unless children are engaged in a structured activity. Older siblings will develop a network of friends outside of the family and should be given ample opportunity to interact with these friends. Interacting with a child with a disability may be hard work, especially if the disabilities are severe or the child is withdrawn. Parents should not expect immediate changes in interaction patterns. Long-lasting changes require time and consistency. In some cases, the disability puts a great deal of distance between siblings who may be close in age. In such cases, reasonable expectations may include acceptance of unequal interactions in which the child without a disability serves as a leader or teacher, rather than a peer, of the child. The more severe the disability, the more difficult it will be to facilitate truly equal interactions between siblings.

Set Realistic Play Time Limits Social interaction between siblings usually occurs in short episodes rather than over extended periods of time. When facilitating interaction through structured play, it is important to keep the play periods rather short. With this in mind, structured play sessions between siblings should incorporate the following guidelines:

- Preschool: 10–12 minutes
- School-age: 10–30 minutes
- Adolescence: 15–60 minutes

Naturally, these times will vary according to the children's abilities and the activity. Again, expecting the social interaction to continue for extended periods of time is simply not realistic. It may be helpful for parents to establish a schedule for regular social interactions. For young children, a daily social interaction period may be favorable. For older children and adolescents, interaction on a weekly basis is more reasonable.

Select Activities and Toys that Lead to Interaction One direct method of facilitating social interaction between siblings is to select activities and toys that will encourage interaction (Brody & Stoneman, 1986; Brody et al., 1982; Brody et al., 1985; Hendrickson, Strain, Tremblay, & Shores, 1981; McEvoy et al., 1988; Stoneman et al., 1984, 1986). Some toys and activities tend to encourage social interaction more than others. Blocks, balls, or trucks, for instance, will naturally facilitate more opportunities for interaction than will crayons, puzzles, or stuffed animals. Activities that can be used by both siblings need to be selected. The parent should locate activities that will be mutually enjoyable and not heighten the child's disability. Some activities and games can be adapted so that both siblings can interact on an equal basis. Sample interactive activities for siblings are listed in Tables 7.1, 7.2, and 7.3.

Arrange the Appropriate Play Environment When children are just beginning to learn to play together, the play environment is an important consideration (McEvoy, Shores, Wehby, Johnson, & Fox, 1990; Stoneman et al., 1987, 1989). The play environment should be free from competing activities, such as television. The focus should be on a few activities; any other play materials should be put away. Naturally, the play environment should be structured to limit interruptions and intrusions from other children. As the children develop their play skills, the environmental arrangements become less critical and should approximate normal conditions.

Praise the Siblings for Interaction When siblings interact with each other, they should be praised by their parents. Praise should be given in a way that will not interrupt the play, yet will communicate pleasure; for example, "You boys are playing so well together, Mom is so proud! Keep it up and I'll be sure to tell Grandma." Praise should always be given in a sincere manner and the specific interaction should be mentioned. "That's good" has less effect than "It's nice to see you sharing your toys" or "I'm glad you helped Tim play with the video game." Various ways to praise siblings for social interaction are listed in Table 7.4.

Praise can be overdone. Parents and teachers are advised to keep praise statements short and to the point. If the praise interrupts the play, it serves the opposite purpose. As the play interaction increases

Table 7.1. Interactive play activities and toys for siblings of preschool age

Playing with balls (e.g., catching, kicking, rolling back and forth)
Playing with blocks
Playing with tinker toys
Playing bean bag games
Acting out stories, television shows, movies
Playing tee ball
Bowling (indoors)
Playing catch with balloons
Playing tea party
Blowing bubbles
Playing spaceship
Playing store
Playing with dolls or action figures
Playing cars and trucks
Playing school
Going for wagon rides
Dancing
Singing
Playing marching band
Playing policeman, fireman, mailman, and so forth
Playing marbles
Having a conversation on a toy telephone
Fixing simple snacks
Pretending to be animals
Using puppets

over time, praise will need to be gradually withdrawn to more natural levels and opportunities; for example, during dinner, note that the children played well together that afternoon. In this way, children still receive the message, but it is given in a more natural way.

Teach Interaction Directly Some children, especially those with disabilities, need specific instruction to learn how to interact. Parents should adhere to the following guidelines:

1. Select an activity for both children that will be of interest to each of them. (The activity should call for interaction.)
2. Set aside a short period of time for the children to learn the activities.
3. Tell and show the children what to do. (Simply telling children what to do is the easiest way to teach play interactions. In some

Table 7.2. Interactive play activities for school-age children

Playing a sport for a team or couple (e.g., badminton, tennis)
Playing ping-pong
Playing video games (two-player or taking turns)
Fixing snacks together
Dancing
Playing fantasy games (e.g., playing Star Wars)
Playing cards
Playing table or board games (e.g., dominoes, checkers)
Playing ball games (e.g., catch, 7-Up, basketball)
Throwing Frisbees
Taking a walk together
Playing tag

cases, parents may need to show the children how to interact by modeling interactive behavior. When modeling, the parent may demonstrate how to share, start an activity, or help the child complete a play action.)

4. Praise the children when they interact.
5. Correct the children for inappropriate play (e.g., negative behaviors, uncooperative play, isolate play). For example, the parent can say, "John, come sit over here next to your sister and share the blocks!"

These five techniques will help to promote sibling interaction and may help to avert some of the typical interaction problems.

Table 7.3. Interactive leisure activities for adolescent siblings

Working on a hobby or arts-and-crafts activity together
Taking a class together (dance, computer)
Going shopping together
Going to a concert together
Going out to eat with each other
Fixing a meal together
Listening to music together
Playing pinball or video games (two-player or taking turns)
Playing a team sport (e.g., basketball, soccer, softball)
Watching a television show together
Going to the movies
Taking a walk together
Playing board games
Playing cards together

Table 7.4. Twenty ways to praise social interactions between siblings

Preschool age

1. "Sharing again? That's super!"
2. "That's a good way to get Tyrone to play."
3. "I'm happy that you are helping your sister."
4. "It's great when you two get along."
5. Give both siblings a kiss.
6. At the end of the pay session, give each sibling a sticker and say, "You play so nicely together."
7. "Wait until Daddy hears what good helpers I have!"
8. "You played with your brother. Good job!"

School age

9. "Oskar, Maria, you're such a great pair when you play like that!"
10. "Mike, it's awfully nice of you to help your brother play."
11. Give both siblings a hug.
12. "Wow! Playing together again? I'm pleased."
13. "Did I ever tell you that you're the greatest helpers I have?"
14. "I like to watch you play together. It makes me feel so happy."
15. "I don't believe it. Sharing and helping each other again!"

Adolescence

16. Write the adolescent sibling a short note to thank him for the interaction with his sister.
17. "Since you included your brother in your game of basketball, I'll let you stay up later tonight. Good job."
18. "Your mother and I are very proud of the way you helped Jeff."
19. "When you play with your sister, you're a great example to the other kids. Thanks."
20. Give the sibling a pat on the shoulder.

TYPICAL SOCIAL INTERACTION PROBLEMS

McDermott (1980) noted that it is a myth that brothers and sisters naturally and easily love one another. Young children are often selfish and primarily concerned with themselves, not their siblings. This natural selfishness can easily escalate into intense problems for families and is an obvious concern for parents.

Parents want their children to be friends with each other. As noted previously, it is through this close and intense friendship that siblings learn from one another. However, parental goals of developing strong sibling friendships can be thwarted if the family does not recognize and prepare for typical social interaction problems common among siblings. Overreacting toward or ignoring sibling interaction problems may only intensify them.

Little (2002) looked at mothers' perceptions of victimization among children with Asperger syndrome and nonverbal learning disorders.

Approximately 75% of the mothers surveyed reported that their children with Asperger syndrome and nonverbal learning disorders had been hit by peers or siblings in the past year and had been emotionally bullied.

Like all families, those with children with disabilities experience sibling rivalry and encounter a full range of social interaction problems (Bryant, 1982; Faber & Mazlish, 1988; McDermott, 1980; Ross & Milgram, 1982). Most sibling conflicts are no cause for alarm. These common problems may be effectively handled with a little planning and deliberate parental intervention. In some cases, however, sibling interactions can be so negative, so intense, and so chronic that parents may need to work closely with professionals to reverse these patterns. Sibling interaction problems, especially in families in which one child has a disability, may be created by jealousy and competition. Jealousy between and among siblings is quite normal. Each sibling desires and seeks the parental attention given to the other (note the research on parental differential treatment in Chapters 2 and 3). In some situations in which parental attention may be unequal due to the severity of a child's disability, the jealousy may, on the one hand, be great. On the other hand, many siblings seem to understand the nature of the disability and the legitimate need for parents to spend extra time and energy on one child. What they appreciate under these circumstances is an acknowledgment of this extra time and energy. It is hard to ask young children to understand why parents need to spend extra time with a child who has a disability. In their eyes, the child is just another sibling who is receiving special attention (i.e., parental differential treatment). Unfortunately, no matter how hard parents try to provide equal attention to all of their children, unequal distribution of attention may simply be a fact of life for a family with a child who has a disability.

Like it or not, all siblings compete with one another for parental attention and outside recognition (e.g., grades, trophies, awards). Competition between siblings is not only natural but also, in most cases, healthy. Competition helps to prepare children for the realities of life. However, when one child has a disabling condition, too much competition for outside recognition may be harmful. When a child has a severe disability, competition between the child and the sibling without a disability typically favors the latter. In such situations, the natural competition between and among siblings may require some parental limits and structure.

Too much jealousy, extensive competition, or unfair competition can cause intense sibling conflict. Jealousy and competition between siblings is usually vented in the form of fighting. Name-calling, shouting matches, wrestling, refusing to share, or taking each other's toys are common fighting styles of siblings with and without disabilities.

STRATEGIES FOR HANDLING SOCIAL INTERACTION PROBLEMS

Although some fighting is to be expected between siblings, parents can and should actively try to limit and to provide reasonable consequences for such fighting.

Limiting Sibling Conflict

Parents should not expect all conflict to be eliminated; conflict is a basic element of human interaction. However, several techniques are helpful in limiting common sibling emotions such as jealousy and competition that often lead to conflict.

Balance the Responsibilities of Siblings Do not elevate one sibling to a "surrogate parent." Although it may be easiest to allow the child without a disability to be in charge, this can cause problems, especially for siblings who are close in age. It is natural to expect the oldest child to provide more direction and leadership; however, all children should receive some experience in making decisions, having responsibility, and being in charge of certain situations. Parents need to select varying activities and situations in which all children, including those with disabilities, can be in charge. In a like manner, the authority a child has over another, especially when one child has a disability, will need to be carefully monitored. When children are given too much authority over others, they may use it to meet selfish aims, which, naturally, intensifies problems between siblings.

Recognize Siblings as Individuals A natural tendency in most families is to compare one sibling's accomplishments with another's. This type of comparing has obvious negative implications for a child who has trouble performing at the same level with siblings. Each child should be recognized individually.

Recognize Each Child's Accomplishments Each accomplishment, no matter how small or unique, needs parental attention. In some families, the parents may pour attention on the accomplishments of the child with a disability and barely recognize a sibling's good grades because they are simply expected. In many cases, it may be easy for parents to overlook a sibling's achievements in favor of the accomplishments of the child with a disability because the parents, themselves, may work harder with the child with the disability to realize his or her accomplishments. Equity in terms of recognition allows siblings to feel valued for their unique contribution to the family system.

Provide Time for Each Sibling In the ideal situation, each sibling has equal access to parents and receives equal attention from them. In reality, this is seldom the case. Children with disabilities typically require more intense parental attention. To overcome some of the problems that result from this unequal distribution of parental attention, parents should set aside special time with each of the siblings, either individually or collectively. Setting up a weekly, or even daily, time period devoted solely to the other children will communicate parental desires to attend equally to each sibling.

Prepare Children for New Siblings The presence of a new brother or sister should never come as a surprise to children. Because their lives will forever be altered by a new arrival, even the youngest child needs some preparation. Parents should talk about the new baby with siblings. Discussions about the new baby's needs, how the family will change, and what to expect from the baby will help the children to include the new sibling in their lives. At these times, parents should actively remind the children how precious and valuable they still are.

Talk About Positive Characteristics Siblings also respond well when parents focus on the positive.

• • • Chloe and Kelly were concerned about their children, Jason, age 11; and Kristen, age 9. The children seemed to talk only in negative terms about Adam, their brother with autism. After dinner and before television on Friday evenings, the parents started a game called "What's so special about . . . ." In the game, each round began by selecting a name (e.g., Mom, Jason, Adam). Each person would write down a response to complete the phrase, "What is so good about . . . ." If responses matched, each person would get a point. Adam was "coached" by his parents. In this way, the children were able to generate lists of each other's positive qualities. After a few weeks, the family devoted a Friday evening to a communal art project, a poster that displayed all of the good qualities of each family member for everyone to see, which was taped to the refrigerator door. Discussing and posting the qualities of each child not only helped the siblings and parents to focus on positive attributes but also helped visiting family members and neighbors to be aware of these good attributes. • • •

Handling Sibling Fighting

Parents need to understand that most siblings outgrow fighting and major conflict. As siblings mature, they move from the simple selfishness of childhood to competition in the early school years and, finally, to collaboration. However, parents need to actively teach their children to limit their fighting and to work cooperatively together. The following 10 strategies are helpful in dealing with fighting between siblings:

1. *Serve as an example.* Parents should strive to handle their own feelings of jealousy and competition in a cooperative manner and, thus, provide a model to the siblings. Although parents should not expect children to immediately imitate their adult behavior, good models should be evident early.

2. *Set limits for siblings.* Parents should establish a reasonable set of rules that govern interactions and should stick to them. Rules such as no throwing, no hurting, no swearing, or no name calling help to clarify the bounds of interactions. Every family will have different rules, and it is a good idea to make these rules explicit and involve the children in setting them if appropriate. This will also help parents in their "referee" role when siblings fight.

3. *Use natural and logical consequences.* When discipline is needed, parents should use a natural and logical consequence. For example, when James and Courtney are fighting over time on an Internet chatroom, the computer could be turned off for 5 minutes to help them learn to reach a compromise.

4. *Always encourage cooperation.* Parents can actively teach their children to be cooperative by praising them when they play together, share, or solve problems in a collaborative fashion. Praise or encouragement lets the siblings know that they will receive increased parental attention via cooperative behavior.

5. *Ignore simple arguments.* Parents should not attempt to intervene during all fights between siblings. A good rule of thumb is to ignore arguments that do not violate established family rules. At the same time, siblings should never be allowed to physically or emotionally hurt each other.

6. *Stay neutral.* If it is unclear who started a fight or what the fight is about, it is wise for parents not to take sides. If both children are fighting, they should be treated equally in terms of the consequences. Taking sides, especially if the side is always that of the child with a disability, will only intensify sibling feelings.

7. *Be consistent.* Teaching siblings to be cooperative instead of argumentative requires consistent and predictable parenting. If parents handle sibling problems inconsistently, siblings will be confused.

8. *Use discipline when needed.* Children need limits and consequences for their behavior. Discipline that is consistent and logical can control fighting between siblings. Several proven methods of discipline can be used to limit fighting:

   Loss of materials or a toy. This is simply the removal of the item with which the children are playing. The item should be returned when the children demonstrate that they can play together cooperatively.

   Loss of a privilege. Excessive fighting might also result in the children losing a privilege (e.g., television, dessert).

   Time out. Time out is short for "time out from positive reinforcement." In this consequence, children are removed from a reinforcing (rewarding) activity or area for a few minutes. Time out should always be used for short durations of time; 3–5 minutes is usually the best. When the children are quiet, they should be allowed to return to the activity. Time out works best if, on their return, the children are praised for cooperative activity or another activity incompatible with fighting. For example, "Now you are sharing your toys. That's what I like to see!"

9. *Share the consequences and alternatives.* A fair warning may help to stop a sibling fight before it escalates into a battle. For example, "I've asked you both to watch television quietly. If I come in again, the television will be shut off for 5 minutes" or, "It would be nice if you'd both stop fighting on your own. If you need me to help you stop, I'll do that by sending you each to your room (where there is not a television!) and taking away your snack. I'll do this in 2 minutes, so it's up to you."

10. *Be creative.* When teenage siblings fight, parents need to have more sophisticated strategies because physically moving an adolescent to a room would never be appropriate. At these ages, consequences that involve privileges are most appropriate and effective. As siblings get older, parents should openly talk with them about any conflict they cannot solve, and suggest alternative strategies for dealing with problems.

SUMMARY

All families, whether they include a child with a disability, occasionally experience problems between and among siblings. These conflicts are a natural part of development and should be expected. If parents expect siblings to automatically love and respect each other, they are setting themselves up for disappointment. In families in which one child has a disability, this is also true. It is unreasonable to expect children to inherently understand another sibling's problems and limitations. Deliberate and consistent parental attention is needed to help siblings to overcome interaction problems and to develop cooperation and appreciation for each other's uniqueness.

8

Siblings as Teachers

"Two years ago, my brother said, 'I want to play baseball like you.' Five minutes later we were outside helping him swing the bat and pitch and catch the ball. The first time he hit it, it went way over my head! Then it was my turn to bat. He pitched it to me and I hit it right back to him and he caught it. I was so amazed that he caught it (with a little help), that I called all of my friends. They were all very amazed. Now I am teaching him how to play basketball. My brother is blind and has cerebral palsy."

—Adolphson, et al., 2003, p. 7

If there is consensus on any one issue regarding brothers and sisters, it is that siblings are responsible for teaching myriad skills to one another. Siblings, because of the nature and intensity of their relationships, provide both information and opportunities for learning various motor, social, and language skills (Dunn, 1983; Lamb & Sutton-Smith, 1982; Perez-Granados & Callahan, 1997a; Sutton-Smith & Rosenberg, 1970;). This "teaching–learning" relationship can be naturally enhanced or hindered depending on varying family circumstances. Families with a child who has a disability may find it necessary and desirable to strengthen this teaching–learning relationship (Itzkowitz, 1989).

Can you remember when you learned something from a sister or brother? Do you remember teaching a particular skill? It might have been breaking in a baseball mitt, making popcorn, tying a shoe, throwing a football, using a hammer, or singing a song. Whatever the task, the memories of sharing skills and information with siblings are powerful and help to form strong and lasting bonds. Consider Michael and Christopher:

• • • Michael, age 9, has finally agreed to teach his younger brother, Christopher, age 6, how to ride a bicycle. They approach the bicycle with a great deal of excitement and anticipation. Michael has a chance to try out his teaching skills, and Christopher will have another opportunity to benefit from his brother's age and skill. Both boys struggle with the task, and after several tense moments, skinned knees, bruised elbows, and five shouting arguments, Christopher pedals the bicycle a wobbly 30 feet before coming to a crash landing. Christopher's eyes light up as he realizes he is on his way to "grownup" bicycling; Michael beams with pride as he shares his brother's success. Both boys run off to tell their mom.

Undoubtedly, Michael and Christopher will long remember this first day of bicycling. It may be a story they will share as adults and even into their later years. Perhaps the details will have blurred, but the feelings of teaching and learning will remain vivid. • • •

However powerful this story is, it does not illustrate the most common teaching and learning situation between siblings. Most teaching–learning occurs in a much less formal, more natural manner. It is probable that neither sibling recognizes his or her participation in this educative process. This informal instruction takes place in everyday situations such as wrestling on the floor, playing with dolls, arguing over a candy bar, having lunch together, or even watching television or playing on the computer. No one plans such learning; it just takes place. These informal, albeit powerful, teaching–learning situations are referred to as *incidental learning.*

To benefit from incidental learning, the learner must have at least three prerequisite skills. First, he or she must be able to interact. Second, the learner must be able to pay attention to the "teacher" (in this case, other siblings), and finally, he or she must be able to imitate in some fashion. Unfortunately, many children with disabilities are excluded from the benefits of incidental learning because they lack these prerequisites. These children will need a more formal approach if they are to benefit from the teaching–learning sibling relationship. A more formal approach implies a situation in which one sibling deliberately teaches the other. Michael's and Christopher's experience with the bicycle is an example of *formal teaching.*

The learning problems often exhibited by children with disabilities demand that the sibling "teachers" have special skills to ensure that the instruction will be successful. Developing these special teaching skills may be a focus of programs aimed at helping siblings with brothers and sisters who have disabilities. These formal teaching programs typically focus on instructing the child so that he or she can learn new skills and/or help the sibling to manage and control inappropriate behavior. Teaching siblings to be effective teachers requires a systematic plan. This chapter explores the various ways in which the teaching–learning relationship between siblings can be strengthened.

FORMAL TEACHING PROGRAMS

Since the early 1980s, considerable effort has been devoted to developing and evaluating ways to include siblings in a formal teaching–learning process. These intervention programs tend to focus on preparing siblings to effectively teach their brothers and sisters how to do specific skills and how to behave in more appropriate ways. This type of intervention program has a number of unique advantages and some potential disadvantages.

Advantages

Many siblings of children with disabilities want to help their brothers and sisters but simply do not know how (Sullivan, 1979). When they try to play with them or teach them, their efforts are rebuked or ignored, or tend to fail in other ways. This is hardly surprising because many of the learning problems exhibited by children with disabilities perplex even the most skilled professionals. The chief objective of programs to develop siblings' teaching skills, then, is to provide the siblings with specific methods that allow them to help their brothers and sisters. This type of training, advantageous to siblings with and without disabilities, can help brothers and sisters to develop more intense and more positive social relationships.

Weinrott (1974) found that siblings who participated in a formal training program greatly improved the quality of their interactions with their sisters and brothers who have disabilities. These siblings began to spend more time with the children and initiated activities to teach the children new skills. Likewise, Schreibman, O'Neill, and Koegel (1983) found that after siblings completed a formal teaching program, they began to make more positive comments about their brothers and sisters with autism. Before the program, they might have commented something like, "She causes problems a lot, but I guess we have to put up with her," but after intervention, their observations were more in the nature of, "She behaves a lot better when we work with her right" (Schriebman et al., 1983, p. 136). The improved quality of these siblings' interactions is likely a direct result of teaching them how to better instruct their brothers and sisters.

Another potential benefit of these intervention programs involves the extension of training to involve the child with a disability. Including siblings in the training significantly boosts the efforts of professionals and parents. In some cases the siblings have an opportunity to augment the instruction provided by professionals (Hancock & Kaiser, 1996). Having the sibling instruct the child in particular skills may help relieve some of the responsibility the child with the disability places on the parents and other family members. Increased instructional time may also help the child with the disability to generalize the skills learned to other daily activities. Teaching siblings to present information and skills in a systematic fashion will help to ensure that the child with a disability receives necessary instruction in many natural environments.

Formal teaching interactions between siblings have been found to help the sibling relationship to grow and develop. Weinrott (1974) demonstrated that siblings trained as teachers shifted from providing custodial care to their brothers and sisters with disabilities to engaging in more educationally related interactions. It seems reasonable that siblings who are trained to teach would spend more time instructing the child in various life skills rather than performing those tasks for their sibling.

Another advantage of this approach rests with the possible ripple effect such instruction between brothers and sisters may provide. Siblings who have been trained as teachers often pass along their skills to other siblings (Weinrott, 1974). Several siblings who have acted as teachers report that they enjoyed the participation in that it allowed them to be involved with their brother or sister in a positive way (Hancock & Kaiser, 1996; James & Egle, 1986; Swenson-Pierce, Kohl, & Egle, 1987; Tekin & Kircaali-Iftar, 2002). Providing younger siblings with a positive model for interaction will certainly influence their subsequent interactions with the child who has a disability and may help to prevent the development of sibling-related problems.

Finally, siblings who learn to systematically teach their brothers and sisters with disabilities may develop a deeper understanding of the learning and social problems faced by the child. These siblings may begin to appreciate parental and professional frustrations with the child's disability. Siblings who learn to teach may develop more reasonable and realistic expectations for the child. Research has shown that parents are more inclined to discuss problems related to the child with the siblings after the siblings attend formal training programs (Weinrott,

1974). Facilitating greater understanding and sharing of family problems is definitely a potential benefit of a formal teaching intervention program.

Disadvantages

Some families and some brothers and sisters may not find the idea of a formal teaching relationship between siblings desirable. If one of the two siblings does not want to participate in the program, he or she should not be forced or coerced to do so. Forcing either sibling to join a teaching program, no matter how well-intentioned, will only lead to greater problems between the siblings. Both children must *want* to participate in order for the program to be successful.

A second potential problem can result from the attention given to the siblings' unequal status. It may not be desirable to identify the child without the disability as "teacher" and the child with the disability as "student." In situations in which the child with the disability is always on the receiving end, he or she may become resentful of the sibling. Likewise, if the sibling is always expected to be a caregiver or the "surrogate parent," additional problems might arise. Skillful parents must balance this give-and-take to provide as balanced a situation between the siblings as possible.

Another potential problem may involve possible sibling exploitation of the child with the disability. Parents need to monitor the application of the siblings' teaching skills to ensure that the siblings do not teach inappropriate behaviors or use the child to perform jobs or chores that they, themselves, should be doing. If Tom Sawyer had employed systematic teaching skills, he may have found ways to get out of more than just whitewashing a fence!

Why Teach Siblings To Teach?

As the previous discussion illustrates, the advantages of formal teaching programs can be significant. Provided that potential problems are averted, instructing siblings in teaching methods can be beneficial not only for the brother or sister with a disability but also for other family members. The following points summarize the goals of, or reasons for, a formal teaching program:

- To foster and/or strengthen positive interaction between siblings in both formal and informal situations
- To enhance the development of positive attitudes between siblings

- To lessen the learning problems and skill deficits experienced by the child with a disability through increased instructional time with siblings who serve as "adjunct" instructors
- To enhance the generalization of learned skills from school settings to home settings and from teachers to family members
- To provide a model for untrained siblings and friends to interact with the child who has a disability

A REVIEW OF TRAINING EFFORTS

The idea of preparing siblings to formally teach their brothers and sisters with disabilities developed as a direct result of successful efforts to involve parents and age-peers in the education of children with disabilities. Reviews of the literature regarding the involvement of parents in teaching these children indicate that parents can be taught to successfully utilize systematic teaching methods (Boyd, 1980; Clements & Alexander, 1975; Johnson & Katz, 1973; Kaiser & Fox, 1986; O'Dell, 1974). In addition, several research studies have indicated that age-peers can be taught to be effective tutors with children who have disabilities (Young, 1981; Young, Hecimovic, & Salzberg, 1983). Given the successful outcomes with parents and age-peers, it seemed logical that siblings could also be involved in the systematic instruction process. Indeed, in the following studies, researchers worked successfully with siblings to teach useful skills to children with disabilities. As Perez-Granados and Callanan have noted, older siblings have unique characteristics that may enhance the teaching–learning process. Older siblings "share both parent- and peer-like qualities, providing younger siblings with more sophisticated points of view while challenging their ideas"(1997b, p. 120).

Study 1 One of the first documented attempts to instruct siblings on how to be teachers was conducted by Bennett (1973). In this study, a preschooler (age 54 months or 4½ years) was systematically trained to teach her younger sister with a hearing impairment (age 30 months or 2½ years) to use plural words (e.g., *fork/forks*). Although limited in its scope, this study demonstrated that when properly instructed, even a preschool-age sibling can be taught to be a systematic teacher.

Study 2 Weinrott (1974) developed a training program for 18 adolescent siblings of younger children with mental retardation. These adolescents attended a 6-week training program held in conjunction with a therapeutic summer camp attended by their sibling with mental retardation. Weinrott's training program consisted of the following activities:

1. Teaching the siblings basic systematic instruction skills, such as providing reinforcement, defining behavior, performing task analysis (breaking a skill down into smaller steps), or using certain prompts or phrases
2. Having the siblings observe individualized teaching sessions conducted with campers
3. Applying learned skills during intensely supervised practice sessions
4. Viewing videotapes of their teaching efforts
5. Receiving detailed feedback from skilled adults in regard to their application of the teaching skills with learners who have disabilities

The siblings also attended workshops on reading readiness, speech, medical considerations, creative dramatics, and the sociology of mental retardation. Throughout the camp program, the siblings were able to successfully apply systematic instruction skills during various teaching sessions. The siblings were also observed using their newly acquired teaching skills in informal settings, such as during mealtime and recreational events.

To evaluate this intensive training program, Weinrott asked the children's parents to complete a questionnaire several months after the training was completed. The questionnaire sought to measure the effects of the training program on general family interaction patterns. The parents reported that the siblings had "moderately" or "vastly" improved the quality of their social interaction with their brother or sister. Weinrott's analysis of this evaluation data indicated that the siblings' interaction shifted from primarily custodial care of the child with a disability to a focus on teaching the child adaptive behavior. In two-thirds of these families, parents reported that siblings were spending more time with the child with mental retardation than they had prior to the initiation of the training. Parents reported that they, themselves, were more willing to discuss problems related to the child after the sibling completed the training. Most of the parents also reported that, after the training, the siblings would comment on the parents' interactions with the child and that this feedback was helpful in maintaining consistency within the family. Parents also reported that the other children in the family who did not participate in the training learned the teaching skills from the trained sibling. Weinrott's program has helped to establish the value of training adolescent siblings to systematically instruct their brothers and sisters with disabilities.

Study 3 In 1975, Cash and Evans described a demonstration project in which three girls (ages 3–6) were taught to modify the behavior of their young siblings with mental retardation. These girls viewed a 6-minute training film that presented aspects of systematic instruction such as modeling, prompting, giving verbal information, praising, and punishment. Cash and Evans evaluated their efforts by observing each girl's ability to teach her sibling before, during, and after the training. The siblings demonstrated more systematic teaching behaviors after the training film than they had before the film.

Study 4 In a similar study, Miller and Miller (1976) included the siblings of a child with a disability in a formal teaching program. Two sisters (ages 9 and 11) of a 4-year-old girl with behavior disorders were successfully taught various strategies to teach their sister to engage in simple play activities. These sisters were instructed in general behavior management techniques such as praising appropriate behavior and ignoring inappropriate behavior. These siblings were then engaged in a speech teaching program. Using their teaching skills, they were able to increase the child's attempts to say words and to decrease inappropriate vocalizations.

Study 5 Colletti and Harris (1977) conducted a series of studies to determine the efficacy of involving siblings in home-based intervention with children with disabilities. In one study, a sister (age 10) was successfully taught to use reinforcement procedures to teach a simple skill to her 9-year-old sister who had autism. In a second study, two brothers (ages 11 and 12) who had a brother (age 9) with severe neurological impairments were taught to provide the child with reinforcement when he correctly responded to several tasks. One sibling taught simple addition skills and the other helped the brother with a disability to write the letters of the alphabet. Once these brothers and sisters learned to use reinforcement, they were able to successfully teach their sibling.

Study 6 A study in 1983 by Schreibman and colleagues demonstrated the effectiveness of teaching behavior modification skills to siblings who had brothers and sisters with autism. In this project, older siblings (ages 8–13) were paired with their brother or sister who had autism (ages 5–8) and were asked to teach a variety of skills (e.g., coin identification, number concepts, letter identification, pronoun discrimination). After their initial teaching attempts, the siblings were shown videotapes that presented information on the use of reinforcement, shaping, chaining, and discrete learning trials. In addition, the siblings received instruction on handling problem behaviors exhibited by the child. Finally, the siblings applied the newly learned skills by teaching a skill to their brother or sister, while receiving corrective feedback from the researchers.

In an evaluation of this effort, Schreibman and her associates found that, after training, all siblings increased their correct use of behavior modification skills. As a consequence of the siblings' increased skills, the children with autism showed steady improvement in the various learning tasks presented. As part of this study, siblings were also observed in less structured, generalized settings. In these settings (e.g., a living room with toys) the sibling and the child with autism were asked to play together, and the siblings' use of teaching skills was scored. The siblings demonstrated that they were able to use the newly acquired skills in these less-formal settings.

Study 7 Lobato and Tlaker (1985) conducted a study to investigate whether a 21-year-old sibling could serve as a teacher to modify the behavior of her 13-year-old brother with severe mental retardation. The sister was instructed in the use of systematic instruction and applied behavior analysis during weekly training sessions. When the sibling began instruction, she taught her brother to brush his teeth and make his bed, tasks that the adolescent could not complete before instruction. Through the sister's use of systematic teaching tactics, her brother was able to master tooth brushing and bed making skills at acceptable levels.

Study 8 In a study by Swenson-Pierce and colleagues (1987), siblings (ages 10–13) were selected to teach their younger brothers and sisters who had moderate to severe levels of mental retardation. Siblings focused their teaching on domestic skills their parents identified as important. Skills taught included making a bed, preparing snacks, and making a sandwich. The siblings were instructed in teaching skills through a five-step program:

1. Explanation of the sibling's role as a teacher
2. Instruction in prompting, time delay, and social praise
3. Instruction in task analysis
4. Role-playing of instructional tactics
5. Actual instruction with the child and feedback

In the last phase of instruction, the researchers provided feedback and suggestions to the siblings to enhance their instructional skills. As a result of this study, siblings demonstrated their ability to learn systematic instruction and the siblings with disabilities increased their competence in the instructed domestic skills. It is important to note that the siblings who participated indicated that "they enjoyed participating in the study and that it did not interfere significantly with their personal time" (Swenson-Pierce et al., 1987, p. 58). Two of the "teachers" reported that they would continue to use their new skills in other areas with their siblings.

Study 9 Hancock and Kaiser (1996) reported a study in which they taught three older siblings to use a natural teaching method to enhance the language skills of their brothers who had developmental disabilities and significant language delays. In this study the siblings (older sisters) were systematically taught to use *milieu teaching procedures* in their home while they played with their younger brothers as a way to enhance language skills. The milieu method (described by Kaiser, Hendrickson & Alpert, 1991) is a way to use natural conversation-based strategies to elicit communication. As a part of their study, they successfully prepared the three older sisters to use this technique during four training sessions that utilized written instructions, discussions, modeling, role-playing, and practicing the teaching tactic with an adult. In all cases the sisters were able to master the teaching techniques and successfully apply these to enhance language skills in play sessions with their brothers. Two of the sisters continued to use these teaching skills in unstructured settings during snack time with their brothers. It is interesting to note that all of the sisters reported that they enjoyed the experience of learning how to help their brothers and learned more about their brothers' skills as a result of participation in the training program.

Study 10 In 2002, Tekin and Kircaali-Iftar described their study in which they instructed siblings to use two different prompting techniques to help their younger siblings with mental retardation to identify animals. The sibling tutors were instructed in a small group session with an adult. The adult described the teaching tactics, modeled both the appropriate teaching techniques and negative examples, and provided guided practice and feedback. All of the sibling tutors mastered the teaching techniques and successfully taught their younger siblings to identify pictures of animals. The researchers noted, "All sibling tutors indicated without hesitation that they enjoyed delivering both procedures and enjoyed being tutors to their siblings with disabilities" (p. 291). As a result of the structured teaching sessions, the siblings described positive interactions with their younger siblings with disabilities.

Study 11 Jones and Schwartz (2004) used siblings and peers (as well as adults) as models to teach novel language skills to children with autism spectrum disorders. The children learned the new skills under the guidance of all three types of teachers, but Jones and Schwartz cautioned that siblings may not always be the best models. One of the sibling teachers, in fact, appeared bored with her teaching task. It is important to understand all of the variables when using siblings as teachers.

Although much research is still needed in regard to the utilization of siblings as teachers, the studies presented here provide an adequate foundation for this type of intervention with siblings and children with disabilities. Each of the studies has systematically added to our knowledge base so that successful instruction using the validated elements of these studies can now be prescribed. The next section of this chapter focuses on specific ways in which parents and professionals can use these research results to establish formal teaching programs for siblings.

ESTABLISHING A SIBLING TEACHING PROGRAM

The decision to use a formal teaching program for siblings should not be regarded lightly. A successful program requires intensive planning and preparation. A poorly planned program will often be more harmful than helpful. As mentioned earlier, the siblings' willingness to participate in the teaching sessions is absolutely critical to success. If Drew does not want to teach his sister Colleen (who has cerebral palsy), forcing the issue is inadvisable. Similarly, if Colleen does not want to be taught by Drew in formal sessions, then other intervention options, such as informal teaching, should be discussed. Sibling willingness is a prerequisite to the commencement of formal training.

When considering this type of formal teaching program, professionals and parents need to address the following questions as a part of the planning process:

- What skills will the sibling need to be an effective teacher?
- How should the sibling learn these skills?
- How should actual teaching sessions be arranged?
- What support will the sibling need?

General Guidelines

Before these questions can be answered, some general guidelines should be followed. These guidelines are designed to ensure that the treatment will meet its goals.

Clarify Teaching Expectations The parent or professional should list answers to the following questions:

- What do you hope to accomplish by using the sibling as a formal teacher?
- Are both children likely to benefit, or are your expectations one-sided?
- How will you know when the goal is attained?

The answers to these questions will guide the development of the intervention program.

Do Not Force Either Child To Participate Children should be willing volunteers. Neither child should be coerced to participate in any way. Teaching sessions should not interfere with favorite activities such as athletics, scouting, music lessons, playing with friends, or watching favorite television shows. Remember that forcing a child to participate will undoubtedly cause more problems in the sibling relationship.

Arrange the Environment so that Success Is Ensured

The tasks that the sibling will teach should be simple and straightforward. (Complex skills should be introduced later or reserved for professionals.) The sibling tutor should be proficient in the task to be taught; therefore, it is wise to have the sibling teach something that he or she already knows how to do well.

Keep the first few teaching sessions brief; limiting the first few sessions to 15 minutes is recommended.

Keep the teaching environment free from distractions. Turn off the television, radio, video games, computers, and stereo. Do not serve snacks while the teaching is in progress. Do not have friends over or talk on the telephone.

Select a specific area for the teaching session. A special place in the house that can be used consistently helps to maintain the uniqueness of the teaching. Inconsistency, such as changing the location, may initially confuse the children and may not convey the message that this is an important activity.

Reward Both Children for Participation It should be clear to both children that their behavior (teaching or being taught) is valued by parents and professionals. Each sibling may need separate rewards. We have found that written notes of appreciation are held in esteem by sibling tutors. These written statements have lasting value; they can be saved and shared with parents and teachers. Parents and professionals should consider giving their own time and undivided attention as a reward for the siblings.

The Sibling Teacher Should Be Older than the Child Generally, at least a 2- to 3-year age difference between the sibling and child with the disability is recommended. A younger sibling tutor, especially one who is not yet an adolescent, may have trouble understanding the role reversal. Using a younger sibling may also cause resentment on the part of the child with the disability.

What Skills Will the Sibling Need?

Past research and demonstration projects make it clear that the most effective skills used to teach siblings are derived from applied behavior analysis. These skills are sometimes referred to as *systematic instruction.* A detailed description of these techniques and how to teach them is beyond the scope of this book; however, complete reviews of these teaching skills and their use in instructing children with disabilities have been presented by Alberto and Troutman (2006) and Sulzer-Azaroff and Mayer (1977) and can be found in most basic textbooks on teaching techniques.

The value of using systematic instruction with learners who have special needs has been well documented (Alberto & Troutman, 2006; Snell, 1987; Whitman, Sciback, & Reid, 1983). All of the skills presented in applied behavior analysis have been empirically derived. In other words, the effectiveness of these skills has been clearly demonstrated in teaching–learning situations and, thus, they can be quickly taught to both adults and children. A specialized degree or certification is not necessary in order to use applied behavior analysis skills effectively. Many of the behavior and learning problems exhibited by children with disabilities have been successfully corrected using these skills. Furthermore, systematic instruction is intended for use in natural environments, such as homes, communities, and schools, as opposed to traditional therapeutic treatment centers (e.g., hospitals and clinics).

The initial skills taught to sibling teachers should be straightforward and, obviously, pragmatic. With siblings, it is not necessary to discuss theories or to compare applied behavior analysis with other treatment tactics. The goal is not to make the sibling a professional, but an effective teacher.

Basic Skills The following *basic* skills should be taught to siblings:

1. *Reinforcement:* Sibling teachers need to use reinforcement effectively in order to encourage their brothers and sisters in learning a skill or behaving in a certain way. The sibling teachers need to use praise and to learn to vary the praise in order to keep reinforcement fresh. They also need to know how to use reinforcement contingently (when the desired behavior has occurred) and consistently. They should demonstrate that they can deliver reinforcement in a timely and meaningful fashion.

2. *Prompting:* It is suggested that siblings engaged in formal teaching need to learn the following skills in producing behavior: *verbal prompting, modeling, cueing, and physical guidance.* In addition, siblings should be taught to use sequential prompting (see Lent & McLean, 1976) and to wait between prompts (see Alberto & Troutman, 2006; Snell & Gast, 1981; Snell and Zirpoli, 1987).

3. *Identification of behaviors:* Siblings need to know how to identify the behaviors that they want their brothers and sisters to learn. In order for instruction to be effective, siblings need their brother or sister's behaviors to be described to them in precise, observable terms (see Mager, 1975).

4. *Task analysis:* Much of what will be taught needs to be broken down into small, achievable components. Siblings should first attempt tasks that are easy to learn. Task analysis that focuses on a performance skill (e.g., buttoning a shirt) as opposed to an academic skill (e.g., adding three digits) should be presented first (see Alberto & Troutman, 2006, for a discussion of task analysis).

5. *Chaining:* Siblings should be taught to use either forward or backward chaining (see Alberto & Troutman, 2006 or Snell & Zirpoli, 1987). Chaining helps to link simple behaviors (e.g., holding a spoon) into complex behavioral repertoires (e.g., self-feeding).

6. *Use of discrete learning trials:* To help organize the teaching sessions, siblings should learn how to present material in discrete trials that

follow an A-B-C pattern (antecedent-behavior-consequence). This pattern can, of course, be applied in other learning situations, including behavior management.

7. *Record keeping:* The sibling should learn simple ways to keep track of the learner's progress. A simple checklist or chart may be helpful.
8. *Tactics to handle problem behavior:* Siblings should learn to ignore or to remove rewards for inappropriate behavior. Aversive tactics, however, should never be used or taught to siblings.

Advanced Skills Once the above skills are mastered, more advanced skills for siblings can be presented. These skills should only be introduced if the sibling expresses an interest in further training. If siblings have not been enthusiastic, they should not be overwhelmed by higher-level techniques. Four advanced skills include the following:

1. *Schedules of reinforcement:* Siblings should know how to use continuous, fixed, and variable schedules of reinforcement and how to alter continuous schedules to fixed or variable ones (see Alberto & Troutman, 2006).
2. *Fading prompts:* As sibling teachers become more advanced they should know how to gradually reduce the assistance, or how to fade the intrusive prompts they use for teaching (see Alberto & Troutman, 2006).
3. *Generalization programming:* Once siblings have demonstrated teaching skills in the formal teaching session, they should learn tactics to teach the child with a disability to transfer newly acquired skills to other situations. Alberto and Troutman (2006) provided an excellent review of these generalization teaching skills.
4. *Graphing:* Graphing helps to make record keeping more useful and more easily interpreted; the sibling should learn to graph data. Again, simple and straightforward methods are encouraged.

How Should Siblings Learn These Skills?

Siblings can be taught to be tutors using a variety of approaches. Simple techniques (e.g., a book that describes teaching skills) to complex methods (e.g., a multiweek training course) have been used to prepare siblings to tutor their brothers and sisters. Unfortunately, determining the best method for training siblings to be tutors is not easily accomplished. The method used to train siblings depends on available resources, the goals of the intervention program, and the number of siblings participating.

Parents and professionals should consider a number of aspects regarding the training of siblings before such a program is initiated. These factors are briefly discussed next.

The Instructor It is essential that the individuals directing and providing the training should have mastered advanced skills in applied behavior analysis. A special education teacher, psychologist, behavior therapist, or social worker may be best able to teach siblings the skills they will need to tutor their brothers or sisters. It may also be possible to recruit professors from a local university to do the training. Many professors, especially those in colleges of education, are skilled in teacher education and are familiar with problems and solutions regarding the education of teachers. Of course, the instructor will need to be familiar with the intervention goals and will need to maintain an enthusiastic approach.

Group versus Individualized Instruction Training siblings in a group is usually more desirable than working with siblings individually. Besides being more cost and time efficient, group training enables siblings to interact with other peers who are learning the same skills. Group instruction also provides an excellent format for allowing the siblings to practice teaching skills with one another before they work with their brothers and sisters.

Written Directions It is always a good idea to provide the siblings with a brief written manual that describes the teaching skills. The use of written manuals has been found to be an effective method for training nonprofessionals in teaching tactics (Clark et al., 1977; Heifetz, 1977). The manual should be written in a manner that will be easily understood by siblings. It should also contain descriptions of the application of these teaching skills with children who have disabilities.

Modeling Lecturing siblings on teaching tactics is not as effective as actually showing them how to teach. In a review of several methods used to teach unskilled people applied behavior analysis skills, modeling was found to be the most effective training method (Green et al., 1976). Siblings should see examples of how reinforcement, prompting, record keeping, task analysis, and so forth are used in the teaching process. Several of the demonstration projects described earlier in this chapter used videotapes to demonstrate proper teaching techniques to siblings.

Practice and Feedback Siblings cannot learn to be effective teachers simply by hearing about, reading descriptions of, or observing examples of teaching skills. They also need opportunities to practice the teaching skills under intense supervision. Practice provides siblings with detailed feedback, which may lessen the sibling's initial frustrations. The sibling can begin by practicing with learners who do not have disabilities. Once the sibling is comfortable in using the teaching skills, practice feedback should occur with the child who has a disability. After the practice session, the instructor should provide detailed feedback on the success of the teaching skills. Videotaping the first few sessions may be helpful in allowing the sibling to judge his or her own performance and to note where improvements need to be made. Practice and feedback sessions are often overlooked, yet they are essential to successful intervention.

Follow-Up Initial mastery of the teaching tactics does not imply that the sibling will be able to carry out a teaching program over an extended period. To eliminate any potential problems, follow-up feedback sessions should be conducted on a regular basis. This means that the instructor will observe various teaching sessions and visit with the sibling. At the very least, telephone or e-mail contact with the sibling should be maintained to answer questions and to help solve any problems encountered by the sibling. Training must be ongoing and long-term rather than a one-time effort.

How Should the Teaching Sessions Be Arranged?

When arranging teaching sessions, the parent and/or professional, along with the sibling and the child with the disability, should *specify the exact skills* that will be taught first. A menu of needed skills like that shown in Figure 8.1 should be developed. The learning tasks should be kept very simple at first to ensure that both children will be successful. The initially targeted skills may not be the most important skills for the child with the disability to learn, but should be chosen to offer the best guarantee of success for both children. After the sibling demonstrates his or her skill as a teacher, more complex skills can be taught.

Next, a *time for formal tutoring* needs to be established. The time selected should be convenient for each person involved and should not interfere with favorite activities. It is not necessary for formal tutoring to occur every day. Three times a week is usually plenty; however, the frequency of the sessions should be decided upon by the siblings and

What Nick **Needs to Learn**
name

1. Names of coins (penny, dime, quarter)

2. Colors (red, yellow, blue, green)

3. Shapes

4. Buttoning shirt

5. Use of pronouns

Teacher: Kelly, Nick's sister
name

What will be taught?

Buttoning his shirt

Colors

Figure 8.1. Sample menu of needed skills.

their parents. Keep the tutoring sessions relatively brief. A 15-minute limit is appropriate for the first few sessions. The time can be gradually increased. In most cases, it is recommended that no tutoring session extend beyond 30 minutes.

Finally, a *special area* of the home should be designated for the tutoring sessions. This will help to establish continuity as well as put a

special distinction on this activity. The area should be generally free from distractions and should be appropriate to the learning task. For example, if the sibling is teaching the child with a disability to dress, this is best done in the bedroom; likewise, learning an academic task may be done in a den or living room with access to a writing surface and books. In addition, the teaching materials used by the siblings will have more significance to both children if they are used only during the teaching sessions.

What Support Will the Sibling Need?

Like many other projects undertaken by brothers and sisters, teaching programs also need to be supported by parents in order to be successful. The type and intensity of support will be as varied as the siblings and children with disabilities participating. A suggested list of considerations for deciding how the teaching program will be supported follows.

Continuing Feedback As mentioned earlier, continued feedback sessions are an integral part of the training process. These feedback sessions also serve to provide ongoing support to both siblings. A regular schedule of feedback should be arranged. The feedback should occur immediately following the teaching session in order to be most effective.

Providing Rewards Both the sibling tutor and the child should be rewarded regularly by the parents, teacher, counselor, or social worker who initiated the teaching sessions. Rewards will vary according to the age of the children, but they should focus on encouragement, praise, and written statements of accomplishments. Occasional special treats (e.g., going for a milkshake, seeing a movie) for the sibling tutor may also offer desirable attention from a parent or other adult.

Posting Results Posting a chart with the results of the completed teaching sessions in a prominent place (e.g., refrigerator door at home, bulletin board at school) is an effective way to solicit positive comments for the siblings. In all of our efforts to foster sibling training, posting results has been the easiest and most effective way to support the teaching sessions. We have found that simple charts, similar to the ones displayed in Figures 8.2 and 8.3, have been successful.

The Daily Diary Another effective way to provide support is to encourage the sibling tutor to maintain a diary of how the teaching is going. A special journal or even a camcorder the sibling can use to

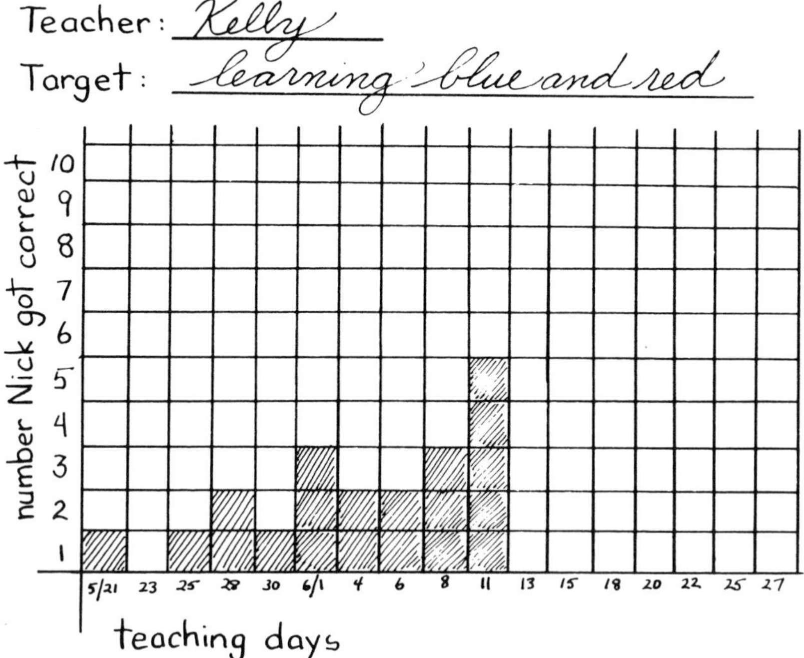

Figure 8.2. Sample progress chart for sibling teaching.

KELLY and NICK'S PROGRESS CALENDAR

MAY learning to button 1984

SUN	MON	TUES	WED	THURS	FRI	SAT
		1	2	3	4 2	5 2
6 3	7 2	8 1 I had practice today	9 2	10 2	11 2	12 3
13 4	14 2	15 1	16 Nick was sick	17 still sick	18 3	19 3
20 3	21 He did ★ one button all by himself! ★ ★	22 2	23 He came to me for 3 help	24 He did 5 buttons by himself 3	25 3	26 3
27 4	28 3 getting better!	29 2	30 Did ★ his whole blue shirt!	31		

How many times each day Kelly worked with Nick.

Figure 8.3. Sample progress calendar for sibling teaching.

record notes and observations can be purchased as a reward for the older sibling. In this way, the sibling is certain to receive special attention and recognition from others while also reflecting on the importance and value of the activity.

SHOULD SIBLINGS BE INVOLVED WITH DISCIPLINE AND BEHAVIOR MANAGEMENT?

• • • "Mommy! Sara just threw my new shoes across the room! Tell her to stop it!"

"Mother, Tanya is making the noises again and it's gross!"

"Dad, Evan is using bad words. Can I spank him, like you do when I say those words?" • • •

All children, whether they do or do not have disabilities, exhibit behavior problems at one time or another. Some children with disabilities exhibit rather frequent and intense behavior problems that cause serious anxiety for the family. It is not unusual for siblings who witness what they believe to be abhorrent behavior to run to parents for action or suggestions on what they should do. In many cases, parents are unable to give clear-cut answers because they did not witness the event. The role of the child without a disability in behavior management and discipline is, at best, controversial.

Like it or not, though, most siblings *are* engaged in teaching and behavior management. Their involvement, however, is usually haphazard. It is beneficial to recognize that siblings can serve as effective teachers in educating their brothers and sisters in proper social behavior. To do this effectively, the sibling needs specific instruction and support similar to those used to teach the child new skills.

Much like teaching new skills to children with disabilities, siblings who are involved in behavior management also need to develop skills derived from applied behavior analysis. Primarily, siblings should be taught the following skills:

1. *Reinforcement:* How to praise their brothers and sisters for good behavior.
2. *Ignoring:* How to ignore inappropriate behavior and how to remove rewards for misbehavior.
3. *Behavioral context analysis:* How to recognize the A-B-C pattern (antecedents-behavior-consequences) of misbehavior.
4. *Recording incidents of misbehavior:* How to keep track of progress and failures.
5. *Handling behavioral emergencies:* How to differentiate a behavioral emergency from common misbehavior and how to know what to do about it.

These five broad categories of behavior management skills can be easily taught to most siblings by either parents or professionals who use these procedures in everyday settings. Obviously, the sibling who has participated in training aimed at teaching new skills to siblings with disabilities does not need much additional training. Other siblings need a more intensive program to learn to use these skills in a systematic fashion. Like the training discussed previously, ample time should be given to the sibling to learn and practice these skills. Feedback and written directions should also be provided. Other guidelines are as follows:

1. If the sibling wants to help with behavior management, have him or her use the skills for a specific behavior (e.g., swearing) as opposed to *all* types of misbehavior.

2. Teach the sibling to attend to the child when the target misbehavior *is not* occurring and to ignore the child when the misbehavior is occurring.

3. Teach the sibling to keep a simple record of misbehavior and to share the data with parents on a frequent and regular basis.

4. Involve the sibling in discussions about discipline and the child with the disability. If the sibling makes viable suggestions, they should be tried and evaluated.

5. Reward the sibling often for ignoring misbehavior and for reinforcing the child's appropriate behavior. Behavior management programs are difficult to implement, even for highly skilled professionals, and children need a great deal of support.

6. *Never* allow the sibling to administer corporal punishment (e.g., spanking). The sibling should be restricted to ignoring and removing attention from the misbehavior.

7. If participation in behavior management is too stressful for the sibling, discontinue it. Suggest another strategy for the sibling so that the responsibility is removed. ("Lou, you've done a great job helping us with Victoria's crying. When she does this again, come and get me, and you can use the computer in the den while I speak with Victoria.")

8. Teach the sibling to recognize behavioral emergencies (e.g., Tim breaks a window, Joe destroys his hearing aid, Tinsley bites her finger) and to immediately report them to parents or other adults.

9. If more than one sibling is available to help, try rotating the behavior management responsibility among the children without disabilities.

10. Be reasonable in your expectations of the sibling. Do not suggest that he or she be involved in handling serious behavior problems. At no time should the sibling be held accountable for the misbehavior of the child with a disability.

Involving siblings in behavior management requires a systematic and planned effort. Success will be more difficult to detect than when siblings are teaching new skills to a brother or sister with a disability. However, if properly prepared, siblings can play a central role in teaching appropriate behavior. Their role should be limited and well supervised, and siblings should be rewarded for their extra effort.

CAPITALIZING ON INFORMAL TEACHING

Thank goodness everything we learn is not a result of formal teaching! Much of what we know is learned in an informal manner. Most likely, in many situations, we are not even fully aware that we are learning and that someone else is teaching. This informal process, described earlier, is referred to as incidental learning. In this process, we learn by observing, encountering, and solving problems; interacting with others; reading; and listening.

Indeed, most of the learning between siblings occurs in a natural, incidental fashion. Neither sibling is fully aware that learning is taking place when they are building a castle out of blocks, wrestling on the floor, arguing over a television show, or sharing a snack together. The learning just seems to take place.

Despite the "incidental" nature of this type of learning, the "teacher" and "learner" are involved in a process that has several unique components. To benefit from incidental learning opportunities, the learner must be able to attend to subtle cues and responses of the teacher and to imitate the teacher. Imitation is a critical prerequisite to benefiting from incidental teaching. Effective incidental teachers, although unaware of the skills they utilize, do, in fact, incorporate aspects of systematic teaching. They model the desired behavior, allow the learner to practice the behavior, and provide feedback to the learner.

Consider the following examples.

• • • Rachel, age 5, and Paul, age 4, are sister and brother who enjoy playing tea party with their stuffed animals.

Rachel: "Paul, bring the babies to the table. Good! Now we can make a cake."

Paul: "Okay. I'll mix it."

Rachel: "Put all the stuff in and stir it like this." [*Demonstrates.*] "Now you do it. Good! Now put it in the oven with me. Good!"

Paul: "Let's feed the babies."

Rachel: "Okay. You can get the cups and I'll get the milk."

Paul: "Real milk?"

Rachel: "No, just pretend, but it's like real milk."

Paul: "Okay." • • •

• • • Nick, age 4, and Chloe, age 2, dig around in their toy box to gather their musical toys together. Nick bangs on the xylophone; Chloe bangs on it, too. Both children laugh. Nick takes Chloe's finger and uses it to play the toy piano, which results in giggling and more laughing. The play continues as both children talk about loud and soft sounds, their Aunt Brittany who plays the harp, and so forth. • • •

Both sets of children are engaged in a teaching–learning process, albeit informally, through these simple and common interactions. The use of systematic instruction tactics can be seen in the directions given, the modeling provided, and the feedback delivered.

Some children, especially those with communication, sensory, motor, intellectual, and/or emotional problems, may have a harder time than most children in deriving the benefits of incidental learning. These children may have trouble attending to siblings or age peers and may not be able to imitate in a natural fashion. They may not be responsive to a sibling's social contact and, thus, may discourage the sibling's informal interactions. Siblings can, however, be taught to enhance this incidental learning process between themselves and their brothers or sisters with disabilities. Likewise, the child with special needs can be taught to attend to the sibling's initiatives and can be taught to initiate interactions with the sibling.

Siblings who have been taught to formally teach their brothers and sisters should have little problem using these skills during the course of the day. Use of reinforcement and prompts is effective in many environments (e.g., grocery store, shopping mall, playground, bathroom, school bus). However, the sibling may need some extra help in learning to apply these skills effectively during such informal times.

To capitalize on the power of incidental teaching between siblings, parents and professionals should

1. Remind sibling "teachers" to use their newly acquired skills (especially reinforcement, prompting, and ignoring) when they are with the child.

2. Reward the sibling when such teaching skills are applied outside of formal teaching situations ("Kelsey, I liked the way you ignored Kyler when he was misbehaving. You're certainly learning to be a good teacher!").

3. Teach the sibling to be persistent when initiating social overtures to the child. First attempts to solicit interactions often fail, and the sibling needs to learn to keep trying.

4. Teach the child with special needs how to attend and respond appropriately to a social overture from his or her sibling.

5. Suggest ways the sibling could use the formal teaching skills in informal ways ("Dan, when Jeremiah shares his toys with Jade, why don't you tell him what a good job he is doing?").
6. Encourage the sibling to spend more time with the child in mutually enjoyable activities ("Let's make some chocolate pudding, and you and Courtney can have a snack together").

FINAL CONSIDERATIONS

This chapter discusses how siblings can serve as teachers for their brothers and sisters. This type of teaching–learning interaction is one powerful way to help facilitate a positive sibling relationship. Other secondary benefits, such as increased skill acquisition and social recognition for both children, are also significant. The limitations and potential problems of such an approach to instruction, however, must not be overlooked. It simply is not for every sibling, and siblings should not be forced to participate in an intervention program. Properly instituted though, a sibling teaching program can be rewarding. The program to instruct siblings how to teach should be well planned, and follow-up training and support should be amply provided to siblings. Teaching children with learning problems is difficult work, and the successful program will recognize this by providing guidance and support to the sibling "teachers."

Earlier in this book, some of the problems between siblings are discussed. One common problem is perceived "inequality" between the children: one brother or sister is perceived as somehow "better" than another. Using siblings as teachers may, in fact, heighten this problem. Parents and professionals need to work hard to minimize this possible side effect by attending to each child's contribution in an equal fashion. "Students" who resent their "teacher" and vice versa do not tend to learn very much from each other. The balance between siblings can be maintained by regularly and frequently recognizing each child's contributions and accomplishments.

In addition to formal teaching approaches, siblings can also work with their brother or sister by helping in behavior management or providing incidental teaching. As with planned teaching of new skills by siblings to a brother or sister with a disability, parents and professionals should be supportive of siblings' efforts in these more informal areas and should provide guidance and feedback on a regular basis.

Siblings at School

Going Beyond Academics to Support Siblings' Unique Needs

"When I was a child there must have been other students at my school who had a brother or sister with a disability. I didn't know of them and they didn't know of me. There was no one I could talk to about my sleepless nights, my embarrassment and loneliness. If only we had known each other through those times, known there were others dealing with similar issues and uncertainties, it would have balanced the negative messages we had from other sources. Such support would be very simple to provide."

—Strohm, 2005, p. 226

• • • Carlos was in the fifth grade at Knowles Elementary School when his sister Elena started public school for the first time. She had attended preschool and kindergarten at a school for children with disabilities. Instead of entering first grade, as Carlos had expected, Elena was assigned to the newly established self-contained Moderate Intellectual Disabilities (MOID) class. The first few days were anything but easy for both of them. Elena seemed to cry all day and screamed when she saw Carlos walking by the room. Carlos felt sorry that his sister was in this class that he thought labeled both him and his sister. No one ever really saw the students in that "special" class unless they were coming to school or leaving at the end of the day. Carlos and Elena hardly ever had a chance to visit at recess or lunch because Elena's class sat separately in the cafeteria and most of the time, they didn't even leave the classroom for art, physical education (PE), or music, like the other students did. No wonder Carlos's friends thought that something was drastically wrong with Elena. Although he knew she had a disability, Carlos had not thought of his sister as "different" before she came to school. It really hurt when he heard some kids point and say "los retardados" (the retards) as they walked past the door to Elena's class. Unfortunately, as a result of the school structure, Carlos's classmates might never get to know his sister as he saw her: a "neat kid" who liked to laugh, listen to music, and play jokes on people.

Carlos's mother asked him to carry Elena's lunchbox and backpack, and to be responsible for the special notebook used for messages from her teacher. She said it was a comfort to know that Elena's big brother was there if she needed him. As much as Carlos wanted Elena at his school, the teasing by the other kids was very difficult to accept. Was something all of a sudden wrong with Carlos because his sister had a disability? No one ever asked for information about Elena. No one tried to understand. Although he knew that some kids teased and made fun of all of the students in the "MOID" class, Carlos did not know how to handle the teasing that was directed at him. Should he ignore it? He didn't want to join the joking and teasing, but maybe that would be best. He found out that anger wasn't the answer when he became involved in a pushing-and-shoving incident that resulted in no recess for two days!

Carlos was already struggling with these feelings when he was asked to be his sister's school aide. He was to bring Elena to her class every morning and pick her up every afternoon. The first time Carlos entered her classroom, he thought it looked like a hospital with all sorts of strange equipment, mats, wheelchairs, and even a special bathroom. When Elena's teacher, Mrs. Pike, asked Carlos if he would like to come to the class and help teach his sister, he didn't know what to do. He expressed concern about missing class time, but Mrs. Pike told him that she had arranged release time so he could help out. How could he say no, even though he didn't want to help teach Elena? Carlos resented the expectation that he was to help escort his sister, carry her things, "stick up" for her, deal with teasing, and now be her teacher. He did these things at home and was wishing for more time at school just for himself. Did he have to do everything because his sister had special needs? Well, he had "special needs" too! After the first month of school, Carlos adamantly told his mother that he wanted Elena to go to a different school!

Carlos's response is hardly surprising. He really loved his sister, but the new demands placed on him by well-meaning teachers and his mother did not take his needs into consideration. Escorting his sister to and from the bus meant that he missed out on a quick game of basketball before class and that his friends went off without him after school. Everything about the new situation seemed structured against success from the very beginning. • • •

• • • Carson and Chandler had a very different school experience. Chandler has Down syndrome and learning disabilities. Carson was in fourth grade when

Chandler started attending her neighborhood school. Chandler's program was truly inclusive. She spent most of her day in class with peers who were typically developing and received speech and physical therapy services in the classroom. Chandler and her classmates ate in the cafeteria; shared the gym and playground; attended assemblies; and visited the media center, computer lab, and art room along with the other first graders. Carson saw her sister often. Chandler loved to hug and it was not unusual for Carson and her sister to hug when they saw each other in the hall. Many of Carson's friends would wave at Chandler, too, when they saw her around the school. Chandler's teacher developed a peer-tutor program to assist her students with special needs. The peer-tutors were chosen through teacher recommendation and received training and support. They would bring Chandler to and from her bus and worked with her in the classroom, library, computer lab, and art room. Chandler even helped with the schoolwide popcorn sale.

Carson was asked to help bring Chandler's medication to school every Monday and return the empty bottle every Friday. Occasionally, she would bring money and special messages to Chandler's teacher, Ms. Mayes. Carson was happy to help Ms. Mayes because she seemed to really care; when Carson came to her room, she asked about Carson's activities, interests, accomplishments, and schoolwork. Ms. Mayes always made time to listen to Carson and did not make too many demands on her time. Of course, there were still some problems to be solved, like when someone would tease the students with disabilities, including Chandler. Once in a while someone would say something mean to Carson that would hurt her feelings or make her angry, but that didn't happen very often and many other students were eager to help out.

Carson saw other students her age serve as peer-tutors and work hard for the privilege of being with the students who had special needs. Every day, Carson observed her sister eating in the cafeteria with other students, listening to a story in the library, or seated with a fourth grader who helped her when she had difficulty paying attention. Carson watched her sister participate in school activities and establish her own friends. She observed many of the adults and children at school caring about Chandler the way she did. Her sister was "different" and would always be different, but with all of her limitations, she could still learn and enjoy school. Carson did not mind helping because she still had her own identity, her own friends, her own time, and because the responsibility was shared, her sister was not such a burden after all (H. Cash, personal communication, May 20, 2005). • • •

The obvious differences between these stories highlight two possible scenarios regarding the special problems faced by siblings in school situations. In the first story, the situation was intensified not only by the

structure of the school program but also by the teachers and parents and the expectations of each. The second story illustrates how siblings can experience positive school interactions with each other when caring adults attend to potential problems and structure situations to respect the needs of each child.

The school-age period for siblings may be the most intense in terms of their special needs. Itzkowitz (1989) found that during this period, siblings had the greatest needs for information and support services regarding their brothers' and sisters' disabilities. Because siblings spend much of their time in school, it is the logical setting for the provision of support services. The school, therefore, has a special responsibility for addressing those needs.

SPECIAL EDUCATION LAWS AND REGULATIONS RELATED TO EDUCATION

The Individuals with Disabilities Education Act (IDEA) Amendments of 1997 (PL 105-17), reauthorized as the Individuals with Disabilities Education Improvement Act of 2004 (PL 108-446), and The Americans with Disabilities Act (ADA) of 1990 (PL 101-336) are two federal laws that define and protect the rights of children with special needs with regard to access to education and participation in community programs such as child care. The trend toward inclusion in service delivery means that a child with a disability will most likely attend the same school and after-school program as siblings without disabilities.

The Individuals with Disabilities Education Improvement Act of 2004 Turnbull, Turnbull, Erwin, and Soodak (2006) identified six key principles that govern the education of students with disabilities: 1) zero reject (no school may exclude a student age 3 through 21 who has a disability.); 2) nondiscriminatory evaluation (to determine whether a student has a disability and if so the type of support needed); 3) free appropriate public education or FAPE (public education programs will be individualized to meet students needs and strengths); 4) least restrictive environment or LRE (students with disabilities must receive education in general education classes with their peers without disabilities to the maximum extent appropriate to the needs of that child, often referred to as *inclusion* or *mainstreaming*); 5) procedural due process (professionals and parents should be accountable to each other); and 6) parent participation (parents and students should participate in making decisions about a student's education). IDEA grants parents the rights to gain access to educational records and to serve on local special education advisory committees.

Unless a child's individualized education program (IEP) requires some other arrangement, the child is to be educated in the (local) school that he or she would attend if the child did not have a disability. Even for students with the most severe disabilities, the local school tends to be the least restrictive setting (Brinker, 1984; Lipsky & Gartner, 1992; Stainback & Stainback, 1992). The law mandates that a child should not be moved from education in age-appropriate regular classrooms solely because of needed modifications in the general curriculum. This policy extends to the provision of nonacademic and extracurricular services and activities, including meals, recess periods, and the services and activities. For more information go to IDEA 2004 Resources (U.S. Department of Education http://www.ed.gov/policy/speced/guid/idea2004.html) or IDEA Law and Resources (Council for Exceptional Children http://www.cec.sped.org/law_res/law/index.php).

The Americans with Disabilities Act of 1990

ADA is a comprehensive, federal civil rights law that prohibits discrimination on the basis of disability. The ADA defines *disability* as a physical or mental impairment that substantially limits one or more major life activities (i.e., working, talking, hearing, seeing, caring for one's self). There are five titles within the ADA including Employment (Title I); State and Local Governments (Title II); Places of Public Accommodation (Title III); Telecommunications (Title IV); and Miscellaneous Provisions (Title V). Businesses, nonprofit agencies, and commercial facilities that serve the public such as private schools, recreation centers, private child care centers, restaurants, hotels, movie theaters, and banks must comply with Title III of the ADA. Child care services provided by government agencies such as Head Start, summer programs, and extended school day programs must comply with Title II of the ADA. Both Title II and

Title III prohibit exclusion, segregation, and unequal treatment on the basis of disability. For example, a child care center must take reasonable steps to integrate a child with disabilities into every activity provided to others. If other children are included in group activities or field trips, children with disabilities should be included as well. Segregating children with disabilities at child care centers is not acceptable under the ADA (U.S. Department of Justice, n.d.).

Opportunity for Inclusion

Families consistently report a desire for choice regarding the educational settings for their children with special needs. When given the opportunity, to the extent possible, most families seem to choose some form of inclusion. Some parents' decisions are based on future goals and some on past experience. Kathy, for example, is passionate about wanting her son Mitch to be included. Her perspective as an adult sibling influences her goals as a parent.

> *"When I was 5, my older brother, Albert, (age 8) was shot in the head, survived, and was never the same. Being the 1960s, not a lot was known about brain injuries, so he was in and out of institutions most of his life. When he would come home to 'visit,' we didn't really know him. He never quite felt like a member of our family. He never quite fit in. Thirty years later, when my son, Mitch, was born with Down syndrome, I vowed to make sure he was always a part of our family, allowing him the same opportunities as his older sister. When school begins this fall, he will be in a 'regular' kindergarten class at the same school as his sister, just as he would have been had he been born 'normal.' I've had to stay active as his advocate to make sure he could stay in a classroom with his peers. Because I've seen the results of someone being excluded from our society because he isn't 'normal,' I know that's not what I want for my son. He deserves a chance just like every other child. It just takes him a little longer to learn."*
>
> —K. Dillon, personal communication, May 20, 2005

SPECIAL PROBLEMS RELATED TO SCHOOL

When a child with a disability enters school for the first time, it poses a potential crisis for the entire family. This is typically the first time the child has been forced to interact with others without the constant protection of parents and siblings. Parents are naturally worried about whether the child will benefit from these opportunities for interaction and from the school experience in general. Will the child be accepted by teachers and other children? Will he or she be able to participate in class activities? Parents are often concerned about their role in preparing the child for school and may worry about how their child will handle new situations and adults.

Likewise, siblings also have a number of special concerns about their brother or sister attending school. How will the brother or sister's attendance at school affect the sibling? Will the others accept the child? Will there be teasing? These special concerns need to be addressed by professionals in order to ensure that the school experience is positive for all of the children. A number of specific sibling concerns are examined in more detail next.

Competition

Competition is healthy in most cases, especially when both children have an opportunity to excel in different areas. However, competition becomes unhealthy when only *one* child is recognized, when one sibling is continually dominant, or when one receives all of the attention. When one child has a disability, competition will most likely favor the sibling without the disability. Unfair competition may result in the child with the disability experiencing extraordinary feelings of jealousy and anger toward a brother or sister. Competition should, of course, be limited. Grades and other school achievements should not be compared. Each child should be recognized for his or her unique accomplishments.

> *"Each of my boys entered the Reflections contest at their schools. Rico wrote an essay, Ryan took pictures, and Rey drew a picture; they each won at the school level in different categories. At the district ceremony, they were all there with their awards. Ryan's was not judged separately; nowhere on his entry did it say 'autism, IEP student, or special needs.' They were really excited for each other."*
>
> —S. Ramirez, personal communication, May 23, 2005

The "Brother's Keeper"

Many siblings worry that they will be expected to help care for their brother or sister at school as they do at home (Michaelis, 1980). Indeed, some siblings are asked to serve as caregivers for the child at school. They are asked to travel with the child, carry messages, keep assignments, interpret the child's communication, and even help instruct the child. This "'brother's keeper" role may impinge unfairly upon siblings' freedom. It may keep a sibling from informal, yet important, social interactions with friends. School may provide the one opportunity for a sibling to have some needed respite from the necessary caregiving that must be performed at home. Expecting the sibling to perform similar caregiving activities at school can unduly burden the sibling with additional responsibilities.

Friends

Siblings often worry about the reactions their school friends and peers will have to their brother or sister with a disability. In some cases, siblings may not have told their friends about their brother or sister. They may be concerned that their friends will reject them if they are too closely associated with the child. Some siblings also worry about the child's relationship with other children. Many siblings are concerned about how other children will treat their brother or sister with a disability. The reactions and acceptance of friends can contribute greatly to sibling adjustment.

"What helped me the most was the acceptance of my own friends. I didn't mind talking to them about Corrie and her school; I willingly answered questions and explained what Down syndrome was."

—F. Last, personal communication, May 25, 2005.

Teasing

Even in the best school situations, children with disabilities often experience teasing by other children. The most typical teasing situations are name-calling, ridicule, or putdowns (Freedman, 2002). The nature and intensity of such teasing may vary, and depends on the children's ages, the climate of the school, and the attitude of the teachers and administrators. Siblings are often concerned about teasing and how they should handle it. Naturally, it is difficult for a sibling to hear jokes and rude remarks about a brother or sister. How should the sibling handle such teasing? Is it best to ignore it, respond with anger, join in, or report it to teachers and parents? How can the sibling defend his or her brother or sister and, at the same time, not risk rejection by peers? How the school handles the teasing affects siblings. What may work in one situation will not in another.

"One day, Anna came home from the after-school program she and her sister attended. Anna witnessed three boys making fun of Lily, which upset her. She told me that she explained to them about Lily's disability but they continued to tease her. Once I brought this up to the after-school program teachers, the problem was quickly resolved."

—L.von Schmeling, personal communication, May 25, 2005

Teasing can get worse as middle school approaches, when students become very concerned about being perceived as different and not fitting in. A sibling whose brother or sister was successfully included for years in elementary school may suddenly experience teasing in middle school. When asked about teasing, Donya, age 12, the younger sister of Elijah, who has autism, noted,

> *"In elementary you weren't allowed to make fun of special needs kids but in middle school the teachers don't do anything about it."*
>
> —J. Graves, personal communication, May 23, 2005

Similarly, teasing may result from unanticipated changes at school.

> *"Lily had been attending our neighborhood school for 3 years and was well-known and loved. What I did not see coming was that the kids in Anna's grade level, the new students who did not know Lily, would be the potential problem."*
>
> —L. von Schmeling, personal communication, May 25, 2005

Most siblings react very negatively to hearing their friends or classmates use the word *retarded,* even if it was not used in regard to their brother or sister. They need to learn how to let others know in a direct and clear way that this language is hurtful and unacceptable. Some siblings ignore teasing, whereas others use humor to defuse it. Sometimes a straightforward answer works best: "You're right. She does have mental retardation. So what? All that means is that her brain doesn't work the way yours or mine does, but she's really smart in other ways."

The most effective way to deal with teasing is for schools to create a climate of acceptance to truly become places where all children are welcome and diversity is celebrated. Demystifying special education and discrediting stereotypes will happen over time in such an environment. As discussed below, the behavior and attitudes of educators along with a clear school policy can influence students' behavior. Parents can take steps to prepare siblings for the inevitable hurt feelings. When children learn effective strategies they can use in teasing situations, their coping skills are strengthened (Freedman, 2002). It is important to recognize that teasing is a problem for many children, with and without disabilities. Programs and materials are available for teachers and parents that would certainly benefit all students, including siblings. One example is a program called *Quit It!* (Froschl, Sprung, & Mullin-Rindler, 1998), which is composed of teacher-initiated and classroom curriculum-based training and support materials. Ten lessons focus on three sequential themes. The accompanying guide for parents offers practical suggestions for promoting friendship and empathy; and it includes a selected bibliography about teasing and bullying. Another example is Sticks and Stones, a web-based activity that includes Internet resources on teasing and bullying (http://www.berksiu.k12.pa/us/webquest/Burkhardt/).

Siblings Attending the Same School

When children with disabilities attend the same school as their brothers or sisters who are typically developing, the situation carries the potential either to increase problems for siblings or to help siblings to see their brother of sister as a valued and contributing member of the school community.

> *"This past school year, the art teacher sponsored 'Art by people with disabilities.' Artwork by several students with disabilities, including Lily, was on a prominent wall right outside the cafeteria. Lily's name was also listed on the wall with her classmates for achieving honor roll all year long. Anna and Max were again able to witness that Lily is a full member of the school just as they are. Anna's name is posted on the wall for reading a certain number of books. While Lily's name may never be posted there, she is recognized for other achievements. Their school does a nice job of recognizing a variety of skills by students rather than only focusing on academics. It is important to note that it is not just Lily's siblings who notice this; it is also the other students who see that Lily achieved some honor. All of this provides for a school environment that is accepting of all people and diverse abilities."*
>
> —L. von Schmeling, personal communication, May 25, 2005

Some siblings do not want to be at the same school as their sibling with special needs, preferring to "be my own person." Although influenced by a variety of factors, it is important to remember that siblings who are not typically developing might express a similar preference. A unique perspective is that of twins and multiples. Schools need to examine their policies regarding twins in which one has a disability. Many times schools require twins to be separated even though parents and siblings' preference is to stay together. One mother became frustrated by the school's repeated attempts to place her 10-year-old twins, Luke and Emily, in different classes.

> *"They don't understand that they are twins and regardless of his disability, they are going to be together. That's part of that twinship. It's just there."*
>
> —E. Spaugh, personal communication, May 24, 2005

Some schools have a policy of not placing twins in the same class. For some siblings, the negative impact of this policy can outweigh the positives. Conversely, when the twin does not want to be in the same class or school as the other, that preference also deserves consideration.

Schools need to recognize that the unique bond reported by twins exists for twins of children with disabilities.

Other Special Situations

In addition to these five major concerns, some special situations may cause added worries:

The "Mysterious" Special Education Program Siblings' knowledge of the special education program at the school may be limited. Depending on the school and the structure of the special education services, the classroom for students with disabilities may have a positive or negative reputation. In some situations, the special education program may consist of a resource room, and in others, a highly specialized self-contained classroom. Siblings may wonder what the child will experience in the room and how his or her education will differ from their own. The special education program typically contains special equipment and materials that may puzzle siblings and, at first appearance, may be frightening. Finally, special education programs are frequented by a full cadre of professionals such as physical therapists, recreational specialists, psychologists, counselors, and social workers. Siblings, like other children who are not directly involved in special education, may be curious as to what these professionals do in school, especially with regard to their brothers or sisters.

Separate versus Inclusive Segregated educational programs are rapidly becoming a service delivery model of the past as more and more children are being welcomed to inclusive public schools. For some children, this transition from separate to inclusive means full participation in general education classes and activities, whereas others may remain in self-contained classes in public schools. Sibling adjustment may be different depending on whether their brother or sister is served in a "mysterious special education class" or a class with typical peers. Siblings, especially, may have adjustment problems and special concerns when their brother or sister suddenly begins to attend their school. The student with the disability, who may be accustomed to the social environment of a separate school, may initially have difficulty adjusting to the environment of an inclusive public school. Naturally, siblings' concerns may be intensified during this period. Special measures to help prepare siblings for these changes may be needed.

Younger Siblings in Class with Older Siblings Special concerns arise when an older brother or sister with a disability is placed in the same classroom with younger siblings. In some cases, the student with a disability is retained a year or attends remedial subjects in a lower grade, which is also attended by a younger brother or sister. Increased competition in terms of grades, friends, and teacher recognition between the siblings may be one result of this arrangement. Both siblings may also find it more difficult to establish independent identities since they are together for a major part of the day.

Stepfamilies

As discussed in Chapter 6, stepsiblings of brothers and sisters with special needs have unique needs. Stepsiblings should be invited to attend school-based programs for children of divorce. Curricula may include teaching communication skills around new roles, rules, and understanding the changes for those in single-parent and stepfamily households. A major resource for stepfamilies is the Stepfamily Association of America (n.d.); their program, Smart Steps for Adults and Children in Stepfamilies is a 12-hour, research-based, educational program curriculum for remarried or partnering couples and their children. Visher and Visher (1988) offered practical suggestions for school support of stepfamilies; some of their suggestions will be helpful to siblings of children with special needs such as encouraging teacher or counselor-led discussion groups for children living in stepfamilies to discuss aspects of disability when appropriate, and to examine class material on "families" and revise as needed to be sure that all types of family groups are represented.

SCHOOL-BASED STRATEGIES

To address the special problems siblings may experience in the school situation, intervention strategies have been developed that focus on the roles of teachers, counselors, principals, and parents; sibling involvement in the IEP and transition planning process; and the school structure.

The Role of Teachers

General education and special education teachers as well as paraeducators play a vital role in helping siblings cope with special problems. The teacher's assistance is enhanced by attention to a number of strategies, highlighted next.

Recognizing the Sibling as an Individual Teachers should respect the individuality of each family member, recognizing individual contributions and strengths. Because some siblings may be preoccupied with the notion that they, too, may be considered by others as having a disability, teachers must be particularly sensitive to a sibling's need to have his or her own achievements and individual differences recognized. This recognition can be conveyed through conversations with the sibling about the sibling's activities, not the activities of the child with a disability. Calling attention to accomplishments, asking questions, and providing words of encouragement and praise communicate a respect for the sibling as an individual.

Demystifying Special Education Special education teachers are in the best position to help siblings to understand what their brother or sister with a disability will experience at school. Michaelis (1980) has suggested two strategies that might help to demystify special education. The first strategy is informal in nature and readily implemented; in fact, it calls for the special education teacher to simply *be available* to the sibling. A brief, guided walk through the classroom and straightforward explanations of materials and content can be very helpful. Friends of the sibling should also be invited to visit. Michaelis's second strategy involves the establishment of a "sibling school." A sibling school is a more structured gathering in which siblings have an opportunity to meet one another and learn about the special education program and the staff who work with their brothers and sisters. The "sibling school" program could be based on the concepts presented in Chapter 5. Another way to demystify special services is to explain all related services in an easy-to-understand manner. Meyer and Vadasy (1996) provided an excellent example of explaining special services in a straightforward manner. Teachers may want to develop brief descriptions of these services. For example, a brief description of physical therapy will help to clarify treatment goals and procedures. Such a description may also be helpful to other professionals and adults in the school.

Involving Siblings in Meetings Turnbull, Turnbull, Erwin, and Soodak (2006) suggested that it may be advantageous to ask older siblings to participate in the development of the IEP or, for young children in early intervention, the individualized family service plan (IFSP). Naturally, this should only be done with permission of the sibling, their parents, and—as appropriate—with the permission of the student with the disability. Siblings should be prepared prior to the meeting so that they understand the reasons and outcomes of the meeting as well as the process itself. These types of educational meetings, which involve planning for the future, are often richer due to the active involvement of brothers and sisters. If siblings do attend IEP, IFSP, or transition services planning meetings, their questions, opinions, or suggestions should be encouraged and respected.

"It's very important to involve your family. The more they're involved, the more they are connected. They can contribute when the going gets tough like at an IEP meeting. Andrew, age 18, is extremely outspoken. He'll ask questions like, 'Why can't this be done?'"

—E. Spaugh, personal communication, May 22, 2005

Being Available to Talk Sometimes siblings need someone to talk to who will understand their special needs and respond in a nonjudgmental manner. Milstead (1988) noted she would have welcomed the comfort of a teacher after learning that she had a sibling with a disability. "Perhaps a teacher could have taken time to chat with me and to assure me that our family would eventually adjust and that our home would return to normalcy" (1988, p. 537). As Michaelis (1980) has also noted, a sibling may have difficulty talking about feelings and problems with parents; therefore, the teacher is a likely and available adult alternative. Someone who will truly listen to problems and concerns and offer practical advice may help a sibling to deal with problems more effectively. The keys to offering support are an understanding manner and a willingness to listen.

Providing "Space" It is also important that educators sense when the sibling would rather not be involved with teachers, especially special education teachers. Some siblings prefer not to be reminded of their sister or brother's disability and actively avoid any association with the teacher. Sensitive teachers will recognize this and not presume that all siblings need or want to be involved with the special classroom or resources.

Talking with Parents When arranging meetings with parents, teachers should remember to schedule separate conferences for each child, or to at least discuss each sibling separately within the same meeting. Conferring about one child at a time helps to reinforce the idea that children, even brothers and sisters, are unique individuals. Parents need to hear about the accomplishments of each child. For instance, by noting the accomplishments of a sibling in an informal meeting with parents, special education teachers can help parents to feel recognized for some of their parenting skills. These positive aspects may have been overlooked in the midst of concentrated efforts to help the child with a disability.

Providing Educational Experiences A wonderful and touching example of sibling involvement was reported by Turnbull and Bronicki (1986). The senior author (then 11 years old), who has a brother with mental retardation, reported on teaching her class about her brother's disability. After the teaching session, a subsequent study was conducted to judge the students' attitudes about mental retardation. Similar class presentations could be organized by general education classroom teachers, provided there is a sibling in the class who is willing to share his or her experiences and knowledge. To ensure success, the sibling's teacher may wish to consult with the special education teacher and parents when planning the project.

STEPPS (Siblings To Educators, Parents, Professionals, and Siblings) is a community-based program for siblings, parents, teachers, teacher educators, service providers, and adult siblings (Cramer et al., 1997). The program goals are to identify the concerns of siblings; to link siblings to existing community resources; to stimulate the development of new opportunities for siblings, parents, and professionals in order to meet the needs of siblings; and to provide motivators through the sharing of resources and ideas. Surveys were distributed to find out from siblings and service providers what they thought siblings needed to know. Survey results show that siblings want

1. Information about disabilities
2. Opportunities to talk about feelings
3. Time to hear about the experiences of other siblings in informal group settings
4. People with whom to share feelings of pride and joy
5. Ways to plan for the future

Activities were then developed including conferences, surveys, fund raising, and program planning. Several community groups sponsored social activities for siblings. To address siblings' need for information, a local librarian who was a member of the group provided bibliographies of books and other resource materials. The bibliographies were shared with school, public and college libraries, and local bookstores, and many of the recommended titles were ordered and even selected for "story hour" at libraries and bookstores. A Sibling Day has become an annual summer school event with school district sponsorship. At Sibling Day, younger children meet with therapists to ask questions and experiment with equipment while adolescents meet to talk about concerns. When brothers and sisters evaluated Sibling Day, they spoke highly of the important time spent with other brothers and sisters.

Disability organizations could be invited to present information at school. A school-sponsored Disability Awareness Day (such as the one just described) or Week is helpful in educating students about disabilities. A sibling could be invited to share about a particular disability and answer questions. Be sure to ask privately because not all siblings would be comfortable with this role. Disability organizations such as the Autism Society of America and the National Fragile X Foundation produce materials for educating peers that may also be useful for siblings and their friends. Parents can be involved as well through sharing information, participating in activities, and providing resources and speakers for school programs.

> *"The entire school's attitude about disabilities can be affected by some education of the typical peers. A lot of the mystery and fear can be relieved this way."*
>
> —C. Dees, personal communication, May 23, 2005

The Role of School Counselors

Many schools now employ professional counselors or social workers to serve the diverse needs of children and adolescents. One role for the school counselor is to establish sibling support groups in schools (Cuskelly, 1999; Dodd, 2004; Dyson, 1998; McLinden, Miller, & Deprey, 1991). As reviewed in Chapters 5 and 6, these support groups can serve to teach siblings new information as well as help them deal with their feelings in a proactive manner.

> *"Anna has loved attending (the sibling) program while I attended the parent meeting. A school counselor led the program and about seven siblings participated. I think Anna felt so positive about it because she was in a room with other kids who walked her walk and understood intuitively her concern, love, and at times, embarrassment for her sister. Just being in a room with other siblings with similar experiences provided an outlet which I could not provide as her mother."*
>
> —L. von Schmeling, personal communication, May 18, 2005

More than any other school professional, the school counselor is in the best position to devote the time and energy needed to establish sibling groups. The counselor is likely to know which children with disabilities have brothers and sisters who can benefit from these special efforts. The counselor is also in a position to be a support for all children and, it is hoped, viewed as a nonthreatening, friendly adult. In establishing a special-based group, the counselor should attend to the suggestions in Chapters 5 and 6. In particular, the school counselor should

1. Determine the goals of the support group (informational or affective).
2. Contact parents to explain the rationale for the group and how it will operate. It may be helpful to host an informational session for parents to answer their questions and to seek their assistance and expertise.

3. Announce the establishment of the group. Children and adolescents should volunteer for these groups. Forcing them to participate will most likely lead to a negative outcome.
4. Explain the goals of the group to the teachers and other instructional personnel.

An evaluation of a support group (Dyson, 1998) identified school-age children's interests and needs for a sibling support group first. The program that developed had four components including learning about the siblings' disabilities, arts and crafts, group discussions with sharing of sibling experiences, and recreational and social times. The students rated strategies to improve relationships with their siblings as the item from the group with the highest impact, followed by awareness of special needs. The most favorite activities were around learning about the disabilities. Dyson suggested that counselors and others may benefit from this model when planning sibling programs.

The SNIP (Sibling Need and Involvement Profile) (Fish, McCaffrey, Bush, & Piskur, 1995) assessment tool helps parents and professionals identify sibling strengths and concerns in five areas including awareness, feelings, play, helping, and advocacy. Counselors may use the SNIP results with siblings or offer them to families as a strategy to encourage family discussions.

The school counselor should not assume that the teachers or other professionals have knowledge or appreciation of sibling concerns. Assisting teachers with appropriate strategies to support siblings will be helpful. One concerned teacher became painfully aware of this problem after the birth of her second child, who was medically fragile.

> *"As an art teacher and life skills teacher, I would have found it helpful to know whether kids I only saw 40 minutes a week were dealing with life-and-death issues at home with a sibling's health on a daily basis."*
>
> —B. MacDonald, personal communication, May 19, 2005

Similarly, parents and siblings stress the need for counselors to have specialized training about sibling needs, concerns, and knowledge of available resources. It is important that the counselor know who the siblings are in a school. Many siblings report feeling "invisible." Most siblings get along well, maintain good grades, and generally have positive relationships at school and are not likely to come to the attention of school counselors. Students are aware of their unique needs for support, yet are unsure about talking with the school counselor.

> *"I didn't think she understood. I'd like a counselor that knew how to handle cases like mine. The counselors really never told us they could do that. So I think they need to be trained . . . "*
>
> —J. Graves, personal communication, May 24, 2005

The Role of Principals

The principal, as the educational leader, defines the nature and tone of the school. Principals play a key role in helping all children to learn and develop their skills and abilities. To support siblings, principals can affirm that brothers and sisters with disabilities are full members of the school community. This affirmation will benefit all children, especially the sibling who may have questions about the child's acceptance. Caring and concerned principals can offer real support and guidance to children who are presented with challenges. Not only can principals make themselves available to talk with siblings but also the simple suggestion, encouragement, or pat on the back from a principal can do much to support siblings. Finally, principals can take the leadership role in meeting special needs of siblings by encouraging and supporting teachers, counselors, and parents in the establishment of special sibling programs. Elizabeth credits the principal at her children's elementary school for her son's success. Luke, who has Down syndrome, was the first child to attend his local school. Now 10, he has been included since kindergarten.

> *"He was the driving force. We were pushing for him to be included, but he [the principal] was the glue that held the IEP together. He was very involved in [developing and reviewing] the IEP and was always willing to listen to what I had to say."*
>
> —E. Spaugh, personal communication, May 23, 2005

The Role of Parents

Parents also play a critical role in ensuring that school-related problems between siblings are minimal. Parents recognize that they must share responsibility with teachers and principals in building successful partnerships that foster inclusion. They are aware that their efforts at home affect what happens at school.

> *"Why should I expect the school to if I'm not willing to include him fully in our lives, in school activities? I can't demand inclusion and then keep him separate in life."*
>
> —S. Ramirez, personal communication, May 24, 2005

• • • Juma and his sister Isoke, who has Asperger syndrome, attend the same school. She receives individual support for math and low vision while the remainder of her day is spent in an inclusive class. She participates fully in school activities and is a member of the school safety patrol. Again, a caring and committed principal made a difference.

"The principal said to give her a chance, and she made it!"

At home, the family provides opportunities for Isoke to build social and organization skills.

"I want the school to do their part, so I have to do my part." • • •

—Anonymous, personal communication, May 24, 2005

Arranging Separate Conferences Like teachers, parents should limit discussions about their children to one child at a time. Most children know when parents go to school to talk with teachers. Each sibling's needs, problems, and achievements should be discussed separately. After parent–teacher conferences, parents should sit down with the individual child and explain the meeting, stressing the positive aspects and noting problem areas discussed.

Being Careful Not To Overburden the Sibling Teachers need to give the sibling "space" at school, and parents need to limit caregiving demands placed on the sibling. Although it may be easier to ask the sibling to deliver messages, carry books and lunches, escort, or interpret, whenever possible parents should avoid expecting the sibling to perform such chores. These chores may interfere with the sibling's activities and/or restrict participation in extracurricular events. In families in which the only possible alternative for providing these needed services is the sibling, the parents should discuss these needs with the sibling and reward the sibling for assuming these extra duties. In large families, responsibilities associated with school should be shared among the siblings.

Participating in School-Related Activities Parents should attempt to provide a balance in terms of attention and resources given to each child. With a child with a disability, the demands for parental time and energy are intense. Meetings with teachers and related medical professionals, medical evaluations, parent groups, and classroom observations may all demand so much parental time that parents cannot attend to the school-related activities of the other sibling. Parental participation in each child's school activities should be kept as equal as possible, even if it means foregoing a classroom observation or volunteer tutoring.

Taking Time to Discuss Schoolwork Some parents have found it helpful to set aside time each week to talk with the sibling about schoolwork and school activities. Setting aside a particular time in the afternoon or evening for this discussion communicates recognition of the sibling's needs as well as his or her uniqueness.

Educational Involvement

Some siblings, especially those who have brothers and sisters with severe disabilities, may wish to take an active role in the school program. The two activities suggested below may allow the sibling to be involved with his or her sibling's school-based educational program or IEP.

Setting Educational Goals Many siblings have specific suggestions for what skills their brothers or sisters should learn. Parents and teachers should involve the sibling in the establishment of learning goals. The sibling can be asked to name skills that the child should learn or to list possible skills by priority. Closely related to the setting of goals is participation in educational assessment activities. Professionals conducting assessments might find it valuable to talk with siblings about the current skills exhibited by the sister or brother as well as behavioral and learning characteristics. Siblings can be a rich source of information, but they are often overlooked in the assessment process. Finally, as noted previously, some siblings may wish to attend educational meetings in which the child's school program is discussed. When parents agree that siblings should participate, they should be welcomed as active members of the child's educational team.

Using Sibling Tutors As discussed in Chapter 8, siblings often make effective instructors who are capable of teaching many skills. If the sibling wishes to be involved in actual teaching, time and resources should be given to ensure that the sibling is well prepared to tutor his or her brother or sister. The guidelines proposed may be found in Chapter 8.

The Transition Plan

IDEA requires early intervention programs to develop transition plans as part of the IFSP for all children receiving services before they reach age 3. IDEA also requires educators to develop transition plans that prepare students for adult life and to include these plans in the individual's IEP (Turnbull, Turnbull, Erwin, & Soodak, 2006). Although IDEA does not require formal transition planning earlier than age 14, all IEP goals and objectives should be set with an eye to how they may affect the child's future school or post-school experiences. Siblings have a unique perspective regarding the strengths, needs, and vision for the future for their brother or sister with special needs. For this reason, sibling participation in adult transition planning meetings and activities should be especially encouraged, as long as the siblings and the person with disabilities are in agreement that this should occur.

Making a Commitment to Inclusion

Making a system-wide commitment to inclusion is essential to ensure its success. In their study of sibling acceptance and interaction, Harry, Day, and Quist concluded, "It is up to schools to foster an atmosphere in which interactions are likely to lead to positive relationships and a sense of membership for all" (1998, p. 297). Furthermore, they advocated for inclusive and continuous school structures so that a full range of activities and opportunities for interaction can occur.

Providing a warm and welcoming environment in which all types of diversity are respected is an important responsibility. As one parent explained,

> *"When the school climate does not support intolerance of any differences and celebrates differences in children, then the child with a disability is accepted and viewed as a member of the student body. It absolutely cannot be something done in one assembly or during a particular month but rather has to be embedded in every aspect of the school program."*
>
> —J. Swett, personal communication, May 18, 2005

Parents recognize and appreciate efforts to foster a positive school climate.

> *"I believe the most important thing the schools have done for my children is to provide a safe and caring environment where all three of them are welcomed. They have modeled appropriate responses to teasing, achievements, and occasionally, Lily's misbehavior. Anna and Max, and really all students, observe the adults in the building and generate their personal responses based upon what the adults model for them."*
>
> —L. von Schmeling, personal communication, May 25, 2005

Parents also report that negative effects on siblings can last a lifetime.

> *"My children [who are typically developing] are now adults and doing well, but the school's lack of empathy, compassion, and support made adolescence so painful for them, and no matter how hard I tried to collaborate, the culture of the district and its leadership was not conducive to change."*
>
> —M. Sampson, personal communication, May 18, 2005

Gallagher and colleagues (2000) looked at siblings' and parents' perspectives on the inclusion of students with moderate or severe disabilities in educational and community settings. Siblings (and parents) shared similar views. They believed that children with disabilities are capable and can function and achieve in the real world. Both groups expressed a desire to have children with disabilities around children who are typically developing as much as possible in order to have models for skills and behaviors, and expressed general satisfaction with the amount and type of inclusion both at school and in the community. Parents and siblings agreed that the students with disabilities model and emulate their siblings who are typically developing. Of note, though, was a general lack of knowledge and involvement of the siblings regarding school inclusion.

The school must be structured so that all students interact on a regular basis. This practice will foster understanding and involvement of all students regarding school inclusion policies. Isolating children or "hiding" special education classes in separate areas perpetuates myths and misinformation about students with disabilities. Having a brother or sister in "the basement" or "special wing" can have a negative effect on a sibling. A strong commitment toward full school inclusion implies that all students can, and are even expected to, participate in the school community. Inclusion implies attending the same classes; going to the cafeteria and playground with other students; attending assemblies, using the library, computer room, and gymnasium; and interacting with many teachers and a variety of students. Seeing the participation of a brother or sister in an accepting school community and their involvement in all aspects of school life can have a profound, positive effect on siblings.

Fostering Schoolwide Awareness School systems can minimize the problems siblings face in the school setting by teaching students and teachers about disabilities. The school community can increase its awareness of the needs and problems experienced by students with disabilities as well as their achievements and contributions. Such training can foster positive attitudes toward students with special needs (Anderson & Milliren, 1983). Letting children who are typically developing try out a wheelchair, be blindfolded, or listen in class while wearing earplugs can help them to experience in a small way what it is like to have a disability. Such activities can help students relate to the person with a disability and their siblings. With understanding, these activities may encourage students without disabilities to help or befriend someone living with disabilities.

Teaching Across Subjects Science, social studies, art, and drama programs, as well as films and books with disability themes can help teach disability awareness. In one school, an elementary art teacher organized an exhibit of art by people with disabilities. Artwork by students and famous people with disabilities was displayed in a prominent place in the school. As positive attitudes toward students with special needs increases, it will most assuredly have a positive impact on their siblings. As a part of this awareness, school leaders should make it clear that teasing students with disabilities or joking about them will not be tolerated. Established policies and procedures regarding teasing and joking will make it easier for siblings to deal with these behaviors. Naturally, no policy will control all teasing or joking, but a school policy may help to prevent some of it and can be a source of support for siblings.

SUMMARY

Children with disabilities will likely attend the same school as their siblings at some point. This situation carries the potential either to increase problems for siblings or to help siblings see their brother or sister as a valued and contributing member of a total school community. To achieve the latter goal, teachers, school counselors, and administrators must play a critical role. Teachers need to recognize and reinforce each sibling's individuality and be available to talk with siblings and explain the special education program. They must also be sensitive to the sibling's need for anonymity and "space," if desired. School counselors must find out who the siblings are and be sensitive to their needs, developing programs and resources as needed. Administrators set the tone of inclusion and diversity for the school. Likewise, parents must be careful to be effective partners in the process. They should not overburden the sibling with extra caregiving demands related to school. Both teachers and parents should provide an opportunity for siblings to become involved in the child's educational program to the extent that the siblings are interested.

Finally, school systems must make concerted efforts to fully integrate all children so that they can participate in all the aspects of school life. Making a commitment to full inclusion will clearly communicate to siblings that their brothers and sisters are valued members of the school community.

> *"Lily unknowingly provides a barometer by which the rest of her family judges this membership. Lily hops on a school bus with her siblings, attends school with her siblings, and participates in other community events with her family. This provides us with a stable and comfortable place from which to confront the challenges that we often experience as a family living with disability."*
>
> —L. von Schmeling, personal communication, May 24, 2005

Siblings as Adults

Building Secure Futures

"My brother, Eric, was in our wedding and cried before the ceremony even began. When my new husband and I prepared to leave the reception, Eric clutched onto me for dear life; I think he thought I was leaving forever. My own children love their Uncle Eric and he is a very big part of their lives as well. He spends weekends with us at our home. When we purchased a home, he came with us and picked out a room in the house that he said was his room. I guess it is just understood that he is a part of our family, not an extension of us. My oldest child is going to be 7 years old this fall and I can already see that he has surpassed my brother mentally, and this is very hard to watch. I can see the normal progression and developmental milestones occurring in my child that Eric will never meet. I think it makes my children better for having the experience with Eric and hopefully they will grow up with a tolerance and understanding their peers may not have."

—L. Dufford, personal communication, May 6, 2005

• • • To Walt, Robert, and Helen, the death of their mother came as no surprise. After their father died, their mother had become melancholy and was prone to colds and flu until her death. These siblings had dealt with the loss of their parents as best they could. Now, they were troubled by the evolution of their new sibling relationship; one that was no longer bound by parents but by each other. Their passage into this new and inevitable sibling relationship was similar to the experience of most siblings in all but one way; Robert has a severe disability.

At an early age, Robert had been placed in an institution. His parents followed the predominant belief at that time that this type of living arrangement was more advantageous for siblings while it would allow Robert to receive specialized education and therapy. When Robert turned 16, he returned home; the advancement in community-based services had finally enabled his family to get the services he needed in his own community. For the past decade, Robert had lived with his mother and frequently visited his siblings, nieces, and nephews. Robert's speech was limited and barely understandable. During family gatherings, he would say, "Good, good, good!" over and over again. After so many years of institutional life, he relished the participation in a thriving family. With his mother's death, Robert and his siblings were faced with a serious dilemma.

Initially, Walt and Helen were confused about their role with Robert. They loved him dearly, but their personal responsibilities to their spouses and children precluded incorporating Robert into their day-to-day life. Immediately after their mother's death, Robert went to live with Helen and her family until a permanent solution could be found.

Over the ensuing months they were consumed with issues and problems associated with Robert's long-term care and treatment. Issues regarding guardianship, finances, Supplemental Security Income (SSI), community-based services, group homes, and permanent care occupied every spare moment. As Walt and Helen began their search for services for Robert, they were overwhelmed with conflicting advice from friends and professionals. Their attorney was unsure about guardianship. Robert's social worker from the county informed them of the waiting list for group-home placement and could not guarantee Robert a spot. As Walt and Helen were commited to keeping Robert in the community, any institutional placement was out of the question. Robert's instructors at the supported employment program suggested a lawsuit to force the county to provide a group home placement for him. The Social Security division needed a "representative payee" if benefits were to continue. A representative of Social Security suggested that Robert's benefits would be terminated once his mother's estate was settled. Needless to say, Walt and Helen were quite confused and often felt helpless, anxious, and afraid of what the future would hold.

Certainly, Walt and Helen thought about Robert's future before the death of their mother, but not in their wildest dreams did they anticipate that providing for his future would be so problematic. They assumed that some social service organization would provide residential and day programs within the community. In the intervening months, Walt and Helen hired an attorney to pursue limited guardianship, which they received. They used their guardianship responsibility to ensure Robert's community placement in supported living and supported employment programs. In consultation with their attorney and an accountant, a financial plan was developed to enable Robert to enjoy the benefits of his mother's estate while still receiving state and federal entitlements.

Robert still visits Walt and Helen often. He usually spends holidays with them and, occasionally, goes on vacation with them. Sitting around with his siblings, their spouses, and his growing nephews and nieces, Robert still says, "Good, good, good!" • • •

Adult siblings who have brothers or sisters with disabilities often face complex issues and problems, as Walt and Helen's story indicates. These problems are uniquely related to the family's situation, past relationships, and services that are available to the adult with the disability. Not all adult siblings have the same experience as Walt and Helen.

Consider Patti and Jackson:

• • • Jackson was born with multiple disabilities and was not expected to live long after his birth. Now, 38 years later, he was still living with his mother, who spent most of her waking hours attending to his needs. His younger sister Patti, an accountant, lived in the same town and visited her brother and mother frequently. Patti has become increasingly concerned about her mother's ability to care for Jackson. She knew that her mother's age and fading health put her brother and mother in an unsafe situation. She also knew that the bond between them was great and that neither of them would agree to separation. She was concerned, not only with her mother's recent need for increased support but also with her older brother's lifelong needs. How could she arrange to help them without sacrificing her personal life and career?

Luckily, Patti located several community services that provided home health care to assist in dressing and bathing Jackson; homemaker services, which provided assistance with household chores; and a nutrition program, which provided periodic meals to Jackson and his mother. Because they lived in an area that supported community living for people with disabilities, Patti was able to help her mother and brother by locating and arranging services rather than by directly providing them herself. • • •

WHAT DO WE KNOW FROM RESEARCH?

Although there is not an extensive research base on adult siblings, the available research supports much of what we know from our clinical and anecdotal obervations and interactions with adult siblings. We know from the research literature that many adult siblings report that their experiences with brothers and sisters who have disabilities have had a profound influence on their adult life. We also know that many adult siblings want and, in fact, do maintain frequent and meaningful contact with their brothers and sisters with disabilities. Many adult siblings report that they were prepared for future involvement because of their discussions with their parents about future life-planning decisions and the information they received about the disability and the availability community services.

Zeitlin (1986) conducted a participant observation study involving 35 adults with mental retardation to assess the nature and intensity of their relationships with their brothers and sisters. Her findings indicate that the vast majority of the adults maintained contact with their siblings. The relationships ranged from very warm with frequent contact and extensive involvement to hostility with neither contact nor involvement. She notes that most of the contact appeared to be hierarchical, with siblings providing assistance to their brothers and sisters. Sisters tended to assume a caregiving role, and in families with multiple siblings, one adult sibling tended to assume most of the responsibility for the brother or sister with the disability. Not unexpectedly, Zeitlin found that the adult siblings' concern for their brothers and sisters followed the desires of their parents. To the adults with mental retardation, the notion of reciprocity in their relationship with a sibling appeared to be important. These adults expressed a desire to return favors and contribute to the relationship.

Burton and Parks (1991) conducted a study with adult siblings that considered their self-esteem, locus of control, and career aspirations. *Locus of control* in this context was defined as the extent to which these adult siblings viewed their control over personal choices and decision-making, which they exert to influence life events. Burton and Parks found that the adult siblings who had brothers and sisters with disabilities had a greater locus of control than siblings who did not have a brother or sister with a disability. They suggest that this may be because their unique experience enabled them to more readily perceive and accept responsibility for their actions. Although they did not find any statistically significant differences between siblings in regard to career aspirations, they noted that twice as many siblings with brothers and sisters who have disabilities were enrolled in helping profession majors in college (e.g., special education, counseling, social work).

Griffiths and Unger (1994) studied 41 pairs of parents and siblings of adult family members with intellectual disabilities to consider future planning for the person with a disability. They report that although almost half of the adult siblings were willing to to assume responsibility for caregiving, the majority of parents were reluctant to have them take on the demands associated with caregiving.

Krauss, Seltzer, Gordon, and Friedman (1996) examined issues surrounding the intergenerational transmission of caregiving provided to people with intellectual disabilities. As parents grow older and eventually die, the issue of how siblings will play a role in providing that care becomes not only a personal, family issue but also it has profound effects on the provision of community-based services. Krauss and her colleagues interviewed numerous adult siblings of people with intellectual disabilities still living with their parents. They found that siblings maintained regular contact, provided emotional support, and were knowledgable of their brother's or sister's needs. A third of the adult siblings they interviewed intended to live with their brother or sister upon the death of the parent. Not unexpectedly, a majority of the siblings who expected to live with the sibling with a disability were sisters. The siblings who reported that they were likely to live with their brother or sister with the disability had discussions with the parents about the future plans for their brother or sister. Also, many of these siblings reported that they expected to serve as the legal guardian for the sibling with a disability.

Seltzer, Krauss, Hong, and Orsmond (2001) reviewed the continuation of family involvement once a person with intellectual disabilities left home for a residential placement. Consistent with other findings, the siblings without disabilities reported that they not only maintained their contact with the brother or sister with a disabilty but also increased their shared activities. These adult siblings also reported that they were more optimistic about the future for their brother or sister once the placement was made. Seltzer and colleagues also found that

> Sibling relationships tend to improve affectively over time, regardless of the place of residence of the adult with mental retardation, although the sibling relationship is closer when the adult continues to live in the parental home. Among those adults who moved, there was an increase in frequency of shared activities and a decrease in the sibling's pessimism about the brother or sister's future care." (2001, p. 190)

Seltzer and her colleagues noted that their study confirms the importance of siblings to the quality of life of adults with intellectual disabilities and urged service providers to recognize the importance of the lifelong sibling bond and to involve siblings as they prepare and evaluate community-based services for adults with disabilities.

Rimmerman and Raif (2001) studied two groups of siblings, one composed of individuals with a brother or sister with intellectual disabilities and the other group made up of individuals who had siblings without disabilities. They found that overall, the adult siblings with brothers and sisters with intellectual disabilities had more frequent and regular contact compared with the adult siblings with brothers and sisters without disabilities. This contact was even more frequent when the parents were no longer living.

CONCERNS OF ADULT SIBLINGS

The concerns of adults who have brothers and sisters with disabilities are somewhat different from the concerns experienced by children or young people with siblings with disabilities. The main issue here is how the adults can attend to their own needs as they mature. Their natural concerns for their spouse or partner, children, aging parents, and careers are often tempered with the added responsibility of being the sibling of a person who has special needs. These adult concerns fall into three broad areas with regard to the sibling with disabilities:

1. Understanding genetics
2. Providing for long-term care
3. Ensuring a quality life

These major concerns are illustrated in Table 10.1 in the form of a number of critical questions often posed by adult siblings.

Table 10.1. Critical questions often posed by adult siblings

Concern	Questions
Genetic	What are my chances of parenting a child with a disability?
	Will I pass a disorder along to my children?
	How can I get specific advice about my genetic concerns?
	How will my spouse/fiancé feel about possible genetic problems?
Long-term care	What will happen when my parents die?
	Who will take care of my sibling?
	Will I be financially responsible for my sibling?
	Should I serve as a guardian?
	What responsibilities does a guardian have?
	Can my parents plan their estate to safeguard my sibling's financial future?
	Will a conservator be needed?
	How can we establish a guardianship or conservatorship?
Helping the sibling	How can I help to improve my sibling's life?
	Can I get involved in services for my sibling?
	How can I advocate for my sibling?

Understanding Genetics and Genetic Counseling

A major concern of most adult siblings who have brothers and sisters with disabilities is the possibility that they, themselves, will give birth to a child with a disability (Tingey, 1988). This concern increases substantially when the brother or sister has had a disability since birth and/or has an identified genetic disorder. Helping siblings with this concern requires a basic knowledge of genetics and the various genetic services available to siblings. Through advances in genetics, many siblings can receive advice and information concerning the risk of having a child with a disability or the risk of passing defective genes to their offspring. Fortunately, genetic counseling has advanced to a stage in which predictability is replacing chance and the prospects for the prevention of many inherited disabilities have dramatically improved (Connor, 1989).

Most adult siblings are concerned about the possibility of having children with a disability if their own brother or sister has a genetic disorder or was born with a disability (S.C. Department of Disabilities and Special Needs, 1994). Having a sibling with disabilities is a known prenatal risk factor for which referral to a genetic counselor is warranted. Many siblings want to take advantage of available genetic counseling, screening services, and prenatal diagnosis. These services cannot guarantee 100% predictive accuracy, nor can they identify the presence of all disabilities. However, they can help to increase a sibling's knowledge of present and potential risks. In other words, genetic counseling and screening can provide the opportunity for the sibling to make informed decisions about pregnancy and procreation. Given the increasing knowledge of genetics as well as the improvements in techniques for diagnosis and treatment of genetic disorders, most adult siblings interested in having a family will benefit from genetic counseling. Because genetic disabilities are many and complex, siblings (independent of the nature of the disability of their brother or sister) should be encouraged to seek genetic counseling.

In 1983, the National Society of Genetic Counselors adopted the following definition of genetic counseling as a profession:

> Genetic counselors are health professionals with specialized graduate degrees and experience in the areas of medical genetics and counseling. . . Genetic counselors work as members of a health care team, providing information and support to families who have members with birth defects or genetic disorders and to families who may be at risk for a variety of inherited conditions. They identify families at risk, investigate the problem present in the family, interpret information about the disorder, analyze inheritance patterns and risks or recurrence and review available options with the family (National Society of Genetic Counselors, 2005).

Roles of Genetics Professionals Genetics professionals include medical geneticists and genetic counselors. Medical geneticists are doctors with specialized training in genetics. Genetic counselors are professionals with postgraduate training and experience in medical genetics and counseling. Other healthcare professionals such as nurses, psychologists, and social workers trained in genetics may be members of a multidisciplinary evaluation team. A medical geneticist must be directly involved when genetic evaluation is sought to establish a diagnosis (GeneTests, 2005).

Genetic counselors can be very helpful in identifying siblings at risk, investigating the disability, interpreting information about the disorder, and analyzing inheritance patterns and risks of recurrence. Genetic counselors coordinate specific genetic testing and are invaluable in reviewing with the sibling options to reduce risks and to provide supportive counseling and referral to community resources.

Steps Involved in a Genetic Evaluation Genetic evaluations usually take place in a doctor's office, hospital, genetics center, or other type of medical facility and may require several visits to complete. The March of Dimes describes the genetic evaluation as including family history taking, physical exam and diagnostic testing, interpretation of medical information and test results, information sharing to facilitate decision making, and referral to appropriate community resources (March of Dimes, 2005). As a part of genetic counseling, the adult sibling typically will construct a family history or pedigree with entry of all medical problems with the help of the genetic counselor. Detailed information about the individual and first-degree (children, siblings, parents) and second-degree relatives (grandparents, aunts, uncles, nieces, nephews) is used to develop this multi-generational family history, often in the form of a pedigree. A pedigree is a chart using standardized symbols to record medical, genetic, and other significant family history. A thorough family pedigree is an essential part of a genetic evaluation (March of Dimes, 2005).

The genetic counselor may also order specific genetic tests. Genetic testing is voluntary and the risks and benefits have to be carefully considered before proceeding. Once the decision is made, usually as part of genetic counseling, testing can be ordered by a medical geneticist, genetic counselor, primary physician, or other specialist to analyze small samples of blood or body tissues. These genetic tests identify changes in chromosomes, genes, or proteins. The testing may include gene tests (DNA testing) and biochemical tests (protein tests) (National Human Genome Research Institute, 2005).

One of the most common uses of genetic testing, carrier testing, can help to identify abnormalities that are linked to inherited disorders. Carrier testing, as the name implies, can confirm if an individual is a carrier of an inheritied disorder that may be passed on to children (GeneTests, 2005). Several hundred genetic tests are available with more under development (U.S. National Library of Medicine, 2005). According to the Genetics and Public Policy Center at Johns Hopkins University, gene discovery and genetic test development will continue to increase in future years, due in part to the significant impact of the Human Genome Project (Genetics and Public Policy Center, 2005). For more information, visit the web site of the National Human Genome Research Institute at www.genome.gov and the Human Genome Project Information at http://doegenomes.org/

A specialized medical exam, called a *dysmorphology exam,* may be performed by a clinical geneticist. The geneticist looks for "unique or unusual physical characteristics that, when taken together, offer clues to the underlying cause of a condition." Measurements of body parts (such as distance between the eyes, or hand and finger measurements) may be taken as well. The dysmorphology exam takes into consideration the ethnic and familial characteristics of the person (Colorado Department of Public Health and Environment, 2005)

Once the nature of the disability is determined, the genetic counselor can provide education to help the sibling to understand the genetics involved in passing along the disability. The goal of genetic counseling is to help siblings make informed decisions concerning their potential children. The genetic counseling process is usually nondirective, providing information and enabling individuals to make their own decisions about parenting (Kolodny, Abuelo, Barsel-Bowers, & Pueschel, 1990). It is important to note that genetic counseling can do much to alleviate fear and anxiety experienced by siblings. Cohen (1985) shared an experience in which genetic counseling helped her to understand her brother's disability and dissipated her concerns about having a child with a disability. Although she recognized that genetic counseling does not offer a guarantee, a confirmation of her "averageness" from testing data served as significant reassurance.

Genetic counseling services are available in all states. A directory of genetic counselors is available from the National Society of Genetic Counselors Executive Office (http://www.nsgc.org). (See Appendix B for more contact information on this organization.)

Genetic Testing and Insurance Genetic testing costs typically range from several hundred to several thousand dollars. Fees vary based on complexity of the test, number of tests, number of family members tested, and other factors. Availability of test results may vary from a few weeks to a few months. Costs and time frame for receiving test results for specific tests can be discussed with the professional who orders the testing. Health insurance may cover the costs of genetic testing under certain conditions. Because testing can be expensive, individuals may find it helpful to check with their insurance company in advance to determine if testing is a covered expense or if there are restrictions or limitations. Some individuals choose to pay for testing themselves to avoid involving their insurance company because of concern about possible discrimination, now or in the future, if insurance companies have genetic testing information. These may be legitimate concerns about the misuse of genetic information that could possibly affect health insurance coverage and future employment.

Genetic Screening *Genetic screening* refers to the identification of known genetic disorders via the evaluation of susceptible individuals in order to identify either those who are affected or who are carriers of the disorder. Genetic screening can be helpful either prenatally or postnatally. For some pregnant couples, prenatal genetic testing for specific conditions may be considered. Prenatal testing during pregnancy can be helpful to expectant couples with an increased risk of having a baby with a genetic or chromosomal disorder. Amniocentesis and chorionic villus sampling (CVS) are two commonly used prenatal testing procedures (GeneTests, 2005).

Genetics Resources The Genetics Education Center at the University of Kansas Medical Center offers an extensive information web site on genetic and rare conditions, including links to genetic counseling sources. It can be found at http://www.kumc.edu/gec/support/

The Genetic Alliance web site (http://geneticalliance.org/) has useful genetic resources for families including information on how to create a family history, explanation of commonly used terms and acronyms (Alphabet Soup: Genetics for Genetics Consumers, at http://www.geneticalliance.org/ws_display.asp?filter=resources_alphabet_soup), and resources in Spanish. In addition, the *Help Me Understand Genetics Handbook,* published by the U.S. National Library of Medicine (Genetics Home Reference, 2006b), is an excellent source of information and resources for siblings who are considering genetic evaluation and/or genetic testing. The book includes seven chapters on genes and how they work, mutations and genetic disorders, genetic conditions and inheritance, genetic consultation, genetic testing, gene theory, the Human Genome project, and genomic research.

Organizations and web sites providing information on genetics such as The American Society of Human Genetics and the Genetics Society of America are listed in more detail in Appendix B.

Choices and Decisions for Adult Siblings We have found that a proper knowledge of genetics combined with the good advice of physicans and genetic counselors can be invaluable for adult siblings who are preparing to start their own families. Numerous siblings have reported to us that such information and genetic counseling has better prepared them to be parents. No doubt, new screening and diagnostic techniques will continue to provide adult siblings with information that they can use to make decisions about parenting. As with many life decisions, some siblings and their spouses will be faced with difficult and complex choices. Decisions made by siblings should be based on thorough up-to-date information and balanced with values and experience.

Providing for Long-Term Care

Eventually, most people face the inevitable fact that their parents will not live forever. Sudden illness or an accident may precipitate an acute realization of parental mortality. When a family has a member with a disability, the ramifications of parental mortality can increase substantially. When parents are no longer around, or are unable to care for the individual with a disability, who will provide for that person's future? As Rimmerman and Raif (2001) noted, aging parents typically hope that their children without disabilities will become more involved in caregiving as the sibling with a disability grows older. In many cases, responsibility for the individual with a disability is awarded to the siblings. Siblings are not always prepared for such a responibility, however. Seltzer (1991) described the results of a survey of 126 siblings who had a brother or sister with developmental disabilities. Only about a third (35%) of these siblings had a thorough discussion with their parents about who would assume future responsibility for their brothers or sisters. The remaining siblings reported that they had talked "a little" or "some" (51%) about the issue, or not at all (14%). Seltzer expressed concern over the lack of information regarding siblings' perceptions of their present and future roles and responsibilities.

Griffiths and Unger (1994), in their interviews with both parents and adult siblings, noted that siblings are typically only minimally involved in the planning process. Without the proper information, issues surrounding long-term care can be very difficult and can engender multiple feelings of guilt, relief, anxiety and uncertainity. Siblings faced with this responsibility will need to be familiar with guardianship, conservatorship, wills, and trusts.

Guardianship Guardianship is a legal relationship between two people, one serving as a guardian and the other as a ward. This legal relationship provides the guardian with the duty and right to act on behalf of the ward in making important decisions. Guardianship is intended for people who have disabilities that render them unable to make decisions that would be in their best interest. Guardianship attempts to protect an individual (the ward) in situations regarding services, finances, residences, and property, while still maintaining that person's individuality. A court may grant a guardian responsibility for an individual's personal affairs (called *guardianship of the person*), financial affairs (called *guardianship of the property*), or both. A *limited guardianship* may also be established in which the guardian only has responsibility for certain areas of decision in the ward's life.

Although guardianship may be necessary for some individuals, for others, the legal situation may be too restrictive. In determining the need for guardianship, siblings should attempt to answer the following questions:

- Is my brother or sister, due to a lack of social, vocational, academic, and personal skills, vulnerable to extraordinary exploitation and/or abuse?
- Does he or she wish to have a guardian?
- Does he or she have property or resources that need management beyond his or her ability?
- Is it likely that the individual will require additional services, will change residence, or will interact with many service agencies?

Answering yes to these questions may indicate that the person would benefit from a legal guardian, even though he or she is an adult.

Who Should Be a Guardian? Selecting the proper guardian for an individual is a serious matter that requires consideration from several perspectives. Often, the guardian is a sibling or other close relative, but this is not necessary. An interested friend may, in some cases, be a better guardian than family members. Other alternatives include public guardianship or corporate (group) guardianship; in the latter, a private agency or organization serves as guardian. This arrangement can offer numerous advantages over individual guardianship because the full resources of a professional group are available to the individual with a disability. Corporate guardianship programs in both the United States and Canada have been reviewed in detail by Apolloni and Cooke (1984).

Recognizing the need for guardianship for many people with intellectual and other disabilites, in 2002 The Arc of the United States and the American Association on Mental Retardation developed a national position statement to serve as a guide to families and communities on the use of guardianships tailored to an individual's needs. They noted that the appointment of a guardian is a serious matter because it limits a person's independence and rights and that such guardianships must be adequately monitored to ensure that the best interests of the individual are protected. Because we believe that this is one of the best, most comprehensive statements on guardianship, it is presented here and should serve as a reference for those siblings considering guardianship.

POSITION

The majority of our constituents can manage their own affairs with informal assistance and guidance from family, friends, and others. If guardianship is essential, it should be used only to the extent necessary with a presumption in favor of limited rather than full guardianship.

Systems Issues

- Appointment of a guardian should be made only to the extent necessary for the protection and welfare of the individual and not for the convenience of the family, the service system, or society.

- Less intrusive alternatives to full guardianship, like limited guardianship or power of attorney, should always be considered first. If used at all, these restrictions on the individual's rights and decision-making powers should be confined to those areas in which the individual clearly cannot understand the serious consequences of his or her decisions or the person lacks foresight.
- Mechanisms to reverse unnecessarily restrictive forms of existing guardianship must be available.
- Since guardianship represents a transfer of the responsibility for exercising an individual's rights, adequate safeguards, including the right to counsel, are needed to assure the individual retains as much decision-making power as possible.
- Members of the judiciary and attorneys need training on alternatives to guardianship for our constituents.
- Individuals placed under guardianship must have legal representation at all stages of the process and must be informed about the possibility and the process to have the guardianship removed.

Guardian Responsibilities

- They should be knowledgeable of services, supports, and systems that could significantly affect the life of the individual, and must be committed to the well-being of the individual, know and understand the individual's needs and wishes, and act in accordance with them whenever possible. Family members are preferable when they meet these criteria.
- They shall take the person's preferences into account.

Oversight

- States should adopt minimum standards for all guardians and require that training and technical assistance be made available.
- Professional guardians (those who serve two or more wards who are not related to each other and receive fees) should be licensed, certified, or registered and should have the appropriate education and skills. They should not be receiving payment for providing other services to the ward.
- The guardians shall be accountable for their actions, and those actions must be reviewed periodically. (The Arc of the United States & AAMR, 2006a)

How Is Guardianship Established? Guardianship is always a legal arrangement and, thus, requires sanction by a court or appointed panel. Specific procedures for establishing guardianship vary according to state statutes. Guardianship should be pursued by parents, siblings, or interested friends who first seek the counsel of an attorney. Attorneys who specialize in family matters have specific expertise on state guardianship laws. Attempting to establish guardianship without the advice of an attorney is not wise.

In many cases, the parents of children with disabilities may wish to appoint a guardian in their will. This is sometimes referred to as a *testamentary nomination of a guardian.* In most states, such nominations are respected, provided that the nominated person agrees to serve in this capacity, does not present any conflict of interest, and is of good character. Nomination of a specific guardian should be thoroughly discussed among the attorney, parents, and the nominated person.

In cases in which a will does not declare a specific guardian or in cases in which the parent is unable to serve as guardian (e.g., due to sickness), one may be appointed via a court petition. In these situations, an interested individual or the person requests that a court appoint a guardian for the person. Typically, the individual who wishes to be appointed as guardian employs an attorney to pursue this legal procedure.

As mentioned, guardianship laws vary according to state law. Usually, the procedure to establish guardianship will entail

1. Appointment of an attorney to protect the interests of the person
2. Evaluation of the individual by a physician and a psychologist
3. Interviews of all parties by a court-appointed "visitor," usually a social worker or counselor, or perhaps a court appointed special advocate, who will make an independent recommendation to the court
4. A court hearing to review the petition and make a judgment

What Does a Guardian Do? The powers given to the guardian by the court vary according to the individual's needs. In some cases, the guardian's power is all-inclusive; in others, it is restricted to specific decision-making areas. This latter form, as mentioned earlier, is called *limited guardianship.* Guardianship powers may include

1. Giving or withholding consent for treatment or intervention and admission to a program
2. Applying for community-based services on behalf of the person
3. Using the person's funds to provide for needs
4. Applying for government assistance for the person
5. Monitoring the person's progress in various treatment programs

Once guardianship is established, the guardian should

1. Allow the individual to participate as fully as possible in all decisions affecting his or her future
2. Interact with the person on a regular basis

3. Solicit professional expertise when necessary to ensure that decisions made for the individual are in the person's best interest
4. Serve as an intermediary for the person with social services and other community representatives or agencies

A guardian does not assume financial responsibility for the individual; however, the guardian will typically manage the person's finances if the individual does not have a conservator. If a conservator has been appointed for the person, the guardian may be asked to report to the conservator all expenses incurred during the guardianship period.

Conservatorship Unlike guardianship, conservatorship has a single focus. A conservator is a person appointed by the court to manage the estate of a person. In some situations, it may be more advantageous for the sibling to become a conservator rather than a guardian. When several siblings are willing to be involved in long-term protection, one sibling can serve as a conservator, managing financial affairs, while another may serve as a guardian. Conservatorship is established in a manner similar to guardianship. An attorney should be retained to legally establish a conservatorship.

Estate Planning A common concern among adult siblings is their financial responsibility in regard to long-term care and interventions for their brother or sister. Proper estate planning by parents may help to alleviate unnecessary worries, and enables all of the siblings, including the person with a disability, to realize the benefits from parental property. Given the rapid changes in social services policy, benefits, and community services, future estate and financial planning are strategic steps to help ensure the family member's future.

Estate and financial planning are typically done by attorneys via wills and trusts. However, Fee (1990) noted that simple wills and special needs trusts are typically insufficient to ensure a secure future for the person with a disability. Fee advocates for a life planning approach, which utilizes a letter of intent (Russell, 1990) that allows the family to specify what they want for the family member in terms of residential, vocational, recreational, religious, medical, and social services. Naturally, the first option is to allow the individual with the disability to be actively involved in specification of future lifestyles and services; however, when the individual has difficulty expressing desires, the family's letter of intent can inform care providers of the preferred future.

Another future planning option for families is the self-sufficiency trust set up in several states to help supplement individuals' government benefits. These trusts are managed in a manner that allows families to set aside resources in a way that does not interfere with the individual's benefits. They are used to provide services and materials to enhance the family member's quality of life.

Apolloni (1989) described a service model called the National Continuity Program that is aimed at supporting long-term financial, advocacy, and guardianship services for people with disabilities. This program serves to assist local advocacy programs in ensuring provision of quality services. The National Continuity Program provides seven key services to participants and their families, as follows:

1. A file is established for each participant and updated to ensure proper services.
2. When a parent dies or becomes permanently disabled, the program monitors a participant's receipt of government benefits.
3. The participant is provided representation at individual habilitation planning sessions with state agencies.
4. The participant is visited twice a month to monitor quality of life standards and to advocate on the individual's behalf.
5. The delivery of all services is monitored and an advocate acts to correct problems.
6. A guardian is ensured when necessary.
7. Legal, dental, and medical services that supplement government services are made available.

In addition to the obvious long-term support that such a program can provide to families, it may offer more immediate support in alleviating some stress about future care for the brother or sister who has a disability.

Ensuring a Quality Life

Not every sibling can be, or is willing to serve as, a guardian or conservator for a brother or sister with a disability. However, an adult sibling can have a significant, positive impact on his or her brother's or sister's quality of life by serving as an advocate. An advocate is a person who promotes the interests of another and helps him or her to enjoy a quality life.

Advocacy Broadly defined, *advocacy* is a set of beliefs that results in action aimed at defending, maintaining, or promoting the best interests of another or a group of people (Neufeld, 1975). An advocate may be another sibling who seeks to protect the human and legal rights of his or her brother or sister. Sibling advocates may be actively engaged in representing the interest of the individual or an entire group of people with disabilities.

Unlike guardians or conservators, advocates typically do not have legal status. Anyone can serve as an advocate, although family members may be best suited for the role. Minimal prerequisites for advocates include the following:

- An interest in the needs of the person with a disability
- A specific knowledge of the needs and resources available to meet those needs
- A willingness to secure needed services
- An ability to be assertive
- A desire to promote the human rights of people
- The courage to help systems change to meet the needs of persons with disabilities

Advocacy can occur at many levels, be pursued with varying intensity, and achieve a multitude of ends. First and foremost, advocacy focuses on the family member and attempts to ensure that he or she will experience a quality life. A dramatic example of vigorous advocacy is the legislation and policies spearheaded by President John F. Kennedy, who had a sister with mental retardation. During his administration, services for people with disabilities were given a definite direction and their resources expanded; thus, they experienced rapid growth. No doubt, President Kennedy's sense of sibling responsibility helped to motivate his advocacy effort. Luckily, siblings do not need to be presidents or even elected officials to be effective advocates. Over the past years we have met a number of adult siblings who have become quite active in advocacy roles. Consider these examples:

• • • Allison is a cashier at a grocery store. Her youngest sister, Mia, who has Turner's syndrome, still attends a public school. Although their mother and father are both alive, Allison attends educational team meetings regarding Mia and is an active team member. Allison has arranged a flexible work schedule with her employer so that she can be involved in Mia's education. She often observes Mia at school and visits with her teachers. Allison enhances her educational advocacy by reading books and articles on special education. • • •

• • • Patrick is an attorney with a private law firm that specializes in corporate law. He recently donated his services to help a group of professionals start a corporation to serve families who have children with disabilities. He was eager to help since his family could have used such services when he was growing up. His advocacy effort, dedicated to his sister who had died, will have a substantial impact on many people with disabilities. • • •

• • • Tessa's busy schedule as a sales representative to large department stores keeps her on the road most weeks. Her advocacy efforts for her brother, Tim, involve her membership in United Cerebal Palsy. Tessa often donates money on behalf of her brother. • • •

• • • Alex is a personnel manager at a large manufacturing company. Each year, the employees select a charitable organization and donate money raised at various company functions. For the last 3 years, thanks to Alex's efforts, the proceeds went to the Foundation for Exceptional Children. No one at his company knows that Alex has a sister with spina bifida. • • •

• • • Marsha and her husband, Rayl, stop by Dan's group home every Sunday and take him to church and dinner. Dan is Marsha's older brother who has Down syndrome. Marsha and Rayl take the opportunity to visit with Dan and monitor his progress and living situation. They often visit with the group home staff to inquire about Dan and the other residents in the home. • • •

• • • Madelyn finds it difficult to get along with her older sister, Sasha, who has visual disabilities. Even though they do not visit on a regular basis, Madelyn keeps track of developments in regard to services to people with disabilities. She often writes her elected officials, especially her state senator, expressing her support for services for people with disabilities in the community. • • •

• • • Darby's brother, Mason, has a learning disability. As a school board member, Darby actively advocates special education services at board meetings. Although Darby is known as an advocate, few people know that his brother has a learning disability. • • •

• • • Amy Claire wanted to do something for her brother, Burton, who is living in a state-operated center for people with disabilities. She decided that her best advocacy effort would be to join the Arc of the United States. Now, Amy Claire regularly attends local chapter and state meetings, volunteers to serve on committees, and assists with chapter events. • • •

• • • Kent loved to play soccer as an adolescent. His brother Chris, who died of muscular dystrophy, never got the chance to play soccer. Kent is now an adult volunteer for a community recreation program that has made a commitment to including children with disabilities. He has joined the Special Olympics program as a volunteer. Every year, he attends the local competition and helps to set up the Fun Run. • • •

• • • Kathy's older brother, Albert, received a gunshot wound to the head as a child and grew up with traumatic brain injury. Now Kathy, whose younger son, Mitch, was born with Down syndrome, advocates actively for full inclusion for Mitch because she's seen the results of someone being excluded and knows she doesn't want that for her son (K. Dillon, personal communication, May 20, 2005). • • •

• • • Gabrielle is a physician at a large metropolitan hospital. Her brother, Morgan, has multiple disabilities. She recently formed and chaired a task force to consider medical ethics involving involuntary euthanasia and newborns with severe disabilities. • • •

• • • Mayira serves as a representative payee for her brother's Social Security benefits. She meets Roberto weekly to go over his finances and to do his banking. Mayira always escorts him to the Social Security office for periodic reviews and to complete new applications. Recently, she helped Roberto apply for food stamps. • • •

• • • Sharon, a professor of special education and a sister to a person with disabilities, organizes special sibling groups at the university to help siblings who have brothers and sisters with disabilities. She organizes positive, upbeat sessions to help other siblings to celebrate their unique relationship. • • •

• • • Miles, a professor of educational psychology, is the brother of Larkie, who has Down syndrome. In his classes of teachers-in-training he stresses human similarities, rather than human differences. He teaches his students

about concepts such as full school inclusion and speaks out against the problems of tracking (i.e., grouping students by ability from year to year) in schools. He makes a commitment to his sister by preparing caring teachers who will respect everyone's right to be a part of school communities. • • •

Advocacy can take on many forms. These examples are just a small sample of the work being done and the various avenues advocates can choose. What unifies these different activities is the desire to help to improve the quality of life experienced by siblings with disabilities or by other people with similar issues.

Self-Determination Everyone with a sister or a brother knows that their sibling has his or her own life to live. Although people love their brothers and sisters and want to support them throughout their lifetimes, once these siblings with disabilities are adults they must be encouraged to live their own lives according to their own perferences. To that end, the self-determination movement in the United States is highlighting the need for adults with disabilities to make their own preferences known about their living arrangements, employment, spiritual life, and recreation choices. Siblings can and should work diligently to protect the preferences of their brother or sister with disabilities, even when at times those preferences may be counter to what the adult sibling desires for him or her. In 2004, the Arc of the United States developed a useful statement on self-determination that should be considered by siblings as they assume more caretaking responsibilities:

Position Statement of the Arc of the United States

People with mental retardation and related developmental disabilities have the same right to self-determination as all people. They must have opportunities and experiences that enable them to exert control in their lives and to advocate on their own behalf.

Issue

Many of our constituents have not had the opportunity or the support to control choices and decisions about important aspects of their lives. Instead, they are often overprotected and involuntarily segregated. Many of these people have not had opportunities to learn the skills and have the experiences that would enable them to take more personal control and make choices. The lack of such learning opportunities and experiences has impeded the right of people with these disabilities to become participating, valued, and respected members of their communities. Furthermore, state monitoring and licensure policies and practices may be contrary to the principles of self-determination.

Position

Our constituents, as Self-Advocates, have the same right to self-determination as all people and must have the freedom, authority, and support to exercise control over their lives. To this end, they

- Must have the opportunity to advocate for themselves with the knowledge that their desires will be heard and respected
- Must have opportunities to acquire skills and develop beliefs that enable them to take greater personal control
- Must be active participants in decision-making about their lives
- Must be supported, assisted, and empowered to vote and to become active members and leaders on community boards, committees, and agencies
- Must have the primary leadership role in setting the policy direction for the self-determination movement
- Must have the option to direct their own care and allocate available resources
- Must be able to hire, train, manage, and fire their personal assistants
- Must have the opportunity to be involved in governmental decisions that have an impact on their lives

Additionally, in working with our constituents

- Families and substitute decision-makers should be supported to understand the concept and implementation of self-determination, including the limits on their powers.
- Disability organizations should make self-determination a priority and include this important concept in their conferences, publications, advocacy, training, services, policies, and research.
- Governments should regularly review and revise laws, regulations, policies, and funding systems to promote self-determination. The affected individuals must be involved in these reviews and revisions. (The Arc & AAMR, 2006b)

SUMMARY

Adult siblings of people with disabilities face a number of unique concerns and challenges. On the one hand, they have lives of their own, often with responsibilities toward their spouses and their own children; on the other hand, they have a bond with their sibling, which has its own set of responsibilities. One sibling raised the issue of the reactions of in-laws; specifically, she believed that her mother-in-law did not seem to accept her because her sister has autism. The sibling noted that she has a real loyalty to her sister as well as a bond and came to the conclusion that it was not worth talking about her sister to her mother-in-law because the woman just didn't seem to want to understand.

As parents age and pass away, the responsibilities toward siblings with disabilities usually increase. The main issue for adult siblings seems to be the delicate balancing act of meeting all of their responsibilities to themselves, their spouses, their children, and to their siblings.

Meeting those special responsibilities leads to a number of concerns unique to adult siblings. A genetic concern has obvious implications for married couples and future children. Concerns about the long-term care for the brother or sister after parents pass away are focused on the responsibilities the sibling may need to assume. Guardianship, conservatorship, and estate planning are all aimed at enabling the person to live as independently and safely as possible while not placing undue burden or hardship on siblings. Advocacy activities also help adults to contribute to the quality of life of their brothers and sisters. Adult siblings who are concerned about the welfare of their sister or brother can help to influence services by actively serving as advocates.

As adult siblings become involved in meaningful and life-long ways, it is important for the sibling to first and foremost consider the needs and desires of his or her brother or sister. As Krauss and her col-

leagues (1996) noted, siblings must be mindful of the choices of the person with a disability in making determinations about their future, especially in regard to where they will live, in addition to the preferences of the family member who may volunteer to share their home.

Finally, it is necessary to reassert a sibling bond at various stages of our lives. Adulthood is a period of uncertainty between siblings. Most adult siblings establish their own families and friends. During this period, the sibling bond may be strained, yet it remains ever present. When one sibling does not or cannot establish a new family or friends, dependency on other siblings and their families may increase rather than decrease. A clear role for adult siblings is to open some space in their lives for their brothers or sisters with disabilities. In doing so, adult siblings reassert their sibling bond and provide testimony to the power of the family.

Capstone Strategies for Parents and Siblings

"Siblings have sought to be more open about their circumstances, their feelings, and their need to be better informed. They have found that they are not alone and indeed have discovered that disability in the family—and the family's reaction to it—is shared by others. Along with discovering that others share this life situation, siblings are speaking out so that parents and professionals will understand their special challenge."

—Seligman and Darling (1997, p. 122)

• • • Six adult siblings sat at the table as the audience, mostly parents and professionals, awaited their guidance. Each sibling came with a different experience. Lori's older sister has Down syndrome and lives in a group home; Cason's brother had Duchenne's muscular dystrophy and died when Cason was 18; Jacque's sister is deafblind and has mental retardation; Sondra's brother has a severe learning disability; Noreen's brother is deaf due to meningitis; and Dan's brother has autism. The panel assembled in an effort to share their experiences and their advice with parents who have children with disabilities and with the professionals who work with them.

After panel members introduced themselves and described their siblings, the moderator posed similar questions to each panelist:

"What do you remember most about growing up with a brother or sister who has a disability?"

"What were some of the problems you faced while growing up?"

"When did you learn about your sibling's disability?"

"What did you learn about your sibling's disability?"

"Did you experience any fears associated with the disability?"

"What were the positive aspects for you or your family?"

Although each sibling grew up with a different set of experiences, had a sibling with a different type of disability, and came from families of a different size and economic status, the commonality of the responses was astounding. The siblings' stories about their problems focused on play and social interactions, their friends, extra family duties and caregiving responsibilities, and their relationships with their siblings as they changed over time. Not surprisingly, the siblings all presented a common litany of benefits they feel that they received as a result of their experiences. They stated that they are more understanding of human problems, that they accept people better, and that they are less judgmental and more easygoing. Several said they had learned to teach; others said they developed patience; still others claimed to have learned to deal effectively with embarrassment. One of the siblings was a teacher and one was a speech pathologist—career choices they attributed to their sibling experiences. Most of the siblings stated that their family communicates more effectively as a result of having a family member with a disability. All of the siblings said their family members are closer, more open, and more honest with each other as a result of their experiences.

In listening to each sibling elaborate on the positive aspects of life with a brother or sister who has a disability, one could call into question the "scientific" value of this exercise. Were these six a representative group of all siblings? They were outspoken and willing to talk to strangers. What about those who are not? Indeed, it would be nearly impossible to tell for sure if the benefits these siblings discussed were a direct result of their special sibling experience; however, the issue of cause was not the point here. What does matter is that these siblings, when given a chance to talk, spoke primarily about the benefits they received. Their negative experiences, although important, seemed to be outweighed by the positive.

The moderator shifted gears a bit and posed another question: "Why, when we know that some siblings have problems, were your experiences so positive? What made the difference?" Almost in unison and without hesitation, the siblings responded, "My parents." The parents of these six were hardly superparents; they were parents who had extraordinary responsibilities and were able to balance, indeed juggle, responsibility effectively. It was unfortunate that none of the parents of the siblings were in the audience to hear these personal testimonials. • • •

Some of the advice from the siblings is presented next. The strategies are broken into two parts that summarize the suggestions for parents and for siblings themselves as set forth by other experienced siblings. Each strategy has been discussed to some extent in the previous chapters of this volume; here, they are simply clarified and succinctly assembled for use by parents and siblings.

The strategies are not listed in any particular order. Each is as important as the next, although not every strategy will be appropriate for every family. Families should read and consider all of the suggestions, choosing those that best meet their individual needs and abilities at a given time. Not every parent or sibling can or should adopt every strategy. Most important, we hope parents recognize that we understand some of the parameters of their unique and often difficult journey and have summarized these suggestions only to assist families in re-evaluating their situation to make positive changes. Balancing and juggling emotions and responsibilities can be done most successfully by utilizing strategies based on the parents' knowledge of themselves and their children.

THIRTY STRATEGIES FOR PARENTS

1. *Be open and honest.* Siblings need parents to be available for questions and to provide straight answers to these questions. If parents don't know the answer, they should say so and work together with siblings to find answers to their questions. Welcome questions from siblings and, if they aren't forthcoming, pose some of your own questions.

2. *Value each child individually.* It is natural to compare children, especially their physical features, strengths, and weaknesses. When one child has a disability, the comparison will almost always be weighed toward the other children and will lead to problems between and among the children. Talk about each child individually.

3. *Limit caregiving responsibilities.* When one child has a severe disability, the siblings may be recruited to perform a number of direct care activities as well as behavior management techniques. Older siblings usually help with childrearing, although these activities may be greatly extended when one child needs extraordinary care. Sharing these responsibilities between family members or utilizing nonfamily helpers when appropriate may foster a workable balance. Remember, siblings always appreciate recognition for these extra caregiving responsibilities.

4. *Use respite care and other supportive services.* Respite care services were designed to help families with the constant and intense caregiving needs of children with disabilities. Respite care can be used to enable parents to spend more time with other siblings. Grandparents

and other family members might also provide respite so that parents and children without disabilities can spend quality time together.

5. *Be fair.* Parents should always attempt to be fair in terms of discipline, attention, and resources. The child with a disability should be treated as normally as possible. Siblings are quick to recognize when parents are acting fairly or unfairly. An important time for parents to be fair is when settling sibling disputes. Always taking one child's side over the other is certain to cause problems between the children.

6. *Put together a library of children's books on disabilities.* One of the best ways in which parents can share information with their children is to provide children's literature for them to read. Local libraries typically carry many books on disabilities and sibling relationships for all ages of children (see Appendix A).

7. *Become familiar with Internet resources for siblings with children and adults with disabilities.* Become familiar with the myriad web resources for siblings and individuals with disabilities. Parents can help their younger children find informative web sites. A wealth of information can be found on the Internet that is constantly being updated. Caution should be exercised so that siblings do not have access to sites that are inaccurate or above their developmental levels. See Appendix B for a list of Internet resources.

8. *Schedule special time with the sibling.* Everyone recognizes that children with disabilities require extra parental time. As siblings mature, they come to realize the necessity of this additional parental attention. Parents can balance this inequity to some extent by scheduling special time for each sibling. For example, one father set aside Thursday evenings from 8:00–9:00 P.M. to play chess. One couple took turns taking their daughter to the movies. Scheduling special times helps to reassert how important each siblings is to his or her parents.

9. *Let siblings settle their own differences.* Fighting between siblings is natural and, in many cases, healthy. It helps the siblings to get to know each other and helps them to work out the rules of cooperative relationships. Always interrupting fights will deny siblings the opportunity to solve their own problems. (Of course, parents should never let siblings hurt one another.)

10. *Welcome other children, friends, and relatives into the home.* The siblings' relationships with others outside of the immediate family

are a universal concern. Parents can minimize potential problems with forming social relationships by providing a home that welcomes other children, relatives, and friends. This sharing provides a powerful model of accepting a child's disability and reasserts the family's willingness to fully participate in community life.

11. *Praise siblings.* All children need parental praise. Siblings should receive acknowledgment and be encouraged when parents notice that they have sacrificed, been patient, or been particularly helpful. Parents should be liberal with their praise; it is a commodity that cannot be exhausted and is always valued. Parental praise will help the siblings to develop a positive self-image.

12. *Recognize that you are the most important, most powerful teacher of your children.* Siblings typically follow the lead set forth by their parents. They model parental behavior. Parents need to recognize the power of their informal lessons and provide an example in terms of their interactions with the child with disabilities. Likewise, they should provide an example in terms of their acceptance of and involvement with people.

13. *Recognize the uniqueness of your family.* When families feel good about themselves and their children, they typically feel no need to make comparisons to other families and other children. Your family is unique and special and should be celebrated for what it is!

14. *Listen to siblings.* Siblings know the child with a disability in a way different from the way their parents know the child. In other words, siblings have a unique relationship. As siblings mature, they will have observations, comments, and suggestions about the child. Their statements and concerns should fall on attentive ears. Active listening also implies that parents attend to unspoken messages and behaviors. Asking the siblings to talk, or in other ways prompting communication between parents and siblings, will let the siblings know that their thoughts and suggestions are valued. Likewise, the child with disabilities should be listened to concerning sibling issues as well.

15. *Involve the siblings.* As siblings mature, they may wish to become actively involved in decisions regarding their brother or sister with a disability. Parents can involve siblings by

    a. Inviting them to attend school meetings (e.g., IEP or transition meetings)

    b. Discussing future plans with them

   c. Soliciting their ideas on treatment and service needs
   d. Having them visit with professionals working with the child
   e. Helping them develop competencies to teach the child new skills
   f. Providing opportunities to advocate for the child

16. *Require the child with a disability to do as much for himself or herself as possible.* When the child performs skills independently, it limits dependency on siblings. Setting the stage for ultimate independence starts with parental expectations that children do as many activities for themselves as is feasible. These expectations clearly communicate that parents recognize the limits of the sibling's responsibilities and provide a foundation for the characteristics of the future relationship between the siblings.

17. *Recognize each child's unique qualities and family contribution.* As often as possible, remind each child of his or her positive qualities and contributions to other family members. Siblings, like the rest of us, cannot hear this too much.

18. *Help establish special sibling programs.* These sibling support groups, organized by age levels, can help siblings to share their feelings and concerns with others in similar situations. Parents should recognize the advantages of siblings' talking with one another and lend their support to efforts that provide such opportunities. Encouraging a parent organization or school to start a "sibling day" or "sibling workshop" will help siblings receive some of the information they need.

19. *Recognize special stress times for siblings and plan to minimize negative effects.* Like parents, siblings experience greater levels of stress at different times. From what we know, it seems that sibling stress may be greatest when

   a. Another child is born
   b. The child goes to school
   c. The sibling starts to date
   d. Friends reject the child
   e. Friends ask questions about the child
   f. The child becomes critically ill or dies

g. Problems related to the child are handled in secrecy
h. Parents die
i. Siblings marry

These tend to be more stressful times, often because of a lack of information and/or communication between the parents and siblings. The stress can be minimized through recognition of potential problems and frank, open discussion about the problems and possible solutions. Siblings may not always recognize why they feel more angry, resentful, frightened, sad, or lonely. Parents can help by opening the door for discussions and mutual problem solving.

20. *Use professionals to help siblings.* Sometimes, siblings need some special support or counseling from teachers, social workers, counselors, and psychologists. If the parent feels that such service is needed, it should be provided in as vigorous a manner as services for the child who has a disability. Luckily, these times are rare because most siblings never need professional help; however, when problems arise, service for the sibling should be sought promptly.

21. *Teach the siblings to interact.* Many siblings need help in learning how to socially interact with their brother or sister who has a disability. Parents should provide recreational activities and materials that their children can enjoy and use together. Parents can teach social interaction by modeling appropriate behavior through their own interactions, as well as by more formal teaching activities (see Chapter 8). Always reward the siblings when they interact with each other. Siblings typically exert much energy and patience when interacting with a brother or sister, and their efforts should not go unnoticed. Occasionally, parents note that siblings are more capable than they are in eliciting positive behaviors from the child who has a disability.

22. *Provide opportunities for a normal family life and normal family activities.* Problems with siblings tend to develop when all of the family's energy and resources are focused on providing care to the child with the disability. In these situations, siblings are denied normal opportunities for personal growth and experience. No outsider can ever determine what comprises "normal" family activities. Each family values a different set of experiences. However, if the family wants to participate in some activities but cannot because of the demands associated with having a child with a disability, extra effort should be taken to ensure that the family does

not have to forgo such activities. This extra effort may mean buying a larger car, adding a special room to the house, modifying traditional activities, or seeking respite services.

Siblings should participate in community activities, like scouting, sports, clubs, and hobby groups, with their parents' encouragement and as much parental participation as possible. Families should have fun together. They should take vacations, pursue special projects, and spend time together. When a child's disability precludes these activities, perhaps grandparents or other family members can help out. Respite care is another possibility, as mentioned in number 4 above. Respite care may, in fact, benefit the siblings more directly than it does the parents. Allowing normal family activities to occur, in spite of a disability, will help to strengthen the family unit.

23. *Do not expect siblings to be saints.* Sometimes parents expect too much from their children who do not have disabilities; for example, they may expect these children to excel and to grow up before their time. Like all people, siblings will occasionally lose their patience, understanding, and compassion. They will become angry at their brother or sister and may even reject him or her. Healthy relationships imply a full range of emotions. Siblings who are always patient and kind are rather rare. Not expecting siblings to be saints allows them to be real, honest people. This means they will fight, argue, compete, laugh, share secrets, and play together as they grow together. The boundaries of typical sibling feelings are rather broad. We cannot expect siblings to behave in extraordinary ways within a narrow definition of acceptable sibling behavior.

24. *Provide understandable answers and repeat them as often as requested.* Siblings, like all people, understand information differently at different times. Parents need to explain disabilities and the ramifications using language and terms understood by the sibling. Most likely, the information will need to be shared many times before it is fully understood. Have patience!

25. *Ask.* So many siblings have told us, "If only our parents had asked, 'Would it be okay if your brother came along?' or 'Would it be okay if you stayed with your sister while I make a run to the store?' or 'Would it be okay if James sat next to you at the movies?' More often than not, when parents ask these kinds of questions, the answer will be yes, but the act of asking reasserts the parents' understanding of the siblings' concerns and needs. Naturally, if

siblings say no, then other plans will need to be made. Ask first and respect the answer.

26. *Let siblings know that they come first sometimes.* Occasionally, it is important to let your other children know that they come first. It is advisable to let your child with the disability know that they will have to wait while you attend to his or her brother or sister.

27. *Let siblings teach you what it is like.* Let your children know that they are having experiences that you did not. Let them know that you want to understand what it is like to have a brother or sister with a disability.

28. *Give siblings a set of strategies.* Some siblings have found it helpful to have a list of actions that they can use to help them with their unique situation. (We have included a list of 20 strategies, generated by siblings, which follows this list. Use the list to create your own set of strategies to share.)

29. *Talk about the future with them.* The future plans for the individual with a disability should not be a mystery. Siblings and, most important—the person with the disability—should be actively engaged in discussing future plans including job placements; living arrangements; and knowledge of wills, trusts, and guardianship.

30. *Don't forget to laugh.* We know several families who have a family laughter book where they write down the funny moments of their life together. These laughter memories come out, especially during stressful times or when the family is just feeling low. Soon one hears, "Remember when . . . ?" or "I was never so embarrassed as when. . . . Now I can really laugh about it!" These laughter memories help to keep the balance for all family members and communicate a powerful message.

TWENTY STRATEGIES FOR SIBLINGS

So what can siblings do to contribute more fully to their family and, in turn, to help themselves? Over the past 25 years we have asked that question of hundreds of siblings young and old. We have been fortunate that they have taught us so much. Here are some ideas that siblings may find helpful.

1. Talk to others, especially parents, teachers, and other siblings, about your feelings and concerns.
2. Read about your brother's or sister's disability in books or through web searches. The knowledge you receive will empower you.
3. Learn from other siblings who have had similar experiences. Sometimes it is easier to follow the lead of others with more experience.
4. Join sibling groups and attend special sessions for siblings.
5. Be willing to teach your parents what it is like to grow up with a brother or sister who has a disability. Remember that most parents have never experienced what you are experiencing.
6. Recognize that your brothers or sisters with disabilities are more like other siblings than they are different. All brothers and sisters embarrass us and make us angry or sad at times.
7. Know that it is okay to have mixed feelings toward your brother or sister. Having these feelings makes you human.
8. Be proud that your special family experience provides you with many opportunities for growth and maturity.
9. Don't be afraid to ask for help when you need it.
10. Teach your friends and others. Remember that many people naturally have questions about people with disabilities and want to learn how they can help. By watching you and your interactions with your brother or sister, they will learn.
11. Be an advocate for people with disabilities. Let others know that your brother or sister is, first and foremost, a person who just happens to have a disability.
12. If your friends tease a person with a disability or say something thoughtless, don't join in. It will only make you feel guilty later.
13. Be kind to your parents. Even though they may make mistakes, know that they love you and that they want the best for you and all of their children.

14. Remember that you are not alone.
15. Keep your sense of humor. Look at the bright side. As in all families, funny things happen. Take time to laugh, smile often, and be happy.
16. Keep a positive outlook. Although it may be easier to make a list of someone's shortcomings, everyone has strengths. Keep a balanced perspective by reminding yourself and your friends about your brother's or sister's good points.
17. When you get older, seek genetic counseling. It cannot hurt and it will usually help you feel more at ease.
18. Remember that your brother or sister, like you, needs to make his or her own way in the world. And, just like you, it is comforting to have a brother or sister whom you can count on when you need him or her.
19. Your brother or sister needs you to be the best sibling you can be. That means getting to know yourself, getting in touch with your feelings, and developing your abilities.
20. Get involved in some way. Your involvement does not need to be extensive or exciting. Small acts will make the world a bettter place for people with disabilities and their families.

All of these strategies, for parents and for siblings, are intended to help families feel that they are not alone in their situations. Brothers and sisters have a unique relationship that can be enjoyed from childhood to adulthood; one that should be celebrated for the unique challenges and joys it brings to individuals' lives.

References

Abramovitch, R., Corter, C., & Lando, B. (1979). Sibling interaction in the home. *Child Development, 50,* 997–1003.

Abramovitch, R., Corter, C., & Pepler, D.J. (1980). Observations of mixed sex sibling dyads. *Child Development, 51,* 1268–1271.

Abramovitch, R., Corter, C., Pepler, D.J., & Stanhope, L. (1986). Sibling and peer interaction: A final follow-up and comparison. *Child Development,* 57, 217–229.

Abramovitch, R., Pepler, D.J., & Corter, C. (1982). Patterns of sibling interaction among preschool-age children. In M.E. Lamb & B. Sutton-Smith (Eds.), *Sibling relationships* (pp. 61-68). Mahwah, NJ: Lawrence Erlbaum Associates.

Abramovitch, R., Stanhope, L., Pepler, D.J., & Corter, C. (1987). The influence of Downs syndrome on sibling interaction. *Journal of Child Psychology and Psychiatry,* 28, 865–879.

Adolphson, T., Baker, M., Fields, P., Jacob, K., Jacob, L., Sartorius, E., et al. (2003). *Beyond the stares.* St. Louis: Delta Gamma Center for Children with Visual Impairments.

Alberto, P.A., & Troutman, A.C. (2006). *Applied behavior analysis for teachers* (7th ed.). Upper Saddle River, NJ: Prentice Hall.

Aldous, J., Klaus, E., & Klein, D.M. (1985). The understanding heart: Aging parents and their favorite children. *Child Development, 56,* 303–316.

Allen, K.E., Hart, B.M., Buell, J.S., Harris, F.R., & Wolf, M.M. (1964). Effects of social reinforcement on isolate behavior of a nursery school child. *Child Development, 35,* 511–518.

Americans with Disabilities Act (ADA) of 1990, PL 101-336, 42 U.S.C. §§ 12101 *et seq.*

Anderson, E.R., Hetherington, E., Reiss, D., & Howe, G. (1994). Parents' nonshared treatment of siblings and the development of social competence during adolescence. *Journal of Family Psychology, 8*(3), 303–320.

Anderson, K., & Milliren, A. (1983). *Structured experiences for integration of handicapped children.* Rockville, MD: Aspen Publications.

Apolloni, T. (1984). Self-advocacy: How to be a winner. *National Information Center for Handicapped Children and Youth Newsletter,* 1–4.

Apolloni, T., & Cooke, T.P. (1975). Peer behavior conceptualized as a variable influencing infant and toddler development. *American Journal of Orthopsychiatry, 45,* 4–17.

Apolloni, T., & Cooke, T.P. (Eds.). (1984). *A new look at guardianship: Protective services that support personalized living.* Baltimore: Paul H. Brookes Publishing Co.

The Arc of the United States and the AAMR (2006a). Guardianship position statement. Retrieved June 1, 2006 from http://www.thearc.org/position-statements.htm.

The Arc of the United States and the AAMR (2006b). Self-determination position statement. Retrieved June 1, 2006 from http://www.thearc.org/position-statements.htm.

Ardelt, M., & Day, L. (2002). Parents, siblings, and peers: Close social relationships and adolescent deviance. *Journal of Early Adolescence, 22*(3), 310–349.

Arliss, L. (1997). Toward a grounded theory of sibling communication during early childhood. *The New Jersey Journal of Communication, 5*(2), 178–201.

Ausubel, D.P. (1958). *Theory and problems of child development.* New York: Grune & Stratton.

Bagenholm, A., & Gillberg, C. (1991). Psychosocial effects on siblings of children with autism and mental retardation: A population-based study. *Journal of Mental Deficiency Research, 35,* 291–307.

Bandura, A. (1977). *Social learning theory.* Upper Saddle River, NJ: Prentice Hall.

Bank, L., Patterson, G., & Reid, J. (1996). Negative sibling interaction patterns as predictors of later adjustment problems in adolescent and youth adult males. In G.H. Brody (Ed.), *Sibling relationships: Their causes and consequences* (pp. 197–229). Stamford, CT: Ablex.

Bank, S., & Kahn, M.D. (1982). Intense sibling loyalties. In M.E. Lamb & B. Sutton-Smith (Eds.), *Sibling relationships* (pp. 251–266). Mahwah, NJ: Lawrence Erlbaum Associates.

Bank, S., & Kahn, M.D. (1997). *The sibling bond.* New York: Basic Books.

Barton, M.E., & Tomasello, M. (1991). Joint attention and conversation in mother–infant–sibling triads. *Child Development,* 62, 517–529.

Battle, C.U. (1974). Disruptions in the socialization of a young severely handicapped child. *Rehabilitation Literature,* 35, 130–140.

Baumann, S., Dyches, T., & Braddick, M. (2005). Being a sibling. *Nursing Science Quarterly, 18*(1), 51–58.

Beckman, P.J. (1983). The influence of selected child characteristics on stress in families of handicapped infants. *American Journal of Mental Deficiency, 88,* 150–156.

Beckman, P.J., & Bristol, M.M. (1991). Issues in developing the IFSP: A framework for establishing family outcomes. *Topics in Early Childhood Special Education, 11*(3), 19–31.

Beckman-Bell, P. (1980). *Characteristics of handicapped infants: A study of the relationship between child characteristics and stress as reported by mothers.* Unpublished doctoral dissertation, University of North Carolina-Chapel Hill.

Begun, A. (1989). Sibling relationships involving disabled people. *American Journal on Mental Deficiency,* 93, 566–574.

Belchic, J.K., & Harris, S.L. (1994). The use of multiple peer exemplars to enhance the generalization of play skills to the siblings of children with autism. *Child and Family Behavior Therapy, 16*(2), 1–25.

Bell, R. (1968). A reinterpretation of the direction of effects in studies of socialization. *Psychological Review, 75,* 81–95.

Belmont, L., & Marolla, F.A. (1973). Birth order, family size and intelligence. *Science, 182,* 1096–1101.

Belmont, L., Stein, Z.A., & Zybert, P. (1978). Child spacing and birth order: Effect on intellectual ability in two child families. *Science, 202,* 995–996.

Benigno, J.P., & Ellis, S. (2004). Two is greater than three: Effects of older siblings on parental support of preschoolers' counting in middle-income families. *Early Childhood Research Quarterly, 19,* 4–20.

Bennett, C.W. (1973). A four-and-a-half year old as a teacher of her hearing impaired sister: A case study. *Journal of Communication Disorders, 6,* 67–75.

Benson, G. (1982, November). *Siblings: Research and implications for family programming.* Paper presented at the 9th annual meeting of The Association for the Severely Handicapped, Denver.

Binger, C. (1973). Childhood leukemia: Emotional impact on siblings. In J. Anthony & C. Koupernik (Eds.), *The child in his family.* New York: Wiley.

Block, J.D., & Bartell, S.S. (2001). *Stepliving for teens: Getting along with stepparents, parents, and siblings.* New York: Price Stern Sloan.

Bodenheimer, C. (1979). For the sake of others. *Journal of Autism and Developmental Disorders, 9*(3), 291–293.

Boer, F. (1990). *Sibling relationships in middle childhood.* Leiden, Netherlands: DSWO University of Leiden Press.

Boisot, T. (2002, January/February). An interview with Michelle on being Ben's sister. *TASH Connections,* pp. 18–19.

Borders, K., Borders, S., Borders, L., Watts, D., & Watts, D. (1982). Our sibling group. *Sibling Information Network Newsletter, 1*(4), 2.

Bossard, J., & Boll, E.S. (1960). *The sociology of child development.* New York: HarperCollins Publishers.

Boyd, R. (1980). Systematic parent training through a home based model. *Exceptional Children, 45,* 647–650.

Brammer, L. (1977). Who can be a helper? *Personnel and Guidance Journal, 55,* 303-308.

Brammer, L., & Shostrom, H. (1982). *Therapeutic psychology: Fundamentals of counseling and psychotherapy.* Englewood Cliffs, NJ: Prentice Hall.

Breslau, N. (1982). Siblings of disabled children: Birth order and age spacing effects. *Journal of Abnormal Child Psychology, 10,* 85–96.

Breslau, N., Weitzman, M., & Messenger, K. (1981). Psychological functioning of siblings of disabled children. *Pedatrics, 67,* 344-353.

Brim, O.J. (1958). Family structure and sex role learning by children: A further analysis of Helen Koch's data. *Sociometry, 21,* 1–16.

Brinker, R.P. (1984). *Executive summary.* Division of Education Policy Research and Services. Princeton, NJ: Educational Testing Service.

Bristol, M.M. (1979). *Maternal coping with autistic children: Adequacy of interpersonal support and effect of child's characteristics.* Unpublished doctoral dissertation, University of North Carolina-Chapel Hill.

Bristol, M.M., Reichle, N.C., & Thomas, D.D. (1987). Changing demographics of the American family: Implications for single parent families of young handicapped children. *Journal of the Division for Early Childhood, 12*(1), 56–69.

Brody, G.H. (1998). Sibling relationship quality: Its causes and consequences. *Annual Review of Psychology, 49,* 1–24.

Brody, G.H., Kim, S., Murry, V.M., & Brown, A.C. (2004). Protective longitudinal paths linking child competence to behavioral problems among African American siblings. *Child Development, 75,* 455–467.

Brody, G.H., & Murry, V.M. (2001). Sibling socialization of competence in rural, single-parent African American families. *Journal of Marriage and Family, 63,* 996–1009.

Brody, G.H., & Stoneman, Z. (1986). Contextual issues in the study of sibling socialization. In J.J. Gallagher & P.M. Vietze (Eds.), *Families of handicapped persons: Research, programs, and policy issues* (pp. 197–217). Baltimore: Paul H. Brookes Publishing Co.

Brody, G.H., & Stoneman, Z. (1987). Sibling conflict: Contributions of the siblings themselves, the parent–sibling relationship, and the broader family system. *Journal of Children in Contemporary Society, 19*(3–4), pages 39–53.

Brody, G.H., & Stoneman, Z. (1994). Sibling relationships and their association with parental differential treatment. In E.M. Hetherington, D. Reiss, & R. Plomin (Eds.),

Separate social worlds of siblings: The impact of nonshared environment on development (pp. 129–142). Mahwah, NJ: Lawrence Erlbaum Associates.

Brody, G.H., Stoneman, Z., Burke, M. (1987a). Family system and individual child correlates of sibling behavior. *American Journal of Orthopsychiatry,* 57, 561–569.

Brody, G.H., Stoneman, Z., & Burke, M. (1987b). Child temperaments, maternal differential behavior and sibling relationships. *Developmental Psychology, 23,* 354–362.

Brody, G.H., Stoneman, Z., & Burke, M. (1988). Child temperament and parental perceptions of individual child adjustment: An intrafamilial analysis. *American Journal of Orthopsychiatry, 58,* 532–542.

Brody, G.H., Stoneman, Z., Davis, C.H., Crapps, J.M. (1991). Observations of the role relations and behavior between older children with mental retardation and their younger siblings. *American Journal of Mental Retardation, 95*(5), 527–536.

Brody, G.H., Stoneman, Z., & Gauger, K. (1996). Parent–child relationships, family problem-solving behavior, and sibling relationship quality: The moderating role of sibling temperaments. *Child Development, 67,* 1289–1300.

Brody, G.H., Stoneman, Z., & MacKinnon, C.E. (1982). Role asymmetries in interactions between school aged children, their younger siblings and their friends. *Child Development, 53,* 1364–1370.

Brody, G.H., Stoneman, Z., & MacKinnon, C.E. (1986). Contributions of maternal child-rearing practices and play contexts to sibling interactions. *Journal of Applied Developmental Psychology, 7,* 225–236.

Brody, G.H., Stoneman, Z., MacKinnon, C.E., & MacKinnon, R. (1985). Role relationships and behavior between preschool-aged and school-aged sibling pairs. *Developmental Psychology, 21*(1), 124–129.

Brody, G.H., Stoneman, Z., & McCoy, J.K. (1992a). Associations of maternal and paternal direct and differential behavior with sibling relationships: Contemporaneous and longitudinal analyses. *Child Development, 63,* 82–92.

Brody, G.H., Stoneman, Z., & McCoy, J.K. (1992b). Parental differential treatment of siblings and sibling differences in negative emotionality. *Journal of Marriage and the Family, 54,* 643–651.

Brody, G.H., Stoneman, Z., & McCoy, J.K. (1994). Forecasting sibling relationships in early adolescence from child temperaments and family processes in middle childhood. *Child Development, 65,* 771–784.

Brody, G.H., Stoneman, Z., McCoy, J.K., & Forehand, R. (1992). Contemporaneous and longitudinal associations of sibling conflict with family relationship assessments and family discussions about sibling problems. *Child Development, 63,* 391–500.

Bronfenbrenner, U. (1977). Toward an experimental ecology of human development. *American Psychologist, 32,* 513–531.

Brown, J.R., & Dunn, J. (1992). Talk with your mother or your sibling? Developmental changes in early family conversations about feelings. *Child Development, 63,* 336–349.

Bruce, E.J., & Schultz, C.L. (2001). *Nonfinite loss and grief: A Psychoeducational Approach.* Baltimore: Paul H. Brookes Publishing Co.

Bryant, B.K. (1982). Sibling relationships in middle childhood. In M.E. Lamb & B. Sutton-Smith (Eds.), *Sibling relationships* (pp. 87–122). Mahwah, NJ: Lawrence Erlbaum Associates.

Bryant, B., & Crockenberg, S. (1980). Correlations and dimensions of prosocial behavior: A study of female siblings and their mothers. *Child Development, 51,* 354–362.

Buell, J., Stoddard, P., Harris, F.R., & Baer, D.M. (1968). Collateral social development accompanying reinforcement of outdoor play in a preschool child. *Journal of Applied Behavior Analysis, 1,* 167–174.

Buhrmester, D. (1992). The developmental course of sibling and peer relationships. In F. Boer & J. Dunn (Eds.), *Children's sibling relationships: Developmental and clinical issues* (pp. 19–40). Mahwah, NJ: Lawrence Erlbaum Associates.

Buhrmester, D., & Furman, W. (1990). Perceptions of sibling relationships during middle childhood and adolescence. *Child Development, 61,* 1387–1398.

Buhrmester, D., & Prager, K. (1995). Patterns and functions of self-disclosure during childhood and adolescence. In K. Rotenberg (Ed.), *Disclosure processes in children and adolescents.* Cambridge, UK: Cambridge University Press.

Burbach, D.J., & Peterson, L. (1986). Children's concepts of physical illness: A review and critique of the cognitive-developmental literature. *Health Psychology, 5,* 307–325.

Burke, P. (2004). *Brothers and sisters of children with disabilities.* Gateshead, Tyne and Wear, Great Britain: Athanaeum Press.

Burke, P., & Montgomery, S. (2000). Siblings of children with disabilities: A pilot study. *Journal of Intellectual Disabilities, 4*(3), 227–236.

Burton, L. (1975). *The family of sick children.* London: Routledge, Kehan Paul.

Burton, S. (1991). *Kidpower.* Moscow: University of Idaho, Idaho Center on Developmental Disabilities.

Burton, S.L., & Parks, A.L. (1991). *The self-esteem, locus of control, and career aspirations of college-aged siblings of individuals with disability.* Moscow: Idaho Center on Developmental Disabilities, The University of Idaho.

Bussell, D.A., Neiderhiser, J.M., Pike, A., Plomin, R., Simmens, S., Howe, G.W., Hetherington, E.M., Carroll, E., & Reiss, D. (1999). Adolescents' relationships to siblings and mothers: A multivariate genetic analysis. *Developmental Psychology, 35*(5), 1248–1259.

Byrnes, C., & Love, M. (1983). Sibling day workshops: A holistic approach. *Sibling Information Network Newsletter, 2*(1), 4.

Calabro, T. (2003). A sibling with disability adds richness—and complexity—to life. Retrieved June 12, 2005, from http://www.post-gazette.com/healthscience/20030325hsiblings2.asp

Caldwell, B.M., & Guze, S.B. (1960). A study of the adjustment of parents and siblings of institutionalized and noninstitutionalized retarded children. *American Journal of Mental Deficiency, 64,* 845–861.

Caro, P., & Derevensky, J.L. (1997). An exploratory study using the Sibling Interaction Scale: Observing interactions between siblings with and without disabilities. *Education and Treatment of Children, 20*(4), 383–403.

Cash, W.M., & Evans, I.N. (1975). Training preschool children to modify their retarded siblings' behavior. *Journal of Behavior Therapy and Experimental Psychiatry, 6,* 13–16.

Cate, I.M.P.T., & Loots, G.M.P. (2000). Experiences of siblings of children with physical disabilities: An empirical investigation. *Disability and Rehabilitation, 22*(9), 399–408.

Cerreto, M., & Miller, N.B. (1981). *Siblings of handicapped children: A review of the literature.* Unpublished paper, University of California-Los Angeles.

Chambers, C.R., Hughes, C., & Carter, E.W. (2004). Parent and sibling perspectives on the transition to adulthood. *Education and Training in Developmental Disabilities, 39*(2), 79–94.

Chintz, S.P. (1981). A sibling group of brothers and sisters of handicapped children. *Children Today, 21–23.*

Cicirelli, V.G. (1972). The effect of sibling relationships on concept learning of young children taught by child teachers. *Child Development,* 43, 282–287.

Cicirelli, V.G. (1976). Mother–child and sibling–sibling interactions on a problem solving task. *Child Development,* 47, 588–596.

Cicirelli, V.G. (1982). Sibling influence throughout the lifespan. In M.E. Lamb & B. Sutton-Smith (Eds.), *Sibling relationships* (pp. 267–284). Mahwah, NJ: Lawrence Erlbaum Associates.

Clark, H.B., Greene, B.F., Macrae, J.N., McNees, N.P., Davis, J.L., & Risley, T.R. (1977). A parent advice package for family shopping trips: Development and evaluation. *Journal of Applied Behavior Analysis, 10,* 605–624.

Clements, J.E., & Alexander, R.N. (1975). Parent training: Bringing it all back home. *Focus on Exceptional Children,* 7(5), 1–12.

Cleveland, D., & Miller, N. (1977). Attitudes and life commitments of older siblings of mentally retarded adults: An exploratory study. *Mental Retardation, 15,* 38–41.

Cohen, B. (1985). Good news genetic counseling. *Sibling Information Network Newsletter, 4*(1), 1.

Colletti, G., & Harris, S.L. (1977). Behavior modification in the home: Siblings as behavior modifiers, parents as observers. *Journal of Abnormal Child Psychology, 5*(1), 21–30.

Colorado Department of Public Health and Environment (2005). What happens during a genetics evaluation? Retrieved September 28, 2005, at http://www.cdphe.state.co.us/ps/genetics/more.html

Conger, K.J., & Conger, R.D. (1994). Differential parenting and change in sibling differences in delinquency. *Journal of Family Psychology, 8,* 287–303.

Connidis, I.A. (1994). Sibling support in older age. *Journal of Gerontology, 49,* S309–S317.

Connor, J.M. (1989). Genetic aspects of prenatal diagnosis. *Journal of Inherited Metabolic Disease, 12,* 89–96.

Connors, C., & Stalker, K. (2003). *The views and experiences of disabled children and their siblings: A positive outlook.* Philadelphia: Jessica Kingsley Publishers.

Conway, A. (1986). A sibling living with schizophrenia: Some personal reflections. *Sibling Information Network Newsletter, 4*(4), 4–5.

Corter, C., Abramovitch, R., & Pepler, D.J. (1983). The role of the mother in sibling interaction. *Child Development, 54,* 1599–1605.

Corter, C., Pepler, D.J., & Abramovitch, R. (1983). Effects of situation and sibling status on sibling interaction. *Canadian Journal of Behavioral Science, 14,* 380–392.

Cowan, E.L., Pederson, A., Babigan, H., Izzo, L.D., & Trost, M.A. (1973). Long term follow-up of early detected vulnerable children. *Journal of Consulting and Clinical Psychology, 41,* 438–446.

Cox, A.H., Marshall, E.S., Mandleco, B., & Olsen, S.F. (2003). Coping responses to daily life stressors of children who have a sibling with a disability. *Journal of Family Nursing, 9*(4), 397–413.

Cramer, S., Erzkus, A., Mayweather, K., Pope, K., Roeder, J., & Tone, T. (1997, September/October). Connecting with siblings. *Teaching Exceptional Children,* 46–51.

Crnic, K.A., & Leconte, J. (1986). Understanding sibling needs and influence. In R. Fewell & P. Vadasy (Eds.), *Families of handicapped children: Needs and supports across the life span* (pp. 75–98). Austin, Texas: PRO-ED.

Cummings, E.M., & Smith, D. (1993). The impact of anger between adults on siblings' emotions and social behavior. *Journal of Child Psychiatry, 34*(8), 1425–1433.

Cuskelly, M. (1999). Adjustment of siblings of children with a disability: Methodological issues. *International Journal for the Advancement of Counseling, 21,* 111–124.

Cuskelly, M., Chant, D., & Hayes, A. (1998). Behaviour problems in the siblings of children with Down syndrome: Associations with family responsibilities and parental stress. *International Journal of Disability, Development, and Education, 45*(3), 295–311.

Cuskelly, M., & Dadds, M. (1992). Behavioural problems in children with Down's syndrome and their siblings. *Journal of Child Psychology and Psychiatry, 33*(4), 749–761.

Cuskelly, M., & Gunn, P. (1993). Maternal reports of behavior of siblings of children with Down syndrome. *American Journal on Mental Retardation, 97*(5), 521–529.

Dallas, E., Stevenson, J., & McGurk, H. (1993). Cerebral-palsied children's interactions with siblings: Influence of severity of disability, age and birth order. *Journal of Child Psychology and Psychiatry, 34*(5), 621–647.

Daniels, D., & Plomin, R. (1985). Differential experience of siblings in the same family. *Developmental Psychology, 21,* 747–760.

D'Arcy, F., Flynn, J., McCarthy, Y., O'Connor, C., & Tierney, E. (2005). Sibshops: An evaluation of an interagency model. *Journal of Intellectual Disabilities, 9*(1), 43–57.

Dauz-Williams, P., Hanson, S., Karlin, S., Ridder, L., Liebergen, A., Olson, J., & Barnard, S. (1997). Outcomes of a nursing intervention for siblings of chronically ill children: A pilot study. *Journal of the Society of Pediatric Nurses, 2*(3), 127-138.

Davis, D., Cahan, S., & Bashi, J. (1977). Birth order and intellectual development: The confluence model in the light of cross-cultural evidence. *Science, 196,* 1470–1472.

Day, R., Lindeman, D., Powell, T., Fox, J.J., Stowitscheck, J., & Shores, R. (1984). The investigation of an empirically derived teaching package for socially withdrawn handicapped children and non-handicapped children. *Teacher Education and Special Education, 7*(1), 46–55.

Day, R., Powell, T., & Stowitschek, J. (1981). *Social competence intervention package for preschool youngsters* (SCIPPY). Logan: Exceptional Child Center, Utah State University.

Deater-Deckard, K., & Dunn, J. (1999). Multiple risks and adjustment in young children growing up in different family settings: A British community study of step-parent, single mother, and non-divorced families. In F.M. Hetherington (Ed.), *Coping with divorce, single parenting, and remarriage: A risk and residency perspective* (pp. 47–64). Mahwah, NJ: Lawrence Erlbaum Associates.

Deater-Deckard, K., & Dunn, J. (2002). Sibling relationships and socioemotional adjustment in different family contexts. *Social Development, 11,* 571–590.

Deater-Deckard, K., Dunn, J., & Lussier, G. (2002). Sibling relationships and social-emotional adjustment in different family contexts. *Social Development, 11*(4), 571–590.

DeHart, G.B. (1999). Conflict and averted conflict in preschoolers' interactions with siblings and friends. In W.A. Collins & B. Laursen (Eds.), *Relationships as developmental contexts: The Minnesota symposia on child psychology* (pp. 281–303). Mahwah, NJ: Lawrence Erlbaum Associates.

DeHart, G., Kilpatrick, L, Betjemann, S., Bernadt, M., Stenger, S., Sullivan, K., et al. (2001). *Conflict and averted conflict between siblings and friends in early and middle childhood.* Poster session presented at the biennial meeting of the Society for Research in Child Development, Minneapolis, MN.

Dodd, L. (2004). Supporting the siblings of young children with disabilities. *British Journal of Special Education, 31*(1), 41–49.

Downey, D.B. (1995). When bigger is not better: Family size, parental resources, and children's educational performance. *American Sociological Review, 60,* 747–761.

Downey, D.B., & Condron, D.J. (2004). Playing well with others in kindergarten: The benefit of siblings at home. *Journal of Marriage and Family, 66,* 333–350.

Dunn, J. (1983). Sibling relationships in early childhood. *Child Development, 54,* 787–811.

Dunn, J. (1985). *Sisters and brothers.* Cambridge, MA: Harvard University Press.

Dunn, J. (1996). Brothers and sisters in middle childhood and adolescence: Continuity and change in individual differences. In G. Brody (Ed.), *Sibling relationships: Their causes and consequences* (pp. 31–46). Stamford, CT: Ablex.

Dunn, J., Deater-Deckard, K., Pickering, K., Golding, J., & the ALSPAC Study Team. (1999). Siblings, parents, and partners: Family relationships within a longitudinal community study. *Journal of Child Psychology, 40*(7), 1025–1037.

Dunn, J., & Kendrick, C. (1979). Interaction between young siblings in the context of family relationships. In M. Lewis & L. Rosenblum (Eds.), *The child and its family.* New York: Kluwer Academic/Plenum.

Dunn, J., & Kendrick, C. (1980). The arrival of a sibling: Changes in patterns of interaction between mother and first born child. *Journal of Child Psychology and Psychiatry and Allied Disciplines, 21*(2), 119–132.

Dunn, J., & Kendrick, C. (1982). *Siblings.* Cambridge, MA: Harvard University Press.

Dunn, J., & Plomin, R. (1990). *Separate lives: Why siblings are so different.* New York: Basic Books.

Dunn, J., & Plomin, R. (1991). Why are siblings so different? The significance of differences in sibling experiences within the family. *Family Process, 30,* 271–283.

Dunn, J.F., Plomin, R., & Daniels, D. (1986). Consistency and change in mothers behavior toward younger siblings. *Child Development,* 57, 348356.

Dunn, J., & Slomkowski, C. (1992). Conflict and the development of social understanding. In C.U. Shantz & W.W. Hartup (Eds.), *Conflict in child and adolescent development* (pp. 70–92). Cambridge, NY: Cambridge University Press.

Dunn, J., Slomkowski, C., & Beardsall, L. (1994). Sibling relationships from the preschool period through middle childhood and early adolescence. *Developmental Psychology, 30*(3), 315–324.

Dunn, J., Slomkowski, C., Beardsall, L., & Rende, R. (1994). Adjustment in middle childhood and early adolescence: Links with earlier and contemporary sibling relationships. *Journal of Child Psychiatry, 35*(3), 491–504.

Dunn, J., & Stocker, C. (1989). The significance of differences in siblings' experiences within the family. In K. Kreppner & R. Lerner (Eds.), *Family systems and life span development* (pp. 289–301). Mahwah, NJ: Lawrence Erlbaum Associates.

Dunn, J., Stocker, C., & Plomin, R. (1990). Non-shared experiences within the family: Correlates of behavioral problems in middle childhood. *Development and Psychopathology, 2,* 113–126.

Dyches, T.T., & Prater, M.A. (2000). *Developmental disability in children's literature.* Reston, VA: Council for Exceptional Children/MRDD.

Dyson, L.L. (1989). Adjustment of siblings of handicapped children: A comparison. *Journal of Pediatric Psychology, 14,* 215–229.

Dyson, L.L. (1996). The experiences of families of children with learning disabilities: Parental stress, family functioning, and sibling self-concept. *Journal of Learning Disabilities, 29*(3), 280–286.

Dyson, L.L. (1998). A support program for siblings of children with disabilities: What siblings learn and what they like. *Psychology in the Schools, 35*(1), 57–65.

Dyson, L.L. (1999). The psychosocial functioning of school-age children who have siblings with developmental disabilities. *Journal of Applied Developmental Psychology, 20*(2), 253–271.

Dyson, L.L. (2003). Children with learning disabilities within the family context: A comparison with siblings in global self-concept, academic self-perception, and social competence. *Learning Disabilities Research and Practice, 18*(1), 1–9.

Dyson, L., Edgar, E., & Crnic, K. (1989). Psychological predictors of adjustment by siblings of developmentally disabled children. *American Journal on Mental Retardation,* 94(3), 292–302.

Dyson, L., & Fewell, R.R. (1989). The self-concept of siblings of handicapped children: A comparison. *Journal of Early Intervention, 13*(3), 230–238.

East, P.L., & Rook, K.S. (1992). Compensatory patterns of support among children's peer relationships: A test using school friends, non-school friends, and siblings. *Developmental Psychology, 28,* 163–172.

Eggebeen, D.J. (1992). Change in sibling configurations for American preschool children. *Social Biology, 39*(1), 27–43.

Eisenberg, L., Baker, B.L., & Blacher, J. (1998). Siblings of children with mental retardation living at home or in residential placement. *Journal of Child Psychology and Psychiatry, 39*(3), 355–363.

Ellifritt, J. (1984). Life with my sister. *Exceptional Parent, 8*(14), 16–21.

Epkins, C.C., & Dedmon, A.M. (1999). An initial look at sibling reports on children's behavior: Comparisons with children's self-reports and relations with siblings' self-reports and sibling relationships. *Journal of Abnormal Child Psychology, 27*(5), 371–381.

Erel, O., Margolin, G., & John, R.S. (1998). Observed sibling interaction: Links with the marital and the mother–child relationship. *Developmental Psychology, 34*(2), 288–298.

Faber, A., & Mazlish, E. (1988). *Siblings without rivalry.* New York: Avon.

Fanos, J.H. (n.d.). Retrieved April 30, 2005, from http://www.cpmc.org/services/sibcnt.html

Farber, B. (1959). Effects of a severely mentally retarded child on family integration. *Monographs of the Society for Research in Child Development, 24,*(2, Serial No. 71).

Farber, B. (1960). Effects of a severely mentally retarded child on family integration. *Monographs of the Society for Research in Child Development, 21*(1, Serial No. 75).

Farber, B. (1964). *Family: Organization and interaction.* San Francisco: Chandler.

Farber, B. (1968). *Mental retardation: Its social context and social consequences.* Boston: Houghton Mifflin.

Farrington, D.P. (1995). The development of offending and antisocial behavior from childhood: Key findings from the Cambridge study in delinquent development. *Journal of Child Psychology and Psychiatry, 36,* 929–964.

Farrington, D.P., & West, D.J. (1993). Criminal, penal and life histories of chronic offenders: Risk and protective factors and early identification. *Criminal Behaviour and Health, 3,* 492–523.

Featherstone, H. (1980). *A difference in the family: Living with a disabled child.* New York: Basic Books.

Fee, R.W. (1990, Fall). The life planning approach. *New Ways,* 18–19.

Feiges, L.S., & Weiss, M.J. (2004). *Sibling stories: Reflections on life with a brother or sister on the Autism Spectrum.* Shawnee Mission, KS: Autism Asperger Publishing Co.

Feigon, J. (1981). A sibling group program. *Sibling Information Network Newsletter, 1*(2), 2.

Feinberg, M.E., & Hetherington, E.M. (2000). Sibling differentiation in adolescence: Implications for behavioral genetic theory. *Child Development, 71*(6), 1512–1524.

Feinberg, M.E., & Hetherington, E.M. (2001). Differential parenting as a with-in family variable. *Journal of Family Psychology, 15,* 22–37.

Ferrari, M. (1984). Chronic illness: Psychosocial effects on siblings-I. Chronically ill boys. *Journal of Child Psychology and Psychiatry, 25,*459–476.

Fewell, R.R. (1986). A handicapped child in the family. In R.R. Fewell & P.F. Vadasy (Eds.), *Families of handicapped children: Needs and supports across the life span* (pp. 3–34). Austin, TX: PRO-ED.

Fialka, J. (1997). *It matters: Lessons from my son.* Huntington Woods, MI: Author.

Fish, T., McCaffrey, F.D., Bush, K., & Piskur, S. (1995). *Sibling need and involvement profile (SNIP).* Available through Nisonger Center Publications Office, The Ohio State University, Columbus, OH 43210–1257.

Fisman, S., Wolf, L., Ellison, D., & Freeman, T. (2000). A longitudinal study of siblings of children with chronic disabilities. *Canadian Journal of Psychiatry, 45*(4), 369–375.

Floyd, K. (1995). Gender and closeness among friends and siblings. *Journal of Psychology, 129*(2), 193–202.

Fotheringham, J., & Creal, D. (1974). Handicapped children and handicapped families. *International Review of Education, 20,* 355–373.

Fowle, C.M. (1968). The effect of the severely mentally retarded child on his family. *American Journal of Mental Deficiency, 73,* 468–473.

Frank, R.A. (1988). Building self-esteem in persons with Down syndrome. In S.M. Pueschel (Ed.), *The young person with Down syndrome* (pp. 205–213). Baltimore: Paul H. Brookes Publishing Co.

Freedman, J.S. (2002). *Easing the teasing: Helping your child cope with name calling, ridicule, and verbal bullying.* New York: McGraw Hill.

Froschl, M., Sprung, B., & Mullin-Rindler, N. (1998). *Quit it! A teacher's guide on teasing and bullying for use with students in grades K–3.* Washington, DC: National Education Association.

Furman, W., & Buhrmester, D. (1985). Children's perception of the qualities of sibling relationships. *Child Development, 56,* 448–461.

Gallagher, P.A., Fialka, J., Rhodes, C., & Arceneaux, C. (2002). Working with families: Rethinking denial. *Young Exceptional Children, 5*(2), 11–17.

Gallagher, P.A., Floyd, J.H., Stafford, A.M., Taber, T.A., Brozovic, S.A., & Alberto, P.A. (2000). Inclusion of students with moderate or severe disabilities in educational and community settings: Perspectives from parents and siblings. *Education and Training in Mental Retardation and Developmental Disabilities, 35*(2), 135–147.

Gallagher, P.A., & Powell, T.H. (1989). Brothers and sisters: Meeting special needs. *Topics in Early Childhood Special Education, 8*(4), 24–37.

Gallagher, P.A., & Rhodes, C.R. (2005). *Siblings in early intervention.* Unpublished manuscript.

Gamble, W.G., & McHale, S.M. (1989). Coping with stress in sibling relationships: A comparison of children with disabled and nondisabled siblings. *Journal of Applied Developmental Psychology, 10,* 353–373.

Garcia, M.M., Shaw, D.S., Winslow, E.B., & Yaggi, K.E. (2000). Destructive sibling conflict and the development of conduct problems in young boys. *Developmental Psychology, 36,* 44–53.

Garner, P.W. (1993). *Social cognitive correlates of preschool children's sibling care-giving behavior.* Poster presented at the biennial meeting of the Society for Research in Child Development, New Orleans.

Garner, P.W., Jones, D.C., & Miner, J.L. (1994). Social competence among low-income preschoolers: Emotion socialization practices and social cognitive correlates. *Child Development, 65,* 622–637.

Garner, P.W., Jones, D.C., & Palmer, D.J. (1994). Social cognitive correlates of preschool children's sibling caregiving behavior. *Developmental Psychology, 30*(6), 905–911.

Gath, A. (1974). Sibling reactions to mental handicap: A comparison of the brothers and sisters of mongol children. *Journal of Child Psychology and Psychiatry, 15,* 187–198.

Gath, A., & Gumley, D. (1987). Retarded children and their siblings. *Journal of Child Psychology and Psychiatry, 28,* 715–730.

Gazda, G. (1978). *Group counseling: A developmental approach.* Boston: Allyn & Bacon.

Geisthardt, C.L., Brotherson, M.J., & Cook, C.C. (2002). Friendships of children with disabilities in the home environment. *Education and Training in Mental Retardation and Developmental Disabilities, 37*(3), 235–252.

GeneTests (2005). About genetic services. Retrieved September 30, 2005, from http://www.genetests.org/servlet/access?id=8888891&key=weMiq4fHNgRAk&fcn=y&fw=S17e&filename=/concepts/primer/primerintro.html

Genetics and Public Policy Center (2005). Retrieved September 30, 2005, from http://www.dnapolicy.org

Genetics Home Reference (2006a): *Genetic testing.* Bethesda, MD: National Library of Medicine; retrieved May 15, 2006, from http://ghr.nlm.nih.gov/info=genetic_testing/show/alltopics

Genetics Home Reference (2006b). *Handbook: Help me understand genetics.* Bethesda, MD: National Library of Medicine; Retrieved May 15, 2006, from http://ghr.nlm.nih.gov/info=understandGenetics

George, R.L., & Christiani, T.S. (1981). *Theory, methods and processes of counseling and psychotherapy.* Englewood Cliffs, NJ: Prentice Hall, Inc.

Glasberg, B.A. (2000). The development of siblings' understanding of autism and related disorders. *Journal of Autism and Developmental Disorders, 30*(2), 143–156.

Gold, N. (1993). Depression and social adjustment in siblings of boys with autism. *Journal of Autism and Developmental Disorders, 23*(1), 147–163.

Goldsmith, H.H. (1993). Nature–nurture issues in the behavioral genetic context: Overcoming barriers to communication. In R. Plomin & G. McClearn (Eds.), *Nature, nurture, and psychology* (pp. 325–339). Washington, DC: American Psychological Association.

Graham-Bermann, S.A. (1991). Siblings in dyads: Relationships among perceptions and behavior. *The Journal of Genetic Psychology, 152*(2), 207–216.

Graliker, B.V., Fishler, K., & Koch, R. (1962). Teenage reaction to a mentally retarded sibling. *American Journal of Mental Deficiency, 66,* 838–843.

Griffiths, D.L., & Unger, D.G. (1994). Views about planning for the future among parents and siblings of adults with mental retardation. *Family Relations, 43,* 221–227.

Grissom, M.O., & Borkowski, J.G. (2002). Self-efficacy in adolescents who have siblings with or without disabilities. *American Journal on Mental Retardation, 107*(2), 79–90.

Gross, J. (2004, December 10). For siblings of the autistic, a burdened youth. *New York Times.*

Grossman, F.K. (1972). *Brothers and sisters of retarded children: An exploratory study.* Syracuse, NY: Syracuse University Press.

Guite, J., Lobato, D., Kao, B., & Plante, W. (2004). Discordance between sibling and parent reports of the impact of chronic illness and disability on siblings. *Children's Health Care, 33*(1), 77–92.

Guralnick, M.J. (1976). The value of integrating handicapped and nonhandicapped preschool children. *American Journal of Orthopsychiatry, 46,* 236–245.

Guralnick, M.J. (Ed.). (1978). *Early intervention and the integration of handicapped and nonhandicapped children.* Baltimore: University Park Press.

Hancock, T.B., & Kaiser, A.P. (1996). Siblings' use of milieu teaching at home. *Topics in Early Childhood Special Education, 16*(2), 169–190.

Hannah, M.E., & Midlarsky, E. (1985). Siblings of the handicapped: A literature review for school psychologists. *School Psychology Review, 14,* 510–520.

Hannah, M.E., & Midlarsky, E. (1999). Competence and adjustment of siblings of children with mental retardation. *American Journal on Mental Retardation, 104*(1), 22–37.

Harland, P., & Cuskelly, M. (2000). The responsibilities of adult siblings of adults with dual sensory impairments. *International Journal of Disability, Development and Education, 47*(3), 293–307.

Harris, I.D. (1964). *The promised seed: A comparative study of eminent first and later sons.* Glencoe, IL: Free Press.

Harris, S. (n.d.). *Siblings of children with autism: An interview with Sandra Harris.* Retrieved January 27, 2005, from http://www.childrensdisabilities.info/autism/interview-harris.htm

Harris, S.L., & Glasberg, B.A. (2003). *Siblings of children with autism: A guide for families.* Bethesda, MD: Woodbine House.

Harris, T.A., Sulzer-Azaroff, B., & McGee, G.G. (1992, May). *Promoting reciprocal interactions between children with developmental delays and their typical siblings through instruction in incidental teaching.* Paper presented at the annual meeting of the Association for Behavior Analysis, San Francisco.

Harris, V., & McHale, S.M. (1989). Family life problems, daily caregiving activities, and the psychological well-being of mothers of mentally retarded children. *American Journal on Mental Retardation, 94,* 231–239.

Harry, B., Day, M., & Quist, F. (1998). "He can't really play": An ethnographic study of sibling acceptance and interaction. *The Journal of The Association for Persons with Severe Handicaps, 23*(4), 289–299.

Hartup, W.W. (1978). Peer interaction and the process of socialization. In M.J. Guralnick (Ed.), *Early intervention and the integration of handicapped and nonhandicapped children.* Baltimore: University Park Press.

Heifetz, L.J. (1977). Behavioral training for parents of retarded children: Alternative formats based on instructional manuals. *American Journal of Mental Deficiency, 82,* 194–203.

Heller, K.W., Gallagher, P.A., & Fredrick, L.D. (1999). Parents' perceptions of siblings' interactions with their brothers and sisters who are deafblind. *Journal of the Association for Persons with Severe Handicaps, 24*(1), 33–43.

Helsels, E. (1985). The Helsels story of Robin. In A.P. Turnbull & H.R. Turnbull (Eds.), *Parents speak out: Then and now* (pp. 94–115). Columbus, OH: Charles E. Merrill.

Hendrickson, J.M., Strain, P., Tremblay, A., & Shores, R.E. (1981). Relationship between toy and material use and the occurrence of social interactive behaviors by normally developing children. *Psychology in the Schools, 18,* 500–504.

Hertz-Lazarowitz, R., Rosenberg, M., & Guttman, J. (1989). Children of divorce and their intimate relationships with parents and peers. *Youth and Society, 21*(1), 85–104.

Hetherington, E.M., Reiss, D., & Plomin, R. (Eds.). (1994). *Separate social worlds of siblings: Impact of nonshared environment on development.* Mahwah, NJ: Lawrence Erlbaum Associates.

Hoffman, M. (1970). Moral development. In P. Mussen (Ed.), *Carmichael's manual of child psychology* (Vol. 2). New York: John Wiley & Sons.

Holt, K. (1958). The home care of severely retarded children. *Pediatrics,* 22(4), 744–755.

Howe, N. (1991). Sibling-directed internal state language, perspective taking, and affective behavior. *Child Development, 62,* 1503–1512.

Howe, N., Aquan-Assee, J., Bukowski, W.M., Lehoux, P.M., & Rinaldi, C.M. (2001). Siblings as confidants: Emotional understanding, relationship warmth, and sibling self-disclosure. *Social Development, 10*(4), 439–454.

Howe, N., Petrakos, H., & Rinaldi, C.M. (1998). "All the sheeps are dead. He murdered them": Sibling pretense, negotiation, internal state language, and relationship quality. *Child Development, 69,* 182–191.

Howe, N., Rinaldi, C.M., Jennings, M., & Petrakos, H. (2002). "No! The lambs can stay out because they got cozies": Constructive and destructive sibling conflict, pretend play, and social understanding. *Child Development, 73,* 1460–1473.

Individuals with Disabilities Education Act Amendments of 1997, PL 105-17, 20 U.S.C. §§ 1400 *et seq.*

Individuals with Disabilities Education Improvement Act of 2004, PL 108-446, 20 U.S.C. §§ 1400 *et seq.*

Internet School Library Media Center. (n.d.). Bibliotherapy and Children's Books. Retrieved March 30, 2005 from http://falcon.jmu.edu/~raseyil/bibliotherapy.htm

Itzkowitz, J.S. (1989). The needs and concerns of brothers and sisters of individuals with disabilities. Unpublished doctoral dissertation, The University of Connecticut.

Jacobs, B.S., & Moss, H.A. (1976). Birth order and sex of sibling as determinants of mother-infant interaction. *Child Development, 47,* 315–322.

James, S.D., & Egle, A.L. (1986). A direct prompting strategy for increasing reciprocal interactions between handicapped and non-handicapped siblings. *Journal of Applied Behavior Analysis, 19,* 173–186.

Jiao, S., Ji, G., & Jing, C.C. (1986). Comparative study of behavioral qualities of only children and sibling children. *Child Development, 57,* 357–361.

Johnson, C.A., & Katz, R.G. (1973). Using parents as change agents for their children: A review. *Journal of Child Psychology and Psychiatry and Allied Disciplines, 14,* 181–200.

Jones, C.B. (2001). *Understanding your special needs grandchild.* Plantation, FL: Specialty Press, Inc.

Jones, C.P., & Adamson, L.B. (1987). Language use in mother–child and mother–child–sibling interactions. *Child Development, 58,* 356–366.

Jones, C.D., & Schwartz, I.S. (2004). Siblings, peers, and adults: Differential effects of models for children with autism. *Topics in Early Childhood Special Education, 24(4),* 187–198.

Kaiser, A.P., & Fox, J.J. (1986). Behavioral parent training research: Contributions to an ecological analysis of families of handicapped children. In J.J. Gallagher & P.M. Vietze (Eds.), *Families of handicapped persons: Research, programs, and policy issues* (pp. 219–235). Baltimore: Paul H. Brookes Publishing Co.

Kaiser, A., Hendrickson, J., & Alpert, K. (1991). Milieu language teaching: A second look. In R. Gable (Ed.), *Advances in mental retardation and developmental disabilities.* (Vol. 4, pp. 63–92). London: Jessica Kingsley.

Kaminsky, L., & Dewey, D. (2001). Sibling relationships of children with autism. *Journal of Autism and Developmental Disorders, 31*(4), 399–410.

Kaminsky, L., & Dewey, D. (2002). Psychological adjustment in siblings of children with autism. *Journal of Child Psychology and Psychiatry, 43,* 225–232.

Kaplan, B.J., & Colombatto, J. (1966). Headstart program for siblings of mentally retarded children. *Mental Retardation 4*(6). 30–32.

Kaplan, B.J., & McHale, F.J. (1980). Communication and play behaviors of a deaf preschooler and his younger brother. *Volta Review, 82,* 476–482.

Kelly, A. (1982). Always been one of us. *Sibling Information Network Newsletter, 1*(5), 3.

Kier, C., & Lewis, C. (1998). Preschool sibling interaction in separated and married families: Are same-sex pairs or older sisters more sociable? *Journal of Child Psychology and Psychiatry, 39*(2), 191–201.

Kirk, S.A., & Bateman, B.D. (1964). *Ten years of research at the Institute for Research on Exceptional Children.* Urbana: University of Illinois.

Kirkman, M. (1986, September). *Sibling relationships with and without a disabled child in the family.* Keynote address to NY Conference on Siblings of Mentally Retarded and Developmentally Disabled Persons, New York City.

Klein, S.D., & Schleifer, M.J. (1993). *It isn't fair: Siblings of children with disabilities.* Westport, CT: Bergin and Garvey.

Knapczyk, D.R. (1989). Peer-mediated training of cooperative play between special and regular class students in integrated play settings. *Education and Training in Mental Retardation, 24*(3), 255–264.

Knott, F., Lewis, C., & Williams, T. (1995). Sibling interaction of children with learning disabilities: A comparison of autism and Down's syndrome. *Journal of Child Psychology and Psychiatry, 6,* 965–976.

Koch, H.L. (1955). Some personality correlates of sex of sibling position and sex of sibling among five– and six-year-old children. *Genetic Psychology Monographs, 52,* 3–50.

Koegel, L.K., Stiebel, D., & Koegel, R.L. (1998). Reducing aggression in children with autism toward infant or toddler siblings. *The Journal for The Association of Persons with Severe Handicaps, 23*(2), 111–118.

Kohl, F., & Beckman, P. (1990). The effects of directed play on the frequency and length of reciprocal interactions with preschoolers having moderate handicaps. *Education and Training in Mental Retardation, 25*(3), 258–266.

Kohn, M., & Rosman, B.L. (1972). Relationship of preschool social-emotional functioning to later intellectual achievement. *Developmental Psychology, 6,* 445–452.

Kolin, K., Scherzer, A., New, B., & Garfield, M. (1971). Studies of the schoolage child with myelomeningocele: Social and emotional adaptation. *Pediatrics, 78,* 1013–1019.

Kolodny, E.H., Abuelo, D.N., Barsel-Bowers, G., & Pueschel, S.M. (1990). Preconceptual genetic screening and counseling. In S.M. Pueschel & J.A. Mulick (Eds.), *Prevention of developmental disabilities* (pp. 37–51). Baltimore: Paul H. Brookes Publishing Co.

Korner, A.F. (1971). Individual differences at birth: Implications for early experience and later development. *American Journal of Orthopsychiatry, 41,* 608–619.

Kosonen, M. (1996). Siblings as providers of support and care during middle childhood: Children's perceptions. *Children and Society, 10,* 267–279.

Kowal, A.K., & Blinn-Pike., L. (2004). Sibling influences on adolescents' attitudes toward safe sex practices. *Family Relations, 53*(4), 377–384.

Kowal, A., & Kramer, L. (1997). Children's understanding of parental differential treatment. *Child Development, 68,* 113–126.

Kramer, L., & Gottman, J.M. (1992). Becoming a sibling: "With a little help from my friends." *Developmental Psychology, 28,* 685–699.

Kramer, L., & Radey, C. (1997). Improving sibling relationships among young children: A social skills training model. *Family Relations, 46,* 237–246.

Krauss, M.W., Seltzer, M.M., Gordon, R., & Friedman, D.H. (1996). Binding ties: The roles of adult siblings of persons with mental retardation. *Mental Retardation, 34*(2), 83–93.

Kutner, L. (2005) When a sibling is disabled. Retrieved April, 2005, from http:www.drkutner.com/parenting/articles/disabled_sib.html

Lamb, M. (1978a). Interactions between 18-month-olds and their preschool-aged siblings. *Child Development, 49,* 51–59.

Lamb, M. (1978b). The development of sibling relationships in infancy: A short term longitudinal study. *Child Development, 49,* 1189–1196.

Lamb, M. (1982). Sibling relationship across the lifespan: An overview and introduction. In M.E. Lamb & B. Sutton-Smith (Eds.), *Sibling relationships* (pp. 1–11). Mahwah, NJ: Lawrence Erlbaum Associates.

Lamb, M., & Sutton-Smith, B. (Eds.). (1982). *Sibling relationships.* Mahwah, NJ: Lawrence Erlbaum Associates.

Larson, J. (1992). Understanding stepfamilies. *American Demographics, 14,* 360.

Lauritsen, J.L. (1993). Sibling resemblance in juvenile delinquency: Findings from the National Youth Survey. *Criminology, 31,* 387–410.

Lefrancois, G.R. (1973). *Of children: Introduction to child development.* Belmont, CA: Wadsworth Publishing.

Lent, J.R., & McLean, B.M. (1976). The trainable retarded: the technology of teaching. In N.G. Haring & R.L. Schiefelbusch (Eds.), *Teaching special children.* New York: McGraw-Hill.

Lipsky, D.K., & Gartner, A. (1992). Achieving full inclusion: Placing the student at the center of educational reform. In W. Stainback & S. Stainback (Eds.), *Controversial issues confronting special education* (pp. 3–12). Boston: Allyn and Bacon.

Little, L. (2002). Middle-class mothers' perceptions of peer and sibling victimization among children with Asperger syndrome and nonverbal learning disorders. *Issues in Comprehensive Pediatric Nursing, 25,* 43–57.

Litzelfelner, P. (1995). Children with emotional disabilities: Perceptions of siblings. *Child and Adolescent Social Work Journal, 12*(4), 263–273.

Lloyd-Bostock, S. (1976). Parents' experiences of official help and guidance in caring for a mentally handicapped child. *Child: Care, Health, and Development, 2,* 325–338.

Lobato, D.J. (1981). *Multiple assessment of a workshop program for siblings of handicapped children.* Unpublished doctoral dissertation, University of Massachusetts.

Lobato, D.J. (1983). Siblings of handicapped children: A review. *Journal of Autism and Developmental Disorders, 13*(4), 347–364.

Lobato, D.J. (1990). *Brothers, sisters and special needs: Information and activities for helping young siblings of children with chronic illnesses and developmental disabilities.* Baltimore: Paul H. Brookes Publishing Co.

Lobato, D., Barbour, L., Hall, L.J., & Miller, C.T. (1987). Psychosocial characteristics of preschool siblings of handicapped and nonhandicapped children. *Journal of Abnormal Child Psychology, 15,* 329–338.

Lobato, D.J., Miller, C.T., Barbour, L., Hall, L.J., & Pezzullo, J.H. (1991). Preschool siblings of handicapped children: Interactions with mothers, brothers, and sisters. *Research in Developmental Disabilities, 12,* 387–399.

Lobato, D., & Tlaker, A. (1985). Sibling intervention with a retarded child. *Education and Treatment of Children, 8,* 221–228.

Lytton, H., & Romney, D.M. (1991). Parents' differential socialization of boys and girls: A meta-analysis. *Psychological Bulletin, 109,* 267–296.

Macfarlane, E. (2001). Growing up with my sister with autism. *Journal of Positive Behavior Interventions, 3*(3), 190–191.

Mackeith, R. (1973). The feelings and behavior of parents of handicapped children. *Developmental Medicine and Child Neurology, 15,* 524–527.

Mager, R. (1975). *Preparing instructional objectives.* Palo Alto, CA: Fearon Publishers.

Mandleco, B., Olsen, S.F., Dyches, T., & Marshall, E. (2003). The relationship between family and sibling functioning in families raising a child with a disability. *Journal of Family Nursing, 9*(4), 365–396.

Mannle, S., & Tomasello, M. (1987). Fathers, sibling, and the bridge hypothesis. In K.E. Nelson & A. VanKleeck (Eds.), *Children's language* (Vol. 6, pp. 23–42). Mahwah, NJ: Lawrence Erlbaum Assoc.

March of Dimes. (2005). Genetic counseling. Retrieved September 25, 2005, from http://www.marchofdimes.com/pnhec/4439_15008.asp.

Martin, M.M., Anderson, C.M., Burant, P.A., & Weber, K. (1997). Verbal aggression in sibling relationships. *Communication Quarterly, 45*(3), 304–317.

Mates, T.E. (1982, July). *Which siblings of autistic children are at greater risk for the development of school and/or personality difficulties?* Paper presented at the National Society for Autistic Children, Omaha, NE.

Mates, T.E. (1990). Siblings of autistic children: Their adjustment at home and in school. *Journal of Autism and Developmental Disorders, 20,* 545–553.

May, J. (2001, March). Enhancing family resilience: Pants first, then your shoes. Retrieved from http://www.fathersnetwork.org/762/html

McCoy, J.K., Brody, G.H., & Stoneman, Z. (1994). A longitudinal analysis of sibling relationships as mediators of the link between family processes and youths' best friendships. *Family Relations, 43,* 400–408.

McCoy, J.K., Brody, G.H., & Stoneman, Z. (2002). Temperament and the quality of best friendships: Effect of same-sex sibling relationships. *Family Relations, 51,* 248–255.

McCubbin, M.A., & McCubbin, H.L. (1993). Families coping with illness: The resiliency model of family stress, adjustment, and adaptation. In C. Danielson, B. Hamell-Bissell, & P. Winstead-Fry (Eds.), *Families, health & illness: Perspectives on coping and intervention* (pp. 21–63). St Louis: Mosby.

McDermott, J. (1980). *The complete book on sibling rivalry.* New York: Wideview Books.

McEvoy, M., Shores, R., Wehby, J., Johnson, S., & Fox, J. (1990). Special education teachers' implementation of procedures to promote social interaction among children in integrated settings. *Education and Training in Mental Retardation, 25*(3), 267–275.

McEvoy, M.A., Nordquist, V.M., Twardosz, S., Heckaman, K., Wehby, J.H., & Denny, R.K. (1988). Promoting autistic children peer interaction in mainstreamed settings using affection activities. *Journal of Applied Behavior Analysis, 21,* 193–200.

McGee, G.G., Almeida, M.C., Sulzer-Azaroff, B., & Feldman, R.S. (1992). Promoting reciprocal interactions via peer incidental teaching. *Journal of Applied Behavior Analysis, 25,* 117. 126.

McGee, G.G., Feldman, R.S., & Morrier, M.J. (1997). Benchmarks of social treatment for children with autism. *Journal of Autism and Develomental Disorders, 27,* 353–364.

McGuire, S., Manke, B., Eftekhari, A., & Dunn, J. (2000). Children's perceptions of sibling conflict during middle childhood: Issues and sibling (dis)similarity. *Social Development, 9*(2), 173–190.

McHale, S.M., Crouter, A.C., McGuire, S.A., & Updegraff, K.A. (1995). Congruence between mother's and father's differential treatment of siblings: Links with family relations and children's well-being. *Child Development, 66,* 116–128.

McHale, S.M., & Gamble, W.C. (1987). Sibling relationships and adjustment of children with disabled brothers and sisters. *Journal of Children in Contemporary Society, 19,* 131–158.

McHale, S.M., & Gamble, W.C. (1989). Sibling relationships of children with disabled and nondisabled brothers and sisters. *Developmental Psychology, 25*(3), 421–429.

McHale, S.M., & Harris, V.S. (1992). Children's experiences with disabled and nondisabled siblings: Links with personal adjustment and relationship evaluation. In F. Boer and J. Dunn (Eds.), *Children's relationships with their siblings: Developmental and clinical implications* (pp. 83–100). Mahwah, NJ: Lawrence Erlbaum Associates.

McHale, S.M., & Pawletko, T.M. (1992). Differential treatment of siblings in two family contexts. *Child Development, 63,* 68–81.

McHale, S.M., Simeonsson, R.J., & Sloan, J.L. (1984). Children with handicapped brothers and sisters. In E. Schopler & G. Mesibov (Eds.), *The effects of autism on the family* (pp. 327–342). New York: Kluwer Academic/Plenum.

McHale, S.M., Sloan, J., & Simeonsson, R.J. (1986). Sibling relationships of children with autistic, mentally retarded, and nonhandicapped brothers and sisters. *Journal of Autism and Developmental Disorders, 16,* 399–413.

McHale, S.M., Updegraff, K.A., Helms-Erikson, H., & Crouter, A.C. (2001). Sibling influences on gender development in middle childhood and early adolescence: A longitudinal study. *Developmental Psychology, 37*(1), 115–125.

McHale, S.M., Updegraff, K.A., Tucker, C.J., & Crouter, A.C. (2000). Step in or stay out? Parents' roles in adolescent siblings' relationships. *Journal of Marriage and the Family,* 62, 746–760.

McHugh, M. (1999). *Special siblings: Growing up with someone with a disability.* New York: Hyperion.

McHugh, M. (2003). *Special siblings: Growing up with someone with a disability* (Rev. ed.). Baltimore: Paul H. Brookes Publishing Co.

McKeever, P. (1983). Siblings of chronically ill children: A literature review with implications for research and practice. *American Journal of Orthopsychiatry, 53*(2), 209–218.

McLinden, S., Miller, L., & Deprey, J. (1991). Effects of a support group for siblings of children with special needs. *Psychology in the Schools, 28,* 230–237.

McMabon, M.A., Noll, R. B., Michaud, L. J., Johnson, J. C. (2001). Sibling adjustment to pediatric traumatic brain injury: A case-controlled pilot study. *Journal of Head Trauma Rehabilitation, 16*(6), 587–594.

Mekos, D., Hetherington, E.M., & Reiss, D. (1996). Sibling differences in problem behavior and parental treatment in nondivorced and remarried families. *Child Development, 67,* 2148–2165.

Meyer, D. (Ed.). (2005). *The sibling slam book: What it's really like to have a brother or sister with special needs.* Bethesda, MD: Woodbine House.

Meyer, D.J., & Vadasy, P. (1996). *Living with a brother or sister with special needs: A book for sibs* (2nd ed.). Seattle: University of Washington Press.

Meyer, D.J., Vadasy, P.F., & Fewell, R.R. (1985). *Living with a brother or sister with special needs: A book for sibs.* Seattle: University of Washington Press.

Meyer, D.J., & Vadasy, P. (1994). *Sibshps: Workshops for siblings of children with special needs.* Baltimore: Paul H. Brookes Publishing Co.

Meyers, R. (1978). *Like normal people.* New York: McGraw-Hill.

Michaelis, C.T. (1980). *Home and school partnerships in exceptional education.* Rockville, MD: Aspen Publications.

Miller, A.L., Volling, B.L., & McElwain, N.L. (2000). Sibling jealousy in a triadic context with mothers and fathers. *Social Development, 9,* 433–457.

Miller, N.B., & Miller, W.H. (1976). Siblings as behavior change agents. In J.D. Kromboltz & C.E. Thoresen (Eds.), *Counseling methods.* Austin, TX: Holt, Rinehart, & Winston.

Miller, S. (1985). Siblings. *Sibling Information Network Newsletter,* 4(3), 4.

Miller, S.G. (1974). An exploratory study of sibling relationships in families with retarded children (Doctoral dissertation, Columbia University). *Dissertation Abstracts International,* 35, 299413–299513.

Milstead, S. (1988). Siblings are people too. *Academic Therapy,* 23(5), 537–540.

Minnett, A.M., Vandell, D.L., & Santrock, J.W. (1983). The effects of sibling status on sibling interaction: Influence of birth order, age spacing, sex of child, and sex of sibling. *Child Development, 54,* 1064–1072.

Minuchin, S. (1974). *Families and family therapy.* Cambridge, MA: Harvard University Press.

Mischel, W. (1970). Sex typing and socialization. In P. Mussen (Ed.), *Carmichael's manual of child psychology.* New York: John Wiley & Sons.

Moser, R.P., & Jacob, T. (2002). Parental and sibling effects in adolescent outcomes. *Psychological Reports, 91,* 463–479.

Munch, S., & Levick, J. (2001). "I'm special, too": Promoting sibling adjustment in the neonatal intensive care unit. *Health and Social Work, 26*(1), 58–64.

Munson, H.L. (1971). Foundations of developmental guidance. Boston: Allyn & Bacon.

Murphy, L., & Corte, S.D. (1989). Siblings. *Special Parent, Special Child, 5*(1), 1-6). (ERIC Document Reproduction Service No. ED 309 605).

Murphy, L., Pueschel, S., Duffy, T., & Brady E. (1976, March/April). Meeting with brothers and sisters of children with Down's syndrome. *Children Today, 5*(2). 20–23.

National Society of Genetic Counselors. (2005). Genetic counseling as a profession. Retrieved September 25, 2005 at www.nsgc.org/about/definition.asp

National Association of Sibling Programs (n.d.) Programs for adult siblings with disabilities. *The NASP Newsletter.* Seattle, WA: Children's Hospital and Medical Center, Sibling Support Project.

National Human Genome Research Institute. (2005). Retrieved September 25, 2005, from http://www.genome.gov/10001191.

Neiderhiser, J.M., Bussell, D.A., Pike, A., Plomin, R., Simmens, S., Howe, G.W., et al. (1999). The importance of shared environmental influences in explaining the overlap between mother's parenting and sibling relationships: Reply to Neale. *Developmental Psychology, 35*(5), 1265–1267.

Neufeld, G.R. (1975). Council as advocate. In J. Paul, R. Wiegerink, & G.R. Neufeld (Eds.), *Advocacy: A role for DD councils.* Chapel Hill: The University of North Carolina.
Newman, J. (1994). Conflict and friendship in sibling relationships: A review. *Child Study Journal, 24,* 119–152.
O'Dell, S. (1974). Training parents in behavior modification: A review. *Psychological Bulletin,* 31, 418–433.
Ogle, P.A. (1982). *The sibling relationship: Maternal perceptions of the nonhandicapped and handicapped/nonhandicapped sibling dyads.* Unpublished doctoral dissertation, University of North Carolina-Chapel Hill.
Opperman, S., & Alant, E. (2003). The coping responses of the adolescent siblings of children with severe disabilities. *Disability Rehabilitation, 25*(9), 441–454.
Ortiz, E., Innocenti, M.S., & Roggman, L. (2005, April). *How much do siblings influence early language development of Hispanic/Latino children?* Poster session presented at the biannual meeting of the Society for Research in Child Development, Atlanta, GA.
Parten, M. (1932). Social participation among preschool children. *Journal of Abnormal Social Psychology, 27,* 243–269.
Patterson, G.R. (1982). *Coercive family process.* Eugene, OR: Castalia Press.
Patterson, L.E., & Eisenberg, S. (1983). *The counseling process* (3rd ed.). Boston: Houghton Mifflin.
Peck, C.A., Donaldson, J., & Pezzoli, M. (1990). Some benefits nonhandicapped adolescents perceive for themselves from their social relationships with peers who have severe handicaps. *Journal of The Association for Persons with Severe Handicaps, 15*(4), 241–249.
Pepler, D.J., Abramovitch, R., & Corter, C. (1981). Sibling interaction in the home: A longitudinal study. *Child Development, 52,* 1344–1347.
Perez-Granados, D.R., & Callanan, M.A. (1997a). Conversations with mothers and siblings: Young children's semantic and conceptual development. *Developmental Psychology, 33*(1), 120–134.
Perez-Granados, D.R., & Callanan, M.A. (1997b). Parents and siblings as early resources for young children's learning in Mexican-descent families. *Hispanic Journal of Behavioral Sciences, 19*(1), 3–33.
Perske, R. (1981). *Hope for families: New directions for parents of persons with retardation or other disabilities.* Nashville: Abingdon Press.
Perske, R. (1990). *Circle of friends.* Nashville: Abingdon Press.
Phillips, R.S.C. (1999). Intervention with siblings of children with developmental disabilities from economically disadvantaged families. *Families in Society: The Journal of Contemporary Human Services, 80*(6), 569–577.
Piers, E.V. (1986). *The Piers-Harris Children's Self-Concept Scale–Revised Manual.* Los Angeles: Western Psychological Services.
Pietrofesa, J.J., Hoffman, A., & Splete, H.H. (1984). *Counseling: An introduction.* Boston: Houghton Mifflin.
Pike, A., Manke, B., Reiss, D., & Plomin, R. (2000). A genetic analysis of differential experiences of adolescent siblings across three years. *Social Development, 9*(1), 96–114.
Pilowsky, T., Yirmiya, N., Doppelt, O., Gross-Tsur, V., & Shalev, R. (2004). Social and emotional adjustment of siblings of children with autism. *Journal of Child Psychology and Psychiatry, 45*(4), 855–865.
Plomin, R., Asbury, K., & Dunn, J. (2001, April). Why are children in the same family so different? Nonshared environment a decade later. *Canadian Journal of Psychiatry, 46,* 225–233.
Plomin, R., & Daniels, D. (1987). Why are children in the same family so different from one another? *Behavioral and Brain Sciences, 10,* 1–16.

Post-Kramer, P., & Nickolai, S. (1985). Counseling services for siblings of the handicapped. *Elementary School Guidance and Counseling, 20*(2), 115-120.

Potter, P.C., & Roberts, M.C. (1984). Children's perceptions of chronic illness: The roles of disease symptoms, cognitive development, and information. *Journal of Pediatric Psychology, 9,* 13–27.

Powell, T.H. (1982). *Parents, siblings, and handicapped children: A social interaction program.* Storrs: The University of Connecticut.

Powell, T.H., & Gallagher, P.A. (1993). *Brothers and sisters: A special part of exceptional families* (2nd ed.). Baltimore: Paul H. Brookes Publishing Co.

Powell, T.H., & Ogle, P.A. (1985). *Brothers and sisters: A special part of exceptional families.* Baltimore: Paul H. Brookes Publishing Co.

Powell, T.H., Salzberg, C., Rule, S., Levy, S., & Itzkowitz, J. (1983). Teaching mentally retarded children to play with their siblings using parents as trainers. *Education and Treatment of Children, 6,* 343–362.

Powell-Smith, K., & Stollar, S. (1997). Families of children with disabilities. In G. Bear, K. Minke, & A. Thomas (Eds.), *Children's needs: Psychological perspectives* (3rd ed.). Bethesda, MD: National Association of School Psychologists.

Prizant, B.M., Wetherby, A.M., & Rydell, P.J. (2000). Communication intervention issues for young children with autism spectrum disorders. In A.M. Wetherby & B.M. Prizant (Eds.), *Children with autism spectrum disorders: A developmental transactional perspective.* Baltimore: Paul H. Brookes Publishing Co.

Pruchno, R.A., Patrick, J.H., & Burant, C.J. (1996). Aging mothers and their children with chronic disabilities: Perception of sibling involvement and effects on well being. *Family Relations, 45,* 318–326.

Pulakos, J. (1989). Young adult relationships: Siblings and friends. *The Journal of Psychology, 123,* 237–244.

Raffaelli, M. (1992). Sibling conflict in early adolescence. *Journal of Marriage and the Family, 54,* 652–663.

Raghuraman, R.S. (2002). Art as a cathartic tool for siblings of children with a hearing loss. *American Journal of Art Therapy, 40,* 203–209.

Ram, A., & Ross, H.S. (2001). Problem solving, contention, and struggle: How siblings resolve a conflict of interests. *Child Development, 72,* 1710–1722.

Rimmerman, A., & Raif, R. (2001). Involvement with and role perception toward an adult siblings with and without mental retardation. *Journal of Rehabilitation, 67*(2), 11–16.

Rinaldi, C., & Howe, N. (1998). Siblings' reports of conflict and the quality of their relationships. *Merrill-Palmer Quarterly, 44*(3), 404–422.

Rinaldi, C.M., & Howe, N. (2003). Perceptions of constructive and destructive conflict within and across family subsystems. *Infant and Child Development, 12,* 441–459.

Rivara, J. (1994). Family functioning following pediatric traumatic brain injury. *Pediatric Annuals, 23,* 38–43.

Rivers, J.W., & Stoneman, Z. (2003). Sibling relationships when a child has autism: Marital stress and support coping. *Journal of Autism and Developmental Disorders, 33*(4), 383–393.

Rodrigue, J.R., Geffken, G.R., & Morgan, S.B. (1993). Perceived competence and behavioral adjustment of siblings of children with autism. *Journal of Autism and Developmental Disorders, 23*(4), 665–674.

Roff, M., Sells, B., & Golden, M. (1972). *Social adjustment and personality development in children.* Minneapolis: University of Minnesota Press.

Ross, H.G., & Milgram, J.I. (1982). Important variables in adult sibling relationships: A qualitative study. In M.E. Lamb & B. Sutton-Smith (Eds.), *Sibling relationships* (pp. 225–250). Mahwah, NJ: Lawrence Erlbaum Associates.

Ross, H.S., Siddiqui, A., Ram, A., & Ward, L. (2004). Perspectives on self and other in children's representations of sibling conflict. *International Journal of Behavioral Development, 28*(1), 37–47.

Rossi, A., & Rossi, P. (1990). *Of human bonding.* New York: Aldine de Gruyter.

Rowe, D.C. (1994). *The limits of family influence: Genes, experience, and behavior.* New York: Guilford Press.

Rowe, D.C., & Gulley, B. (1992). Sibling effects on substance abuse and delinquency. *Criminology, 30,* 217–233.

Rowe, D.C., & Plomin, R. (1981). The importance of nonshared environmental influences in behavioral developments. *Developmental Psychology, 17,* 517–531.

Russell, M. (1990, Fall). Writing the letter of intent. *New Ways,* 20–25.

Rust, J., Golombok, S., Hines, M., Johnston, K., Golding, J. & The ALSPAC Study Team. (2000). The role of brothers and sisters in the gender development of preschool children. *Journal of Experimental Child Psychology, 77,* 292–303.

Sameroff, A.J., & Chandler, M.J. (1975). Perinatal risk and the continuum of caretaking casualty. In M.F.D. Horowitz et al. (Eds.), *Review of child development research* (Vol. IV). Chicago: University of Chicago Press.

Samuels, H. (1980). The effect of an older sibling on infant locomotor exploration in a new environment. *Child Development, 51,* 607–609.

Sandler, A. (1998). Grandparents of children with disabilities: A closer look. *Education and Training in Mental Retardation and Developmental Disabilities, 33,* 350–356.

San Martino, M., & Newman, M. B. (1974). Siblings of retarded children: A population at risk. *Child Psychiatry and Human Development, 4*(3), 168-177.

Schachter, F.F. (1982). Sibling deidentification and split-parent identification. In M.E. Lamb & B. Sutton-Smith (Eds.), *Sibling relationships: Their nature and significance across the lifespan.* Mahwah, NJ: Lawrence Erlbaum Associates.

Schachter, F.F., & Stone, R.K. (1985). Difficult sibling, easy sibling: Temperament and the within-family environment. *Child Development, 56,* 1335–1344.

Schaefer, E., & Edgerton, M. (1979, November). *Sibling Inventory of Behavior.* Caroline Institute for Research on Early Education of the Handicapped, University of North Carolina-Chapel Hill.

Schaffer, E., & Edgerton, M. (1981). *Short description of the Sibling Inventory of Behavior.* Unpublished manuscript, University of North Carolina-Chapel Hill.

Schaefer, H.R., & Emerson, P.E. (1964). Patterns of response to physical contact in early human development. *Journal of Child Psychology and Psychiatry, 5,* 1–13.

Schipper, M.T. (1959). The child with Mongolism in the home. *Pediatrics, 24,* 132–144.

Schneider-Corey, M., & Corey, G. (1987). *Groups: Process and practice* (3rd ed.). Pacific Grove, CA: Brooks/Cole.

Schreiber, M., & Feeley, M. (1965). Siblings of the retarded: A guided group experience. *Children, 12*(6), 221–225.

Schreibman, L., O'Neill, R.E., & Koegel, R.L. (1983). Behavioral training for siblings of autistic children. *Journal of Applied Behavior Analysis, 16*(2), 129–138.

Schvaneveldt, J.D., & Ihinger, M. (1979). Sibling relationships in the family. In W.R. Burr, R. Hill, F.I. Nye, & I.L. Reiss (Eds.), *Contemporary theories about the family* (Vol. 1, pp. 453–467). New York: The Free Press.

Seligman, M. (1983). Siblings of handicapped persons. In M. Seligman (Ed.), *The family with a handicapped child: Understanding and treatment* (pp. 147–174). New York: Grune & Stratton.

Seligman, M., & Darling, R.B. (1997). *Ordinary Families, Special Children* (2nd ed.). New York: The Guilford Press.

Seltzer, G.B. (1991). *Stress, health, and social support among families and care-givers of older adults with developmental disabilities.* Cincinnati, OH: Research and Training Center Consortium on Aging and Developmental Disabilities.

Seltzer, G.B., Begun, A., Seltzer, M.M., & Krauss, M.W. (1991). Adults with mental retardation and their aging mothers: Impacts of siblings. *Family Relations, 40,* 310–317.

Seltzer, M.M., Greenberg, J.S., Krauss, M.W., Gordon, R.M., & Judge, K. (1997). Siblings of adults with mental retardation or mental illness: Effects on lifestyle and psychological well-being. *Family Relations, 46,* 395–405.

Seltzer, M.M., Krauss, M.W., Hong, J., & Orsmond, G.I. (2001). Continuity or discontinuity of family involvement following residential transitions of adults who have mental retardation. *Mental Retardation, 39*(3), 181–194.

Senapti, R., & Hayes, A. (1988). Sibling relationships of handicapped children: A review of conceptual and methodological issues. *International Journal of Behavioral Development, 11*(1), 89–115.

Shertzer, B., & Stone, S.C. (1980). *Fundamentals of counseling* (3rd ed.). Boston: Houghton Mifflin.

Shores, R.E. (1981). *Social competence intervention project: Final report.* Nashville, TN: Vanderbilt University. (U.S. Office of Education Grant No. 0007802088).

Shores, R.E. (1987). Overview of research on social interaction: A historical and personal perspective. *Behavior Disorders, 12*(4), 233–241.

Siddiqui, A.A., & Ross, H.S. (1999). How do sibling conflicts end? *Early Education and Development, 10*(3), 315–332.

Siegal, M. (1987). Are sons and daughters treated more differently by fathers than by mothers? *Developmental Review, 7,* 183–209.

Simeonsson, R.J., & Bailey, D.B. (1983, September). *Siblings of handicapped children.* Paper presented at National Insitute of Child and Human Development (NICHD) Conference on Research on Families with Retarded Children.

Simeonsson, R.J., & McHale, S.M. (1981). Review: Research on handicapped children: Sibling relationships. *Child: Care, Health, and Development, 7,* 153–171.

Simeonsson, R.J., & Simeonsson, N.E. (1981). Parenting handicapped children: Psychological aspects. In J.L. Paul (Ed.), *Understanding and working with parents of children with special needs* (pp. 51–88). New York: Holt, Rinehart, & Winston.

Slade, J.C. (1988). Why siblings of handicapped children need the attention and help of the counselor. *The School Counselor, 36,* 107-111.

Slomkowski, C., Rende, R., Conger, K.J., Simons, R.L., & Conger, R.D. (2001). Sisters, brothers, and delinquency: Evaluating social influence during early and middle adolescence. *Child Development, 72,* 271–283.

Snell, M.E. (1987). *Systematic instruction of persons with severe handicaps.* Columbus, OH: Charles E. Merrill.

Snell, M.E., & Gast, D.L. (1981). Applying time delay procedure to the instruction of the severely handicapped. *Journal of The Association for the Severely Handicapped, 6*(3), 3–14.

Snell, M.E., & Zirpoli, T.J. (1987). Intervention strategies. In M. Snell (Ed.), *Systematic instruction of persons with severe handicaps* (pp. 110–149). Columbus, OH: Charles E. Merrill.

Soutter, J., Hamilton, N., Russell, P., Russell, C., Bushby, K., Sloper, P., et al. (2004). The golden freeway: A preliminary evaluation of a pilot study advancing information technology as a social intervention for boys with Duchenne muscular dystrophy and their families. *Health and Social Care in the Community, 12*(1), 25–33.

Stainback, S., & Stainback, W. (1992). Schools as inclusive communities. In W. Stainback & S. Stainback (Eds.), *Controversial issues confronting special education* (pp. 29–43). Boston: Allyn & Bacon.

Stainback, W., & Stainback, S. (1987). Facilitating friendships. *Education and Training in Mental Retardation, 22*(1), 18–25.

Stepfamily Association of America. (n.d.). Retrieved on May 8, 2005 from http://www.saafamilies.org/faqs/myths.htm

Stepfamily Foundation. (n.d.). Retrieved on May 12, 2005 from http.//www .stepfamily.org

Stewart, J.C. (1986). *Counseling parents of exceptional children* (2nd ed.). Columbus, OH: Charles E. Merrill.

Stewart, R.B., Mobley, L.A., VanTuyl, S.S., & Salvador, M.A. (1987). The firstborns adjustment to the birth of a sibling: A longitudinal assessment. *Child Development, 58,* 341–355.

Stocker, C., Dunn, J., & Plomin, R. (1989). Sibling relationships: Links with child temperament, maternal behavior, and family structure. *Child Development, 60,* 715–727.

Stocker, C.M., & McHale, S.M. (1992). The nature and family correlates of preadolescents' perceptions of their sibling relationships. *Journal of Social and Personal Relationships, 9,* 179–195.

Stoneman, Z., & Brody, G.H. (1982). Strengths inherent in sibling interactions involving a retarded child: A functional role theory approach. In N. Stinnett, B. Chesser, J. DeFrain, & P. Knaub (Eds.), *Family strengths: Positive models for family life* (pp. 113–129). Lincoln: University of Nebraska Press.

Stoneman, Z., & Brody, G.H. (1984). Research with families of severely handicapped children: Theoretical and methodological considerations. In J. Blacher (Ed.), *Severely handicapped young children and their families* (pp. 179–214). Orlando, FL: Academic Press.

Stoneman, Z., & Brody, G.H. (1993). Sibling temperaments, conflict, warmth, and role asymmetry, *Child Development, 64,* 1786–1800.

Stoneman, Z., Brody, G.H., Davis, C.H., & Crapps, J.M. (1987). Mentally retarded children and their older same-sex siblings: Naturalistic in-home observations. *American Journal of Mental Retardation, 92,* 290–298.

Stoneman, Z., Brody, G.H., Davis, C.H., & Crapps, J.M. (1988). Childcare responsibilities, peer relations, and sibling conflict: Older siblings of mentally retarded children. *American Journal of Mental Retardation,* 93, 174–183.

Stoneman, Z., Brody, G.H., Davis, C.H., & Crapps, J.M. (1989). Role relations between children who are mentally retarded and their older siblings: Observations in three in-home contexts. *Research in Developmental Disabilities, 10,* 61–76.

Stoneman, Z., Brody, G.H., Davis, C.H., Crapps, J.M., & Malone, D.M. (1991). Ascribed role relations between children with mental retardation and their younger siblings. *American Journal of Mental Retardation, 95*(5), 537–550.

Stoneman, Z., Brody, G.H., & MacKinnon, C. (1984). Naturalistic observations of children's activities and roles while playing with their siblings and friends. *Child Development, 55,* 617–627.

Stoneman, Z., Brody, G.H., & MacKinnon, C.E. (1986). Same-sex and cross-sex siblings: Activity choices, roles, behavior, and gender stereotypes. *Sex Roles, 15*(9/10), 495–511.

Stoneman, Z., & Crapps, J.M. (1990). Mentally retarded individuals in family care homes: Relationships with the family-of-origin. *American Journal on Mental Retardation, 94,* 420-430.

Stormshak, E.A., Bellanti, C.J., & Bierman, K.L. (1996). The quality of sibling relationships and the developmental of social competence and behavioral control in aggressive children. *Developmental Psychology, 32*(1), 79–89.

Strain, P.S., Cooke, R.P., & Apolloni, T. (1976). *Teaching exceptional children: Assessing and modifying social behavior.* New York: Academic Press.

Strain, P.S., & Fox, J.J. (1981). Peers as behavior change agents for withdrawn classmates. In B.B. Lahey & A.E. Kazdin (Eds.), *Advances in clinical child psychology* (Vol. 4). New York: Plenum Press.

Strain, P.S., Shores, R.E., & Timm, M.A. (1977). Effects of peer social initiations on the behavior of withdrawn preschool children. *Journal of Applied Behavior Analysis, 10,* 289–298.

Strain, P.S., & Timm, M.A. (1974). An experimental analysis of social interaction between a behaviorally disordered child and her classroom peers. *Journal of Applied Behavior Analysis, 7,* 583–590.

Strohm, K. (2005). *Being the other one: Growing up with a brother or sister who has special needs.* Boston: Shambhala.

Strully, J.L., & Bartholomew-Lorimer, K. (1988). Social integration and friendship. In S.M. Pueschel, (Ed.), *The young person with Down syndrome* (pp. 65–76). Baltimore: Paul H. Brookes Publishing Co.

Stubblefield, H.W. (1965). Religion, parents, and mental retardation. *Mental Retardation, 3,* 4, 8–11.

Sturgess, W., Dunn, J., & Davies, L. (2001). Young children's perceptions of their relationships with family members: Links with family setting, friendships, and adjustment. *International Journal of Behavioral Development, 25*(6), 521–529.

Sullivan, R.C. (1979). Siblings of autistic children. *Journal of Autism and Developmental Disorders, 9*(3), 287–298.

Sulzer-Azaroff, B., & Mayer, G.R. (1977). *Applying behavior analysis procedures with children and youth.* New York: Holt, Rinehart, & Winston.

Summers, J.A., Behr, S.K., & Turnbull, A.P. (1989). Positive adaptations and coping strengths of families who have children with disabilities. In G.H.S. Singer & L.K. Irving (Eds.), *Support for caregiving families: Enabling positive adaptation to disability* (pp. 27–40). Baltimore: Paul H. Brookes Publishing Co. 119

Summers, M., Bridge, J., & Summers, C. R. (1991, Summer). Sibling support groups. *Teaching Exceptional Children,* 20-25.

Summers, M., Hahs, J., & Summers, C.R. (1997). Conversational patterns of children with disabled and nondisabled siblings. *Applied Psycholinguistics, 18,* 277–291.

Sutton-Smith, B., & Rosenberg, B.G. (1968). Sibling consensus on power tactics. *Journal of Genetic Psychology, 112*(1), 63–72.

Sutton-Smith, B., & Rosenberg, B.G. (1970). *The sibling.* New York: Holt, Rinehart, & Winston.

Swenson-Pierce, A., Kohl, F., & Egle, A. (1987). Siblings as home trainers: A strategy for teaching domestic skills to children. *Journal of The Association for Persons with Severe Handicaps, 12*(1), 53–60.

Taunt, H.M., & Hastings, R.P. (2002). Positive impact of children with developmental disabilities on their families: A preliminary study. *Education and Training in Mental Retardation and Developmental Disabilities, 37*(4), 410–420.

Taylor, L.S. (1974). *Communication between mothers and normal siblings of retarded children: Nature and modification.* Unpublished doctoral dissertation, University of North Carolina-Chapel Hill.

Tekin, E., & Kircaali-Iftar, G. (2002). Comparison of the effectiveness and efficiency of two response prompting procedures delivered by sibling tutors. *Education and Training in Mental Retardation and Developmental Disabilities, 37*(3), 283–299.

Teti, D.M., & Ablard, K.E. (1989). Security of attachment and infant-sibling relationships: A laboratory study. *Child Development, 60,* 1519–1528.

Tew, B., & Laurence, K.M. (1973). Mothers, brothers, and sisters of patients with spina bifida. *Developmental Medicine and Child Neurology, 15,* 69–76.

Tiedemann, G.L., & Johnston, C. (1992). Evaluation of parent training program to promote sharing between young siblings. *Behavior Therapy, 23,* 299–318.

Tingey, C. (1988). Cutting the umbilical cord: Parental perspectives. In S.M. Pueschel (Ed.), *The young person with Down syndrome: Transition from adolescence to adulthood* (pp. 5–22). Baltimore: Paul H. Brookes Publishing Co.

Tomasello, M., & Mannle, S. (1985). Pragmatics of sibling speech to one-year-olds. *Child Development, 56,* 911-917.

Travis, G. (1976). *Chronic illness: Its impact on child and family.* Stanford: Stanford University Press.

Tremblay, A., Strain, P.S., Hendrickson, J.M., & Shores, R.E. (1981). Social interactions of normal preschool children: Using normative data for subject and target behavior selection. *Behavior Modification, 5*(2), 237–253.

Trevino, F. (1979). Siblings of handicapped children: Identifying those at risk. *Social Casework, 60,* 488–493.

Tucker, C.J., Barber, B.L., & Eccles, J.S. (1997). Advice about life plans and personal problems in late adolescent sibling relationships. *Journal of Youth and Adolescence, 26,* 63–76.

Tucker, C.J., McHale, S.M., & Crouter, A.C. (2001). Conditions of sibling support in adolescence. *Journal of Family Psychology, 15*(2), 254–271.

Tucker, C.J., McHale, S.M., & Crouter, A.C. (2003). Dimensions of mothers' and fathers' differential treatment of siblings: Links with adolescents' sex-typed personal qualities. *Family Relations, 52,* 82–89.

Turkheimer, E., & Waldron, M. (2000). Nonshared environment: A theoretical, methodological, and quantitative review. *Psychological Bulletin, 126*(1), 78–108.

Turnbull, A.P., & Bronicki, G.J. (1986). Changing second graders' attitudes toward people with mental retardation: Using kid power. *Mental Retardation, 24,* 44–45.

Turnbull, A.P., & Turnbull, H.R. (1990). *Families, professionals, and exceptionality: A special partnership* (2nd ed.). Columbus, OH: Charles E. Merrill.

Turnbull, A.P., & Turnbull, H.R. (2001). *Families, professionals, and exceptionality: Collaborating for empowerment* (4th ed.). Columbus, OH: Merrill Prentice Hall.

Turnbull, A., Turnbull, R., Erwin, E.J., & Soodak, L.C. (2006). *Families, professionals, and exceptionality: Positive outcomes through partnerships and trust* (5th ed.). Upper Saddle River, NJ: Pearson Merrill Prentice Hall.

United States Department of Health and Human Services. (1980). *Learning together: A guide for families with genetic disorders.* Washington, DC: U.S. Government Printing Office (DHHS Publication No. HSA 80–5131).

United States Department of Justice. (n.d.). Commonly asked questions about child care centers and the Americans with Disabilities Act. Retrieved on April 3, 2005 from http://www.usdoj.gov/crt.ada.htm

Unruh, S.G., Grosse, M.E., & Zigler, E. (1971). Birth order, number of siblings, and social reinforcer effectiveness in children. *Child Development, 42,* 1, 153–163.

Updegraff, K.A., McHale, S.M., & Crouter, A.C. (2002). Adolescents' sibling relationship and friendship experiences: Developmental patterns and relationship linkages. *Social Development, 11*(2), 182–204.

U.S. National Library of Medicine (2005a). Genetics home reference: Genetic testing. Retrieved September 28, 2005, from http://ghr.nlm.nih.gov/info=genetic_testing /show/alltopics

U.S. National Library of Medicine (2005b). Help me understand genetics. Retrieved September 28, 2005, from http://ghr.nlm.nih.gov/info=genetic_testing/show/alltopics

Vandell, D.L., & Bailey, M.D. (1992). Conflicts between siblings. In C.U. Shantz & W.W. Hartup (Eds.), *Conflict in child and adolescent development* (pp. 242–269). Cambridge, NY: Cambridge University Press.

Vandell, D.L., & Wilson, K.S. (1987). Infants interactions with mother, sibling, and peer: Contrasts and relations between interaction systems. *Child Development, 58,* 176–186.

Van Hasselt, V.B., Hersen, M., Whitehill, M.B., & Bellack, A.A. (1979). Social skills assessment and training for children: An evaluation review. *Behavioral Research and Therapy, 17,* 413–437.

Van Riper, M. (2000). Family variables associated with well-being in siblings of children with down syndrome. *Journal of Family Nursing, 6*(3), 267–286.

Vespo, J.E., Pedersen, J., & Hay, D.F. (1995). Young children's conflicts with peers and siblings: Gender effects. *Child Study Journal, 25*(3), 189–212.

Visher, E.B., & Visher, J.S. (1988). *Old loyalties, new ties: Therapeutic strategies with stepfamilies.* New York: Bruner/Mazel.

Volling, B.L., Herrera, C., & Poris, M.P. (2004). Situational affect and temperament: Implications for sibling caregiving. *Infant and Child Development, 13,* 173–183.

Volling, B.L., McElwain, N.L., & Miller, A.L. (2002). Emotion regulation in context: The jealousy complex between young siblings and its relations with child and family characteristics. *Child Development, 73,* 581–600.

Wagner, M.E., Schubert, H.J.P., & Schubert, D.S.P. (1985). Effects of sibling spacing on intelligence, interfamilial relations, psychosocial characteristics, and mental and physical health. In H.W. Reese (Ed.), *Advances in child development and behavior* (Vol. 19, pp. 149–206). New York: Academic Press.

Walker, L.S., Garber, J., & Van Slyke, D.A. (1995). Do parents excuse misbehavior of children with physical or emotional symptoms? An investigation of the pediatric sick role. *Journal of Pediatric Psychology, 20*(3), 329-345.

Wasserman, R. (1983). Identifying the counseling needs of siblings of mentally retarded children. *Personnel and Guidance Journal, 61,* 622-627.

Weinrott, M.R. (1974). A training program in behavior modification for siblings of the retarded. *American Journal of Orthopsychiatry, 44,* 362–375.

Weiss, J.H. (1970). Birth order and physiological stress response. *Child Development, 41,* 461–470.

White, L. (2001). Sibling relationships over the life course: A panel analysis. *Journal of Marriage and Family, 63,* 555–568.

White, P.G. (n.d.). Long-term effects of childhood sibling loss. Retrieved June 12, 2005 from http://www.counselingstlouis.net.effects.html

Whitman, T.L., Sciback, J.W., & Reid, D.H. (1983). *Behavior modification with the severely and profoundly retarded.* New York: Academic Press.

Widmer, E.D., & Weiss, C.C. (2000). Do older siblings make a difference? The effects of older sibling support and older sibling adjustment on the adjustment of socially disadvantaged adolescents. *Journal of Research on Adolescence, 10*(1), 1–27.

Wikler, L. (1983). Chronic stresses of families of mentally retarded children. *Family Relations,* 30, 281–288.

Willenz-Issacs, I. (1983). Brothers and sisters are special: A Kendall Program at the Kendall Demonstration School. *Sibling Information Network Newsletter, 2*(1), 2.

Wilson, J., Blacher, J., & Baker, B.L. (1989). Siblings of children with severe handicaps. *Mental Retardation, 27*(3), 167–173.

Wishart, J.G. (1986). Siblings as models in early infant learning. *Child Development,* 57, 1232–1240.

Wood, M.J., Vaughn, B.E., & Robb, M.D. (1988). Social-emotional adaptaption and infant–mother attachment in siblings: Role of the mother in cross-sibling consistency. *Child Development, 59,* 643-651.

Woolett, A. (1986). The influence of older siblings on the language environment of young children. *British Journal of Developmental Psychology, 4,* 235–245.

Young, C.C. (1981). Children as instructional agents for handicapped peers: A review and analysis. In P.S. Strain (Ed.), *The utilization of classroom peers as behavior change agents.* New York: Plenum Press.

Young, C., Hecimovic, A., & Salzberg, C.L. (1983). Tutor-tutee behavior of disadvantaged kindergarten children during peer teaching. *Education and Treatment of Children, 6*(2), 123–135.

Zajonc, R.B., & Bargh, J. (1980). Birth order, family size and decline in SAT scores. *American Psychologist, 35,* 662–668.

Zatlow, G. (1982). A sister's lament. *Sibling Information Network Newsletter, 1*(5), 2; reprinted from 1981 Citizens Future.

Zetlin, A.G. (1986). Mentally retarded adults and their siblings. *American Journal of Mental Deficiency, 91*(3), 217–225.

Zuk, G.H., Miller, R.L., Bartram, J.B., & Kling, F. (1961). Maternal acceptance of retarded children: A questionnaire study of attitudes and religious background. *Child Development, 32,* 525–540.

Related Literature and Media

A note about the categories following each book's description: the letters "N," "F," or "B" stands for Nonfiction, Fiction, or Biography; the age of target audience is indicated by school level (e.g., "Elementary" for elementary school children, "High" for high school students); the symbol + indicates a book written by a sibling or that has contributions by a sibling; the symbol # indicates a bilingual book (including foreign languages and Braille).

BIBLIOGRAPHIES

Attitude toward disability: A bibliography of children's books. Santa Monica, CA: Pediatric Projects, Inc.

Dyches, T.T. & Prater M.A. (2000). *Developmental disability in children's literature: Issues and annotated bibliography.* Reston, VA: Council for Exceptional Children/MRDD.

Friedberg, J.B., Mullins, J.B., & Sukiennik, A.W. (1992). *Portraying persons with disabilities: An annotated bibliography of nonfiction for children and teenagers.* Portsmouth, NH: Libraries Unlimited.

Icon Health Publications. (2004). *Dyslexia: A medical dictionary, bibliography, and annotated research guide to Internet references.* San Diego, CA: Icon Health Publications.

Siblings, A bibliography of children's books. Santa Monica, CA: Pediatric Projects, Inc.

Ward, M. (2002). *Voices from the margins: An annotated bibliography of fiction on disabilities and differences for young people.* Westport, CT: Greenwood Press.

LITERATURE FOR CHILDREN

General Disabilities

Carlisle, K. (1994). *The special raccoon: Helping a child learn about handicaps and love.* Far Hills, NJ: New Horizon. | This story gives readers information about what it means to be physically and mentally challenged. **| F | Preschool-elementary**

Craymer, S. (1992). *There's a blue square on my brother's school bus.* Studley, VA: The Wishing Room, Inc. | This story explains disability from a sibling's point of view. **| Preschool-elementary**

Gifaldi, D. (2001). ***Ben, king of the river.*** **Morton Grove, IL: Albert Whitman & Co. |** Chad narrates this story about his family's first camping trip and life with Ben, his brother who has developmental disabilities. The book includes tips for siblings of children with special needs. **| F | Elementary**

Hale, N. (2004). ***Oh brother! Growing up with a special needs sibling.*** **Washington, DC: Magination Press. |** Based on the experiences of a real-life family. Becca discusses finding the right kind of friends, getting quality time with parents, the struggles of balancing the responsibilities of caring about a special needs sibling without becoming another parent, and more. **| F | Elementary-middle**

Huegel, K. (1998). ***Young people with chronic illness: True stories, help, and hope.*** **Minneapolis, MN: Free Spirit Publishing. |** Written in a conversational, sympathetic tone, and full of upbeat quotes. Advice is concise and well organized, showing how siblings' experiences can help others cope with chronic illness. **| N | High**

Klayman, G. (1996). ***Our new baby needs special help: A coloring book for families whose new baby has problems.*** **Omaha, NE: Centering Corporation. |** This is a coloring book for young siblings whose new baby brother or sister may or may not come home from the hospital. The book illustrates a child first learning about the new baby's special needs, the parents finding out the baby has a serious health problem, and a visit to the NICU. **| F | Preschool–elementary**

Lozoff, B. (2002). ***The wonderful life of a fly who couldn't fly.*** **Charlottesville, VA: Hampton Roads Publishing Co. |** This book tells the story of a young fly born without wings who learns to enjoy the short life she's been given. Though she never flies, she learns that Mother Nature never makes a mistake and, by enjoying all the beautiful things around her, she can "fly." **| F | Elementary**

Meyer, D. (1997). ***Views from our shoes: Growing up with a brother or sister with special needs.*** **Bethesda, MD: Woodbine House. |** This book describes the lives and emotions such as embarrassment, anger, and jealousy, of 45 siblings ranging in age from 4 to 18 who have brothers and sisters with special needs. The siblings share how they get along in a family that is different and how they love and protect their siblings with disabilities. **| N | All ages | +**

Meyer, D.J. (2004). ***The sibling slam book: What it's really like to have a brother or sister with special needs.*** **Bethesda, MD: Woodbine House. |** This innovative book is based on answers to a series of questions asked to teens about what it is like to grow up with a brother or sister with disabilities. Whether positive or negative, the young authors' honest answers reflect the multidimensional sibling relationship. **| N | High | +**

Meyer, D., & Vadasy, P. (1996). ***Living with a brother or sister with special needs: A book for sibs.*** **Seattle: University of Washington Press. |** This book focuses on the emotions that brothers and sisters experience and the questions they ask when they have a sibling with special needs. The book discusses specific disabilities in "kid-friendly" terms, and the good and the not-so-good aspects of having a sibling who has special needs, and it offers suggestions for how to make life easier for all family members. **| N | Elementary**

Mills, J.C. (2003). ***Little tree: A story for children with serious medical problems.*** **Washington, DC: Magination Press. |** This story provides hope and inspiration to children with serious illness or injury and valuable guidance to parents as well as relaxation exercises they may teach their children. New to the second edition is a Note to Parents by author and psychologist Jane Annunziata, Psy.D. **| F | Elementary**

Rogers, F. (2000). *Extraordinary friends.* East Rutherford, NJ: Puffin Books. | This story by the late Fred Rogers, the famous children's television personality, focuses on children who use equipment such as wheelchairs and special computers, and suggests ways to facilitate their interaction with other children. **| N | Preschool-elementary**

Thompson, M. (1992). *My brother, Matthew.* Bethesda, MD: Woodbine House. | This book is narrated by a young boy who describes the ups and downs of day-to-day life as he and his family adjust to life with his new brother, Matthew, who is born with a disability. This story may help other siblings share their feelings and reassure them that their role in the family is very important. **| F | Elementary-middle | +**

Asthma and Allergies

Gosselin, K. (1997). *SPORTSercise!* Valley Park, MO: JayJo Books. | When Justin and Ashley's team competes in the school's SPORTSercise competition, they learn that they can still participate in all sporting activities even though they have asthma and that proper precautions can prevent exercise-induced asthma. **| N | Elementary-middle**

Gosselin, K. (1998). *ABCs of asthma: An asthma alphabet book for kids of all ages.* Valley Park, MO: JayJo Books. | This fun and educational alphabet book matches each letter of the alphabet with corresponding words that are associated with asthma. It explains asthma and asthma triggers and treatments and offers encouragement to children who have asthma. **| N | Elementary**

Gosselin, K. (1996). *Zooallergy: A fun story about allergy and asthma triggers.* Plainview, NY: JayJo Books. | This color-illustrated story helps children learn about allergy testing and asthma and allergy triggers. Justin goes to the doctor to get tested for allergies, and afterward, he and his friend Ashley go to the zoo. While there, they make a game of discovering allergy and asthma triggers such as animal fur, dust, and dander. **| F | Elementary**

London, J., & Westcott, N.B. (Illust.). (1997). *The lion who had asthma.* Morton Grove, IL: Albert Whitman & Co. | Sean may roar like a lion, but he has asthma, and sometimes it's hard for him to breathe. His family helps provide treatment and soon Sean is once again King of the Jungle. **| F | Preschool-elementary**

Weiss, J.H. (2003). *Breathe easy: Young people's guide to asthma* (2nd ed.). Washington, DC: Magination Press. | Completely updated, this practical guide is filled with information, tips, checklists, resources, diagrams, and illustrations to help young people learn to control their asthma, gain self-confidence, and live with asthma to the fullest extent possible. **| N | Middle-high**

Autism Spectrum Disorders

Band, E.B., & Hecht, E. (2001). *Autism through a sister's eyes: A young girl's view of her brother's autism.* Arlington, TX: Future Horizons, Inc. | This book for younger readers is told by a girl whose older brother has Asperger syndrome. The narrator shares her frustrations, fears, and memories of fun moments with her brother. **| N | Preschool–elementary | +**

Branon, B. (1998). *Timesong*. Las Vegas, NV: Huntington Press. | *Timesong* tells the story of a three-legged coyote named J.B. who befriends a boy named Tom who has autsim. After his father dies, Tom withdraws and becomes isolated. J.B. lifts Tom's sorrow with a simple explanation of immortality. **| F**

Bleach, F. (2001). *Everybody is different: A book for young people who have brothers or sisters with autism*. Shawnee Mission, KS: Autism Asperger Publishing Company. | This book gives answers to the many questions asked by brothers and sisters of young people on the autistic spectrum. In addition to explaining characteristics of autism, it offers helpful suggestions for making family life more comfortable for all family members. **| N | Elementary**

Choldenko, G. (2004). *Al Capone does my shirts*. New York: Putnam Juvenile. | It's 1935, and 12-year-old Moose finds himself the new kid in the most unusual of places: Alcatraz Island. Joining a band of kids whose fathers work in the prison system, Moose must face the challenge of having to explain the strange behavior of his teenage sister, who would be considered today to have autism. An honest look at the mixed feelings of siblings, including embarrassment over sexuality issues and resentment over having too much responsibility for a sibling with special needs. **| F | Middle**

Cullen, D.T. (1999). *Trevor Trevor*. Higganum, CT: Starfish Specialty Press. | The main character, Trevor, is a child with impressive, though isolated skills. Unfortunately, Trevor's classmates see his differences and not his strengths. A caring and sensitive teacher makes the difference. **| F | Elementary**

Edwards, B., & Armitage, D. (1999). *My brother Sammy*. Brookfield, CT: Millbrook Press, Inc. | The narrator of this picture book longs for a brother who can talk to him, build towers with him, and join his friends at play. His younger brother Sammy, who has autism, mimics his speech, knocks down his building blocks, and lies alone on the grass staring at the leaves on trees. Their relationship changes when the older boy tries doing things Sammy's way and seeing things through Sammy's eyes. **| F | Elementary**

Ellis, D. (2001). *Looking for X*. Toronto: Groundwood-Douglas and McIntyre. | Eleven-year-old Khyber lives with her mother and twin brothers who have autism in a low-income area in Toronto. In addition to her problems at school, she must face trying to understand her mother's decision to send her brothers to a group home, getting expelled after being accused falsely of vandalism, and searching for her homeless friend, "X." **| F | Middle**

Ellis, M., & Loehr, J. (Illust.). (2005) *Keisha's Door/Las Puertas de Keisha*. Round Rock, TX: Speech Kids Texas Press. | An older sister can't understand why her little sister, Keisha, won't play with her. The family finds out that Keisha has autism and goes to see a therapist who helps them understand autism. Text is written in both English and Spanish. **| F | Elementary | #**

Ellis, M., & Loehr, J. (Illust.). (2005) *Tacos Anyone?/¿Alguien quiere tacos?* Round Rock, TX: Speech Kids Texas Press. | Michael is a 4-year old boy with autism. His older brother, Thomas, doesn't understand why Michael behaves the way he does. The boys start to have fun together after a therapist teaches Thomas how to play with Michael. Text is written in both English and Spanish. **| F | Elementary | #**

Gagnon, E., & Myles, B.S. (1999). ***This is Asperger syndrome.*** **Shawnee Mission, KS: Autism Asperger Publishing Company. |** This book gives the reader an experience of the world from the perspective of a young child with Asperger syndrome. The simple text is accompanied by lively illustrations. **| N | Elementary–middle**

Gartenberg, Z.M. (1998). ***Mori's Story: A book about a boy with autism.*** **Minneapolis, MN: Lerner Publications Company. |** This book tells the story of the childhood of Moriel Gartenburg, the author's brother, who has autism. **| N | Elementary | +**

Gray, C., & White, A.L. (Eds.). (2002). ***My social stories book.*** **London: Jessica Kingsley Publishers. |** The short narratives in *My Social Stories Book* take children step-by-step through basic activities such as brushing your teeth, taking a bath, and wearing a safety belt in the car. These stories form a useful primer for all children as well as children who are on the autism spectrum. **| F | Preschool–elementary**

Hoopman, K. (2001). ***Blue bottle mystery: An Asperger adventure.*** **London: Jessica Kingsley Publishers. |** Ben and Andy are friends who attend the same school. Ben doesn't always understand the way other people interact with him. He eventually receives the diagnosis of Asperger syndrome. **| F | Elementary–middle**

Hoopmann, K. (2003). ***Haze.*** **London: Jessica Kingsley Publishers. |** Kathy Hoopmann, author of the "Asperger Adventures" series for children, has written a novel for teenagers. Weaving the facts of Asperger syndrome into the story of a teenager named Seb, this fast-paced book is appropriate for teenagers of all ages and abilities. **| F | High**

Hoopman, K. (2001). ***Of mice and aliens: An Asperger's adventure.*** **London: Jessica Kingsley Publishers. |** Ben is learning to cope with his newly diagnosed Asperger syndrome. When Spick, an alien, crash-lands in Ben's back yard and knows nothing about Earth's rules and norms, it is up to Ben and his friend Andy to help him survive. **| F | Elementary–middle**

Jackson, L., & Attwood, T. (2002). ***Freaks, geeks, and Asperger syndrome: A user's guide to adolescence.*** **London: Jessica Kingsley Publishers. |** Jackson, a 13-year-old from the UK, is one of seven children. He has Asperger syndrome, one of his brothers has attention-deficit/hyperactivity disorder, and another has autism. Jackson's conversational and humorous text offers helpful insights into the challenges faced by those with AS. Written for adolescents with AS and their families. **| N | Middle–high | +**

Katz, I., Ritvo, E., & Borowitz, F. (Ilust.) (1993). ***Joey and Sam: A heartwarming storybook about autism, a family, and a brother's love.*** **West Hills, CA: Real Life Storybooks. |** Although Joey sometimes finds it difficult to have a younger brother like Sam, who has autism, Joey is proud when Sam's special class performs at a school assembly. **| F | Preschool–elementary | +**

Landalf, H., & Rimland, M. (Illust.). (1998). ***The secret night world of cats.*** **Lyme, NH: Smith & Kraus. |** Illustrated by an individual with autism, this fantasy tale describes many kinds of cats in different colors and sizes in a variety of amazing settings. **| F | Elementary**

Lears, L. (1998). ***Ian's walk: A story about autism.*** **Morton Grove, IL: Albert Whitman & Co. |** A young girl realizes how much she cares for her brother Ian, who has autism, when he gets lost at the park. **| F | Elementary | +**

Levinson, M., & De Groat, D. (2001). ***And don't bring Jeremy.*** **New York: Henry Holt and Company. |** This novel for young adults describes some of the decisions and dilemmas faced by siblings of children with special needs. **| F | High | +**

Messner, A.W. (1999). ***Captain Tommy.*** **Arlington, TX: Future Horizons. |** This story tells how one young boy becomes involved with a classmate with autism and becomes an important contributor to his life. **| F | Elementary**

Peralta, S. (2002). ***All about my brother: An eight-year-old sister's introduction to her brother who has autism.*** **Shawnee, KS: Autism Asperger Publishing Company. |** Eight-year-old Sarah Peralta gives the reader a look into the world of her younger brother who has autism and is nonverbal. Through simple descriptions of Evan's everyday behavior, Sarah encourages others to approach autism without apprehension. **| N | Preschool–elementary | +**

Prizant, B.M. (Ed.). (1997). ***In our own words: Stories by brothers and sisters of children with autism and PDD.*** **Fall River, MA: Adsum, Inc. |** This book helps teens to better understand autism and to live with the challenges of living with sibling who has autism. **| N | Middle | +**

Rodowsky, C.F. (2004). ***Clay.*** **New York: Farrar Straus Giroux. |** Eleven-year-old Elsie gradually makes clear that she and her younger brother, Tommy, who has autism, have been stolen away from their father by their emotionally unstable mother. When Tommy becomes seriously ill while their mother is at work, Elsie's courage saves not only her younger brother but also herself. **| F | Elementary–middle**

Rosenberg, M.S. (2001). ***Coping when a brother or sister is autistic.*** **New York: Rosen Publishing Group. |** This book provides information about autism and related disorders along with diagnosis, intervention, and advocacy. It also addresses the ups and downs of being a sibling of a child with autism and offers advice about dealing with negative feelings, stressed parents, and curious neighbors. **| N | Middle | +**

Rosenberg, M.S. (2000). ***Everything you need to know when a brother or sister is autistic.*** **New York: Rosen Publishing Group, Inc. |** This book helps teens better understand autism and learn to cope with the challenges of living with a sibling who has autism. **| N | Middle | +**

Sprecher, J., & Forrest, J. (Illust.). (1997). ***Jeffrey and the despondent dragon.*** **Muskego, WI: Special Kids. |** The author wrote this bedtime story for his son, Jeffrey, who was diagnosed with autism spectrum disorder (ASD) at age 2. It tells the story of a boy who tries to help a fire-breathing dragon who has lost his fire. **| F | Elementary**

Thompson, M. (1996). ***Andy and his yellow Frisbee.*** **Bethesda, MD: Woodbine House. |** This book is about Andy, a boy with autism, who is fascinated with motion. Andy has a talent for spinning his Frisbee and it is this behavior that intrigues a new classmate. **| F | Preschool–elementary | +**

Watson, E. (1996). ***Talking to angels.*** **San Diego: Harcourt and Brace Company. |** This personal story of the author/artist's young sister who has autism shows her as a girl who has a rich imagination despite her inability to behave and communicate "normally." She seems to hear and see things within her head and murmurs as if talking softly to angels. **| F | Preschool-elementary | +**

Wilson, R. (1999). ***The legendary blobshocker.*** **Arlington, TX: Future Horizons. |** This colorful picture book was written and illustrated by a 9-year-old boy with pervasive developmental disorder-not otherwise specified (PDD-NOS). The story is about a Blobshocker named Henry who travels from outer space to Earth in order to find a more comfortable place to live. **| F | Preschool-elementary**

Cancer

Hamilton, V. (1999). ***Bluish.*** **New York: Blue Sky Press. |** Three girls, Bluish, Dreenie, and Tuli, become unlikely friends as they confront issues of illness, ethnicity, culture, need, and hope. **| F | Elementary**

Slote, A. (1992). ***Hang tough, Paul Mather.*** **New York: Harper Collins Children's. |** A boy with leukemia who pitches on a baseball team is determined to get in as much time on the mound as possible. His illness has put him into the hospital several times already, and his parents are so worried that they've forbidden him to play. But Paul's team needs him, and he won't give up without a fight. **| F | Elementary-middle**

Celiac Disease

Kruszka, B.J. (2004). ***Eating gluten-free with Emily: A story for children with celiac disease.*** **Bethesda, MD: Woodbine House. |** Written by the mother of a child with celiac disease who has the disease herself, this book offers a reassuring look at celiac disease in language that a child can easily understand. This book's positive message will be a huge boost to children with celiac disease, especially those who have been recently diagnosed. **| N | Preschool-elementary**

Cerebral Palsy

Carter, A.R., & Carter, C.S. (Photographer). (2000). ***Stretching ourselves: Kids with cerebral palsy.*** **Morton Grove, IL: Albert Whitman. |** Carter offers a brief description of cerebral palsy (CP), followed by photographic essays about four children, Emily, Nick, Tanner, and Leslie, who have different forms of CP with different degrees of disability. **| N | Elementary**

Metzger, L. (1992). ***Barry's sister.*** **New York: Atheneum. |** Metzger has woven what is almost an allegory on families of children born with physical disabilities. All of the elements are here: the pity, shunning, and mockery displayed by those whose lives have been touched by disability; the isolation; the conflicting emotions; and the relief at finding others who share their problems. **| F | Middle-high**

Perske, R. (1986). ***Don't stop the music.*** **Nashville: Abingdon Press. |** This book generates an action-packed adventure as it shows how people with disabilities contribute positively to the community. Joe and Jessica, two teens with cerebral palsy, become key elements in cracking an auto-theft ring. The reader will be amazed as Joe and Jessica use their wits and their motorized wheelchairs to capture the thieves, while making some very special friends along the way. **| F | Middle-high**

Wanous, S. (1995). ***Sara's Secret.*** **Minneapolis, MN: Carolrhoda Books. |** Sara's secret is her brother Justin, who was born with cerebral palsy and has an intellectual disability. Experience has taught her that kids who know about her brother are sometimes cruel, and she's determined not to let Justin become a joke or to be teased about him in her new school. But keeping her secret isn't easy. It takes a teacher's decision to begin a classroom discussion of disabilities to make her face up to her feelings. **| F | Preschool–elementary**

Deaf and Hard of Hearing

Addabbo, C. (1998). ***Dina the deaf dinosaur.*** **Stamford, CT: Hannacroix Creek. |** Because her parents would not learn sign language, Dina the deaf dinosaur runs away from home and becomes friends with an owl, a mole, and a chipmunk. The author of this book is deaf. **| F | Preschool–elementary**

Blatchford, C.H. (1995). ***Nick's mission.*** **Minneapolis, MN: Lerner Publications. |** This suspenseful story is about 12-year-old Nick and his mission to save a lake. Nick's hearing loss affects his life, but it never affects his character. **| F | Elementary–middle**

Hodges, C., & Yoder, D. (Illust.). (1995). ***When I grow up.*** **Hollidaysburg, PA: Jason & Nordic Publishers. |** Jimmy, who is deaf, attends Career Day where he meets deaf adults with varied and interesting careers who communicate using sign language. Includes diagrams that illustrate signs for some of the words in the text. **| F | Elementary**

Lakin, P. (1994). ***Dad and me in the morning.*** **Morton Grove, IL: Albert Whitman & Co. |** A young deaf boy awakens to the light of his special alarm clock, puts in his hearing aids, and tiptoes to awaken his father. Together they walk to the beach, observing nature. Jacob and his father share "lots of ways of talking...signing or lipreading or just squeezing each other's hands." **| F | Elementary**

Lowell, G.R., & Brooks, K.S. (Illust.). (2000). ***Elana's ears, or how I became the best big sister in the world.*** **Washington, DC: Magination Press. |** Lacey is the family dog. One day, her life of luxury is disrupted when a new baby comes home. When the family realizes that this baby can't hear, the baby's "sister" Lacey is there to help protect her and become her hearing ear dog. **| F | Preschool–elementary**

Millman, I. (2003). ***Moses goes to the circus.*** **New York: Francis Foster Books. |** Moses, who is deaf, and his family are going to the Big Apple's Circus of the Senses with acts specially designed for people who are deaf and hard of hearing and/or blind. Moses' little sister, Renee, isn't deaf but is learning sign language. Moses loves teaching her, and illustrations of some of the signs they use are included. **| F | Preschool–elementary**

Piper, D. (1996). ***Jake's the name, sixth grade's the game.*** **Unionville, NY: Royal Fireworks Press. |** Jake is a pretty typical sixth grader, has a knack for getting into trouble and irritating his mother, and he's deaf. **| F | Middle**

Shreve, S.R. (1993). ***Gift of the girl who couldn't hear.*** **New York: William Morrow. |** Eliza, who is a gifted singer, helps her friend Lucy, who has been deaf since birth, learn to sing so she can try out for the seventh-grade musical. **| F | Elementary**

Slier, D. (1995). ***Word signs: A first book of sign language.*** **Washington, DC: Gallaudet University Press. |** This board book provides words, illustrations, and sign language for common objects. **| N | Preschool**

Diabetes

Beatty, M.D. (1997). *My sister Rose has diabetes.* Santa Fe, NM: Health Press. | James and Rose, brother and sister, help to reduce the sense of devastation family members may feel when a child is first diagnosed with diabetes by showing how manageable the disease can be. Written and illustrated specifically for young readers, this 23-page book is endorsed by Juvenile Diabetes Foundation, American Diabetes Association, and the Joslin Diabetes Center. **| N | Elementary-middle**

Haines, S. (1994). *Donnie makes a difference.* Boise, ID: Writer's Press Service. | Donnie, who has diabetes, is a football fan—actually—a football nut. He wants desperately to make a contribution to his team. A story about perseverance to inspire children of all ages. Includes teacher lesson plans and a resource guide. **| F | Elementary-middle**

Down Syndrome

Carter, A.R., Young, D. (Illust.) & Carter, C. (Illust.). (1997). *Big brother Dustin.* Morton Grove, IL: Albert Whitman. | Dustin, a young boy with Down syndrome, is excited when he learns that his mother is going to have a baby. Dustin makes it his job to find just the perfect name for his baby sister, but the choices he comes up with are not quite right. **| F | Elementary**

Carter, A.R., Young, D. (Photographer), & Carter, C. (Illust.). (1999). *Dustin's big school day.* Morton Grove, IL: Albert Whitman. | This story follows Dustin, a second grader who has Down syndrome, through his school day. He attends a general education school and classes supplemented by visits to a speech therapist and an occupational therapist. Dustin is an engaging young man who is more similar to his friends than he is different. **| F | Elementary**

Dodds, B. (1993). *My sister Annie.* Honesdale, PA: Caroline House Boyds Mills Press. | In Charlie's family, "not normal is normal." Embarrassed by his older sister, Annie, who has Down syndrome, and his younger twin sisters, 11-year-old Charlie struggles to balance the demands of his particular family with his own preoccupations. **| F | Elementary-middle**

Fox, P. (1997). *Radiance descending.* New York: DK Publishing. | Paul can spin mental circles around his younger brother, Jacob, and he's tired of the way his parents focus all of their attention on his brother just because Jacob has a disability. Paul focuses all of his energy on ignoring Jacob. Slowly, though, Paul begins to wonder if, perhaps, *not* thinking about Jacob is only another way of thinking about him. **| F | Middle**

Mazer, H. (1998). *Wild kid.* New York: Simon & Schuster Children's Books. | Sammy's troubles keep escalating. He goes off to the store by himself, which is forbidden, and his new bike is stolen. Chasing the thief, Sammy becomes lost. Then Kevin, a "wild" kid who holds him captive in the woods, asks him if he's "dumb." Sammy says, "No, I'm Down's. I'm young for my age. I'm a special person." Mazer describes Sammy's world, his awful predicament, his magnificent spirit, and his incredible determination. **| F | Elementary-middle**

Rickert, J.E., & McGahan, P. (Photographer). (2001). ***Russ and the almost perfect day.*** **Bethesda, MD: Woodbine House. |** Russ's day takes an interesting turn when he's faced with a tricky decision at school. **| F | Preschool-elementary**

Rickert, J.E., & McGahan, P. (Photographer). (1999). ***Russ and the apple tree surprise.*** **Bethesda, MD: Woodbine House. |** After Russ, a 5-year old boy with Down syndrome, picks a basket of apples and helps his mother and grandmother make a pie, his grandfather invites him into the backyard for a surprise. **| F | Preschool-elementary**

Rickert, J.E. (1999). ***Russ and the firehouse.*** **Bethesda, MD: Woodbine House. |** This story begins as Russ goes "on duty" for the day. He helps inspect the fire equipment—the ax, fire hydrant, flashlight, ladders, fire truck—to make sure that it's all working well. After Russ and the firefighters finish cleaning, everything in the firehouse is sparkling—except for Russ, who's just a little bit wet! **| F | Preschool-elementary**

Rottman, S.L. (2003). ***Head above water.*** **Atlanta, GA: Peachtree Publishers. |** High school junior Skye Johnson faces many challenges. She's trying to qualify for the state swimming competition; she's being pursued by a hunky football star; and she bears the brunt of the responsibility for the care of Sunny, her 19-year-old brother who has Down syndrome, while her single mother is at work. **| F | Elementary-middle**

Stuve-Bodeen, S., & DeVito P. (Illust.) (1998). ***We'll paint the octopus red.*** **Bethesda, MD: Woodbine House. |** Six-year-old Emma has big dreams for her new baby brother. When she learns that he has Down syndrome, she worries that he won't be able to do many of the fun things she'd imagined they'd do together. Slowly, however, Emma learns that there are many things her brother can and will be able to do. **| F | Preschool-elementary**

Stuve-Bodeen, S. (2005). ***The best worst brother.*** **Bethesda, MD: Woodbine House. |** Emma misses the adoring baby brother Isaac used to be. Now that he's older, he's a pain. Emma thinks Isaac would be more fun if he'd hurry up and learn some of the sign language she and her mom are trying to teach him. **| F | Preschool-elementary | +**

Testa, M., & Paterson, D. (1994). ***Thumbs up, Rico!*** **Morton Grove, IL: Albert Whitman. |** Rico, a boy with Down syndrome, narrates this chapter book for young readers. During the course of the book, Rico befriends a boy who initially calls him "dummy," learns to consider his sister's needs as well as his own, and finds the resources within himself to improve his drawing ability. **| F | Elementary-middle**

Woloson, E. (2003). ***My friend Isabelle.*** **Bethesda, MD: Woodbine House. |** Isabelle and Charlie are friends. They both like to draw, dance, read, and play at the park. They both like to eat Cheerios. They both cry if their feelings are hurt. And like most friends, they are also different from each other. Isabelle has Down syndrome. Charlie doesn't. This charming tale encourages readers to think about what makes a friendship special. **| F | Preschool-elementary**

Emotional and Behavioral Problems/ Attention-Deficit/Hyperactivity Disorder

Corman, C.L., & Trevino, E. (1995). ***Eukee, the jumpy, jumpy elephant.*** **North Branch, MN: Specialty Press. |** Eukee is a smart little elephant who likes to chase butterflies, blow bubbles, and do cartwheels. He always feels jumpy inside, however, and can never finish the march at school. Unhappy that he doesn't have any friends, he consents to a visit to the doctor where he learns he has attention-deficit/hyperactivity disorder (ADHD). **| F | Preschool–elementary**

Gehret, J. (1992). ***I'm somebody, too.*** **Fairport, NY: Verbal Images Press. |** The dynamics of the plot involve everyday activities from which relationships and feelings grow. In addition, the book offers suggestions for siblings on how to deal with frustration. **| F | Middle–high**

Gordon, M. (1992). ***My brother's a world-class pain: A sibling's guide to ADHD/hyperactivity.*** **DeWitt, NY: GSI Publications. |** A book for the siblings of those affected with ADHD. Siblings frequently bear the brunt of a child's impulsiveness and distractibility related to ADHD. This story highlights the important role siblings play, shows siblings how to understand ADHD and how to have their own feelings addressed. **| N | Elementary–high**

Janover, C. (1997). ***Zipper: The kid with ADHD.*** **Bethesda, MD: Woodbine House. |** Zach, a fifth-grader who has ADHD, has trouble concentrating and controlling himself until a retired jazz musician who believes in him gives him the motivation to start trying to do better. **| F | Elementary–middle**

McIntyre, T. (2003). ***The behavior survival guide for kids: How to make good choices and stay out of trouble.*** **Minneapolis, MN: Free Spirit Publishing. |** Kids labeled with behavior challenges struggle every day—with their peers, teachers, parents, and themselves. It's no fun to be labeled, and nobody wants to have behavior problems. Often kids who get in trouble frequently don't know how else to act. This book can help them improve their behavior and their lives. **| N | Elementary–high**

Penn, A. (2003). ***A.D.D., not B.A.D.*** **Washington, DC: Child and Family Press. |** Jimmy Jumping Bean can't sit still, and his fellow students just can't understand why. With the help of their teacher, Jimmy's classmates are able to put themselves into Jimmy's shoes—both literally and figuratively. Inspired by the author's own son, this warmly illustrated tale offers children ages 5–9 accurate, yet age-appropriate insights into attention deficit disorder and its associated behaviors. **| F | Preschool–elementary**

Epilepsy

Epilepsy Foundation of America. (1992). ***Brothers and sisters: Just for you.*** **Landover, MD: Epilepsy Foundation of America. |** This guide looks at the effect that epilepsy has on the other children in the family. It has two sections: the first half is written specifically for siblings to read; the second half is for parents and other adult family members. **| N | All ages**

Swanson, S.M. (1994). ***My friend Emily.*** **Boise, ID: Writers Press Service. |** Emily, a self-confident child who enjoys life, shows that kids with epilepsy are just like other kids. **| F | Elementary**

Fragile X

Heyman, C. (2003). ***My eXtra special brother: How to love, understand, and celebrate your sibling with special needs.*** **San Francisco: National Fragile X Foundation. |** Sixteen-year-old Carly Heyman writes about living with and loving her older brother who was born with fragile X syndrome. The young author entertains and teaches the reader about many of her experiences with her brother. She shares her struggles, frustrations, and finally her joys as she learns the skills to cope with her brother's limitations. **| N | High | +**

O'Connor, R. (1995). ***Boys with fragile X syndrome.*** **San Francisco, CA: National Fragile X Foundation. |** This children's book is designed to enlighten siblings, friends, classmates, and educators about the characteristics of fragile X. The author is a developmental specialist and has more than 10 years' experience in the development of intervention plans for children with fragile X syndrome. **| N | All ages**

Steiger, C. (1998). ***My brother has fragile X syndrome.*** **San Francisco, CA: National Fragile X Foundation. |** Written by 8-year-old Charles, this book describes his life and experience with his older brother who has fragile X syndrome. This personal narrative makes a great addition to any family's reading list as they live with a child with fragile X syndrome. **| N | Elementary | +**

Grief/Loss

Grollman, E., & Johnson, J. (2001). ***Child's book about death.*** **Omaha, NE: Centering Corporation. |** This book provides a gentle explanation of how everything and everyone dies. **| N | Elementary**

Munoz-Kiehne, M . (2000). ***Since my brother died/Desde que murio mi hermano.*** **Omaha, NE: Centering Corporation. |** A child talks about how things are different since his brother died. In the end, the child realizes that his brother will always be alive in his heart. Includes both English and Spanish translation of sections for caregivers, teachers, and parents. **| N | Middle-high | #**

Riches, G., & Dawson, P. (2000). ***An intimate loneliness: Supporting bereaved parents and siblings.*** **Berkshire, England: Open University Press. |** Explores how family members attempt to come to terms with the death of an offspring or brother or sister. Examines the importance of social relationships in helping adjusting to death. **| N | Middle-adult**

Ruiz, R.A. (2001). ***Coping with the death of a brother or sister.*** **New York: Rosen Publishing Group. |** Nothing seems as difficult to face as a death in the family, but for young people, facing the death of a sibling is among the most painful of life's struggles. Ruiz speaks sympathetically about emotional grief that children face after a loved one has died, and discusses how other young people have handled grief. **| N | Middle-high**

Schwiebert, P., & DeKlyen, C. (2005). ***Tear soup*** **(3rd rev. ed.). Portland, OR: Grief Watch. |** Grandy has suffered the loss of someone close (who is not identified), and deals with her feelings by mixing up a batch of "Tear Soup." She finally freezes it with the intention of tasting it from time to time. When her grandchild asks what he will do when she dies, she tells him she will leave him her recipe for the healing soup. **| F | Middle**

Sims, A. (1996). ***Am I still a sister?*** **Big A & Co. |** This book was written when Allie was 11 and reflects the child-wise discoveries she made after her baby brother died. "I learned that death is all right for some, but terrible for others. Some think death is a release from life. Others aren't ready to leave. Some do not have a choice." **| N | Elementary | +**

Temes, R., & Carlisle, K. (1992). ***The empty place: A child's guide through grief.*** **Far Hills, NJ: Small Horizons. |** A boy whose sister has died describes his and another friend's feelings of loss, fear, and guilt after they both lost a sibling. **| Elementary**

Traisman, E.S. (1994). ***A child remembers.*** **Omaha, NE: Centering Corporation. |** This book includes pages for remembering favorite stories and favorite things of the person a child lost and art pages for drawing. **| N | Preschool–middle**

Yeomans, E., & Derosa, D. (2000). ***Lost and found: Remembering a sister.*** **Omaha, NE: Centering Corporation. |** An honest portrayal of a young girl's experiences and feelings after her sister Paige dies. Readers commend the book for not sugarcoating the experience. **| N | Preschool–elementary**

Intellectual Disabilities

O'Connor, B. (2003). ***Me and Rupert Goody.*** **New York: Farrar, Straus & Giroux. |** Eleven-year-old Jennalee is jealous when a "slow-thinking" African American arrives in her Smoky Mountains community and claims to be the son of Uncle Beau, the owner of the general store and Jennalee's only friend. **| F | Middle**

Powell, R. (2003). ***Tribute to another dead rock star.*** **New York: Farrar Straus & Giroux. |** Grady, the 15-year-old narrator, returns to his hometown of Seattle 3 years after the death of his mother, a famous hard rock musician, to speak at a concert performed in her memory. While there, he stays with his half-brother, Louie, who has an intellectual disability, and Louie's born-again-Christian family. The half-brothers' artless conversations allow Grady time to reflect on Debbie's rise to fame as well as her self-destructive behavior. **| F | Middle–high**

Pulver, R., & Wolf, E. (1999). ***Way to go, Alex!*** **Morton Grove, IL: Albert Whitman. |** Carly feels the dual emotions that many siblings of special needs children feel. She's frustrated with her older brother, Alex, whose "brain doesn't work," and is ashamed of her feelings. When her parents enroll Alex in the upcoming Special Olympics, Carly helps him train and then cheers him on despite her pessimism. **| F | Elementary**

Tashjian, J. (1997). ***Tru confessions.*** **New York: Henry Holt & Co. |** Trudy "Tru" Walker learns a lot about herself and her twin brother Eddie, who has developmental disabilities, when she enters her video documentary about her brother in a teen video competition. Also made into a made-for-television film. **| F | Middle**

Learning Disabilities

Banks, J.T. (1995). ***Egg-drop blues.*** **Boston, MA: Houghton Mifflin. |** This novel is about sixth-grader Judge Jenkins, who is recently diagnosed with dyslexia and is struggling with learning. When his mother threatens to send him to a different school next year unless he shows that he can succeed at Plank Elementary, Judge pins his hopes on winning the Einstein Rally. He tussles with packaging his egg for a safe landing in the egg drop competition and keeping his twin brother and rally partner out of trouble until the contest begins. **| F | Elementary**

Cobb, J. (2001). ***Learning how to learn: Getting into and surviving college when you have a learning disability.*** **Washington, DC: Child Welfare League of America. |** Written for high school and college students with learning disabilities, this thorough, down-to-earth manual, designed in an LD-friendly format, gently steers students through the process of applying to college, selecting the right classes, and succeeding academically. **| N | High-college**

Griffith, J. (1997). ***How dyslexic Benny became a star.*** **Dallas, TX: Yorktown Press. |** A fifth-grader who is frustrated and humiliated because he can't read as well as his classmates becomes a star on the football field, and when he is diagnosed with dyslexia, he finds that he has a whole team of people ready to help. **| F | Elementary-middle**

Isdell, W. (1993). ***A zebra named Al.*** **Minneapolis, MN: Free Spirit Press. |** Julie is an eighth-grader who has trouble in math. Frustrated, she rests her head on her book and is awakened by an Imaginary Number who suddenly appears in her room. When she follows the Number through a mysterious portal, she enters a strange land of mathematics, where she meets a zebra named Al. **| F | Elementary-middle**

Janover, C. (2000). ***How many days until tomorrow?*** **Bethesda, MD: Woodbine House. |** A realistic portrait of a young adolescent boy with a learning disability struggling to find himself. Young readers will see themselves in Josh as he copes with frustration and loneliness. His ingenuity and bravery help him to avert disaster and gain respect. **| F | Elementary-middle**

Root, A., & Gladden, L. (1995). ***Charlie's challenge.*** **Austin, TX: Printmaster Press. |** Charlie excels at some school activities but struggles with other school activities. After his doctor determines that he has a learning disability, his teacher implements some learning strategies that help Charlie's performance and confidence. **| F | Elementary**

Schlieper, A. (1994). ***Best fight.*** **Morton Grove, IL: Albert Whitman & Co. |** Jamie repeatedly gets into fistfights with the other fifth-graders. He attends a special class for reading, and his peers tease him about his disability. Mr. Wilson, the principal, eventually delivers an unusual punishment to Josh for his fighting: He must show up to Mr. Wilson's office for a week after school to talk about his "burden." Mr. Wilson gives Jamie practical ways to deal with the teasing of his classmates and a sensible way of internalizing his disability. **| F | Elementary-middle**

Smith, S.L., & Booz, B. (Illust.). (1994). ***Different is not bad, different is the world: A book about disabilities.*** **Longmont, CO: Sopris West. |** A book of wonderful illustrations to prove that being "different" is quite okay. Children (with and without disabilities) will see that people who are different have different ways of accomplishing everyday tasks, but can do almost anything in their own way. **| N | Elementary**

Physical Disabilities

Berenstain, S., & Berenstain, J. (1993). ***The Berenstain Bears and the wheelchair commando.*** **New York: Random House, Inc. |** Harry, a new student at Bear Country School who has a disability and uses a wheelchair, has trouble making friends until the others discover that he is really very much like them. **| F | Elementary**

Benton, H. (1996). ***Whoa, Nellie!*** **Columbus, OH: Open Minds. |** Part of the Best Friends series, this book features Kathryn, a girl with a physical disability who uses a wheelchair. **| F | Elementary-middle**

Harshman, M. (1995). ***The storm.*** **New York: Cobblehill Books. |** Though confined to a wheelchair, Jonathan faces the terror of a tornado all by himself and saves the lives of the horses on the family farm. **| F | Elementary**

Heelan, J.R. (1998). ***Making of my special hand: Madison's story.*** **Atlanta, GA: Peachtree Publishers. |** Madison, who was born without a left hand, takes readers through the process of being fitted for her prosthesis. Children will have no problem understanding how the myo-electric hand starts out as a plaster cast, how it is fitted and refitted, and how an occupational therapist teaches Madison to work the battery and use her new hand. **| N | Elementary**

Heelan, J.R. (2000). ***Rolling along: The story of Taylor and his wheelchair.*** **Atlanta, GA: Peachtree Publishers. |** Taylor describes his condition, aspects of his daily activities at home and at school, and his desire for independence. While he has been trained to use a walker, he prefers a wheelchair as it enables him to go faster and not tire as quickly. The book also includes some discussion of his physical-therapy sessions. **| N | Elementary**

Holcomb, N. (1992). ***Andy finds a turtle.*** **Hollidaysburg, PA: Jason & Nordic Publishers. |** Andy's physical therapist calls him a turtle one day when he is feeling uncooperative, and thus begins a search to find a turtle, during which Andy becomes a hero and learns something important about himself. **| F | Preschool-elementary**

Holcomb, N. (1992). ***Andy opens wide.*** **Hollidaysburg, PA: Jason & Nordic Publishers. |** Andy, who is 5 and has cerebral palsy, has difficulty opening his mouth at mealtime, until his frustration leads to a discovery. **| F | Preschool-elementary**

Holcomb, N. (1992). ***Fair and square.*** **Hollidaysburg, PA: Jason & Nordic Publishers. |** Kevin wants to play and win or lose fair and square instead of others letting him win. His occupational therapist teaches him to play using a computer and a capability switch. At last he knows the joy of winning fair and square against the computer. **| F | Preschool-elementary**

Loski, D., & Sniffen, L.M. (Illust.). (1995). ***Dinosaur hill.*** **Boise, ID: Writers Press. |** In the town of Maysville, Kentucky, a young girl named Sarah dreams of exploring the giant wooded hill she views daily from her bay window—where she sits in a wheelchair. When she finally gets the chance to climb it on horseback, she discovers a mystery in the form of a deserted mansion. **| F | Elementary-middle**

Meyers, C., & Morgan, C. (Illust). (1999). ***Rolling along with Goldilocks and the three bears.*** **Bethesda, MD: Woodbine House. |** The classic folktale retold with a special-needs twist. In this version, Baby Bear uses a wheelchair, goes to physical therapy, and ultimately makes friends with Goldilocks. **| F | Preschool-elementary**

Moran, G., & Westcott, N.B. (1994). ***Imagine me on a sit-ski.*** **Morton Grove, IL: Albert Whitman |** Billy, who uses a wheelchair, never imagined himself able to ski, so he's very excited when he discovers that he and his classmates are going to have a chance to learn. He describes his experiences at Snow Valley, where people with physical disabilities are trained by instructors to use adaptive equipment. Billy describes how the equipment works as well as his adventures on the slopes. **| F | Elementary**

Osofsky, A. (1992). ***My buddy.*** **New York: Henry Holt and Co. |** A young boy with muscular dystrophy goes to a special camp where he is paired with an intelligent golden retriever who performs everyday tasks that are too difficult for physically challenged people. When they leave camp, the dog is able to help his human friend dress, attend school, shop, and play. **| F | Elementary**

Ratto, L. (1992). ***Coping with a physically challenged brother or sister.*** **New York: Rosen Publishing Group. |** This book offers a variety of positive suggestions on how to approach problems that might be faced by those with disabled siblings. A list of organizations for specific disabilities and an extensive list for further reading are appended. **| N | High**

Russo, M. (1992). ***Alex is my friend.*** **New York: Greenwillow Books. |** From the time Ben is coming in a stroller to the park where they first meet, Alex and Ben are close friends. At age 5, Ben notices that he's getting much taller than Alex, and Mama explains that Alex will always be unusually small. After he undergoes a special back operation, Alex sometimes needs a wheelchair; at the end of the story the boys remain friends and can appreciate each other's strengths. **| F | Elementary**

Tuitel, J., Lamson, S.E., & Sharp, D. (Illust.). (2000). ***Searching the noonday trail.*** **Muskegon, MI: Cedar Tree. |** Part of the Gun Lake Gang Adventure series, this book features a boy with cerebral palsy who uses a wheelchair. One of the authors, J. Tuitel, also has CP and uses a wheelchair. **| F | Elementary–middle**

Useman, S., Useman, E., & Phillo, C. (Illust.). (1999). ***Tibby tried it.*** **Washington, DC: Magination Press. |** Tibby the tree swallow cannot fly because he has a crooked wing, but the other animals teach him skills that come in handy when a baby robin falls from its nest. **| F | Preschool–elementary**

Schizophrenia

Knoll, V. (1992). ***My sister then and now.*** **Minneapolis, MN: Carol Rhoda Books. |** Ten-year-old Rachael describes how her 20-year-old sister's life with schizophrenia has affected the family. Rachael expresses her own feelings of sadness and anger. This book presents some basic information on mental illness and its effect on family members in a style that is accessible to younger readers. **| N | Elementary | +**

Speech Impairment

Small, D. (1992). ***Ruby Mae has something to say.*** **New York: Crown Publishers. |** Ruby Mae Foote's dream of delivering a message before the United Nations is thwarted by her inability to speak clearly without garbling and mixing up her words. Her nephew's wacky invention, the "Bobatron," gives Ruby Mae the confidence to conquer public speaking. **| F | Elementary**

Spina Bifida

Lutkenhoff, M., & Oppenheimer, S.G. (1997). ***SPINAbilities.*** **Washington, DC: Spina Bifida Association. |** Medical professionals offer practical, no-nonsense advice to individuals with Spina Biffida on managing daily and long-term healthcare, and strategies for success at school and on the job, now and down the road. **| N | High**

Senisi, E.B. (2002). ***All kinds of friends, even green!*** **Bethesda, MD: Woodbine House. |** The teacher gives Moses and his class an assignment to write about a friend. His friend Katie has an iguana named Zaki who is missing toes, making it hard for her to walk and climb. Moses decides to write about Zaki because he and Zaki have a lot in common. They both have special needs. More than just a story about friendship, this book looks at difference in a clever yet subtle way. **| F | Preschool-elementary**

Tourette Syndrome

Buehrens, A. (1990). ***Hi, I'm Adam.*** **Duarte, CA: Hope Press. |** Adam Buehrens is 10 years old and has Tourette syndrome (TS) and ADHD. Adam tells this story from a child's viewpoint, how it feels to have the symptoms of TS when no one, including himself, knew why he was making noises and jerky movements and having temper tantrums. Adam relates the problems of getting a diagnosis, school problems, the side effects he had with some of the medications, and how he has now come to terms with his disorder. **| B | Preschool-middle**

Visual Impairment

Adolphson, T. (2004). ***Beyond the stares.*** **St. Louis: Delta Gamma Center. |** This book was written by a group of children and young adults from St. Louis, ages 9–15, who have brothers and sisters who are blind or visually impaired as well as other disabilities. This informative and inspirational book is a collection of their stories. **| N | Elementary-middle | +**

Bloor, E. (2001). ***Tangerine.*** **New York: Scholastic Paperbacks. |** Although legally blind, Paul Fisher can see better than most people. He can see the lies his parents and brother live out, day after day. No one ever listens to Paul, though—until the family moves to Tangerine. In Tangerine, even a blind, geeky, alien freak can become cool and even a hero! **| F | Middle-high**

Chamberlin, K. (1997). ***The night search.*** **Hollidaysburg, PA: Jason & Nordic, Publishers. |** Heather, who is blind, resists using her white cane until her puppy wanders off. **| F | Elementary**

Day, S., & Morris, D. (Illust.) ***Luna and the big blur.*** **Washington, DC: Magination Press. |** Nearsighted Luna hates wearing glasses, and she hates her name. When her father tells her that she is special and that she was actually named after the moon, she immediately cheers up and announces that she doesn't mind wearing glasses anymore. **| F | Preschool-elementary**

Gardner, S., & Spurlock, J. (Illust.). (1997). ***Eagle feather.*** **Boise, ID: Writers Press. |** About a blind Native American boy in the mid-19th century. **| F | Elementary-middle**

Jones, J. (n.d.) ***My baby brother's eyes.*** **|** This book was written by a mother trying to help her young daughter understand her little brother's visual impairment. (It is available in print and in Braille by special request. Contact Jane Jones, 590 Cumberland Place, Nanaimo, British Columbia, V9T 4S5, Canada, (250) 751-8141.) **| Preschool | #**

Karim, R. (1994). ***Mandy Sue day.*** **New York: Houghton Mifflin Co. |** Mandy Sue's father gives each of his children a day off from their farm chores and their homeschooling lessons to enjoy the days of Indian summer, and today is Mandy Sue's day. She describes her activities in detail as she feeds and grooms her horse, Ben, saddles and bridles him, and goes for a ride in the country. Readers learn late in the story that Mandy Sue is blind. **| F | Middle**

Lang, G. (2001). ***Looking out for Sarah.*** **Boston: National Braille Press. |** Told from a guide dog's perspective, this book shows the relationship between a guide dog and a young woman who is blind. **| F | Elementary**

Martin, Jr., B., Archambault, J., & Rand, T. (Illust.). (1995). ***Knots on a counting rope.*** **New York: Henry Holt. |** Boy-Strength-of-Blue-Horses was born blind. With the help of his grandfather, he teaches his horse to run the trails. They enter a race, and although the boy does not win, his grandfather tells him that he has "raced darkness and won." **| F | Preschool–elementary**

Schulman, A. (1997). ***T.J.'s story: A book about a boy who is blind.*** **Minneapolis, MN: Lerner. |** A book about a 9-year-old boy who has been blind since birth. He describes his life, including reading Braille, using a cane, and playing games with his friends and family. **| B | Elementary–middle**

LITERATURE FOR PARENTS AND ADULT SIBLINGS

General Disabilities

Baker, B.L., & Brightman, A.J., with Blacher, J.B., Hinshaw, S.P., Heifetz, & Murphy, D.M. (2004). ***Steps to independence: Teaching everyday skills to children with special needs*** **(4th ed.). Baltimore: Paul H. Brookes Publishing Co. |** A classic family resource, this book gives parents of children from age 3 through young adult some important life skills training strategies. A basic teaching overview is supplemented with a comprehensive step-by-step guide to teaching seven different types of skills.

Batshaw, M.L. (2001). ***When your child has a disability: The complete sourcebook of daily and medical care*** **(Rev. ed.). Baltimore: Paul H. Brookes Publishing Co. |** This valuable guidebook provides expert advice and information on specific disabilities, including mental retardation, autism, Down syndrome, communication disorders, ADHD, and cerebral palsy. Explores key topics such as legal rights, nutrition, behavior, and transition to adulthood.

Falvey, M.A. (2005). ***Believe in my child with special needs! Helping children achieve their potential in school.*** **Baltimore: Paul H. Brookes Publishing Co. |** This upbeat, reassuring handbook is an invaluable resource to share with parents of a school-age child with a disability. It demystifies complicated issues, encourages parents to celebrate abilities and recognize possibilities, and helps parents be successful advocates throughout their child's education.

Klein, S.D., & Scheleifer, M.J. (Eds.). (1993). ***It isn't fair: Siblings of children with disabilities.*** **Westport, CT: Greenwood Publishing Group. |** The 32 articles in this short book were published in *Exceptional Parent* magazine between 1972 and 1992. The book presents a unique personal and historical perspective on families who have a child with a developmental disability.

McHugh, M. (2003). ***Special siblings: Growing up with someone with a disability*** **(Rev. ed.). Baltimore: Paul H. Brookes Publishing Co. |** In this absorbing and candid book, the author reveals her experiences growing up with a brother with cerebral palsy and mental retardation—and shares what others have learned about being and having a "special sibling." Personal memories blend with research and enlightening interviews with more than 100 siblings and experts. | +

Meyer, D.J., & Vadasy, P.F. (1994). *Sibshops: Workshops for siblings of children with special needs.* Baltimore: Paul H. Brookes Publishing Co. | Children who have brothers and sisters with special needs have three needs of their own—needs that are often overlooked. This practical resource details Sibshops, the award-winning program that brings together children between the ages of 8 to 13 to express their good—and maybe not so good—feelings about having brothers and sisters with disabilities.

Safer, J. (2002). *The normal one: Life with a difficult or damaged sibling.* New York: Free Press | Drawing on concrete examples from her own life and also from her interviews with 60 other siblings, Safer identifies the key experiences that few siblings of individuals with disabilities escapes including being labeled "the normal one," premature maturity, survivor guilt, compulsion to achieve, the fear of contagion, and jealousy. | +

Siegel, B., Silverstein, S., Elliott, G.R., & Silverstein, S. (2001). *What about me? Growing up with a developmentally disabled sibling.* New York: Da Capo Press. | The author, a physician, gives a first-person account of his experiences as the older brother of a sibling with autism. Now a developmental psychologist, Siegel discusses family approaches to disabilities based on clinical interviews with approximately 1,000 families. | +

Autism Spectrum Disorders

Feiges, L.S., & Weiss, M.J. (2004). *Sibling stories: Reflections on life with a brother or sister on the autism spectrum.* Shawnee Mission, KS: Asperger Publishing Company. | The authors present a unique collection of interviews with individuals of all ages who have a brother or sister with autism spectrum disorder (ASD). Interview topics include the family impact of ASD, increased responsibility for typical siblings, the emotional impact on siblings who are typically developing, and the positive aspects of having a brother or sister with ASD. | +

Harris, S.L., & Glasberg, B.A. (2003). *Siblings of children with autism: A guide for families.* Bethesda, MD: Woodbine House. | This book offers information and guidance about the impact of having a family member with autism on siblings. The new edition addresses family concerns and questions and gives advice on how to increase sibling interaction and when to seek professional help.

Karasik, P., & Karasik, J. (2003). *The ride together: a brother and sister's memoir of autism in the family.* New York: Washington Square Press. | Siblings Paul and Judy Karasik tell their life stories growing up with their brother David, who has an especially severe form of autism. The authors show what it is like to grow up with autism from the sibling's perspective. | +

Koegel, L.K., & LaZebnik, C. (2004). *Overcoming autism.* New York: Viking Books. | Lynn Kern Koegel, Ph.D., a well-known and highly respected expert on autism interventions, shares her professional advice while coauthor Claire LaZebnik, a professional writer whose son has autism, provides insight into the daily life of parents coping with autism.

Naseef, R.A. (2001). ***Special children, challenged parents: The struggles and rewards of raising a child with a disability.*** **Baltimore: Paul H. Brookes, Publishing Co. |** Told from a father's perspective, this story is a moving account of a family's journey with their son Tariq who has autism.

Neisworth, J.T., & Wolfe, P.S. (2004). ***The Autism encyclopedia.*** **Baltimore, MD: Paul H. Brookes Publishing Co. |** This comprehensive encyclopedia includes more than 500 terms, alphabetically listed and clearly described. Autism experts have contributed essential terminology and information from various disciplines. Two appendices describe assessment tools and curricula and list autism-related study centers and organizations.

Overton, J. (2003). ***Snapshots of autism: A family album.*** **London: Jessica Kingsley Publishers. |** A mother uses the calendar events in a key year in the life of her son Nicholas, who is diagnosed with autism on his birthday, to discuss the roller coaster of emotions that accompanies life with her son.

Behavior Disorders/ADHD

Monastra, V.J. (2004). ***Parenting children with ADHD: 10 lessons that medicine cannot teach.*** **Washington, DC: American Psychological Association. |** This book gives parents a framework for building a successful parenting program at home based on the author's extensive experience evaluating and providing interventions to children and teens with attention-deficit/hyperactivity disorder (ADHD).

Down Syndrome

Kingsley, J., & Levitz, M. (1994). ***Count us in: Growing up with Down syndrome.*** **New York: Harcourt Brace & Co. |** The authors, two young men with Down syndrome, discuss their friendship, having Down syndrome, marriage, children, becoming independent, and their hopes and dreams for the future. They speak openly about their feelings about having been treated differently because of having an intellectual disability.

Rogers, C., & Dolva, G. (1999). ***Karina has Down syndrome: One family's account of the early years with a child who has special needs.*** **London: Jessica Kingsley Publishers. |** From their initial reaction to learning that their daughter has Down syndrome to the present, Karina's parents have experienced the challenges and joys of raising a child with special needs. They describe the activities, services, and programs they used to help her develop to her full potential and reach the goal they have for her full community participation.

Fragile X Syndrome

Weber, J.D. (1999). ***Children with fragile X syndrome: A parents' guide.*** **Bethesda, MD: Woodbine House. |** This guide, written by parents, doctors, therapists, and teachers, gives a complete introduction to fragile X syndrome and an in-depth look at the issues and concerns of children and their families.

Grief/Loss

Ashton, J., & Ashton, D. (1996). ***Loss and grief recovery: Help caring for children with disabilities, chronic or terminal illness.*** **Amityville, NY: Baywood Publishing Co. |** Written by a mother who had a son with cerebral palsy who died at age 14, this book is designed to help parents grieve the loss of a child who had a disability or chronic illness.

Davies, B. (1998). ***Shadows in the sun: The experiences of sibling bereavement in childhood.*** **Levittown, PA: Brunner/Mazel. |** This comprehensive guide to understanding sibling bereavement offers practical guidelines to those who seek to help grieving siblings, children, and families.

Fanos, J. (1996). ***Sibling loss.*** **Mahwah, NJ: Lawrence Erlbaum Associates. |** This book examines how the grief of sibling loss differs from that caused by the loss of a parent, child, or friend. Fanos's study of sibling reactions shows that the death of a brother or sister can trigger very strong reactions that approach the intensity of posttraumatic stress disorder (PTSD).

Scherago, M.G. (1999). ***Sibling grief.*** **Redmond, WA: Medic Publishing Co. |** This book offers information to parents on how they can help the child who is grieving the loss of a brother or sister. It addresses the importance of sharing grief and parents as role models, and describes what is helpful and what is not as siblings cope with to their sibling's death.

Wolfelt, A. (2002). ***A child's view of grief: A guide for parents, teachers, and counselors.*** **Omaha, NE: Centering Corporation. |** This informative, easy-to-read book explains how children and adolescents grieve after someone dies. Answers many questions parents and caregivers may have.

Intellectual Disabilities

Kaufman, S.Z. (1999). ***Retarded isn't stupid, Mom!*** **(Rev. ed.). Baltimore: Paul H. Brookes Publishing Co. |** In this fast-paced, engaging story, a mother frankly reveals the feelings that result from her determination to help her daughter Nicole live an independent life. This anniversary edition highlights Nicole's adult years and reflects on the changes in society's attitudes toward people with disabilities since Nicole's birth.

Simon, R. (2002). ***Riding the bus with my sister: A true life journey.*** **Boston: Houghton Mifflin. |** Writer Rachel Simon details her time spent riding buses with Beth, her younger sister who has developmental disabilities, and how through the experience the sisters' relationship changes for the better. The book has been made into a Hallmark Hall of Fame movie. **| +**

Mental Illness

Moorman, M. (2002). ***My sister's keeper: Learning to cope with a sister's mental illness.*** **New York: W.W. Norton. |** This true story tells the experiences of a woman, Margaret, who grew up with a sister with schizophrenia and how her sister's illness affected her own life in many ways. After the death of their mother, Margaret is the only one responsible for her sister. Ultimately, this is a story about the strength of the love between two sisters in the face of adversity. **| +**

Physical Disabilities

Panzarino, C. (1994). ***The me in the mirror.*** **Seattle: Seal Press. |** Connie Panzarino is a woman with Spinal Muscular Atrophy Type III. She tells of her struggles and triumphs, relationships with family, and her pioneering work in the disability rights movement.

Spina Bifida

Lutkenhoff, M. (1999). *Children with spina bifida: A parents' guide*. Bethesda, MD: Woodbine House. | A comprehensive guide for parents of children with spina bifida that provides information, guidance, and support to help meet their child's often intensive needs from birth through childhood.

Visual Impairment

Holbrook, M.C. (1996). *Children with visual impairments: A parents' guide*. Bethesda, MD: Woodbine House. | Discovering and learning about a young child's visual impairment can be a scary and lonely time for parents, but this guide for families of children with mild to severe visual impairment provides just the support and guidance parents need.

FILMS/TELEVISION PROGRAMS/DOCUMENTARIES WITH SIBLING THEMES

Arost, L. (Producer), & Lagomarsono, R. (Director). (2002). *My sister's keeper*; [Television broadcast]. United States: Hallmark Hall of Fame. | This true story about the lives of two sisters, Margaret and Judy Moorman, is based on Margaret Moorman's book about her sister, who has bipolar disorder. When their mother dies, Margaret, a New York art director, becomes responsible for her sister's care. **| Not rated**

Badalato, B. (Producer), & Chechihk, J.S. (Director). (1993). *Benny & Joon* [Motion picture.] United States: MGM. | Comedy about a brother and sister, Benny and Joon, who are looking for love and a "normal" life. Although never explicitly stated, Joon appears to have schizophrenia. The films show the effects of her disability on Benny, who cares for her. Their lives are changed when a young man falls in love with Joon. **| PG**

Blomquist, A.C. (Producer), & Hallström, L. (Director). (1993). *What's eating Gilbert Grape?* [Motion picture]. United States: J&M Entertainment, Paramount Pictures. | The story is told from the perspective of Gilbert Grape, a teenager who must care for both his obese mother and younger brother Arnie, who has a cognitive impairment. When Gilbert falls in love with Becky, a new girl in town, he struggles to make time for a life of his own while meeting the demands at home. **| PG-13**

Cairo, J.C. (Producer), & Reeve, C. (Director). (2004). *The Brooke Ellison story*. [Television broadcast]. United States: Jaffe/Braunstein films. | Based on a true story about Brooke Ellison, an 11-year-old girl who became paralyzed from the neck down after being hit by a car and required a ventilator to breathe. The film depicts her incredible determination and how with the support of her family, including her older sister and younger brother, she was able to finish high school and graduate Magna Cum Laude from Harvard. **| PG**

Farrell, M. (Producer), & Young, R.M. (Director). (1988). *Dominick and Eugene*. [Motion picture]. United States: MGM. | Dominick and Eugene Luciano are fraternal twin brothers. Eugene is a medical student who plans to care for Dominick, who has developmental disabilities. The film depicts the impact of mental retardation on sibling relationships and the challenges for adult siblings of balancing caregiving and future plans. **| PG-13**

Guber, P. (Producer), & Levinson, B. (Director). (1988). ***Rain man.*** **[Motion picture]. United States: MGM. |** This is an award-winning story about Charlie Babbitt and his older brother Raymond. After the death of their father, Charlie returns to his hometown and reunites with Raymond, who has autism and has lived in an institution since the death of their mother many years ago. The brothers learn about one another on a cross-country road trip. **| R**

Hamovitch, S. (Producer and Director). (2004). ***Without apology*** **[Video Documentary]. United States: One-Eyed Cat Productions. |** Susan Hamovitch uses film to tell the story of Alan, her brother with severe disabilities, who was born and raised in the 1950s at a time when such children were routinely placed in institutions. Alan was sent to one such state-run institution and was rarely spoke of in her family again. A story of one family, their challenges, and Alan's eventual move to a group home, the movie traces changes in our society toward people with developmental disabilities. **| Not rated**

Hoberman, D. (Producer), & Marshall, G. (Director). (1999) ***The other sister.*** **[Motion picture]. United States: Walt Disney Video. |** This heartwarming story about Carla Tate, a young woman who has developmental disabilities, who returns home after years of living at a private boarding school and dreams of going to college and living independently. At age 24, Carla moves out of her parents' home and goes to college, where she meets Danny, who also has mental retardation. Danny and Carla fall in love and get married. **| PG-13**

Hoen, P. (Director). (2002). ***Tru confessions.*** **[Television broadcast]. United States: Disney Productions. |** Based on the novel by the same name, Trudy "Tru" Walker dreams of two things: becoming a television host and helping her twin brother Eddie, who has developmental disabilities. She chooses to make a documentary about her brother as her entry in a cable television contest for teens. Through making the film, Tru learns about herself and gains a deeper understanding of Eddie. When finished, the film also helps the family become closer. **| Not rated**

Saito, S. (Producer), & Houston, A. (Director). (2005). ***Riding the bus with my sister.*** **[Television broadcast]. United States: Hallmark Hall of Fame. |** True story based on the book by Rachel Simon. Rachel is a busy New York fashion photographer and her sister Beth, who has developmental disabilities, has lived independently for years with the ongoing support of their father. Rachel comes home to look after her sister when their father dies. Their relationship deepens over the course of several months when Rachel joins Beth in her favorite pasttime, riding city buses. **| Not rated**

Weisberg, R. (Producer), & Aronson, J. (Director). ***Sound and fury*** **(2000). [Documentary]. United States: New Video Group. |** This film is about three generations of two families, connected through marriage, who each have family members who are deaf. Themes include Deaf culture, deaf identity, what is or is not a handicap, being a minority, and parental decision-making. Family members debate the appropriateness of cochlear implants for two of the children. **| Not rated**

Web Sites for Disability in Films

Films Involving Disabilities: http://www.disabilityfilms.co.uk

This site includes an extensive list of feature films involving people with disabilities. It is directed towards teachers, students and anyone who has an interest in how disability is represented in films. Each category is split into categories of major and minor films.

Information and Services for Siblings and Parents

Adaptive Environments Center
374 Congress Street
Suite 301
Boston, Massachusetts 02210
Phone: 617-695-1225
Fax: 617-482-8099
http://www.adaptenv.org

Administration on Developmental Disabilities (ADD)
Administration for Children and Families
U.S. Department of Health and Human Services
Mail Stop: HHH 405-D
370 L'Enfant Promenade, S.W.
Washington, DC 20447
Phone: 202-690-6590
http://www.acf.dhhs.gov/programs/add/

Alexander Graham Bell Association for the Deaf and Hard of Hearing, Inc.
3417 Volta Place, NW
Washington, DC 20007
Phone: 202-337-5220
TTY: 202-337-5221
Fax: 202-337-8314
http://www.agbell.org

American Association on Mental Retardation (AAMR)
444 North Capitol Street, N.W.
Suite 846
Washington, DC 20001-1512
Phone: 202-387-1968
Toll-free: 800-424-3688
Fax: 202-387-2193
http://www.aamr.org

American Cleft Palate-Craniofacial Association/Cleft Palate Foundation
1504 East Franklin Street
Suite 102
Chapel Hill, North Carolina 27514-2820
Phone: 919-933-9044
http://www.cleftline.org

American Foundation for the Blind (AFB)
11 Penn Plaza
Suite 300
New York, New York 10001
Phone: 212-502-7600
Fax: 212-502-7777
http://www.afb.org

American Society for Deaf Children (ASDC)
P.O. Box 3355
Gettysburg, Pennsylvania 17325
Phone/TTY: 717-334-7922
Parent Hotline: 800-942-ASDC
Fax: 717-334-8808
http://www.deafchildren.org

American Speech-Language-Hearing Association (ASHA)
10801 Rockville Pike
Rockville, Maryland 20852
Phone: 301-897-5700
Voice/TTY for Professionals & Students: 800-498-2071
Voice/TTY for the Public: 800-638-8255
Fax: 301-571-0457
http://www.asha.org

The Arc of the United States (formerly Association for Retarded Citizens of the United States [ARC])
1010 Wayne Avenue, Suite 650
Silver Spring, Maryland 20910
Phone: 301-565-3842
Fax: 301-565-3843 or 301-565-5342
http://www.thearc.org

ARCH National Respite Network
Chapel Hill Training-Outreach Project, Inc.
800 Eastowne Drive, Suite 105
Chapel Hill, North Carolina 27514
Phone: 919-490-5577
Fax: 919-490-4905
http://www.archrespite.org

Association for Education and Rehabilitation of the Blind and Visually Impaired (AERBVI)
1703 N. Beauregard Street, Suite 440
Alexandria, Virginia 22311
Phone: 703-671-4500
Toll-free: 877-492-2708
Fax: 703-671-6391
http://www.aerbvi.org

Association for Spina Bifida and Hydrocephalus (ASBAH)
42 Park Road
Peterborough
PE1 2UQ
United Kingdom
Phone: +44 173 355 5988
Fax: +44 173 355 5985
http://www.asbah.org

Autism Society of America (ASA)
7910 Woodmont Avenue, Suite 300
Bethesda, Maryland 20814-3067
Phone: 301-657-0881
Toll-free: 800-3AUTISM
http://www.autism-society.org

Autism Speaks
2 Park Avenue
11th Floor
New York, New York 10016
Phone: 212-252-8584
Fax: 212-252-8676
http://www.autismspeaks.org

Best Buddies
100 SE Second Street, #1990
Miami, Florida 33131
Phone: 305-374-2233
Toll-free: 800-89BUDDY
Fax: 305-374-5305
http://www.bestbuddies.org

Brain Injury Association of America
8201 Greensboro Drive
Suite 611
McLean, Virginia 22102
Phone: 703-761-0750
Toll-free: 800-444-6443 (Family Helpline)
http://www.biausa.org

Canavan Foundation
450 West End Avenue
Suite 10C
New York, New York 10024
Toll-free: 8770-4-CANAVAN
http://www.canavanfoundation.org

The Candlelighters Childhood Cancer Foundation
National Office
P.O. Box 498
Kensington, Maryland 20895-0498
Phone: 301-962-3520
Toll-free: 800-366-CCCF
Fax: 301-962-3521
http://www.candlelighters.org

Center for Effective Collaboration and Practive (CECP)
1000 Thomas Jefferson St., N.W.
Suite 400
Washington, DC 20007
Phone: 202-944-5300
Toll-free: 888-457-1551
TTY: 877-334-3499
Fax: 202-944-5454
http://cecp.air.org/

Children and Adults with Attention-Deficit/Hyperactivity Disorder (CHADD)
8181 Professional Place
Suite 150
Landover, Maryland 20785
Phone: 301-306-7070
Fax: 301-306-7090
National Resource Center on ADHD: 800-233-4050
http://www.chadd.org

Children's Tumor Foundation
95 Pine Street, 16th Floor
New York, New York 10005
Phone: 212-344-NNFF (6633)
Toll-free: 800-323-7938
Fax: 212-747-0004
http://www.ctf.org

Clearinghouse on Disability Information
Office of Special Education and Rehabilitative Services
Communication and Media Support Services
550 12th Street, S.W., Room 5133
Washington, DC 20202-2550
Phone: 202-245-7307
TTY: 202-205-5637
Fax: 202-245-7636
http://www.ed.gov/about/offices/list/osers/codi.html

The Council for Exceptional Children (CEC)
1110 North Glebe Road, Suite 300
Arlington, Virginia 22201
Voice phone: 703-620-3660
TTY: 866-915-5000
Toll-free: 888-CEC-SPED
FAX: 703-264-9494
http://www.cec.sped.org

Cure Autism Now! Foundation
5455 Wilshire Boulevard
Suite 715
Los Angeles, California 90036-4234
Phone: 323-549-0500
Toll-free: 888-8-AUTISM
Fax: 323-549-0547
http://www.canfoundation.org

Cystic Fibrosis Foundation (CFF)
6931 Arlington Road
Bethesda, Maryland 20814
Phone: 301-951-4422
Toll-free: 1-800-FIGHT CF
Fax: 301-951-6378
http://www.cff.org

Dysautonomia Foundation
315 West 39th Street
Suite 701
New York, New York 10018
Phone: 212-279-1066
http://www.familialdysautonomia.org

Easter Seals
230 West Monroe Street
Suite 1800
Chicago, Illinois 60606
Phone: 312-726-6200
Toll-free: 800-221-6827
TTY: 312-726-4258
Fax: 312-726-1494
http://www.easterseals.com

Epilepsy Foundation of America
4351 Garden City Drive
Suite 406
Landover, Maryland 20785-7223
Phone: 301-459-3700
Toll-free: 800-332-1000
http://www.epilepsyfoundation.org

Exceptional Parent
EP Global Communications
551 Main Street
Johnstown, Pennsylvania 15901
Toll-free: 877-372-7368
http://www.eparent.com

Families and Advocate Partnership for Education Project (FAPE Project)
PACER Center
8161 Normandale Boulevard
Minneapolis, Minnesota 55437-1044
Phone: 952-838-9000
Toll-free: 888-248-0822
http://www.fape.org

Fraxa Research Foundation
45 Pleasant Street
Newburyport, Massachusetts 01950
(978) 462-1866
http://www.fraxa.org

Federation for Children with Special Needs
1135 Tremont Street, Suite 420
Boston, Massachusetts 02120
Phone: 617-236-7210
Toll-Free (in MA): 800-331-0688
Fax: 617-572-2094
http://www.fcsn.org

Federation of Families for Children's Mental Health
1101 King Street, Suite 420
Alexandria, Virginia 22314
Phone: 703-684-7710
Fax: 703-836-1040
http://www.ffcmh.org

Genetics Education Center
University of Kansas Medical Center
Information for Siblings and Family Members of Individuals with Genetic Conditions/Rare Conditions
http://www.kumc.edu/gec/support.html

Inclusion International (II)
c/o The Rix Centre
University of East London
Docklands Campus
4-6 University Way
London E16 2RD
United Kingdom
Phone: +44 208 223 7709
Fax: +44 208 223 7411
http://www.inclusion-international.org

International Dyslexia Association (IDA)
Chester Building
8600 LaSalle Road
Suite 382
Baltimore, Maryland 21204
Phone: 410-296-0232
Fax: 410-321-5069
http://www.interdys.org

International Rett Syndrome Association
9121 Piscataway Road
Clinton, Maryland 20735
Phone: 301-856-3334
Toll-free: 1-800-818-RETT
Fax: 301-856-3336
http://www.rettsyndrome.org

Juvenile Diabetes Research Foundation International
120 Wall Street
New York, New York 10005-4001
Phone: 1-800-533-CURE
Fax: 212-785-9595
http://www.jdrf.org

Kids on the Block
9385-C Gerwig Lane
Columbia, Maryland 21046
Phone: 410-290-9095
Toll-free: 800-368-KIDS
Fax: 410-290-9358
http://www.kotb.com

Little People of America (LPA)
5289 NE Elam Young Parkway
Suite F-100
Hillsboro, Oregon 97124
Toll-free: 888-LPA-2001
http://www.lpaonline.org

Learning Disabilities Association of America (LDA)
4156 Library Road
Pittsburgh, Pennsylvania 15234-1349
Phone: 412-341-1515
Fax: 412-344-0224
http://www.ldanatl.org

The Leukemia & Lymphoma Society
1311 Mamaroneck Avenue
White Plains, New York 10605
Phone: 914-949-5213
Fax: 914-949-6691
http://www.leukemia.org

March of Dimes Birth Defects Foundation
1275 Mamaroneck Avenue
White Plains, New York 10605
Phone: 914-428-7100
http://www.marchofdimes.com

Mothers United for Moral Support (MUMS)
150 Custer Court
Green Bay, Wisconsin 54301-1243
Phone: 920-336-5333
Toll-free (parents only): 877-336-5333
Fax: 920-339-0995
http://www.netnet.net/mums/

Muscular Dystrophy Association (MDA)
National Headquarters
3300 E. Sunrise Drive
Tucson, Arizona 85718
Phone: 800-572-1717
http://www.mdausa.org

National Alliance for Autism Research (NAAR)
See **Autism Speaks**
http://www.autismspeaks.org

National Association of the Deaf (NAD)
814 Thayer Avenue
Silver Spring, Maryland 20910-4500
Phone: 301-587-1788
TTY: 301-587-1789
http://www.nad.org

National Organization for Rare Disorders (NORD)
55 Kenosia Avenue
PO Box 1968
Danbury, Connecticut 06813-1968
Phone: 203-744-0100
TTY: 203-797-9590
Fax: 203-798-2291
http://www.rarediseases.org

National Association for Visually Handicapped (NAVH)
22 West 21st Street
6th Floor
New York, New York 10010
Phone: 212-889-3141
Fax: 212-727-2931
http://www.navh.org

National Disability Rights Network (NDRN)
900 Second Street, NE, Suite 211
Washington, DC 20002
Phone: 202-408-9514
TTY: 202-408-9521
Fax: 202-408-9520
http://www.ndrn.org

National Ataxia Foundation (NAF)
2600 Fernbrook Lane
Suite 119
Minneapolis, Minnesota 55447
Phone: 763-553-0020
Fax: 763-553-0167
http://www.ataxia.org

National Center for Learning Disabilities (NCLD)
381 Park Avenue South, Suite 1401
New York, New York 10016
Phone: 212-545-7510
Toll-free: 888-575-7373
Fax: 212-545-9665
http://www.ncld.org

National Center for Stuttering (NCS)
200 East 33rd Street
New York, New York 10016
National Stutterers' Hotline:
800-221-2483
http://www.stuttering.com

National Center on Birth Defects and Developmental Disabilities (NCBDD, a division of the Centers for Disease Control and Prevention [CDC]) Centers for Disease Control and Prevention
1600 Clifton Road
Atlanta, Georgia 30333
Phone: 404-639-3534
Toll-free: 800-311-3435
http://www.cdc.gov/ncbddd/

National Council on Disability (NCD)
1331 F Street, NW
Suite 850
Washington, DC 20004
Phone: 202-272-2004
TTY: 202-272-2074
Fax: 202-272-2022
http://www.ncd.gov

National Dissemination Center for Children with Disabilities (NICHCY)
P.O. Box 1492
Washington, DC 20013
Phone/TTY: 800-695-0285
Fax: 202-884-8441
http://www.nichcy.org

National Down Syndrome Congress (NDSC)
1370 Center Drive, Suite 102
Atlanta, Georgia 30338
Phone: 770-604-9500
Toll-free: 800-232-NDSC
http://www.ndsccenter.org

National Down Syndrome Society (NDSS)
666 Broadway
New York, New York 10012
Toll-free: 800-221-4602
Fax: 212-979-2873
http://www.ndss.org

National Federation for the Blind (NFB)
1800 Johnson Street
Baltimore, Maryland 21230
Phone: 301-659-9314
Fax: 410-685-5653
http://www.nfb.org

National Fragile X Foundation
P.O. Box 190488
San Francisco, California 94119
Phone: 925-938-9300
Toll-free: 800-688-8765
Fax: 925-938-9315
http://www.fragilex.org

National Institute of Mental Health (NIMH)
Office of Communications
6001 Executive Boulevard, Room 8184
MSC 9663
Bethesda, Maryland 20892-9663
Phone: 301-443-4513
Toll-free: 866-615-6464
TTY: 301-443-8431
Fax: 301-443-4279
http://www.nimh.nih.gov

National Mental Health Association (NMHA)
2001 N. Beauregard Street, 12th Floor
Alexandria, Virginia 22311
Phone: 703-684-7722
Toll-free: 800-969-NMHA (6642)
TTY: 800-433-5959
Fax: 703-684-5968
http://www.nmha.org

National Multiple Sclerosis Society
733 Third Avenue, 6th Floor
New York, New York 10017
Phone: 212-986-3240
Toll-free: 800-344-4867
http://www.nmss.org

National Organization on Disability (NOD)
910 16th Street, NW
Suite 600
Washington, DC 20006
Phone: 202-293-5960
Toll-Free: 800-248-ABLE
TTY: 202-293-5968
Fax: 202-293-7999
http://www.nod.org

National Parent Network on Disabilities
1600 Prince Street
Suite 115
Alexandria, Virginia 22314
Phone: 703-684-NPND
http://www.npnd.org

National Rehabilitation Information Center (NARIC)
4200 Forbes Boulevard, Suite 202
Lanham, Maryland 20706-4829
Phone: 301-459-5900
Toll-free: 800-346-2742
TTY: 800-346-2742
Fax: 301-459-4263
http://www.naric.com

National Reye's Syndrome Foundation (NRSF)
723 East Mulberry Street
Bryan, Ohio 43506
Phone: 419-636-2679
Toll-free: 800-233-7393
Fax: 419-636-9897
http://www.reyessyndrome.org

National Tay-Sachs and Allied Diseases Association (NTSAD)
2001 Beacon Street
Suite 304
Brookline, Massachusetts 02135
Toll-free: 800-906-8723
Fax: 617-277-0134
http://www.ntsad.org

Osteogenesis Imperfecta Foundation
804 W. Diamond Ave, Suite 210
Gaithersburg, Maryland 20878
Phone: 301-947-0083
Toll-free: 800-981-2663
http://www.oif.org

Pediatric Brain Tumor Foundation of the United States
302 Ridgefield Court
Asheville, NC 28806
Phone: 828-665-6891
Toll free: 800-253-6530
Fax: 828-665-6894
http://www.pbtfus.org

Prader-Willi Syndrome Association
5700 Midnight Pass Road, Suite 6
Sarasota, Florida 34242
Toll-free: 800-926-4797
http://www.pwsausa.org

President's Committee for People with Intellectual Disabilities (PCPID)
Room 701
The Aerospace Center
370 L'Enfant Promenade, S.W.
Washington, DC 20447
http://www.acf.hhs.gov/programs/pcpid/

Quality Mall
150 Pillsbury Drive SE, Room 204
Minneapolis, Minnesota 55455
Phone: 612-624-6328
Fax: 612-625-6619
http://www.qualitymall.org

Rainbows
2100 Golf Road
Suite 370
Rolling Meadows, Illinois 60008
Phone: 847-952-1770
Toll-free: 800-266-3206
Fax: 847-952-1774
http://www.rainbows.org

Siblings for Significant Change
350 Fifth Ave., Room 627
New York, New York 10118
Phone: 212-643-2663
Toll-free: 800-841-8251
Fax: 212-643-1244

Sibling Support Project
The Arc of the United States
6512 23rd St., N.W., Suite 213
Seattle, Washington 98117
Phone: 206-297-6368
http://www.thearc.org/siblingsupport

SIBS
Meadowfield
Oxenhope, West Yorkshire BD22 9JD
United Kingdom
Phone: +44 153 564 5453
http://www.sibs.org.uk

Sickle-Cell Disease Association of America, Inc.
(formerly the National Association for Sickle Cell Disease [NASCD])
16 S. Calvert Street, Suite 600
Baltimore, Maryland 21202
Phone: 410-528-1555
Toll-free: 800-421-8453
Fax: 410-528-1495
http://www.sicklecelldisease.org

Spina Bifida Association of America (SBAA)
4590 MacArthur Blvd., N.W., Suite 250
Washington, DC 20007-4226
Phone: 202-944-3285
Toll-free: 800-621-3141
http://www.sbaa.org

Stuttering Foundation of America
3100 Walnut Grove Road
Suite 603
P.O. Box 11749
Memphis, Tennessee 38111-0749
Phone: 901-452-7343
Toll-free: 800-992-9392
http://www.stutteringhelp.org

TASH (formerly the Association for Persons with Severe Handicaps)
29 W. Susquehanna Avenue, Suite 210
Baltimore, Maryland 21204
Phone: 410-828-8274
Fax: 410-828-6706
http://www.tash.org

Tourette Syndrome Association (TSA)
42-40 Bell Boulevard
Bayside, New York 11361-2861
Phone: 718-224-2999
Toll-free: 800-237-0717
http://www.tsa-usa.org

Tuberous Sclerosis Alliance (TSA)
801 Roeder Road, Suite 750
Silver Spring, Maryland 20910
Phone: 301-562-9890
Fax: 301-562-9870
Toll-free: 800-225-6872
http://www.tsalliance.org

United Cerebral Palsy (UCP)
1660 L Street, N.W., Suite 700
Washington, DC 20036
Phone: 202-776-0406
Toll-free: 800-872-5827
TTY: 202-973-7197
Fax: 202-776-0414
http://www.ucp.org

Williams Syndrome Association
P.O. Box 297
Clawson, Michigan 48017-0297
Phone: 248-244-2229
Toll-free: 800-806-1871
Fax: 248-244-2230
http://www.williams-syndrome.org

INTERNET RESOURCES

Family Village: A Global Community of Disability-Related Resources | http://www.familyvillage.wisc.edu
Waisman Center
University of Wisconsin-Madison
1500 Highland Avenue
Madison, Wisconsin 53705-2280

Internet Resources for Special Children (IRSC) | www.irsc.org/
IRSC provides information to those who care for, support, and provide services to individuals with special needs. Internet links are listed for a variety of disability-related categories. The web site provides Online Communities where parents or providers can ask questions and meet others who may have the same questions or experiences.

Wrightslaw | http://www.wrightslaw.com

WEB SITES FOR SIBLINGS

Asperger-teens | http://health.groups.yahoo.com/group/aspergers-teens/
This message board is for teens with Asperger syndrome and their family including brothers, sisters, and parents.

Autism Sibs | http://groups.yahoo.com/subscribe/autism_sibs/
This list is for siblings of adults and children with autism to discuss growing up with their brother or sister.

SibKids Listserv | http://www.thearc.org/siblingsupport/sibkids-listserv
SibKids listserv is especially for young brothers and sisters of people with special health, developmental, and emotional needs.

Sibling Connection and Heartbeat | http://www.counselingstlouis.net/
The Sibling Connection and Heartbeat are for siblings who have lost a brother or sister. Sibling Connection is written by a psychotherapist and includes articles about dealing with the loss of a sibling at any age, resources, and a message board. Heartbeat was created by a 14-year-old dealing with the loss of a sibling.

SibNet Listserv | http://www.thearc.org/siblingsupport/sibnet-listserv
SibNet is a listserv especially for adult brothers and sisters of people with special health, developmental, and emotional needs.

SuperSibs! | http://www.supersibs.org
SuperSibs! provides education, information, resources and support to brothers and sisters of children who have cancer.

Index

Page numbers followed by *f* indicate figures; those followed by *t* indicate tables.